ACCLAIM for BOOKS by JAMES WINTER

Once the hinge of democracy, the media now specialize in 'junk food news'—Winter's analysis is strong. —*Globe and Mail*

Democracy's Oxygen is an important book...it enhances the political discourse on a critical subject and refutes the view that those concerned with corporate control of the news are wacky conspiracy-seekers. Clearly, one doesn't have to believe in any kind of grand conspiracy to see why ownership of the news media by a handful of people can't be good for democracy. —*Literary Review of Canada*

Winter's book is an invaluable reference tool. Its research is particularly strong in the profiles of Black, his fellow baron Paul Desmarais, and the publishing giant Québecor. —*Quill & Quire*

The combination of Winter's deep desire for fundamental political and media reforms, and his relentless examples backed up by facts, figures and quotations makes his a distinct voice at a distinct intersection. —*Barrie Zwicker, Media Critic for Vision TV*

In the increasingly stifling atmosphere of Canadian democracy, Winter's book is a breath of fresh air. Winter—admirably—writes in direct and accessible language. —*Canadian Dimension*

Democracy's Oxygen by media critic James Winter, is a timely release. Winter's main point that the left needs to develop and vastly expand its own media is undeniable. —*Briarpatch*

A fact-packed examination of the influence of ideology and ownership in the media. One of the best things about Winter's work is that it stands outside the loop, where the flatness of the media landscape isn't so evident. —*Now Magazine*

Winter presents a well-documented case that Black has a definite political agenda, and his acquisition of newspapers the world over is a conscious grab for political power. —*Hour Magazine*

James Winter has hit on a hot topic. Contains truths which only those in an advanced state of denial could ignore. —*Ottawa Citizen*

This book is a must for all of us concerned about the direction in which Canada is heading. —*Howard Pawley, Former Premier of Manitoba*

This book is about nothing less than the corporate takeover of public expression. Read it. —*Maude Barlow, Council of Canadians*

BLACK ROSE BOOKS

is proud to have published the following books

by JAMES WINTER

COMMON CENTS
Media Portrayal of the Gulf War and Other Events (1992)

DEMOCRACY'S OXYGEN
How the Corporations Control the News (1997)

MEDIATHINK (2002)

and as a contributor to

FILTERING THE NEWS
Essays on Herman and Chomsky's Propaganda Model (2005)

RADICAL MASS MEDIA CRITICISM
A Cultural Genealogy (2005)

BOUND BY POWER
Intended Consequences (2006)

Lies the Media tell Us

This book is dedicated to the indomitable people of Haïti and Cuba.

You are an example to the world.

Lies the Media tell Us

James Winter

BLACK
ROSE
BOOKS

Montreal/New York/London

Black Rose Books No. KK357

National Library of Canada Cataloguing in Publication Data

Winter, James P. (James Patrick), 1952-

Lies the media tell us / James Winter

Includes bibliographical references and index.

13 digit ISBN 978-1-55164-253-6 : 10 digit ISBN: 1-55164-253-0 (bound)
13 digit ISBN 978-1-55164-252-9 : 10 digit ISBN: 1-55164-252-2 (pbk.)

1. Mass media and public opinion. 2. Mass media--Social aspects.
3. Mass media criticism. I. Title.

P94.W55 2005   302.23   C2004-905034-6

BLACK ROSE BOOKS

C.P. 1258	2250 Military Road	99 Wallis Road
Succ. Place du Parc	Tonawanda, NY	London, E9 5LN
Montréal, H2X 4A7	14150	England
Canada	USA	UK

To order books:

In Canada: (phone) 1-800-565-9523 (fax) 1-800-221-9985
email: utpbooks@utpress.utoronto.ca

In the United States: (phone) 1-800-283-3572 (fax) 1-651-917-6406

In the UK & Europe: (phone) 44 (0)20 8986-4854 (fax) 44 (0)20 8533-5821
email: order@centralbooks.com

Our Web Site address: http://www.blackrosebooks.net

A publication of the Institute of Policy Alternatives of Montréal (IPAM)

Printed in Canada

CONTENTS

ACKNOWLEDGMENTS

THANKS, AS ALWAYS, to my publisher Dimitri Roussopoulos and to Linda Barton of Black Rose Books. Your patience is virtuous.

Thanks to Robert Babe and Valerie Scatamburlo-D'Annibale, for reading some draft chapters and making valuable suggestions. Any remaining errors are my own.

Thanks to Sandy Vanzetten and Sharron Wazny, for your daily help in getting my act together. And to Irv Goldman, who started down this path with me, so many years ago.

Thanks to Jane McArthur and Brenna Wolf, two wonderful people and excellent Graduate Assistants.

Thanks to my students. For those who have said this course has changed your lives, *you* have changed your lives. Well done.

To our children, Andrew Morgan, Kieran Winter, Kaeleigh Winter, and honey boy Aidan Winter Robertson: you are our pride and joy. We love you as much as the sun and the moon and the stars.

To our families, who are always there for us, and for whom we are always here: especially Ken and Marg Winter; Bert and Sandra Morgan.

Finally, to Lisa, whose love is a source of constant amazement: I love you more than I can ever express.

James Winter, LaSalle, Ontario, May 2007

INTRODUCTION

WHEN TWO OF MY CHILDREN, Kieran and Kaeleigh, were about five and three years old, they took part in a demonstration and protest in Chatham, Ontario, supporting some striking workers. This would have been in about 1996. There was marching and singing and guitar playing, and it was a good example of labour solidarity. In fact, one of the songs we sang was the labour anthem: "Solidarity Forever." The chorus goes like this: "Solidarity forever, solidarity forever, solidarity forever, the union makes us strong."

That evening when we returned home to Windsor, I was in the kitchen making dinner, and Kaeleigh announced she was going to the bathroom off the kitchen where, a few moments later I heard her singing in her sweet voice: "Unidarity forever, Unidarity forever, the human makes us strong." I was standing in the kitchen chopping vegetables, with tears streaming down my cheeks.

Over the years the kids have been to many demonstrations and protests, in keeping with our commitment to social justice. I remember young Kieran once made the front page of the *Windsor Star*, as he sat at a demonstration with his face sporting anti-Mike Harris stickers. I've always thought it's important to nurture values such as solidarity and equality, while trying to be careful not to be pushy: ultimately, everyone has to choose their own path.

The downside to all this became apparent early on, when the children would jokingly take up pretend placards and march around the kitchen shouting, "We want ice cream! We want ice cream!" If workers have rights, then children have rights too, don't they? Of course, parents are responsible for supervising children's nutrition, but some things are open to negotiation.

Ironically, those of us who discuss discipline, manners, and respect with our children are faced with a contradiction when we also want them to stand up for their rights, think independently, and question authority. As parents, "good behaviour" frequently translates into respectful silence as in the adage: "children should be seen and not heard." In my observation, a major part of child-rearing seems to involve teaching children to listen, obey, and conform, so they'll be less trouble to us as we go about our busy lives. I've thought of this as I've heard myself saying, "Do you have your listening ears on?" I've heard parenting gurus advise parents to hold the child's face with both hands, forcing them to look into your eyes and to listen and then to repeat what they're being told, to be sure they understand—and obey.

Here are three sample excerpts from a recent article in a parenting magazine:

If compliance is the goal, listening is certainly the first step: A child who hasn't heard dad tell him to unload the dishwasher isn't likely to do it...

Get down to your child's height and look him in the eye to be sure he gets the message.

Winnipeg's Sho McDowell, mother of Alexandria, nine, Daniel, seven, and Neil Andrew, five, has her own method to ensure her crew is truly listening: "My one and only trick is when I have something I want them to do, and I think they aren't listening, they have to repeat back to me what I said and what they think it means."[1]

Droopy Pants Legislation

I am a staunch advocate for teachers and our public school system. Of course, parents' desires for quiet, order, and compliance with one or two kids gets magnified many times when it comes to teachers struggling with education cutbacks and up to 35 active children in a classroom. One result is that *conformity* is the rule of the day in our schools. Like parents, some teachers or administrators hit the panic button when they see a kid with spiked or dyed hair, or a t-shirt with a slogan they don't like. We need rules preventing objectionable slogans and behavior, but it sometimes borders on the bizarre.

In 2004 and 2005, legislators in Florida, Virginia and Louisiana introduced three separate "droopy pants bills," in an attempt to outlaw baggy pants which allow teen's underwear to show. The Florida bill would have meant up to ten days in jail and a $50 fine. None of the bills were approved, but the fact that they were introduced is telling. The Virginia bill passed the house legislature, but was defeated in the State Senate.² And at Greenbriar High School in Evans, Georgia, student Mike Cameron was suspended in 1998 for wearing a Pepsi t-shirt on a school-designated "Coke Day." The school was hoping to win $500 in a CocaCola-sponsored contest.³

Educators, like legislators, are looking for conformity. Students with C-grades don't raise an eyebrow, but arriving three minutes late means a trip to the principal's office. Those who don't conform are weeded out using a variety of techniques, from the fourth-grader who is labeled as a "behavioral problem," to more sophisticated methods at the university level. Noam Chomsky summed it up:

> [G]iven the external power structure of the society in which they function now, the institutional role of the schools for the most part is just to train people for obedience and conformity, and to make them controllable and indoctrinated—and as long as the schools fulfill that role, they'll be supported.⁴

So, the conformity seeps over from the behavioural area, to the academic content. Part of maintaining order becomes having students taking notes rather than asking questions. After all, if students can question your academic authority, might they not question your authority to discipline? This assembly-line model for learning leads to rote memorization and regurgitation. Students who do the best are those who can best parrot back what is sometimes merely dogma, to the teacher or professor. Questioning authority or otherwise causing trouble inevitably leads to one form or another of punishment, from a poor grade to time spent in the office. These lessons extend all the way up the ladder of education, from primary school to graduate school work.

Internalized Beliefs

A few years ago I was contacted by a doctoral student in sociology at a large comprehensive university in southern Ontario. After seven years of doctoral studies, his professors abandoned him, meaning that now he would never graduate. The reason? His dissertation results didn't agree with his professors' ideological bias. I read his dissertation and it was perfectly acceptable. He kept rewriting his thesis as instructed by his advisory committee, until he realized that what they *really* wanted him to do was to change his findings to agree with their political perspective. This student had integrity, and was rewarded with expulsion after seven years' work. As I write these words, he is enrolled in a doctoral program in Europe, has published several refereed journal articles from his dissertation, and expects to formally defend his dissertation later in 2007.

Faced with these sorts of demands, most graduate students naturally capitulate. What choice do they have, really? Ironically, this student was replicating research by American academic and famed dissident Noam Chomsky. I say it's ironic because Chomsky has actually warned students and academics that this is what will happen to them if they challenge the status quo rather than conforming.

Chomsky tells the story of Norman Finkelstein, a graduate student at Princeton who documented the fraud in a book which was popular and favorably reviewed, only to be punished by his professors and ignored by academic journals and the mass media. Even though Finkelstein was eventually allowed to graduate, he was ostracized and prevented from obtaining an academic position.[5] After giving several other examples, Chomsky summarizes the situation:

> [I]n the universities or in any other institution, you can often find some dissidents hanging around in the woodwork—and they can survive in one fashion or another, particularly if they get community support. But if they become too disruptive or too obstreperous—or you know, too effective—they're likely to be kicked out. The standard thing, though, is that they won't make it within the institutions in the first place, particularly if they were that way when they were young—they'll simply be weeded out somewhere along the line. *So in most cases, the people who make it through the institutions and are able to remain in them have already internalized the right kinds of beliefs: it's not a problem for them to be obedient, they already are obedient, that's how they got there.* And that's pretty much how the ideological control system perpetuates itself in the schools—that's the basic story of how it operates, I think (emphasis added).[6]

So, the higher up you go in academia, the more you learn to conform. And, as Chomsky notes, the people who teach in universities, part of the "intelligentsia," are the most indoctrinated of all, because it's our job to teach others to conform. In previous books I've referred to this conforming and obedient mindset as *Common Sense* or *MediaThink*, to underscore the key role also played in this process by the mainstream corporate media.

More than a half century ago in what was by far his best book, Marshall McLuhan criticized, somewhat enviously, the relatively vast sums of money spent on the "unofficial education system" of the mass media, particularly advertising.[7] Increasingly, the formal education system of our schools has become a mere subset of the mainstream media, a process heightened by expanding corporatization, and privatization, which are part of the "external power structure" to which Chomsky refers.

A Disney View of History

One estimate has it that about 75 percent of classroom time and 90 percent of homework time is related to textbook use. University and school texts are predominantly mass-produced by the giant international publishing houses, with names like Time-Warner-AOL (Warner Books), Viacom (Simon & Schuster) and Bertelsmann AG (Random House, Ballantine, Bantam, Doubleday, Knopf, etc.) Four publishers dominate textbook publishing in the U.S., accounting for about 70 percent of texts.

As the author of *Lies My Teacher Told Me* writes, regarding American history texts, "the books actually make students stupid,"[8] in part because children, like most adults, "do not readily retain isolated, incoherent, and meaningless data."[9] Newspapers and magazines target teachers and students with "education" programs using media content to foment current and future readership. Canned content in the form of films, documentaries and regular television programs form an increasing proportion of the curriculum, with both good and bad effects. Students increasingly rely on the Internet and worldwide web for their research, and although there is good alternative information available, the bulk of the information—and information providers—are the same.

Academia is a place, ideally, where we can have reflection, study, even dreaming. This is where independent and critical analysis of society, the corporate, political, religious, artistic, commercial, and even educational aspects, may take place. With encroaching corporate sponsorship, government cutbacks, and "academic freedom" bills which do the reverse, this ability is being lost. In part, the corporate advertising money which McLuhan decried, has encroached, making education just another part of the corporate system. Now, some professors can be paid what the advertising people get, but at what cost? This is most clearly evident in the area of medical education, as we will see in Chapter Three.

Another gigantic problem with the education system is that there is nowhere to study issues of enormous significance to society. In universities, the disciplines or subject areas have been divided in a way that effectively precludes the pursuit of some very important questions. Economics departments study abstract mathematical models of how "free enterprise" economies potentially could work; political science departments study election voting patterns and electoral "horse race" statistics; sociology departments study crime in the ghettos, or gambling addictions.[10] But in the age of corporate globalization, for example, what discipline is devoted to studying its impact on the world population, or alternatives? Who is studying and explaining the World Trade Organization, or the impact of trade agreements on jobs, or the environment, or sovereignty and democracy? These vital areas for study are all but ignored by mainstream academia, in favor of topics more suited to winning corporate and government grants, and promoting student employment. Critical analysis of the vitally important WTO, IMF, and FTAA is left to the paltry resources of a small number of dedicated researchers.[11]

Throughout the educational system, our textbooks and our teachers use what James Loewen calls, "a godlike tone," and as a result, it rarely occurs to students to question. He quotes a former student:

> In retrospect I ask myself, why *didn't* I think to ask, for example, who *were* the original inhabitants of the Americas, what was *their* life like, and how did it change when Columbus arrived? However, back then everything was presented as if it were the full picture, so I never thought to doubt that it was.

As examples, Loewen uses the partial and biased portrayal of Helen Keller, who became a radical socialist, and went from being admired and celebrated, to being disparaged and condemned. Or, President Woodrow Wilson, a white supremacist who invaded and colonized Nicaragua, Cuba, the Dominican Republic, Haïti, and other countries. But U.S. textbooks say, "President Wilson was urged to send military forces into Mexico to protect American investments and to restore law and order." As a result, says Loewen, author of *Lies My Teacher Told Me*, "most high school seniors are hamstrung in their efforts to analyze controversial issues in our society," they have what he calls, "a Disney view of history."

Why the title *Lies the Media Tell Us*? There are two reasons: in 1992 I wrote a book which discussed media portrayal of such issues as the Persian Gulf War, and the election and government by Bob Rae and the NDP in Ontario. The book's title was *Common Cents*, and I can recall one interviewer asking me what the title meant. Of course, this meant the interviewer hadn't read the book, because the title was explained in the introduction. (It was all about the common sense perspective, or conventional wisdom parroted by the news media. I used "cents" instead of "sense" to signal the economic context, the political economy of news media.) Next I wrote *Democracy's Oxygen*, and then co-wrote *The Big Black Book*, and then wrote *MediaThink*. For this book, I thought I'd just try to state the obvious, as jarring as it may be for some. After all, these examples clearly illustrate that the media are telling us lies. The second reason is that I wanted to connect the book to

Lies My Teacher Told Me, because the very real sins of the education system are also the sins of the news media. And why wouldn't they be? Academics teach journalists and publishers alike. And every day, the news media teach professors, teachers, students, and everyone else.

Media Literacy

It's within this educational context that I introduced a media literacy course in the mid-nineties. I began teaching the course once a year to maybe fifty students. More recently, I've taught 400 students in a year, and it's usually around 300. The course is aimed at correcting for media biases, the lies media tell us. It's also partially in reaction to the conservative nature of academia itself, which largely tends to reinforce conventional wisdom, and teach conformity. I wanted to teach a course which would be an exception. Because this book covers a number of the topics in the course, it's written for my students. But it's also for curious members of the public, who are open to having their conventional views challenged.

In the course, I put forward some unconventional notions, such as, "we are all feminists," or "we are all environmentalists"—or at least, we should be. I think much of the blame for how we see feminism or environmentalism, rests with the mainstream media.[12] (See Chapter Two.) I argue that pharmaceutical companies with the help of MDs and Hollywood celebrities—and some university professors —have turned us into pill poppers. And that it's a corrupt and despicable business. (See Chapter Three.) More controversially, I also dissect some of the entertaining animated films produced by Disney and others, pointing to their sometimes blatant sexism, racism, and stereotyping. Perhaps more challenging, I ask students to reconsider the stated foreign policy goals of the U.S., and increasingly Canada. Is it all about liberation and democracy, or access to oil? (Chapter Four.) And what about corporate globalization? Is it a Global Village, or Global Pillage? (Chapter Five.) And then, in the category of "what-drugs-is-this-prof-on?" I ask students to suspend their disbelief, and consider the possibility that: Canada is not a democracy, while Cuba is. I don't ask them to *believe* this heresy, but just to listen to some arguments and perhaps do their own investigation if they are interested. They don't have to adopt these views, but I ask them to be aware of the arguments. And *just to consider the very possibility of what it might mean* if this wild notion is actually true.

As Mark Twain said, "It ain't what you don't know that gets you into trouble. It's what you know for sure, that just ain't so."

NOTES

1. Donna Papacosta, "Now Hear This: From toddlers to teens, tips on talking to your kids," *Today's Parent*, Sept. 3, 2003. http://www.todaysparent.com/behaviordevelopment/allages/article.jsp?content=20030903_141855_4224.

2. Frank Cerabino, "Lawmakers took a pass on one stupid law," *Palm Beach Post*, May 11, 2005.

3. Liza Featherstone, "Hot-Wiring High School," *The Nation*, June 21, 1999. After students' rights groups got involved and held press conferences, high school officials backed down, admitted they made a mistake, and erased the suspension from the student's record.

4. Noam Chomsky, quoted in Peter Mitchell and John Schoeffel, *Understanding Power: The Indispensable Chomsky*, The New Press, N.Y., 2002, p. 237.

5. Mitchell and Schoeffel, *Understanding Power*, p. 245.

6. *Ibid*, p. 249. Emphasis added.

7. Marshall McLuhan, *The Mechanical Bride: Folklore of Industrial Man*, Ginko Press, Corte Madera Ca, 2001. (Originally published in 1951.)

8. James W. Loewen, *Lies My Teacher Told Me: Everything Your American History Textbook Got Wrong*, Touchstone, N.Y., 1995, p. 17.

9. A. B. Hodgetts and Paul Gallagher, *Teaching Canada for the '80s*, Toronto, OISE, 1978, p. 20, cited in Loewen, *Lies My Teacher Told Me*, p. 301.

10. Chomsky provides a few of these examples and then concludes, "In fact, there is no academic profession that is concerned with the central problems of modern society." Quoted in Mitchell and Schoefel, *Understanding Power*, p. 242.

11. Aside from Chomsky, a few examples would include: the indefatigable Maude Barlow of the Council of Canadians, Tony Clarke, Murray Dobbin, Michael Albert and colleagues at Z-Net, Michel Chossudovsky of Concordia, and Bruce Campbell and associates at the Canadian Centre for Policy Alternatives.

12. I discuss Feminism in "Feminism Did It," *MediaThink*, Black Rose Books, Montreal, 2002.

Chapter One

HOW IT WORKS

OUR DIRECT EXPERIENCES ARE relatively limited, when compared to what we're exposed to in the media. Take the example of political leadership. How many of us have met Canadian prime minister Stephen Harper, or U.S. president George Bush, personally? Relatively few. How many know them well enough on a personal basis to judge whether or not we like them? Hardly any. And yet, many of us *have* formed opinions about them and their governments and their policies. We love them, we hate them, we're ambivalent. Where did we get these opinions? From the media. The same thing holds whether it's bombings in London, the latest on the Middle East, war in Iraq, Anna Nicole Smith, economics: from GDP to inflation rates or unemployment levels, *et cetera*. Our first-hand experience is limited and so we learn about these things through the media.

Unless we live in a bubble, we spend most of our waking hours with one form of media or another, from the moment the radio wakes us up and we read the newspaper, to when we watch television news before bed. We read books, chill with the television, surf the web, or listen to music. We spend about half of a work week—on average about 20 hours—watching television. When we're not *directly* exposed to the media, we may be *indirectly* exposed, when we talk to someone and they relay something they've seen or heard. Lunchroom conversations are loaded with indirect news and entertainment programming. Even in university classes the lecture material probably originated in, or is making its way *into*, a textbook or journal article.

The other day my dad, who's eighty, emailed to tell me about an interesting article in the *Toronto Star*. He sends me lots of informative material, along with some questionable jokes. The internet seems to be a bonanza for jokes. The day before sending that article, my dad sent me some blatant (pro-U.S.) Iraq war propaganda, encouraging us to support their troops, with photos depicting how uncomfortable some of the troops are when they bed down for the night. "Stop complaining about your lot in life. Look how bad these guys have it, fighting for freedom and democracy"—that sort of thing. (I was tempted to find and send photos of murdered civilians: "If you think soldiers are uncomfortable, how do you think these dead civilians feel?" But I didn't.)

So, here was my dad circulating to his family and friends a little war propaganda probably designed by someone in the Pentagon. The second-hand media influence has reached new heights, courtesy of the Internet.

Now, if you have personal experience with any of these things, then you can put the media depictions in some kind of context. Some people have a story written about them, or are quoted in a story, and they know the difference between what they said in its entirety and what gets reported. A newspaper journalist once came to my office and interviewed me for about an hour and then quoted *one sentence* of what I said in that hour in the story he wrote. Another (television) journalist once interviewed me and I explained to him the two sides of the issue, as I saw them. When I watched the TV news that night, he'd edited out one side—the one he didn't like—and left me to promote the position he favoured.

Perhaps you've been to an event, a protest or demonstration or something. When you read about it in the newspaper the next day, you can put what you read into context. If there are distortions, you can make allowances, or dismiss what you've read altogether. That's where our first-hand personal experience comes in. The unfortunate thing is that we may not have much personal experience with the issues covered in the media.

So, media help us to formulate our views, ideas, beliefs, and oftentimes they actually shape our views because what they tell us is all we know about an issue. Or, we are influenced by others who, in turn, have gotten their views from the media.

Although alternative media exist, especially with the advent of the Internet, the vast majority of people continue to rely on the mainstream media for their information. For news, people either go to places like Yahoo or Google News, or Alta Vista, which almost exclusively search the mainstream sources, or people go to mainstream news web sources themselves, such as: CNN.com, CBC.ca, the *Globe and Mail* or the *Toronto Star*. Here are the top 15 web sites visited by Canadians, as of March, 2007:

Top 15 Web Sites

1. Google.ca

2. Microsoft Network (MSN) msn.com

3. Yahoo! yahoo.com

4. Google google.com

5. Thefacebook facebook.com

6. YouTube youtube.com

7. Windows Live live.com

8. Myspace myspace.com

9. WikiPedia wikipedia.org

10. Msn.ca

11. EBay ebay.com

12. EBay Canada ebay.ca

13. Blogger.com

14. Government of Canada gc.ca

15. Microsoft Corporation microsoft.com[1]

The first thing to note is that only one of these is truly Canadian: #14, the Canadian government web site. One has to wonder what this means for Canadian culture. The 2006 Gemini Award for top Canadian web site went to "Sons of Butcher," an animation TV program built around the band by the same name. The 2005 award went to CTV's "Canadian Idol." And, of course, none of these are news sites specifically, although you can get news stories at Yahoo, or MSN, but these are primarily web search sites.

So, excluding these, what are the top news sites? In Canada, the top 12 are as follows, listed by their overall ranking:

Top Twelve News Sites

20. CNN

26. BBC Newsline Ticker

27. Canada.com (CanWest Global)

29. CBC TV

36. *Globe and Mail*

60. *Toronto Star*

61. Canoe.com (Sun newspapers)

65. Canoe.ca (Sun newspapers)

71. CNET.com

72. World press.com

85. CTV News

86. *New York Times*[2]

Alternative media web sites are buried far down the list. The top one I could find in spring, 2007, was Indymedia.com, which ranked 3,162nd Alternet.org was 8,375th commondreams.org ranked number 11,312th amongst all web sites visited. *Counterpunch* was ranked 21,472nd while, the *Nation* was 21,607th and ZMag was 25,776th. The Canadian alternative Rabble.ca was number 274,683, while *This Magazine* was 1,095,542nd and Straightgoods.ca was ranked 657,258th.

The Free Marketplace of Ideas

If indeed the news media are responsible for many of the ideas we hold, especially about faraway places and events, then what becomes paramount is where these popular media come from, and where they get "our" ideas. The 17th Century British poet John Milton is credited with the notion that ideally, we live in a rough-and-tumble marketplace of ideas, where truth and falsehood clash, and truth inevitably triumphs. Serious scholars have demonstrated that it wasn't true in Milton's time—when he himself worked as a censor—and it certainly isn't true in our times.[3] But some people still promote the view that we are surrounded by diverse views and clashing opinions. We can ignore huge corporate media mergers, they say, because the Internet has saved the day, and we are now inundated with voices.

It's important that the media provide us with diverse and opposing views, so we can choose the best available options. Let's take the example of going to war. War should be a last resort, obviously, undertaken when all other options have failed. So, when someone is threatening to go to war, or trying to convince us—if they seek our approval—and mounting a huge public relations campaign to justify it, the news media have a responsibility to question everything. They should be providing the most intense scrutiny on our behalf, so the public can see the other side of things. Otherwise, we may be drawn into unnecessary wars, or wars fought for reasons other than those presented by governments and generals. Most of the time, the media fail to perform this crucial role. We now know, for example, that the media didn't do this with the U.S. invasion of Iraq in 2003. Even the large, so-called "liberal" American media such as the *New York Times* and *Washington Post* (let alone Fox and CNN) later admitted that they were cheerleaders for the Pentagon rather than watchdogs for the public interest. The *Washington Post*, when it went back to look at its own role about 18 months after the U.S. invaded Iraq, concluded that its own coverage, "looks strikingly one-sided at times."[4]

As part of that newspaper's assessment, Karen DeYoung, a *Washington Post* reporter and former assistant managing editor, summed things up: "We are inevitably the mouthpiece for whatever administration is in power. If the president stands up and says something, we report what the president said."[5]

This role—that of stenographers for power—now adopted by the news media, has important consequences, beginning with the waging of unnecessary wars, or wars fought for very different reasons than those provided, with all of the accompanying death and destruction. It also undermines to the point of absurdity a more idealistic role of the press, where it would keep people widely informed and serve the interests of democracy. Over the years, practicing journalists have referred to this crucial, ideal media role as providing the "hinge" or the "glue that holds together our democratic society." I parodied this usage in the title of an earlier book, *Democracy's Oxygen*. Here's how one prominent journalist described their role:

> Our job is to try to reflect reality…the media are…a socially and professionally responsible agent for the public…our job…is to provide a searchlight probing for truth through the confusing, complicated, cascading avalanche of fact and fiction.[6]

There is a tremendous difference between this journalistic ideal of a probing searchlight for truth, and being the U.S. President's mouthpiece. The risk you run when you don't have media which are independent of government, is that undemocratic forms of government develop, as we saw with: Hitler, Mussolini, Papa Doc Duvalier, Ferdinand Marcos or General Suharto. We need the police to function independently of politicians if we are to avoid a police state. We also need the media to be independent critics, the so-called *fourth estate*, (press) or *fifth estate* (broadcasting), critiquing governments, and the economic elite, for the rest of us. So, the news media role in society is crucial.

The Myth of Competition

According to conventional wisdom, just as the free marketplace of ideas produces diverse viewpoints, the free marketplace of economic transactions produces increased competition. If we can only do away with the government interference in the marketplace, the proponents of neoliberalism argue, everything will be fine. Keep those ham-fisted politicians out of things, leave economics to corporations and the "unseen hand of the marketplace," in the words of Adam Smith, an eighteenth-century philosopher who was dredged up and distorted to justify the merger mania of the last hundred years. Well, this is really an enormous triumph of public relations over reality, spin-doctoring at its most effective. For example, here's how the British magazine the *Economist* and Toronto's *Globe and Mail* reacted to the concentration threats posed by Bill Gates of Microsoft and Rupert Murdoch of News Corp., in the mid-1990s.

> A public desire for common standards, big-company muscle and sheer entrepreneurial flair are combining to create scary monsters with names like [Bill] Gates and [Rupert] Murdoch. The best way to deal with them is to watch them closely—*but never underestimate the capacity of natural economic forces to keep them in check, or of regulators' remedies to go wrong in practice.* Changing technology and the appetites of today's baby monsters should be enough to cope even with Gates (emphasis added).[7]

Here we have a succinct statement of the conventional wisdom, or what I have elsewhere called, "mediathink": the free marketplace, simply described as "natural economic forces," is supreme. Any attempt at regulation is foolish. And, of course, this all reflects "public desire," so it's really a democratic development. The Rupert Murdochs in the news business and the Bill Gates's in other businesses benefit equally from this mindset.

Just a few years later, the U.S. Justice Department brought an anti-trust case against Microsoft, and in April, 2000, Federal Judge Thomas Penfield Jackson ruled that Microsoft was a bullying monopolist which engaged in "predatory" business practices, "placed an oppressive thumb on the scale of competitive fortune," and "trammeled the competitive process." Two months later, the judge ordered that Microsoft be broken up into two separate companies. Of course, money talks, and the judge was removed from the case and his replacement eventually settled for rapping Bill Gates on the knuckles. As of

2004, Microsoft was an industrial giant with 50,000 employees worldwide and annual revenues of more than $37 billion.

> The company controls 90 percent of the market for computer operating systems and 95 percent of the market for office software... It already provides 30 percent of the software that allows graphics, sound, video, and animation to be delivered over the Internet, and is seeking to expand that market. It is also making inroads in new areas such as business software and mobile devices such as wireless phones.[8]

As for Australian/American media mogul Rupert Murdoch, his News Corporation controls the Fox Network, magazines, the *New York Post,* film and cable in the U.S., a lot of the press in the U.K. and Australia, magazines, television and satellite in China, book publishing, music, sports and MySpace.com. His potential worldwide audience "reach" is 4.7 billion. In the U.S., the Federal Communications Commission, which was chaired by Michael Powell, son of former U.S. Secretary of State Colin Powell, rewarded Murdoch for his media openly campaigning for George W. Bush, by voting 3-2 to allow his News Corp. to buy control of Hughes Electronics and its DirecTV satellite operation in a deal valued at $6.6 billion, in 2001. According to Alexander Cockburn,

> Murdoch offers his target governments a privatized version of a state propaganda service, manipulated without scruple and with no regard for truth. His price takes the form of vast government favors such as tax breaks, regulatory relief (as with the recent FCC ruling on the acquisition of Direct TV) monopoly markets and so forth.[9]

In every area of the economy, from telecommunications to raw materials, agriculture, retail merchandising, banking, the unseen hand has overseen dwindling competition. Mammoth international box stores and WalMarts have squeezed out competitors as consumers are lured by (some) lower prices and one-stop shopping. While there is competition, prices remain competitive. But once the competition is gone, monopoly pricing follows, where retailers charge what the market will bear.

The conclusion we are left with from all of this is that the unfettered competition of the free marketplace fosters concentration, oligopolies and monopolies. For example, in Canadian food retailing, in July 2005 Metro Inc. Bought up A&P Stores, for $1.7 billion. A&P already owned Dominion Stores and Food Basics. Metro owns Loeb, and Super C. The only other food giant is Loblaws, which owns

Zehrs, No Frills, Value-Mart, Provigo—and—well, you get the point. It's the same story with drug stores and corner stores and gasoline, *et cetera*.

Historically, these monopolies have long been with us. In the Canadian context, in 1588 Jacques Cartier's nephew Jacques Noel obtained a monopoly on furs and mines in what was to become Canada. Examples include the Hudson's Bay Company charter in 1670, (HBC owned all of what is now Alberta and Saskatchewan, at the time of Confederation) and the Canadian Pacific Railway monopoly clause in 1880. The public has been protected from these monopolies and their price-gouging, when governments have intervened on the other side of things. A notable example was at the end of the 19th century in the U.S., when huge monopolistic trusts had formed in 200 industries, including beef, copper, life insurance, sugar, tobacco, steel, and most notably the Standard Oil trust headed by John D. Rockefeller. In 1910, Rockefeller's net worth was equal to nearly 2.5% of the whole U.S. economy, the equivalent of nearly $250 billion in today's terms, or, relatively, at least twice as much as Bill Gates.[10]

Opposition to the trusts, especially amongst farmers protesting the high cost of rail transport to take their products to the cities, led to the passage of the first anti-trust law—The Sherman Act—in 1890. More than 20 years later, after a campaign led by "muckraking" journalists, Standard Oil was brought before the courts. The historic 1911 decision broke up Rockefeller's company into six oil companies, now reduced to four: Exxon, Mobil, BP, and Chevron.[11]

The Muckrakers

What changed things were the so-called "muckrakers," the journalists who exposed the fraud, political corruption and injustices of the robber barons. For example, the *Atlantic Monthly* published *The Story of a Great Monopoly*, about the railroads, and Standard Oil, which said in part,

> Our treatment of "the railroad problem" will show the quality and calibre of our political sense. It will go far in foreshadowing the future lines of our social and political growth. It may indicate whether the American democracy, like all the democratic experiments which have preceded it, is to become extinct because the people had not wit enough or virtue enough to make the common good supreme.[12]

Ida Tarbell, Upton Sinclair, Will Irwin and others penned more than a thousand muckraking articles in magazines such as the *Atlantic Monthly*, *McClures*, *Colliers* and *Everybody's*, in the first decade or so of the 20th century, inciting public outrage and spurring reform. This is how journalism ideally functions, as watchdogs for the public interest, blowing the whistle on greed and disparity, "afflicting the comfortable and comforting the afflicted," in the words of Finley Peter Dunne.

> The muckrakers helped bring about an unprecedented era of reform which included pioneering legislation aimed at restoring free competition to the economy and protecting the food supply along with other measures designed to stop the excesses and abuses of corporate greed.[13]

Without an adversarial press, the avarice may know no bounds. The question becomes, then, if a campaign by an independent press is what may spur people and governments to action, what happens when the press is no longer independent?

Media Ownership

Like the other areas of business, the news media have been ravaged by mergers and buy-outs in recent years, resulting in concentration levels which are exceedingly high, by comparison with other countries. A little more than a hundred years ago, at the time of the trust-busting legislation against robber barons, there were about 120 daily newspapers in Canada, with the same number of owners. Today, we have fewer dailies—about a hundred—with just a handful of owners. Five chains controlled 80 percent of daily newspaper circulation in 2003. And these same owners also control broadcast licenses and web portals and other media. For example, CTVglobemedia consists of Canada's largest private television network, CTV, with 24 stations spread across the country, as well as a prestigious national newspaper, the *Globe and Mail*. It owns a share of the Toronto Maple Leafs and Toronto Raptors. And it owns 17 specialty channels, from MTV, to TSN, Discovery Channel, to ROBTV, and the Comedy Network. And, it owns the Atlantic Satellite Network. In July 2006, CTVglobemedia offered to take over CHUM Limited for $1.4 billion, a deal which was approved by the federal competition bureau in March, 2007. This will add the number three television broadcast system, the CityTV network, as well as 21 specialty channels such as MuchMusic, Bravo!, and SPACE, and all of CHUM's 33 radio stations.[14]

This phenomenal concentration of ownership would have been unthinkable just a few years ago. And, it has brought together ostensible competitors, for example, the *Toronto Star's* parent company, Torstar, owns 20 percent of CTVglobemedia, owners of the *Globe and Mail*. What should one think, in reading about the CTVglobemedia takeover in the *Globe and Mail*, or even the *Toronto Star*? Are these relatively unbiased accounts, or will they be tainted by the lines of ownership? How will these newspapers report on CTV, or its competitors?

The media companies are largely controlled by powerful families, reminiscent of the Family Compact from the 19th century. For example Ted Rogers owns 91 percent of the voting shares in Rogers Communications Inc. Canada's wealthiest family, Ken Thomson's heirs, hold 40 percent of the shares of CTVglobemedia, through the Woodbridge Co. The Asper family owns 89 percent of voting shares at CanWest Global Communications Inc., which has one-third of national newspaper circulation, the number two private TV network, Global, and more, including, if it is approved by the CRTC, the $2.3-billion acquisition of television and film producer, Alliance Atlantis Communications Inc., which brings us all of the "CSI" programs.

At the *Toronto Star*, three families control 65 percent of the voting shares. The Peladeau family controls 64 percent of the shares of Quebecor, which owns Sun Media. Alan Waters' estate holds 88 percent of the shares at CHUM (at least until that CTVglobemedia deal is finalized), while Henri Audet controls 73 percent of the shares at Cogeco cable. "You can fit everyone who controls significant Canadian media in my office," Vince Carlin, chair of the School of Journalism at Ryerson University in Toronto, told the *Washington Post* recently. "This is not a healthy situation."

It's not just the degree of concentrated ownership, but who is involved. These owners are among the top ten wealthiest people in the country. I'm reminded of that quote from John Jay, an author of the Federalist Papers and the first chief justice of the U.S. Supreme Court who said, "The people who own the country ought to govern it." Other media owners in the top ten wealthiest list, in addition to the leading Thomson family ($22 billion), include Paul Desmarais of Power Corporation, ($4 billion), the Irving brothers of New Brunswick, ($5 billion), Jimmy Pattison of Vancouver, ($4.2 billion), and Ted Rogers ($2.2 billion). Apparently, media ownership is both influential *and* profitable.

One thing that's clear is that there will be no muckraking done in *these* media properties. There are other tangible negative consequences when small groups control so much. For example, the Asper family at CanWest Global fired

Russ Mills, the publisher of the *Ottawa Citizen*, in 2002. Why? Mills said it was because he allowed the *Citizen* to run a series of articles critical of then-prime minister Jean Chrétien, and an editorial calling for his resignation. The Aspers are close friends to Chrétien, especially the family patriarch Israel "Izzy" Asper, who died the following year, in 2003. Asper was the former leader of the Liberal party in Manitoba.

As Mills pointed out in a subsequent opinion column he wrote in the *Globe and Mail*, these actions had a 'chilling effect' on newsrooms across the country, especially because of CanWest's extensive holdings. "At the worst," Mills wrote, "my firing could send a serious chill across the newsrooms of CanWest papers, causing editors and other journalists to be excessively cautious in their political coverage and commentary." He went on to refer to "the climate of fear that must exist at the CanWest newspapers today." Publishers, editors and journalists knew that to keep their jobs, they should refrain from criticizing the Chrétien Liberals.

What's most unusual about this incident, under corporate control of the media, is that it was handled in such a ham-fisted manner and became such a public issue. Normally, as journalist Linda McQuaig pointed out in the *Toronto Star*, an incident like this would have been quickly swept under the carpet, with Mills promoted to a vice presidency, or a given a golden handshake, his silence bought and paid for.

UNDER THE ASPER THUMB

To comment on the conduct of elected officials is at the core of journalism in democratic countries, says ousted publisher Russell Mills

By Russell Mills, *Globe and Mail*, June 19, 2002

Last Sunday evening, my 30-year career with the *Ottawa Citizen* came to an abrupt end when I was fired by David Asper, chairman of Canwest Global's publications committee, for failing to seek approval from CanWest headquarters for the publication of an editorial that called for the resignation of the Prime Minister.

The editorial resulted from a long article published the same day reporting that Prime Minister Jean Chrétien had lied repeatedly in the case that has become known as Shawinigate. In my mind, there was no CanWest policy that required preapproval of such material.

continued

The company offered me a financial settlement that was only available if I would portray my departure as a retirement and sign an agreement not to discuss the situation. I refused. I said that I had not spent 30 years in journalism attempting to pursue the truth in order to leave on a lie.

If I was being fired, I wanted to be able to say so.

I am very concerned about my former colleagues who are with the CanWest newspapers. At the very least, my firing must have created great uncertainty about which editorials must be approved at the Winnipeg head office before publication.

Clearly, it seems, editorials seeking the resignation of the Prime Minister must go to Winnipeg before they can be published in any of the 14 Southam newspapers. But does strong criticism of the Prime Minister that stops short of asking for his resignation require approval? Does calling for the resignation of another cabinet minister require approval? Are the rules different for provincial or municipal officials? Are there any other sacred cows?

Today, no one can be sure of the answers to these questions and, as we have seen, the penalty for guessing wrong can be dismissal.

Since freedom of the press ultimately lies in the hands of the proprietor, CanWest has the right to run its newspapers as it sees fit. How it wants to do this, however, is quite unclear. Policy seems to be made on the fly and enforced capriciously.

In appearances before the CRTC, the Heritage Committee of the House of Commons, and in other public forums, executives of CanWest have given explicit guarantees that they will protect the editorial independence of their newspapers. The CanWest definition of independence appears to be quite different from the way most journalists and citizens would define it. Commentary on the conduct of elected officials is at the core of journalism in democratic countries. If much of this commentary requires corporate approval in advance of publication, this would be a significant limitation on the independence of newspapers.

At the worst, my firing could send a serious chill across the newsrooms of CanWest papers, causing editors and other journalists to be excessively cautious in their political coverage and commentary. Most journalists need their jobs and can't afford to be fired.

continued

Excessive caution would be damaging not only to journalism but to democracy in Canada. In a democracy, the people are ultimately sovereign and they need thorough and accurate information and commentary if they are to judge the conduct of the public officials they have put in power. This is the most important responsibility of Canada's newspapers and news broadcasters. Such information and commentary cannot be provided through government apparatus, nor can it be provided properly in the.climate of fear that must exist at the CanWest newspapers today. Journalists should not have to fear risking their livelihoods and the security of their families in order to do the essential job of keeping Canadians informed.

This is not an issue that can be dealt with by government. News media that relied on government for protection from proprietors would lack independence from government. Getting government involved could be worse.

It is up to individual Canadians to take action to protect the quality and independence of the information and commentary they require in order to be good citizens of a democracy.

Russell Mills was editor of the Ottawa Citizen from 1977 to 1986, publisher of the Citizen from 1986 to 1989 and from 1992 to 2002, president of the Southam Newspaper Group from 1989 to 1992, and past chairman of the board of the Canadian Newspaper Association.

CanWest Global: A Case Study in Control

This was not the first time CanWest, whose motto is, "inform, enlighten, entertain," was in hot water. In January, 2002, organizations representing journalists across Canada called for a parliamentary inquiry into media concentration, especially at CanWest Global. The Canadian Association of Journalists (CAJ) and the Quebec Federation of Professional Journalists (QFPJ) denounced actions of the media giant as "a disturbing pattern of censorship and repression of dissenting views."

CAJ vice president Paul Schneidereit said the federal government needed to examine the issue of media ownership concentration: "We feel it's time for the elected officials of this country to be looking at what the repercussions [of media concentration] are for the general public." The Quebec provincial government has said it might introduce legislation to force "a plurality of opinion" and diverse sources of information, according to culture minister Diane Lemieux.

The Newspaper Guild of Canada demanded that CanWest "immediately cease its attack on divergent opinions." The Guild—the largest journalists' union in North America—called in February 2002 for the Winnipeg-based media conglomerate to adopt principles that would respect the editorial autonomy of each paper and its columnists, and allow editors, rather than corporate headquarters, to make news judgments.

In 2000, CanWest bought up the Hollinger and Southam newspaper holdings from conservative media mogul Conrad Black. In 2001, it acquired majority control of Black's *National Post*, a Toronto-based Canada-wide daily. In addition to the *National Post*, CanWest now owns 11 large city dailies, 120 smaller dailies and weeklies, and the Global TV network, Canada's second-largest private broadcaster. The company also has private TV networks in Australia, New Zealand and Ireland, among other holdings.

CanWest set off the media furor in December, 2001, with its decision to require all of its daily newspapers to run corporate editorials produced in its Winnipeg head office. Initially, the company sent out one editorial weekly, but said this would eventually increase to three times a week. The company also said locally-written material should not contradict the corporate line handed down in its editorials. Ownership and management clashed with journalists and columnists who cringed under the new controls.

Journalists at CanWest's *Montreal Gazette* led the resistance, holding a brief "byline strike," keeping their names off articles, putting up a website to rally support, and enlisting the support of the union and other journalists. The *Montreal Gazette's* publisher, Michael Goldbloom, had earlier resigned over what he called CanWest's "centralized management style."

Izzy Asper, then chair of CanWest, told the CanWest Global annual shareholders meeting on January 30, 2002, that "on national and international key issues we should have one, not fourteen, editorial positions." But this reversed the guarantee of local autonomy the newspaper chains promised regulators when they were allowed to amass their empires, gobbling up independent dailies from the 1970s through the 1990s. Even during Conrad Black's ownership, Southam was still running a "Statement of Editorial Independence" in its annual report in 1995. The annual report said,

> For more than a century, Southam has proudly upheld its policy of editorial independence on all matters involving news and opinion. In the widely different environments in which Southam operates across the country, publishers and editors make their own editorial decisions.

And, as recently as 2001, in a brief to a House of Commons committee, CanWest said, "Each of our metropolitan and local newspapers is a strong player in its own community. Each is relentlessly local in its coverage and fiercely independent in its editorial policy. Under CanWest's ownership, that will not change."

Carnage at CanWest Global

In July, 2002, forty former senior management people at Southam, which was taken over by CanWest, took out an ad in several non-CanWest daily newspapers, urging CanWest to change its policy about not allowing contrary opinions. The group, which included publishers and a former CEO of Southam, said the policy was adversely affecting diversity of opinion in the country. The ad claimed the editorial policy limits "diversity of voices that is the essence of free speech, democracy and pluralism."[15]

Initially, the Asper family, which owns CanWest, arrogantly dismissed the widespread criticism of their actions. CanWest publications committee chair David Asper borrowed lyrics from the rock group REM: "I can say to our critics and especially to the bleeding hearts of the journalist community that it's the end of the world as they know it—and I feel fine," he said in a speech in January, 2002. By mid-February, however, the company backtracked somewhat, announcing that it would not go beyond imposing one editorial per week.

John Miller, director of Ryerson's newspaper journalism program, told the *Washington Post* that CanWest newsrooms have become demoralized. "It is not so much the national editorial, but the fact that everyone has been sent the message they have to watch what they write," Miller said. "If it goes against what is perceived as the Asper line, then some stories aren't going to get written, or some stories will be written and then they will be killed."[16]

Author and Southam columnist Lawrence Martin's contract was not.renewed in 2001, because of his criticism of then-Liberal Prime Minister Jean Chrétien—a friend of Izzy Asper.

Toronto Sun columnist Peter Worthington was critical of the Aspers and had his column pulled from the *Windsor Star*, a Southam paper, as a result. "I got a rather embarrassed call from the *Windsor Star*...saying they had been ordered to drop my column and not run [it] under any circumstances," Worthington told the *Toronto Star*.

Doug Cuthand, a First Nations columnist for the *Regina Leader Post*, wrote an essay in January, 2002 that was sympathetic to the plight of Palestinians in the West Bank, comparing them to Canada's indigenous peoples. The Aspers, who are "well known for their unstinting support of Israel," according to the *Toronto Star*, had the column killed. In November, 2002, Izzy Asper wrote a half-page opinion column which was run in all of his daily newspapers, in which he ranted and raved, exhorting the (other) news media to "End [their] media bias against Israel." In the column, Asper wrote that the "big lie" in the "world media" is that the Middle East conflict is not about territory and Palestinian Statehood, but rather, "it is a war to destroy Israel and kill or expel or subjugate all the Jews."[17]

Stephen Kimber, a columnist for 15 years with the *Halifax Daily News*, quit in January, 2002 after his column was killed by corporate headquarters. Kimber wrote in the column, which was eventually published in the *Globe and Mail*, that the Asper family, which made its fortune in the television business, appeared to consider their newspapers not only as profit centres and promotional vehicles for their television network but also as private, personal pulpits from which to express their views. Kimber claimed that:

> The Aspers support the federal Liberal Party. They're pro-Israel. They think rich people like themselves deserve tax breaks. They support privatizing health care delivery. And they believe their newspapers...should agree with them.[18]

Kimber told the *Toronto Star*, "I think that they could have gotten away with the 'national editorials' policy. But it's clear now that what they really wanted to do was stifle other people's opinions."

Stephanie Domet, another freelance columnist for the *Halifax Sunday Daily News*, resigned a few days later after writing a column in support of Kimber for the *Coast*, a Halifax weekly, a column later posted on the CBC's website.

Four reporters at CanWest's *Regina Leader Post* were suspended for five days in early March, 2002, for talking to outside media, and another six were given letters of reprimand after they withdrew their bylines in protest over an incident of censorship at the newspaper. Management at the *Leader Post* had censored a story by reporter Michelle Lang about a speech critical of CanWest by the *Toronto Star's* Haroon Siddiqui.

In March, 2002, the International Federation of Journalists accused CanWest of corporate censorship and victimizing journalists who were trying to defend professional standards. "If this had happened in Eastern Europe 15 years ago there would have been widespread protests from media owners and journalists' groups," the IFJ said in a press release. "The issues today are no different—the fight for editorial freedom and protection from censorship."

In 1991, after acquiring a 20 percent stake in New Zealand's TV3, Izzy Asper gathered 200 employees of the station in the cafeteria and astounded them by asking a journalist, "You—what business do you think you're in?"

The journalist replied that "the business we're in is to make sure our audience gets the most carefully researched news and information possible." Asper asked the same question of the drama and entertainment departments and got similar answers.

"You're all wrong," he told them. "You're in the business of selling soap."

Dan Rather and "Rathergate"

The U.S. equivalent of the Russ Mills story involves former journalism icon Dan Rather, the anchor for "CBS Evening News," who has been called the "Dean of American television journalism." Rather worked at CBS for 44 years, covering the Kennedy assassination, the Vietnam War, and 9/11. He replaced Walter Cronkite as anchor in 1981, a position he held until March, 2005. After that he was re-assigned to "60 Minutes," and produced a few stories with them before he was let go altogether in June, 2006, at age 74. Rather was no radical. In fact, journalism professor Robert Jensen wrote a scathing assessment of the incompatibility of Rather's brand of patriotism with honest journalism, indeed, he described Rather's position as "morally indefensible."[19]

Jensen was referring to Dan Rather's pronouncements on patriotism, first enunciated on the "David Letterman Show" on Sept. 17, 2001, when he said: "George Bush is the president. He makes the decisions, and, you know, it's [sic] just one American, wherever he wants me to line up, just tell me where, and he'll make the call." This interview was controversial because of the amount of emotion Rather displayed, struggling to keep from weeping on air. A few days later, in an interview on "CNN Tonight" with Howard Kurtz, Rather was asked if he thought journalists might be reluctant to criticize the Bush Administration, out of a fear of a public backlash. He replied, "I want to fulfill my role as a decent human member of the community and a decent and patriotic American. And therefore, I am willing to give the government, the president and the military, the benefit of any doubt here in the beginning." A few days later Rather gave an interview to former NBC and CBS reporter Marvin Kalb, in which he said, "As a journalist, I never want to place a single American fighting man or woman's life in danger. And I'm fully prepared to give the government military spokesman [sic] the benefit of every reasonable doubt on that score." So, apparently, Rather will go along, not just with the U.S. President, but with military spokespersons, refraining from the tough questioning inherent to good journalism. All of this demonstrates Rather's conservative, rather than progressive, nature.

In September, 2004 CBS's "60 Minutes II" ran an exposé on George W. Bush's National Guard Service, and how his congressman father pulled strings to get him in the National Guard as a pilot, in 1968, instead of serving in Vietnam, despite scoring 25% on his pilot aptitude test. Some of the documents used in the story were photocopies and fax copies, and hence it was very difficult to prove their authenticity. After the story aired, the internet lit up with blogs in a PR campaign in which right-wing conservatives attacked Rather, his producer Mary Mapes, CBS and "60 Minutes." Although the story about Bush is true, and it was published in the *Guardian* and on the BBC in Britain as early as 1999, the controversy centred on Rather and "60 Minutes" allegedly using some forged documents, and not doing adequate fact-checking. Because they could not definitively *prove* some of the documents they used were *not* forged, Rather, Mapes and others at "60 Minutes" took the fall.

More importantly, the spin doctors in the 2004 Republican re-election campaign managed to turn the real issue—the concrete and irrefutable evidence of Bush's draft dodging—into an attack on the allegedly 'liberal' news media, with their supposed vendetta against Bush. Three people at "60 Minutes" lost their jobs shortly thereafter, and Rather lost his job in 2006.[20]

Ironically, and prophetically, Rather the uber patriot had spoken earlier about his fears of what can happen to those who are not patriotic enough: necklacing.

"It is an obscene comparison. You know I am not sure I like it. But you know there was a time in South Africa that people would put flaming tires around peoples' necks if they dissented. And in some ways the fear is that you will be necklaced here, you will have a flaming tire of lack of patriotism put around your neck. Now it is that fear that keeps journalists from asking the toughest of the tough questions... And again, I am humbled to say, I do not except myself from this criticism."[21]

In the same way that what happened to Russ Mills had a chilling effect in newsrooms across Canada, what happened to Dan Rather and others at CBS had a chilling effect across the U.S. The lessons: don't be critical of the prime minister, or the president. What kind of journalism does this leave us with?

Business Interests

A number of years ago I noticed a peculiar article in the Report on Business of the *Globe and Mail*. The article discussed how the *Globe* was going to be better-serving its advertisers. How? By winnowing out readers with the wrong demographics. A popular misconception about the press is that they want to have the largest circulation possible. It's kind of a populist, even democratic type of notion: the idea that the press tries to appeal to as many of us as it can. So, at first blush, this article was almost shocking. The *Globe* was announcing that it would no longer deliver its newspaper to subscribers in *the wrong* neighbourhoods. That is, poor folks who don't have enough money to be attractive to advertisers.

If you understand how newspapers and other media work, it actually makes perfect sense. You see, we all have this misconception that media *sell news to audiences*. In fact, what they do is *sell audiences to advertisers*. The news, as Ken Thomson's dad Roy was fond of saying, "is just filler in between the ads." The reality is most clear in private broadcasting, where audiences don't pay anything, directly, for the news. So it's evident that what's being sold is the audience, as this is the only transaction taking place. Later, the audience pays money to the advertisers for their products, and the circle of life is complete.

Virtually the same thing happens in newspaper journalism, where advertisers pay for about 80 percent of the product and readers pay the rest. Well, in a sense the *Globe* cut back its subscriptions because the advertisers weren't willing to subsidize those readers—they weren't worth it, in terms of their purchasing power. On the other hand, newspapers like the *Globe* provide free copies of their newspapers to hotels and airlines, because these readers are well off, the business class, and "worth" subsidizing 100 percent, instead of the usual 80 percent.

Under this arrangement, what takes on unusual significance is creating "the buying mood" for readers. Things that might affect this mood are discouraged, if not censored. For example, airlines will not run their ads near to news about airline crashes. In television, serious programming is sometimes cut because advertisers find it too critical. Sometimes advertisers ask to preview programming, to make sure it's okay. It might affect the buying mood. If audiences become use to being critical, become good at it, then they might just turn their critical minds to the advertisements and the products. Where would it all end? Better instead to keep that "don't worry, be happy!" mindset. Give 'em sitcoms.

Chrysler Corp. (now Daimler-Chrysler)'s ad agency, PentaCom, a division of BBDO North America, sent out a contract with the following clause, to at least fifty magazines, in 1996:

> In an effort to avoid potential conflicts, it is required that Chrysler Corporation *be alerted in advance of any and all editorial content that encompasses sexual, political, social issues or any editorial that might be construed as provocative or offensive.* Each and every issue that carries Chrysler advertising requires a written summary outlining major theme/articles appearing in upcoming issues. These summaries are to be forwarded to PentaCom prior to closing in order to give Chrysler ample time to review and reschedule if desired… As acknowledgment of this letter we ask that you or a representative from the publication sign below and return to us no later than February 15 (emphasis added).[22]

As Russ Baker of the *Columbia Journalism Review* points out, this isn't Chrysler merely pursuing its own narrow economic interests, it's reaching out into "sexual, political, social issues" and beyond into anything that *might be* "provocative or offensive." To whom? PentaCom's President and CEO David Martin explained to the *Wall Street Journal*, "Our whole contention is that when you are looking at a product that costs $22,000, you want the product to be surrounded by positive things. There's nothing positive about child pornography."[23]

Chrysler is not alone in this. Other documented offenders include Colgate-Palmolive, which won't allow "offensive" sexual content or material that's "antisocial or in bad taste;" Procter & Gamble, which doesn't want its ads near anything about "gun control, abortion, the occult, cults, or the disparagement of religion." Other offenders include Kmart, Revlon, IBM, AT&T, Ford. Kimberly-Clark, maker of Huggies diapers demands in writing in its ad-insertion orders, that Huggies ads only be placed "adjacent to black and white happy baby editorial." Nothing as controversial as a discussion of the pros and cons of inoculating babies against diseases. One editor says, "sometimes we have to create editorial that is satisfactory to them."[24]

In September 2004, 61 American journalism and law professors sent a letter to the *American Society of Magazine Editors* asking it to "safeguard the integrity of magazines." The professors argued that allowing advertising to work its way into editorial content is a fundamental threat to press freedom and the integrity of journalism: "If magazines become mere tout sheets for products and the interests of those who sell them, then every story will be suspect, and the reading public may have nowhere to turn for information that is truly independent of reigning commercial interests," the professors wrote.[25]

At the *Kingston Whig-Standard*, in 1990 the editors made the mistake of running a review of a book written about how to sell your own home, on the front page of the Real Estate/Homes section. The wrath of the real estate industry came down on them, as realtors pulled their ads, reportedly costing the newspaper at least $1/4 million.[26] Not long afterwards, the newspaper was sold to the Southam chain (now CanWest Global).

At KTVO-TV in Missouri, the station lost an advertiser in 2004 who was upset by a news story which quoted a competitor who was not an advertiser.

> Crystal Amini-Rad, its vice president and general manager, was quick to see the error of her ways. "From now on," she decreed in a memo that included an apology to the sales staff, news reporters will "have access to an active advertiser list...of sources which you can tap into" for expert opinion and industry comment. Oh, and one more thing: reporters "should always go" to the station's advertising sources "first."[27]

Automotive Champions

On April 6, 2005 automotive columnist and Pulitzer prize winner Dan Neil of the *Los Angeles Times* wrote in a column that General Motors Chairman and CEO Rick Wagoner should be fired for incompetence. Citing "factual errors" in reporting, the next day General Motors withdrew its advertising from the *Times*, a reported $10 million (U.S.) yearly. The boycott lasted four months, which, doing the math, would cost the newspaper $3.3 million (U.S.) In early August, 2005 an undisclosed agreement was reached between GM and management at the *Times*.[28]

These examples belie a prevailing myth in journalism, that corporate ownership may affect profits and the business side of things, but it leaves the editorial or news side untouched. To anyone who is not in an advanced stage of denial this is immediately and overwhelmingly false. Two further examples from the *Windsor Star* are illustrative. In the first instance, on March 1, 1994, publisher Andre Préfontaine pulled from the second, home delivery edition, an editorial page column by regular columnist Gord Henderson. Henderson merely raised some reasonable questions about the wisdom of Chrysler Corp. paying American executives bonuses ranging from 75 to 100 percent of their salaries. At a time when CAW workers were allowed raises of 1.5 percent, the top 200 American executives were given 100 percent. Shouldn't someone have been allowed to comment?

By censoring Henderson's column (included below, slightly abridged) from the late edition, the publisher lent credence to those who view the press as a corporate lapdog rather than a public watchdog. Shortly before this incident occurred, Chrysler paid an estimated $300,000 for an advertising spread in the *Windsor Star*. According to one reporter with the *Star*, "Columnists should have the freedom to write opinion pieces. [This example] stands out because a journalist should be able to state an opinion but he couldn't. That was frightening. And our columnists tend to be more right-leaning."[29]

BAD CHOICES WILL HAUNT CHRYSLER

By Gord Henderson, *Windsor Star*. Windsor, ON, Mar 1, 1994. pg. A.6
LIBRARY NOTE: This column was not published in the final edition.

Far be it from me to bite the hand that feeds all of us.

I remember the bad times. I remember all too well the fear and anxiety on the faces of Chrysler executives who came to Ottawa 14 years ago looking for government help to save a desperate automaker.

The Chrysler miracle, the transformation of a corporate basket case into the industrial success story of the 1990s, has been Windsor's miracle as well. Its huge profits are this city's life insurance policy.

But it still boggles the mind how a corporation smart enough to earn $3.8 billion US in one year could do something this shortsighted.

The parent corporation, in doling out huge performance bonuses to its senior executives in the U.S., has sent the worst possible message to the people who make its immensely popular vehicles.

In effect, it has told Chrysler employees everywhere that it has two compensation standards: one for the folks who produce its cars and trucks and another for the suits in the executive offices...

continued

THE STORY THAT made the lasting impression, the one clipped and saved for the next set of contract talks, revealed that Highland Park paid bonuses matching last year's salaries to 200 top executives.

According to a Detroit News report that quoted unnamed Chrysler executives, another 100 executives just below the top level received bonuses of 75 to 85 per cent of annual pay. It said the 1993 bonuses were the largest payments ever from the company's executive bonus pool and were made because it exceeded profit, customer satisfaction and quality improvement targets.

Outraged UAW officials termed the bonuses "total greed," and warned that they caused "a hell of a step backward" in labour relations. Chrysler UAW members received bonuses equalling about 10 per cent of their annual pay, approximately $4,300 US.

If this news didn't sit well with the UAW, imagine how it struck CAW officials, who spent months last summer hammering out a Chrysler Canada contract that included a five-per-cent wage hike over three years.

"This is just ridiculous. Where's the equity?" fumed Ken Lewenza, first vice-president of CAW Local 444. He said Windsor Chrysler workers are up in arms over it. "This really ticks them off."

Walt McCall, manager of corporate public relations for Chrysler Canada, stressed that the Canadian subsidiary has a separate salaried bonus system based on profit sharing. "All I can really confirm is that our Canadian officers receive bonuses also. I can't say what they are."

McCall said the CAW was offered profit sharing in the last two sets of contract talks but rejected it both times...

What's interesting is that the CAW leadership isn't screaming for a share of the loot. That's how the union would have responded 15 or 20 years ago, by demanding money.

BUT IN 1994, a sophisticated labour organization recognizes the direct link between productivity and job security. It wants Chrysler to remain a winner.

It's insisting, and this should be music to an executive's ear, that Chrysler plough every spare dollar into readying the company for future challenges.

"We're saying put it (the bonus money) back in. Re-invest it," said Lewenza.

"The reality is that when the company is making money, it should be preparing for five and 10 years down the road."

continued

FROM A TAXPAYER point of view, seeing Chrysler Corp. executives handed huge cash bonuses is a little hard to swallow.

Less than a year ago, Ontario announced a $30-million retraining contribution as part of an expansion and retooling of the minivan plant to build both the regular and stretch versions. A nearly bankrupt province scraped up millions of dollars to improve the workforce of a Canadian subsidiary that recently announced a $418-million profit.

Meanwhile, the parent corporation has money for lavish executive bonuses.

You could argue that it's nobody else's business how Chrysler spends its mega-earnings. If it chooses to double the income of its top executives, so be it. This isn't 1980, and the company is no longer a hardship case.

Still, it's hard to believe that a firm which has done so many things right wouldn't be concerned about the impact on its workforce of being seen to have a double standard.

You don't build morale in the trenches with tales about the good life being enjoyed by the generals back at headquarters.

If Chrysler Corp. truly values restraint, not to mention teamwork, a 100-per-cent bonus for the lucky few is one strange way to show it.

An action by James Bruce, former editor of the *Star* and Préfontaine's successor as publisher, was even more problematical because it applied to the news rather than commentary. On February 5, 1996, the *Star* ran a CP wire service story out of Montréal which mildly criticized car dealers. The story, which ran on Page D7, provided tips on car buying and reported on a study by the Automobile Protection Association, which found in a test that seven out of nine Montréal car dealers mislead customers. Although the story reported on these findings, the criticism was muted, and the story contained a rebuttal by the president of the Canadian Automobile Dealers' Association. Nevertheless, Bruce says "I went ballistic," reportedly screaming at his editors for allowing the story to run.[30] He admitted he had not received a single complaint. The next day, Bruce published a letter of apology on Page 4, which began: "On rare occasions a story finds its way into the newspaper which does not meet the high ethical and journalistic standards of balance, fairness and factual accuracy which we set for ourselves at the *Windsor Star*." After briefly describing the story, he continued: "The story was a discredit to the dealers and employees of members of the Windsor Essex County Dealers Association, who adhere to the highest of ethical standards and provide their customers with first rate standards of service." Bruce concluded by saying, "The *Star* apologizes to the dealers, their sales people and readers for any false impressions which the story may have created."[31]

Journalists at the newspaper were so riled up over the car dealer incident that they demanded a meeting with the editor and publisher, who agreed. According to some who were present, the publisher defended his position by saying that he had recently attended a human rights workshop sponsored by the CAW, and that stereotyping occupational groups such as car dealers was unacceptable! Bruce said afterwards, "I don't believe that any group in society should be stereotyped. Over the years, car dealers have been stereotyped, they have been characterized as a bunch of crooks." He went on to add that:

> I thought it was a very, very poor piece of journalism, which should
> not be in our newspaper. I have absolutely no apologies to make for
> the decision that I personally took at six o'clock the next morning.
> That decision was to respond and to be pro-active in the situation."

To rectify the situation, acting editor Doug Firby vowed that in future, management would read each and every story. This would ensure that no such thing would happen again.

The most striking thing about this incident is that it makes it clear that anything which is even remotely critical of advertisers is not going to make it into the newspaper. Additionally, as a letter writer subsequently pointed out, the article in question did in fact meet the three standards of "balance, fairness and factual accuracy" which the publisher said the *Star* sets for itself. It's not at all clear that the publisher's letter meets those same criteria, especially where he wrote that *all* local car dealers "adhere to the highest of ethical standards and provide their customers with first rate standards of service." What is his authority for making this claim? The wire service story was based on a field experiment conducted at nine Montréal dealerships. Publisher James Bruce's sweeping generalization appears to have been based on nothing more than the claims made in the car dealers' advertisements in his own newspaper. I am not aware of any evidence which indicates that car dealers and salespeople are different from other occupational groups. There is however plenty of evidence which indicates that some salespeople mislead their customers. In fact, the

Better Business Bureau has, in the past, indicated that car dealers are at the top of their complaints list.[32] To deny this and apologize to car dealers for what amounts to a balanced and factual story, is to take the business of toadying to advertisers to new heights.

STORY FAILED TO MEET STAR'S STANDARDS

Montreal-based wire story on dealer survey unfairly implicates local dealers, *Star* publisher says

By James Bruce, *Windsor Star*. Windsor, ON, Feb 6, 1996. pg. A.4

On rare occasions a story finds its way into the newspaper which does not meet the high ethical and journalistic standards of balance, fairness and factual accuracy which we set for ourselves at the *Windsor Star*.

Such a story appeared on Page D7 on Monday, under the headline How to drive a bargain when buying a car.

This story, which was sent to newspapers from across Canada by the Canadian Press, was based on a survey done by George Iny, president of the Montreal-based Automobile Protections Association. It questioned the integrity and honesty of a few auto dealerships who were surveyed in Montreal.

Although the story did not involve any Essex County Dealers, it may have by implication cast aspersions on their business practices. The story was a discredit to the dealers and employees of members of the Windsor Essex County Dealers Association, who adhere to the highest of ethical standards and provide their customers with first rate standards of service.

The *Star* apologizes to the dealers, their sales people and readers for any false impressions which the story may have created.

In another incident, Chrysler Canada instituted an advertising boycott at the *Montreal Gazette*, when that newspaper ran an article which quoted a commentator as saying that then-Chrysler president Yves Landry was "hypocritical" for calling for quotas on Japanese car imports, because Chrysler itself imports and sells Japanese vehicles such as the Eagle Talon and Plymouth Laser.

CHRYSLER REPORT COSTS *GAZETTE* ADS
'Very harmful' story assailed

By Barrie McKenna, *Globe and Mail*, June 22, 1991

Montreal PQ—Angered by an article suggesting president Yves Landry was a hypocrite for supporting import quotas, Chrysler Canada Ltd. has yanked its advertising from the *Montreal Gazette*.

"Fair comment is fair comment," Chrysler spokesman Walt McCall said from Windsor, Ont., yesterday. "We'll take that anytime. But this was not fair."

Mr. McCall said a May 18 story in the *Gazette* was "a gross distortion" of remarks Mr. Landry made earlier to a Calgary business group.

He would not say how much Chrysler spends on ads in the newspaper nor how long the ban would last.

"It was more of an editorial than a story," Mr. McCall said. "It's been very harmful to us."

In his speech, Mr. Landry called for a halt to the erosion of North American car makers' domestic market share, better access to Japanese markets and a 60-per-cent content rule on Japanese cars made here. He also urged Ottawa to impose quotas against the Japanese.

The *Gazette's* story, running under the headline, "Casting the wrong stone," pointed out that Chrysler and other major North American car makers are themselves large-scale importers of Japanese-made vehicles. Chrysler, for example, sells the Eagle Talon and Plymouth Laser, both made by its Japanese partner Mitsubishi Motors Corp. Chrysler owns a stake in Mitsubishi.

This was part of what Chrysler objected to.

Gazette publisher David Perks said the newspaper has not yet received official word about any ads being pulled.

"We hope we have no problem with Chrysler," he said. "They are a valuable customer."

Mr. Perks said an advertiser has every right to place ads where and when it wants. He noted that the newspaper published a response from the company in a letter to the editor.

But Mr. McCall said that was not enough. "A letter does not make up for the harm caused by the original story and it does not get the same play."

continued

The move by Chrysler comes as U.S. politicians are calling for an investigation into all so-called transplant plants established by the Japanese in Canada.

A preliminary U.S. customs finding has found that Honda Motor Co. Ltd. of Japan escaped duties by exaggerating the North American content of Civics made in Ontario. Honda has denied the finding.

While relatively rare, ad boycotts do occur. Earlier this year, Canadian Airlines International Ltd. of Calgary pulled its ads from the *Financial Post* in protest over what a spokesman said was the newspaper's "alarmist approach" to the airline industry.

These are not isolated events, but they don't receive much publicity. Reporter John Asling, who has worked for the former Thomson and Southam chains, recounted numerous incidents of corporate and advertiser influence, in what he described as "backscratch journalism."[33] Rob Reid, then-city editor of the *Timmins Daily Press* remembers in the 1980s when Maurice Switzer was publisher, and a national story came over the wire which was vaguely critical of McDonalds restaurants. "We ran the story as a small brief. Switzer reamed out the wire editor for running the story," Reid said.[34]

What's abundantly clear from these examples is that the news is not written for readers, it's written to please advertisers. It's really a wonder anything *even remotely critical* of advertisers ever gets in. And what's important to understand is that *any corporation is a potential advertiser*. As former journalist and media educator Ben Bagdikian notes, corporations are the "sacred cows" of the newsroom. Here's what an excellent journalist, Antonia Zerbisias of the *Toronto Star*, wrote during the Hurricane Katrina disaster in the summer of 2005:

> On the day before [hurricane] Katrina struck the Gulf coast, I blogged my concerns about how the levees would fail. I learned about that horrendous possibility from public broadcasting—in this case a PBS documentary in 2002. No commercial broadcaster warned Americans because they would never do anything to upset advertisers. Hence, you'll see very little serious investigative journalism on any commercial network—including those in Canada. Which is why we need the CBC.[35]

The Diminishing CBC

A number of factors including smaller budgets, less public money, more money from advertising, and flak from private networks and conservative "free market" lobbyists such as the Fraser Institute have steadily eroded the influence and credibility of public broadcasting. Government cuts over the years, leading to greater reliance on advertising support for the CBC, make it harder to distinguish it from the commercial services. At a certain point the argument becomes: why do we need a public broadcaster? What is it doing that is different? This argument has resonance with the widely promoted belief that public enterprise is inefficient and bad while private is good. Privatization hysteria makes it seem as though we are ready to do away with the public broadcaster. The public broadcaster is not as beholden to corporate interests, and has the potential—not always realized—to carry more balanced and open-minded reporting which may even occasionally challenge the corporate agenda.

The ability of the CBC or TVO, *et cetera*, to present an alternative is qualified by a number of influences. First, in the case of CBC-TV, it remains a commercial network in the sense that an increasing proportion of its funding comes from advertising dollars, as public financing dries up. As a result, it is driven by similar economic concerns to those of the corporate media. Second, its upper management and board of directors are appointed by the government of the day, inevitably leading to political appointments, and views at the top which are in sync with those of the corporations, politicians and commercial media. Third, many of the people who work in the CBC move back and forth from corporate to public media, bringing with them the same news values. Fourth, the news decision-makers at CBC rely on wire service sources which are largely compiled by the Canadian Press (CP) news service, which in turn is produced by its member daily newspapers. Fifth, the news workers at the CBC evaluate their own performance by reference to the corporate press and broadcasting outlets. Hence, while morning programs on CBC radio compare quite favourably with the mindless drivel of commercial radio stations, in the final analysis they are little better than a *Toronto Star* of the airwaves. While somewhat better than the others they are ultimately promoting the same corporate views, frequently quoting the same people in the commercial news media, academia or government. What we really need is a *Canadian Dimension* or *This Magazine* or rabble.ca, or *Z Magazine* of the airwaves.

One example will illustrate. Noam Chomsky tells the story of how he is treated as a pariah by the American media, but he is usually given some more attention and even some favorable reception by the Canadian media, as long as he confines his criticism to U.S. foreign policy. The moment he brings the Canadian government's despicable actions into focus, he is cut off at the knees by the Canadian media as well. He tells the story of appearing on Peter Gzowski's morning program on CBC radio, and criticizing Lester Pearson over Canada's involvement in Vietnam. "Canada was probably the leading military exporter in the world per capita, enriching itself on the destruction of Indochina," Chomsky said. Gzowski was "infuriated," throwing "a tantrum," launching into a harangue and not letting Chomsky elaborate or continue. The CBC switchboard lit up with thousands of phone calls from listeners, many of whom were furious with Gzowski for not hearing Chomsky out. To appease the listeners, the producers arranged for another interview in which Gzowski was suitably contrite, and gave Chomsky a chance to air his views. But, Chomsky says it was the last time he was on the program.[36]

While it is imperfect, the CBC is also, as the annual Gemini Awards demonstrate, usually head and shoulders above the private competition. When the public broadcaster provides excellent journalism, the profit-oriented corporate networks look bad by comparison. This fact may play a role in the desire by CanWest Global, for example, to have CBC sold off to private bidders such as itself. Having gobbled up the independent private stations, the media barons have long turned their eyes to the public stations as one of the few remaining areas of expansion. (The other being international opportunities, which are rapidly, if not entirely, diminishing.)

Working hand-in-glove with the media barons are the policy makers and their minions on the CRTC and at the Department of Heritage, whom the politicos have appointed. The other private media, such as the newspapers, cooperate by promoting the general ideals and the specific actions needed to undermine the CBC.

In August 2005, CBC management locked out its news journalists union, disrupting news coverage in the ensuing weeks. Once again, the federal Liberal government and CBC management were looking for major concessions and cutbacks, including "flexibility" to contract out production and services to the private sector. As they did in 1996, the CBC unions said that unlimited out-sourcing amounts to privatization of the CBC through the back door.

Public broadcasting can potentially avoid one of the largest pitfalls of news reporting: the bias in favour of advertisers, and corporations generally.

That's why programs such as "Marketplace," which takes a critical consumer perspective, are found on CBC and not CTV or Global.

Additionally, since our big corporate media are owned by the very wealthy, this will be reflected in other ways in news content, and public policy. An example is "income trusts."

We Trust Income Trusts

Another example, briefly, is that of "Income Trusts." The way this controversy has been covered in the corporate media reveals, in a more direct and apparent way, the elite interests which underlie news media coverage.

Corporations which are redefined as "income trusts," are not required to pay taxes on profits. They have been around in Canada since the 1980s, but they've grown in a spectacular way in the past few years, as business discovered what a gold mine they represent. In 1995, they had a market value of $1.3 billion. Five years later, there were 70 trusts, worth $10 billion. In 2005 there were more than 225 trusts worth $170 billion. Why the growth? Well, income trusts are not taxed. As economist Jim Stanford with the Canadian Auto Workers put it, their "sole reason for existence is legalized tax evasion."[37]

No other government in the world has this kind of tax-free policy. Because of the obvious controversy over these trusts, in September, 2005, Liberal government finance minister Ralph Goodale announced a review of the tax issues surrounding income trusts, but two months later and with an election imminent, he pulled the plug on the consultation process. Goodale announced that instead of taxing income trusts, as some expected, he was cutting the taxes shareholders pay when they receive corporate dividends, to help "level the playing field" between corporations and trusts.

In other words, if you have a problem with a tax loophole which is costing the treasury plenty of money, the best way to deal with this, according to the Liberals, is to open up another loophole which will cost even more.

Instead of creating a controversy, however, this decision received accolades in the news media. Quoting jubilant business analysts, the media were universally pleased with this decision. For example, a Canadian Press story in the *Toronto Star* was headlined, "Investors cheer Ottawa's dividend and trust move." The article pointed out that the tax rate payable on corporate dividends "will drop by more than a third for people in the top income bracket." Although the Federal Finance Department estimated (conservatively?) that the decision would cost the public treasury $300 million a year, this was described as "a very cheap way to settle this contentious issue." This CP/*Toronto Star* article reported that "Bay Street was almost unanimous in applauding Goodale." But the media reports were not almost unanimous, they *were* unanimous.[38] Analysts were overjoyed, the stock market soared in reaction, and things couldn't have been better. The only question asked was, just how good an investment is an Income Trust, for stockholders?[39]

The corporate bias in this reporting is readily apparent. Soon, the conflict of interest became apparent as well, as BCE Inc., then Canada's largest media conglomerate, announced its transformation into an Income Trust, followed by its subsidiary Telus, and selected CanWest Global newspapers.[40] What was good for the goose, was also good for the gander. It's little wonder the gander was so positive about corporate raiding of the federal treasury, to the tune of hundreds of millions if not billions of dollars in taxes.

Then, things really started to get out of hand. The loss of federal revenue from income trusts was estimated at $500 million for 2006 alone, which would rise by another $300 million with the conversions of Telus and Bell Canada. The Conservative government said this would increase into the billions of dollars a year if left unchecked. (Oops.) The provinces also are losing revenues, with one estimate putting the total net loss to all governments at $1.1 billion for 2006.[41] Nice windfall, but who's going to pave the roads and pay for health care and education? In fall, 2006, the minority Conservative government of Stephen Harper decided to set a date for closing the Income Trust tax loophole because it would soon be crippling the federal treasury. The news media, including the CBC, roundly condemned the decision.[42] Largely ignoring the blatant problems caused by this corporate tax giveaway, the news media helped the opposition Liberal party to turn it into a controversy over Harper's flip-flop on the issue, and what would happen to senior citizens' pension investments. The real story was still more new general corporate tax cuts, and the way the Conservatives' legislation delayed closing the tax loophole until 2011, giving corporate Canada plenty of time to profit handsomely, at our expense.

Labour As a Four-Letter Word

If corporations are sacrosanct, or untouchable, then the obvious test case rests with labour, which is the "other side" in the regular battles with management and ownership. The first thing to note regarding labour coverage is that labour reporters have disappeared, even in labour towns such as Windsor Ontario. While business sections have expanded, filling up with stock market reports and stock exchange information, business news and opinion columns, labour no longer warrants a single reporter. When *Globe and Mail* labour reporter Lorne Slotnick was reassigned back in 1989, management told him "the paper is no longer interested in covering developments in collective bargaining or the activities of organized labour." Instead, the newspaper's management wanted coverage of "the 'good' things that are happening at non-union establishments, as well as stories about workplace 'trends'—apparently from a management point of view," Slotnick said.[43] At the time, the *Globe* had more than 30 reporters covering business, a figure which has since grown.

A litmus test for journalistic objectivity is the coverage of a strike or lockout at a newspaper. These case studies show how well the newspaper can put aside biases, to report objectively. Casual observation of reporting during recent significant strikes/lockouts, such as the prolonged one at the *Calgary Herald* in 1999-2000, or the five-and-a-half-year-long *Detroit News* and *Free Press* strike ending in 2000, indicates that management's perspective is predominant. Columnists write, defending their decision to cross picket lines, while the other side isn't seen or heard, for example when Catherine Ford of the *Calgary Herald* wrote that hers was an "ethical decision" to refuse to strike.[44] Commentators from elsewhere in the newspaper chain or business are run in the newspaper, who happen to agree with management's perspective.[45] Any editorials obviously represent management's views.[46] Deciding what letters to print is always a subjective exercise. So, the commentary in the newspaper is heavily biased toward management.

What about the news stories? Well, perhaps we can judge from the December 6, 1999 story, two months into the *Calgary Herald* dispute. "Strike Nears Second Month..." Here, newspaper management uses the views of a business professor, described as a "labour expert," to claim that the "union [is] in a tough place." This view is foregrounded, put in the headline and at the top of the story. Additionally, notice that the expert is quoted for his views on the battle strategy of the strike, rather than its merits. He's not asked, for example, what he thinks of management's position that union seniority will not be allowed. Next, we learn that 33 journalists have crossed the picket lines, "including some high-profile columnists." Then Peter Menzies, editor-in-chief is quoted, who says its "hard to see how they're [the union] going to get out of this," backing up the views of the labour expert. Menzies goes on to say that the strike is about control of the newspaper.

We next hear from newspaper publisher Dan Gaynor, with a lengthy quote about "the pursuit of excellence," and a critique of seniority rights. After all of this, finally, a Vancouver-based union executive is given three brief sentences in response, wherein she repeats the seemingly reasonable position by management that they merely want to be able to keep "the best and the brightest." It's not explained that without union seniority, reporters can be fired on a whim, or because of a vendetta by management. Then it's back to Gaynor, the publisher, for a rebuttal, and then finally, a few brief comments from a local 26-year-old striker, followed by another comment from the union rep. The union/striker side of things has been backgrounded at the end of the story, what's sometimes called 'the back of the bus,' but the reporter and newspaper can claim there is 'balance' in the story. Of course, this position is ludicrous, a fact which is proven by journalism's own convention of "inverted pyramid" writing, where the most important elements of the story are put at the top, while what follows is less and less important. This allows for editors to cut the bottom off stories for space considerations, if necessary. And, it explains why newspapers are not written in a narrative, chronological style, with the most important information at the end. Newspaper marketing research also demonstrates that readers frequently only read the headline and first few paragraphs of a story, never getting to the labour side of the story. This story is obviously heavily weighted toward management views.

STRIKE NEARS SECOND MONTH, NO TALKS AND NO END IN SIGHT
Union in a tough place, labour expert claims

By Joan Walters, *Calgary Herald*, AB, Dec 6, 1999. pg. C.4

A month-long strike for a first contract at the Calgary Herald, one of Southam's leading western newspapers, shows all the signs of being a long, drawn-out dispute, an Alberta labour expert says.

"I think the union is in a tough place," Prof. Allen Ponak of the University of Calgary faculty of management said Friday.

"They've been replaced, the paper is still operating, the revenue streams are still there and this is a time of year when revenue is very high," he said. "And from a consumer point of view, to buy a newspaper, you don't have to cross a picket line. This makes it a completely different dispute."

continued

About 150 members of the Communications, Energy and Paperworkers Local 115A, employed in the Herald newsroom, and 65 production employees with the Graphic Communications International Union have been on strike since Nov. 8 for a first contract with the paper. The union was certified in the fall of 1998.

There is wide agreement among all parties that this will be a long, difficult haul. Thirty-three journalists, including some high- profile columnists, have crossed the picket lines.

"It's hard to see how they're going to get out of this," said Peter Menzies, named editor-in-chief in a reorganization of Herald management earlier this year.

"It (the strike) seems to be about control," said Menzies who, with new publisher Dan Gaynor, Herald management, and a cadre of Southam managers from across the country, continues to publish full editions every day.

"(The employees) acknowledge management's right to control the content of the paper. But they feel seniority is required so that senior journalists feel confident enough to stand up and challenge management on its decisions."

Union officials agree seniority is the dominant issue, as does Gaynor, who was publisher of the St. Catharines Standard when that Ontario Southam daily went on strike over wages in a first contract dispute in 1998.

"First and foremost, it's important we have an editorial department that encourages initiative and is motivated by pursuit of excellence and that we have a framework for encouraging that," Gaynor said.

"I don't think seniority contracts—last-in, first-out language—does anything to support that. As a matter of fact, I think it can foster a very different culture."

Joy Langan, a Vancouver-based executive of the CEP, says the union has proposed "basic seniority language that's in every other newsroom contract in Canada.

"We believe that when you give 30 years to the company you should be able to expect some respect for that contribution," Langan said. "The company has consistently said no, we want to be able to keep the best and the brightest."

Gaynor said the Herald proposes that "all of our decision-making would be based on merit, on job performance. So if there were layoffs, and none are planned, we could retain our very best rather than laying off in order of seniority."

continued

Gaynor contends that, in his experience, seniority language "is problematic." "And here, in a first contract, we have an opportunity to make sure it doesn't become problematic here."

Brian Brennan, a 26-year Herald writer and member of the bargaining committee, says Gaynor's response signals to him there may be a larger agenda in play.

"That sort of suggests we have become a kind of test case," Brennan said. He believes the Herald will ultimately be the battleground for all the forces hovering around the dispute.

"Frankly, I think seniority is a red herring," Brennan said. "The real issue is they don't want to have a collective agreement or a union in the building."

Langan said the CEP believes Southam picked Alberta as a place "to draw a line in the sand...because of the labour laws in Alberta. If we lose here, that will have a spin-off impact as contracts get negotiated in other papers."

The Calgary Herald dispute involves a more complex set of forces and has featured deep divisions: union accounts of egotistical managers, failed journalism ethics and sycophantic public posturing. On the other side, management describes a nucleus of senior workers so locked into their past that the venerable daily had become a caricature—unable to capture the glory, guts and thinking of the city it was supposed to reflect.

Talks between the company and the GCIU have been scheduled for Dec. 13. No talks have been scheduled between the company and the CEP.

This kind of thing is not unusual. In his study of the *New York Times*, Daniel Chomsky describes how management reined in a reporter who didn't put labour's views at the back of the bus.

Publisher 'suggestions' have special force. A complaint or proposal from the publisher resonates throughout the institution and can establish new policies. Unsympathetic treatment of labour unions in the news pages, for instance, may reflect the attitudes of ownership. In fact, when Russell Porter gave too much prominence to the views of workers, the publisher [Arthur Hays Sulzberger of the *New York Times*] was irate. 'I would appreciate it if you would let me know how Mr. Porter happened to write his story as he did this morning', Sulzberger instructed James. Porter had written a story on the sale of a newspaper. After the first three paragraphs Porter included a re-sponse from the newspaper's unions. He defended his story on the grounds that the views of union leaders were a significant part of the story. Management was not persuaded. Porter was informed that 'Management's judgement is against him', a particularly stern warn-ing in the circumspect language of internal communications at the *Times*. Porter's editors acknowledged that labour's perspective was a part of the story, 'but it could better have come further down in it'. It is not likely that Porter made that mistake again. And it is not likely that other reporters repeated that error either.[47]

With regard to the prolonged Detroit newspapers strike, professors Robert Picard and Stephen Lacy conducted a study and concluded:

> The use of a newspaper to promote management's business inter-ests is not new to strikes nor journalism, but it marked the Detroit strike from early on. Although it is tempting for management to use all the resources, including the voice of the newspaper, during a dis-pute, this can rapidly lead to one-sidedness in reporting about the dispute and a loss of fairness. When this occurs, readers will detect the bias... Using the newspaper for business propaganda will create the impression that newspaper companies are just another business with no interest in hiring independent journalists. Once people per-ceive a newspaper as biased in its coverage of one area, it becomes easy for them to see bias in other coverage areas.[48]

An excellent study of reporting on labour is Dr. Erin Steuter's doctoral research. Steuter examined coverage of striking Irving Oil Refinery workers in New Brunswick. What makes her case study so important is the fact that the Irving Group of Companies has monopoly ownership of the New Brunswick media, in-cluding all four English-language daily newspapers. As one might anticipate, the coverage showed a very clear bias against the workers, and in favor of man-agement and ownership. What's more, other Canadian newspapers such as the *Globe and Mail*, also reported on the strike from a management-perspective, deni-grated the strikers, and refused to criticize the powerful Irving family.[49]

The news media are quite clearly biased when reporting on an in-house strike or lockout. There's also considerable evidence that they're biased when it comes to reporting on strikes or lockouts elsewhere. For example, a study of the news coverage of the Ontario teachers' strike of 1997 concluded that, "On the whole, the coverage portrayed the teachers' action as an affront to the law and socially acceptable standards of political action, as well as the main cause for considerable harm and inconvenience to the public and the business community."[50]

A study of press coverage during the 1997 UPS strike in the U.S. found that *USA Today* "focused almost exclusively on the inconvenience caused by the strike to businesses and consumers, with a minimal discussion of the issues at stake...*USA Today* also actively justified UPS [management] practices ...and represented UPS as an icon of American society." Despite this coverage, "public sympathy favored the strikers," over UPS management, by a margin of 55 percent to 27 percent.[51]

All these findings accord with the observations on strike/lockout reporting made by American academics Michael Parenti and William Puette.[52]

- Strikes are depicted as senseless acts which could be avoided through discussion.
- Labour, not management, is unwilling to negotiate in good faith.
- Management makes "offers" while labour makes "demands."
- The impact on the economy and the inconvenience caused to the public is highlighted, while little is said about the deeper cause of strikes.
- Offers that reflect favorably on the company are emphasized, while concessions are not mentioned.
- Workers appear to be irrational, greedy, and self-destructive.
- Large salary increases and stock options of management are not mentioned, while emphasis is on supposed high wages of labour.
- Public support for the strikers is neglected.
- The state, police etc., are regarded as neutral arbiters rather than corporate property protectors and strikebreaker bodyguards.

This overwhelmingly negative coverage of labour during so-called "labour disputes" (Why aren't they 'management disputes?' or management-labour disputes?) contributes to the bad rep the labour movement and working people generally, have with the public(!) After all, most of us are workers rather than managers or owners, and our sympathies should lie with our own kind. And while labour leaders are subject to many of the same flaws as corporate or political leaders, they can be: arrogant, autocratic, overbearing, *et cetera*, the unions and leaders have their positive side as well—not the least of which is that they can represent a bulwark against the ravages of corporatism.

A Harris Poll released just before Labour Day in 2005 started like this: "Most American adults overall, most employed adults and, surprisingly, many union households rate labour unions negatively." Now, we don't want to place too much emphasis on what the pollsters say, given all of their bias,[53] but it would be foolish to deny that there are some negative views towards unions out there. (Incidentally, the Harris Poll's press release distorted their own findings, making the results appear more negative towards unions than they were. The results showed an improvement in public views toward unions, whereas the Harris Poll alleged that views are becoming more negative. Some press reports compounded the problem by omitting positive poll results altogether.)[54]

Close examination of the media demonstrates quite clearly that reporting on labour is just the tip of the iceberg—there are numerous other biases which flow from the corporate structure, management influences and other causes. We'll turn to more of these after looking at the role of journalists themselves.

The Role of Journalists

It is a remarkable sign of voluntary discipline under alleged freedom that in much of the public and academic debates over the role of journalists in society, there are just two possibilities. Depending on the side you take, journalists are either liberal-minded critics of government and big business, who go overboard, or they are fairly balanced and objective and criticize the establishment just about the right amount. These are the boundaries of the debate. The very idea that journalists might be too cozy with power, that they might be 'embedded' with more than the military, is just beyond the limits of reasonable thought. Anyone who even raises this spectre is summarily dismissed as a conspiracy theorist.

Although journalists are portrayed as a bunch of 'lefties' by owners such as Conrad Black, or the Asper family, they tend to hold conventional views, and to be white, middle or upper-middle class males. Journalists are a product of a state- and corporate-run selection system that is operative throughout politics, culture and education. Children are trained to defer to experts, to repeat what they're told by learned authorities, and to suppress their own doubts and independent conclusions. As children and adults rise up the educational and career ladder they're rewarded and selected for obedience and subservience (such as the willingness, for example, to put aside reservations and do as they're told for the sake of career advancement). Winners are intelligent and free-thinking, but only within certain parameters.[55]

A concerted campaign, spearheaded by rightist ideologues and based in the United States has successfully promoted the view that news media journalists are "leftist" in their political beliefs, a mythology which supposedly justifies the "balancing" effect of right-wing commentators and indeed, right-wing networks such as Rupert Murdoch's Fox.[56] Allegedly, surveys have shown that most journalists vote Democratic in U.S. presidential elections, leading conservatives to argue that a liberal bias permeates the news media. This claim is then supported by anecdotal evidence, such as allegations that Dan Rather of CBS distorted evidence in an attempt to undermine George W. Bush.

However, academic studies of national, Washington-based journalists in the U.S. demonstrate that these journalists are mostly "centrist" in their political orientation, and that in fact, on issues ranging from corporate power to free trade, Social Security and Medicare, to health care and taxes, "journalists are actually more conservative than the general public."[57]

But there's another crucial problem with the notion that media content is liberal or left. As journalist Robert Parry points out, this larger fallacy is the notion that working journalists set the news agenda.

> In reality, most journalists have about as much say over what is presented by newspapers and TV news programs as factory workers and foremen have over what a factory manufactures. That is not to say factory workers have no input in their company's product: they can make suggestions and ensure the product is professionally built. But top executives have a much bigger say in what gets produced and how. The news business is essentially the same.[58]

This sense of individual journalistic responsibility is reinforced by the periodical, sensational scandals involving the actions of individual journalists, such as Janet Cooke, Stephen Glass, and Jayson Blair. In 1981 Janet Cooke of the *Washington Post* invented an eight-year-old heroin addict and wrote a Pulitzer Prize-winning feature story about him. Stephen Glass was a *New Republic* reporter who invented a number of feature stories in the late 1990s. In 2003, Jayson Blair quit the *New York Times* after it was learned he fabricated all or part of about 36 stories he wrote over a period of several months. Then there is Judith Miller of the *New York Times*, and Dan Rather and Mary Mapes of CBS. The emphasis on these "notorious" individuals means that the role of journalists is spotlighted, while editors, publishers and ownership toil away out-of-sight in the back rooms. As discussed above Mary Mapes was fired by CBS (which is owned by Viacom) in early 2005 because of allegations that she (and Dan Rather) unknowingly used forged documents in a story on George W. Bush's record with the U.S. National Guard. Mapes later wrote about the panel appointed by CBS executives to investigate what happened.

> In the end, the panel prepared a document that read more like a prosecutorial brief than an independent investigation. And I think no one was happier to receive this condemnation of its employees than the executives at Viacom. Now they could present themselves to the Bush administration as victims of irresponsible, out-of-control journalists, not as an operation that was actually doing some tough reporting. Gosh, it had all been a terrible accident.[59]

Journalists' role is exaggerated, notwithstanding the presence of their bylines or names in the credits on stories that appear. Here is an account by Nicholas Johnson, former chairman of the Federal Communications Commission in the U.S., the equivalent to the Canadian Radio-television and Telecommunications Commission (CRTC):

> The story is told of a reporter who first comes up with an investigative story idea, writes it up and submits it to the editor and is told the story is not going to run. He wonders why, but the next time he is cautious enough to check with the editor first. He is told by the editor that it would be better not to write that story. The third time he thinks of an investigative story idea but doesn't bother the editor with it because he knows it's silly. The fourth time he doesn't even think of the idea anymore.[60]

This tendency toward self-censorship is supported by working professionals in the industry. For example, according to Dennis Mazzocco, who spent 20 years with ABC TV and other broadcast media in the U.S., "when you work in broadcasting, it is very hard not to become an agent for the political-economic interests of those who employ you… There is little room for independence on the job or off, due to the tremendous competition for the ever-decreasing number of jobs available in the broadcast industry."[61]

> According to Sandra Precop, a producer with CBC radio in Windsor and a former newspaper journalist, columnist and editor,

> You get people within the newsroom anticipating what they think somebody wants. I think that can be a problem. In fact, I've seen that

happen. Someone will say, 'Fred will love this story: this is the kind of stuff he really likes.' Fred is the editor, publisher, whatever. And that's the story that they put on the front page. That's a decision made in anticipation that the person who made the decision is going to please someone higher up because this is the kind of story that Fred wants. But Fred never said anything.[62]

Windsor Star reporter Craig Pearson, who wrote a Master's thesis on the sociology of news and corporate influences, says, "there are certain stories that just are not going to be printed. You might as well not even propose a story on newspaper profits—it's not going to get in."[63]

More than forty-five years of research into the sociology of news supports the anecdotal accounts of Nicholas Johnson, Dennis Mazzocco, Sandra Precop, and Craig Pearson. As U.S. academic Michael Parenti put it, "in the final analysis, the news is not what reporters report but what editors and owners decide to print."[64] In the news industry as in other industries, decisions are made by owners, either directly or indirectly. Here is Nicholas Johnson again, on the implications of ownership:

The First Amendment rights belong to the owners, and the owners can exercise those rights by hiring people who will hire journalists who don't rock the boat, who don't attack advertisers, who don't challenge the establishment. That's a form of censorship.[65]

Owners hire publishers who reflect their views, and who in turn hire and promote managers, who then hire and promote editors and journalists. According to the aforementioned Sandra Precop, who was also employed at the Southam -owned *Windsor Star* for 19 years, working her way up to assistant city editor,

I think, realistically, people tend to hire or promote people who tend to remind them of themselves…I think publishers hire editors who are like themselves. And editors hire lower level editors who are like them, to some extent, and it's a nice middle class place, like *The Windsor Star*. So you're going to get middle class values.[66]

Writing about his days working as editor for legendary *Toronto Star* publisher Beland ("Bee") Honderich, author Peter C. Newman describes the way he and Honderich were in sync. Although the progressive ideals held by the *Star's* founder Joseph Atkinson, as well as Honderich and Newman, are almost nonexistent these days, the principle holds: you hire underlings who will do your bidding.

Bee and me [sic] in fact had few quarrels because we agreed on basic principles. I was impressed that Honderich was convinced, as I was, that politics ought to be fuelled not by the exercise of power or the expenditure of money but by the quest for ideas. His sedate populism flowed from its founding spirit, "Holy Joe" Atkinson, who had advocated social justice, the equitable distribution of wealth, state support for the disadvantaged. He wanted a proud, independent Canada, and urged Ottawa to "kick the Yankee poachers out of Hudson Bay." These were Honderich's core beliefs—as well as my own.[67]

If Newman didn't agree with Honderich, he would not have been hired to do the job. Journalists who do not demonstrate "the right stuff" simply are not going to go anywhere. They won't be promoted to editor, they won't get the choice assignments, and they are lucky these days if they can even keep their job. The reason for this is simple. In the words of David Radler, former president of Hollinger International and partner to Conrad Black,

I don't audit each newspaper's editorials day by day, but if it should come to a matter of principle, I am ultimately the publisher of all these papers, and *if editors disagree with us, they should disagree with us when they're no longer in our employ.* The buck stops with the ownership. I am responsible for meeting the payroll; therefore, I will ultimately determine what the papers say and how they're going to be run (emphasis added).[68]

This is a candid if somewhat chilling admission in an industry where testimonials to the "local autonomy" of chain newspapers have been *de rigueur* during decades of monopolistic expansion which has left only a handful of cities on the continent with independent ownership or competing daily newspapers. Still, Radler's perspective is not unique, as indicated by this comment from Otis Chandler, publisher of the mighty *Los Angeles Times.* "I'm the chief executive. I set policy and I'm not going to surround myself with people who disagree with me...I surround myself with people who generally see the way I do."[69] Or, here is another Canadian example: John Bassett, once publisher of the defunct *Toronto Telegram*, and *Montreal Gazette*, was asked by a TV interviewer, "Is it not true you use your newspaper to push your own political views?" Bassett replied, "Of course. Why else would you want to own a newspaper?"[70] *New York Times* publisher Arthur Hays Sulzberger clearly made this point about management control in a letter he wrote to Bassett, saying that even the smallest hint of independence was illusory.

He recalled that his predecessor as publisher Adolph Ochs used to hold editorial meetings with editorial writers, giving the appearance that an open, deliberative process existed. 'He would go around the table, asking what each one planned to write about the following day.' 'Actually, of course, the assignment had already been made by the chief editor', and 'the major questions of editorial policy' had already been decided. The formal mechanisms were largely irrelevant; it was in small, informal discussions between the publisher and his most trusted subordinates 'that the course of the paper was really set'.[71]

Hiring, firing and promoting by publishers and management, while obviously crucial, are only the most important starting points for content control and effective socialization in the newsroom. Story assignments and deciding what gets covered each day from numerous possibilities, is a management function. Producers and assignment editors tell reporters what to cover. Often they indicate to reporters how important a story is. Sometimes this is just a matter of telling the reporter how long the story should be, other times it is more direct. At the *Windsor Star*, an assignment editor has been known to write the notation "Small Moo" (somewhat important) or "Big Moo" (very important) on the reporter's assignment sheet. This indicates that the story is a "must," a sacred cow, a special request by someone higher up in news management. One news manager has commented, "Every newspaper has sacred cows and everyone knows what they are."[72] These are what Ben Bagdikian called, "the sacred cows," primarily corporations.[73]

If someone says "J.B. [then-publisher James Bruce] wants this," you know it's pretty important," says one *Windsor Star* reporter. "If the editor wants it, you know it's important... You get an idea of what makes it onto the front page. A story on the plight of urban poverty would not be deemed that important. Pro-development, or deficit cutbacks are generally seen on the front page.[74]

Sociologist David Altheide indicates that management will frequently "frame" a story within a particular news frame or "predefined story angle," or what he calls the "news perspective," which fits the circumstances of a particular story "to prior conclusions, beliefs and practices."[75]

Management also may directly affect the general tone and content of the news. For example, soon after publisher André Préfontaine came to the *Wind-*

sor Star, the paper dramatically increased coverage of crime and accidents. According to one staff reporter,

> When Préfontaine came, the coverage of car crashes increased. At one point, people were saying, "what's going on here?" They were concerned that the roads were unsafe, or whatever. But it was the same number of crashes, we were just putting them on the front page more often.[76]

Here are some other ways in which newsroom management has been found to influence reporters' stories. These are based upon the sociology of news literature,[77] and also field studies and interviews conducted with my students over the years, and my own discussions with and observations of journalists during the course of more than 25 years of research. These are in addition to the above-mentioned management roles of: owning papers, setting policies, and hiring and promoting employees.

1. Management assigns stories, and has a veto over any that journalists themselves initiate.

2. Management decides story "importance," in terms of length, time or play.

3. Management may frame the story within a particular angle or perspective.

4. Management may suggest sources or contacts to interview or leads to follow.

5. When the reporter hands in a story, it may have to be rewritten by the reporter, to the editor's specifications. The emphasis might be changed, new material added, and/or some material dropped.

6. When the reporter is finished with a story, it is copy edited, which may mean significant additional changes.

7. At any time the story may be dropped altogether, for various reasons, without much explanation other than space constraints.

8. If the story makes it into the paper, an editor decides placement: whether it will go on the top of page one, or if it will be buried in the comic section. Additional cuts to content may be made, owing to space considerations or other reasons.

9. Management also decides what the headline will be, which is crucial. This is the first (and sometimes last) thing people learn about the story.

10. At some newspapers, if reporters object to changes made to the story, they may remove their byline. They have no other control over the story at that point, and no right at all to insist that the management version not appear in the paper.

The Cult of Objectivity

While most journalists no longer claim to be entirely "objective" in their work, they do say that they strive for balance, which can amount to the same thing. The roots of objectivity in journalism reach back to commercial initiatives, the advent of the wire services late in the 19th and early 20th centuries, and the recognition that blatantly partisan reporting would not have mass market appeal to hundreds of newspapers simultaneously.

Journalism mythology aside, the ownership and management influences we've discussed obviously don't leave very much room for the news to be objectively reported. An example is the priority given to management views instead of labour's opinions during a strike. One convention journalists use to support their contention of impartiality is the reliance on sources to provide opinions. This way, journalists may claim they are not really 'saying' anything themselves, but merely reporting on what is said by others. Again, on the surface, this appears to work to the reporters' advantage: they report on newsmakers. In addition to Hollywood celebrities, this includes government, politicians generally, CEOs and the corporate elite generally, lawyers, educators, *et cetera*. Sometimes, average members of the public-at-large will even be consulted in polls or "streeters," which are—purportedly at least—haphazard interviews with men or women walking down the street. Although this may appear straightforward, in reality it conceals a number of built-in biases. For example, which street are you on, and is it nearby the newspaper office, the business district, outside of a factory, or in a more dangerous area of town? As Italian theorist Antonio Gramsci commented, "objectivity" essentially amounts to "support for the status quo."

In-Sourcing Rather Than Out-Sourcing

This raises the key question: whom do they quote and why? Do opinions just fall out of the sky? Research conducted for decades now indicates, pretty consistently, that journalists tend to interview conservative, wealthier white males.[78] A recent review of the literature commented, "More than 30 years of research documents the media's long-standing dearth of news source diversity."[79] One study on ABC's "Nightline" reported "Nightline," "serves as an electronic soapbox from which white, male, elite representatives of the status quo can present their case. Minorities, women and those with challenging views are generally excluded."[80]

This means women's views are under-represented, along with visible minorities, progressive thinkers, and the less-well-off. If a journalist is working on a story about the economy, for example, she will probably interview an economist with one of the major banks, or a conservative academic, rather than a progressive academic or labour economist, or even someone like popular economist Linda McQuaig. In other words, she'll seek out someone with views consistent to her own, and those of her editors, and the owners. Journalist don't go out and 'find' the news, or ask people what it is: instead, they seek out people who will confirm their perspective—or, in the event they differ—management's perspective, on events. So, a story about income trusts will tend to reflect a particular perspective, as we have seen.

This problem has been heightened by mergers and downsizing in media industries which result in fewer employees, with less time on their hands. This makes them even more susceptible to press releases and video news releases which predominantly come from corporations. In addition, the primarily conservative and corporate think tanks and policy institutes now flood the news media with "studies" and opinion pieces, which largely revolve around the benefits of the free market system, the problems with "big government," the hysteria of global warming extremists, the greedy labour unions, and so on.

Just A Few Other Problems

Briefly, I'll list a few of the other serious problems with what and how the news media report. Some of these are addressed in subsequent chapters. It's clear, however, that the muckrakers of yore have become the stargazers of today, owned by and beholden to conglomerates. Rather than exposing corporate foibles, today's news media have largely been bought up and sold out. Here are a few more of the lies the media tell us:

- Distracting us from important news with 'Junk Food News' about the lives of the rich and famous, stars and celebrities, crazes and fads, *et cetera*.

- Focusing too much attention on some stories, such as Anna Nicole Smith's death, life support for Terri Schiavo, Elian Gonzalez, Princess Diana, or the trials of Scott Peterson and O.J. Simpson.

- Ridiculing environmentalists who are concerned about the earth, while promoting the views of pseudo-'scientists' who are in the pay of industry.

- Ignoring and downplaying climate change phenomena such as global warming.

- Downplaying and ignoring serious health risks posed by substances such as lead and toxic chemicals, because of support for industries.

- Selling us on prescription drugs, through biased reporting of benefits.

- Presenting the disastrous U.S. health care system as a preferred alternative to universal, relatively inexpensive Canadian health care.

- Promoting consumption and consumerism as a way of life, with devastating consequences on a personal and global level.

- Pretending that so-called "western-style democracies" such as Canada and the U.S. really are democratic.

- Indicating that popular, democratically-elected Third-World governments are "dictatorships."

- Obfuscating the readily-apparent reasons for events such as 9/11 and the London bombings of 2005.

- Portraying Cuba and Venezuela as dictatorships.

- Ignoring the U.S.-sponsored coup d'etat in Haïti, in 2004, and treating it as if it was a local rebellion resulting in president Aristide's resignation and flight.

In my book *Democracy's Oxygen*, I listed more than 50 of these biases, which I called "media-think truisms" and which are a part of the conventional wisdom promoted by the news media. With a few small editing changes, I've listed them below. Not much has changed.

A Sampling of Lies the Media Tell Us
Economics

1. That which governs least, governs best. The unfettered free market system is the fairest and best guiding principle.

2. Public ownership such as crown corporations are wasteful and inefficient, serving no real useful purpose.

3. Private enterprise, while sometimes given to excess, is the core of our society and is beyond questioning.

4. Democracy and capitalism are synonymous and interchangeable. You can't have one without the other.

5. When it comes to corporation size, the bigger the better.

6. The global economy is as inevitable as the rising sun.

7. We need huge national companies with little or no competition, in order to compete internationally.

8. In order to be lean, mean and competitive, companies must lay people off and eliminate inefficiencies.

9. Canadian employees, with (relatively) high salaries and benefits, are the most costly inefficiency of all.

10. Producing goods where labour is cheapest is an inevitable development under globalization and the free market.

11. Transferring jobs to low-wage, no benefit, non-unionized Third World countries will help those countries. There are no negative effects abroad or at home.

12. Job losses in Canada due to company relocations elsewhere are minimal, and where this happens they are menial jobs and people here are better off without them.

13. Job losses under globalization are a temporary thing, during a period of restructuring. Eventually, better paying, high tech jobs will be available for everyone.

14. It's not yet clear what these jobs are, how to train people for them, or who will offer the jobs. These are mysteries.

15. High levels of unemployment are not cause for alarm, but are "structural." High unemployment helps to keep inflation down by putting a brake on unreasonable wage demands.

16. The shift from full-time manufacturing jobs to low paying, part-time service jobs, is another inevitable, short term product of the global economy.

17. A company has to make profits. The more profit it makes, the better the company.

18. People who are wealthy got there because of ability and deserve our respect and admiration.

19. People who are poor got there because of their own inability. They should have charity in the form of food banks, but only if they're desperate.

20. People on unemployment assistance, welfare, or who are homeless, with few exceptions, are there because they are too lazy to look for work.

21. Government debts are mostly due to lavish social programs which we can no longer afford.

22. We all pay far too much in taxes, thanks to overspending by bloated governments.

23. Interest rates are determined by complex international forces, over which we have no control.

24. Sometimes the Bank of Canada is forced to raise interest rates to protect the Canadian dollar.

International Affairs

25. Canadians pay out far too much in aid to foreign countries, and most of the time the money doesn't reach its target. Charity begins at home.

26. Occasionally, a tyrant in some part of the world threatens democracy and has to be put in his place, for the good of the world community and those in his own country.

27. Recently, these tyrants have included: Jean-Bertrand Aristide, Fidel Castro, Saddam Hussein, Manuel Noriega, Daniel Ortega, Ayatollah Khomeini, Muhammar Ghaddafi, among others.

Environment

28. Environmental "problems" are largely invented by hysterical global warming fanatics.

29. Global warming is doubtful. If it does exist, humans aren't responsible and there's nothing we can do about it without ruining our economies.

Feminism

30. A small group of radical feminists is constantly whining about problems which either don't exist, or which are relatively small problems that we are already doing our best to solve.

31. Violence against women, while unfortunate, is relatively small scale and, let's face it—some women bring it on themselves.

32. Since society "judges" people based on their merits, those who don't succeed, including women, are just not capable enough.

33. Feminists "have it in for" all men, whereas we know that many men are nice guys who neither hate nor abuse women.

Universities

34. A small group of "politically correct" people is trying to turn Canada into a police state, where you can't even think innocent thoughts anymore.

35. Professors on university campuses are a bunch of radical Marxists who are corrupting our youth.

36. Universities have to get more practical and down-to-earth and train people for jobs rather than all of this pie-in-the-sky stuff.

Culture

37. The CBC is too expensive. It should be sold off to private companies which can do a better job at no cost to the public.

Minorities

38. Native peoples are well cared for on reserves, and would be better off if it wasn't for their corrupt leaders, or if they would do something for themselves instead of relying on government handouts and complaining.

39. Immigration laws in Canada are too lax. We let people from minority cultures in, and they take advantage of our generous social programs.

40. Because of their small numbers and different views, Gays and Lesbians in Canada only deserve media coverage when they hold demonstrations or if they are dying from AIDS or something.

Working People

41. Labour struggles are senseless, avoidable contests which are created by unions' unwillingness to negotiate in good faith.

42. Companies make wage "offers," while defiant, sometimes even militant unions, will boycott talks and reject management offers.

43. Workers, especially those on strike, are irrational, greedy and self-destructive.

44. Executives and management receive high salaries because they deserve them. There is no point in questioning these, or comparing these to what workers are asking for.

45. Strikes are always caused by greedy unions. What's sad about this is the negative impact strikes have on the public. The fact that unions will inconvenience the public at the drop of a hat is further evidence that workers are selfish.

46. During strikes, the police and other government agencies such as the courts are neutral referees for the public interest. This role includes protecting corporate properties and acting as bodyguards for strike-breakers.

47. Labour unions protect and encourage unproductive, overweight, lazy, and insubordinate workers.

48. Our failure to compete internationally is due to big, powerful unions which have forced employers to pay exorbitant union wages to unproductive workers.

49. Although some very poor and abused workers (particularly women and immigrants) may need to form unions to protect themselves, big unions don't represent workers' interests.

50. Union leaders or "bosses," because they do not come from the educated, cultured and privileged classes, are more likely to be corrupted by the power they achieve than are business or political leaders.

51. Unions have outlived their usefulness. Employers are enlightened and wouldn't abuse their workers. If they do try, there are government laws to protect workers.

52. Unions actually promote conflict with management, as a means of justifying their own existence.

The Media

53. Freedom of the press is essential to our democracy, and is the basis of an informed public.

54. The news media are independent, socially responsible watchdogs who look out for the public interest.

55. Most journalists are leftists, and consequently conservative owners are needed to balance things so the public receives objective reporting.

A Cabal?

Some of those on the right wing of the political spectrum have charged that those who make these sorts of allegations about the media are "conspiracy theorists," that we see plots, cabals and conspiracies everywhere. The image that is conjured up is that of smoke-filled back rooms, where the robber barons secretly plot their next campaign. Media content is what it is, this theory goes, because of heavy-handed manipulation. It's actually quite the opposite, as Chomsky has pointed out. The way the news media work is endemic to capitalism.

> It's precisely the opposite of conspiracy theory, actually—in fact, in general this analysis tends to downplay the role of individuals: they're just replaceable pieces. *Look, part of the structure of corporate capitalism is that the players in the game try to increase profits and market shares—if they don't do that, they will no longer be players in the game. Any economist knows this: it's not a conspiracy theory to point that out, it's just taken for granted as an institutional fact... That's the opposite of conspiracy theory...* For people to call it "conspiracy theory" is part of the effort to prevent an understanding of how the world works, in my view— "conspiracy theory" has become the intellectual equivalent of a four-letter word: it's something people say when they don't want you to think about what's really going on (emphasis added).[81]

Saying someone is a conspiracy theorist is like calling them "anti-American." If you criticize U.S. foreign policy, you're anti-American. Well, it seems to me that a lot of Americans qualify. Both these labels are *ad hominem* attacks: a way to dismiss someone's ideas without considering them, by simply attacking them in person.

Perhaps I may indulge myself with a brief personal example, which will give me the opportunity to mention Conrad Black. In the early 1990s, I was raising an alarm about newspaper baron Conrad Black, saying that he was a scourge on journalism, he was hellbent on monopolizing the news media and shifting them to the far right to reflect his political views, and that his miserly approach to business was not only bad for employees but bad for business. And indeed, in hindsight he did do these things, he shifted the practice of journalism in Canada, he shifted the news media to the right, and government policy along with them. So, in this respect he was a success. But in business, he was a failure, a man who dissembled and sold off Massey Ferguson and Dominion Stores, and whose only newspaper creation the *National Post*, has lost tens of millions of dollars. A decade later, it's still not profitable. The guy is an obvious crook, with an inflated ego, and he is on trial in the spring of 2007 for embezzling millions from his companies. Maude Barlow and I even wrote a book about this to try to bring what was happening to people's attention. (So great was Black's reputation, the awe and fear that he inspired, that a university student working at the bookstore in the Ottawa airport was instructed by the manager to take our books off the display when word circulated that Lord Black was passing through the airport.) Well, many journalists attacked us and demonized us and accused us of conspiracy theory. For more than 30 years in the business, Conrad Black was attacking workers, "demanning" as he called it, or "drowning the kittens." He consistently attacked working people, and unions, most notably through his vicious supervision of the *Calgary Herald* strike in 1999-2000.

Through all this Conrad Black was the darling of the media, invited to lecture to their conferences and interviewed by Peter Gzowski and Pamela Wallen, while they feted him and worshipped at his feet. In furious email exchanges, Kirk LaPointe, then editor of the *Hamilton Spectator,* and others fiercely defended Black. (Soon after, LaPointe went to work more directly for Black at the *Post*, demonstrating that sycophancy has its rewards. When LaPointe briefly returned to the *Spectator*, he bragged to a student journalist that "Barbara Amiel even called my wife and told her how important I was to the next generation in leadership at Hollinger.")[82] But when the allegations finally came out about Black stealing from the corporate shareholders, the roof caved in, and he became a pariah. At this writing, he stands charged with lining his own pockets to the tune of about $84 million (U.S.) in company money, arraigned on eight counts of fraud and facing, possibly, 40 years in jail. By this point, David Olive of the *Toronto Star* felt free to write that, "For all his renown, Conrad Black didn't amount to much…in the end, he proved to be a conspicuous underachiever."[83] That would have been heresy in 2004: people would have treated David Olive as if he was on drugs. After all, this is the man Peter C. Newman celebrated as *The Establishment Man*, in his book by that title.

The lesson in this is that you can do what you like to working people, employees, and unions in general, but be kind to the shareholders. As David Olive demonstrates, now it's become conventional wisdom even amongst some journalists that Black was neither a beacon of business ethics, nor of journalistic practices. But when we were sounding the alarm and pointing to his unsavory views, his past, and his actions, we were dismissed as "conspiracy theorists."

NOTES

1. Alexa traffic rankings, www.alexa.com, March 16, 2007.

2. Alexa traffic rankings, www.alexa.com, March 16, 2007.

3. In *Deterring Democracy*, for example, Noam Chomsky writes, regarding Milton's *Areopagitica*, "Milton himself explained that the purpose of the tract was 'so that the determination of true and false, of what should be published and what should be suppressed, might not be under the control of...unlearned men of mediocre judgment,' but only 'an appointed officer' of the right persuasion, who will have the authority to ban work he finds to be 'mischievous or libellous' 'erroneous and scandalous,'..." Quoted in Noam Chomsky, *Deterring Democracy*, Verso, N.Y., 1991, p. 402, footnote 13.

4. Howard Kurtz, "An Inside Story: Prewar Articles Questioning Threat Often Didn't Make Front Page," *Washington Post*, August 12, 2004. See also, Norman Solomon, *Wars Made Easy: How Presidents and Pundits Keep Spinning Us to Death*, John Wiley & Sons, N.Y., 2005; and Valerie Scatamburlo-D'Annibale, "In 'Sync': Bush's War Propaganda Machine and the American Mainsteam Media," in Jeffrey Klaehn (Ed), *Filtering The News: Essays on Herman and Chomsky's Propaganda Model*, Black Rose Books, Montreal, 2005, pp. 21-62.

5. Kurtz, "An Inside Story."

6. Knowlton Nash, "The Imperfect Necessity," *content* magazine, Jan./Feb., 1988, pp. 7-11.

7. Editorial, "How dangerous is Microsoft?" *Globe and Mail*, reprinted from the *Economist*, July 10, 1995, p. A11.

8. "Microsoft," Historylink.org online encyclopedia, Washington State. http://www.historylink.org/essays/printer_friendly/index.cfm?file_id=2294.

9. Alexander Cockburn, "I Am Thy Father's Ghost:" A Journey into Rupert Murdoch's Soul, *Counterpunch*, December 27/28, 2003.

10. Steve Schifferes, "Trustbusters: A history lesson," BBC News Online: In Depth: Microsoft," Feb 15, 2000, http://news.bbc.co.uk/1/low/in_depth/business/2000/microsoft/635257.stm.

11. Steve Schifferes, "Trustbusters."

12. Henry Demarest Lloyd, "Story of A Great Monopoly," *Atlantic Monthly*, March, 1881.

13. "The Dismantling of the Standard Oil Trust," The Linux information project, 2004. http://www.bellevuelinux.org/standardoil.html.

14. The merger was scheduled to begin hearings before the CRTC, for final approval April 30, 2007.

15. Canadian Press, "Former Southam brass slams CanWest editorial policy: National editorials menace 'free speech, democracy and pluralism,' statement says," *Toronto Star online*, June 5, 2002. See also, Nicholas Keung, "Ad critical of CanWest policy," *Toronto Star*, June 6, 2002.

16. DeNeen Brown, "Canadian Publisher Raises Hackles: Family is Accused of Trying to Restrict Local Newspapers' Autonomy," *Washington Post* Foreign Service, January 27, 2002.

17. For a critique of Asper's article and his allegations, see Robert Everton, "Israel Asper And Israeli Propaganda," in Jeffery Klaehn (Ed), *Filtering The News: Essays on Herman and Chomsky's Propaganda Model*, Black Rose Books, Montreal, 2005.

18. Stephen Kimber, "Why I won't write for the Aspers," *Globe and Mail*, January 7, 2002.

19. See Robert Jensen, "Dan Rather and the Problem with Patriotism: Steps Toward the Redemption of American Journalism and Democracy," in Jeffery Klaehn, (Ed), *Filtering The News: Essays on Herman and Chomsky's Propaganda Model*, Black Rose Books, Montreal, 2005, p.126.

20. Cf. Gregory Palast, "Dan Crashes, Bush Flies High," an excerpt from *Armed Madhouse*, Penguin, N.Y., 2006, http://www.gregpalast.com/dan-crashes-bush-flies-high/; Mary Mapes, "Inside the 'Memogate' Affair," *Vanity Fair*, December, 2005.

21. "Dan Rather says U.S. patriotism leads some journalists to self-censorship," Associated Press report, May 16, 2002. Cited in Jensen, "Dan Rather..." in Klaehn (Ed).

22. Quoted in, Russ Baker, "The Squeeze," in Alison Alexander and Janice Hanson, (Ed) *Taking Sides: Clashing Views on Controversial Issues in Mass Media and Society*, 8th Edition, McGraw-Hill/Dushkin, Dubuque, Iowa, 2005, p. 142.

23. Quoted in Baker, "The Squeeze," p. 147.

24. Quoted in Baker, "The Squeeze."

25. Quoted in Anna-Christina Di Liberto, "Redrawing the line: Despite vigilance, advertorial content gains credibility in Canadian publishing," *Ryerson Review of Journalism*, Spring, 2005.

26. Murray Hogben, "Selling it Yourself," A book review of *Sold! By Owner*, written by Lynn Larabie, *Kingston Whig-Standard*, May 12, 1990. See Charlene Yarrow, "Hail and Farewell to the Whig," *Ryerson Review of Journalism*, Summer 1993.

27. Gloria Cooper, "Darts & Laurels," *Columbia Journalism Review*, Sept./Oct. 2004.

28. Steven Cole Smith, "Mr. Nice Guy: The Pontiac G6 Gets a Bad Review—and So Does the Author," *The Inside Line*, www.edmunds.com, April 18, 2005.
http://www.edmunds.com/insideline/do/Columns/articleId=105386.

29. Interview, February 15, 1996.

30. James Bruce, interview, April, 1996.

31. See Ian Jack, "How to drive a bargain when buying a car," *Windsor Star*, February 5, 1996, p. D7; James Bruce, "Story failed to meet Star's standards," *Windsor Star*, February 6, 1996, p. A4.

32. See for example, Allan Woods, "Car dealerships, movers top complaints list," *Globe and Mail*, July 5, 2002.

33. John Asling, "Backscratch journalism on the Bay of Quinte," in Barrie Zwicker and Dick MacDonald, eds, *The News: Inside the Canadian Media*, Ottawa: Deneau Publishers, 1984.

34. Quoted in Doug Smith, "Man Bites Newspaper," *This Magazine*, Sept., 1992, p. 18.

35. Antonia Zerbisias, "Leaders leave CBC prone and bleeding; Lockout opens door to political sniping," *Toronto Star*, Sept. 14, 2005.

36. Peter Mitchell and John Schoeffel (Eds) *Understanding Power: The Indispensable Chomsky*, The New Press, N.Y., 2002, p. 290.

37. Jim Stanford, "Bonnie and Clyde's Income Trust," CAW No.109, October 11, 2005, http://www.caw.ca/news/factsfromthefringe/issue109.asp.

38. Norris, Gary. "Investors cheer Ottawa's dividend and trust move," *Toronto Star*, CP, November 24, 2005.

39. Ray Turchansky, "Alarm bells sound over income trusts," *Edmonton Journal*, February 4, 2006.

40. Paul Delean, "BCE shareholders OK shift of assets to income trust: Eastern Canadian land-line operations," *National Post*, June 8, 2006; Mark Evans, "Telco trust wave: BCE's rivals may decide to follow its lead," *National Post*, March 9, 2006; Barbara Schecter, "Canwest Income trust for some papers: CanWest stands firm behind *National Post*," *Windsor Star*, February 8, 2006.

41. Eric Beauchesne, Juliet O'Neill and Norma Greenaway, "Tories will tax income trusts: But gov't will reduce corporate income taxes," Saskatoon *Star-Phoenix*. November 1, 2006.

42. Cf. Sean Silcoff, "Markets brace for chaos in wake of trust ruling: Tories to unveil tax on payouts," *Calgary Herald*, November 1, 2006; Lisa Schmidt, "Ottawa moves to tax income trusts: New rules outrage Alberta energy industry," *Calgary Herald*, November 1, 2006; Steven Chase, "Income Trusts: Party's Over: Tories break key election promise with sudden distribution tax to plug hole in its revenues," *Globe and Mail*, November 1, 2006, pg. A.1; "Income trust tax will hurt Manitoba businesses: income fund," www.cbc.ca/canada/manitoba/story/2006/11/02/mba-income.html, CBC, November 2, 2006; "Income trust tax angers Alberta oil patch: Calgary lawyer," www.cbc.ca/canada/story/2006/11/02/trust-reaction.html, November 2, 2006; "Liberals demand PM apologize over income trust 'double-cross'," www.cbc.ca/canada/story/2006/11/02/trust-harper.html, November 2, 2006.

43. Lorne Slotnick, "To all concerned in the labour movement," an open letter published on April 19, 1989, and subsequently published in James Winter, (Ed) *Silent Revolution: Media, Democracy, and the Free Trade Debate*, University of Ottawa Press, Ottawa, 1990, p. 163-164.

44. Cf. Columns by Catherine Ford, "Refusal to strike a question of ethics," *Calgary Herald*, Nov. 9, 1999; and "A bitter, divisive sectarian feud," *Calgary Herald*, Nov. 19, 1999.

45. Cf. Terence Corcoran, "Herald strike ignites pundits," *Financial Post* [note:Terence Corcoran is editor of the Financial Post]. *Calgary Herald*, Nov. 27, 1999.

46. "Publisher's letter: A message to *Calgary Herald* readers and subscribers from Herald publisher Dan Gaynor," *Calgary Herald*, Nov 9, 1999.

47. Daniel Chomsky, "The Mechanisms of Management Control at the *New York Times*," *Media, Culture & Society*, vol. 21: pp. 586-7.

48. Robert Picard and Stephen Lacy, "Commentary: Lessons From the Detroit Newspaper Strike, *Newspaper Research Journal*, Winter/Spring 1997, Vol. 18, issues 1/2.

49. Erin Steuter, "The Irvings Cover Themselves: Media Representations of the Irving Oil Refinery Strike, 1994-1996," *The Canadian Journal of Communication*, Vol.24:4, 1999.

50. Joshua Greenberg, "Tories, Teachers and the Media: Politics of Education Reform; News Discourse and the 1997 Ontario Teachers' Strike," *Journalism Studies*, 5:3, 2004, pp. 366.

51. Deepa Kumar, "Mass Media, Class, and Democracy: The Struggle over Newspaper Representation of the UPS Strike," *Critical Studies in Media Communication*, 18:3, September, 2001, p. 287. The author did find a shift in coverage in some newspapers but not all, as a result of a massive union effort, offering up some hope in this respect to the labour movement.

52. Michael Parenti, *Inventing Reality: The Politics of the Mass Media*, St. Martin's Press, N.Y., 1986; William Puette, *Through Jaundiced Eyes: How the Media View Organized Labour*, ILR Press, N.Y., 1992.

53. I discuss some examples of this in, "The Poll as Cudgel," in *MediaThink*, Black Rose Books, Montreal, 2002, p. 162.

54. Harris Poll, "Negative Attitudes to Labour Unions Show Little Change in Past Decade, According to New Harris Poll," PRNewswire, August 31, 2005. UPI, "Business News: Survey finds labour unions viewed dimly," Aug 31, 2005, Monsters and Critics.com, http://news. monstersandcritics.com/business/printer_1045127.php.

55. Noam Chomsky, quoted on www.medialens.org.

56. For a debunking of the Liberal media myth, cf. Eric Alterman, *What Liberal Media? The Truth about Bias and the News*, Basic Books, N.Y., 2003; and Eric Alterman, "What Liberal Media," *Nation*, February 6, 2003, http://www.thenation.com/doc/20030224/alterman2.

57. Cf. Jeff Cohen, "Maybe the Public—Not the Press—Has a Leftist Bias," *Extra!*, www. fair.org, July 5, 1998.

58. Robert Parry, "In Search of the Liberal Media," Extra!, www.fair.org July/August, 1998.

59. Mary Mapes, "Inside the 'MemoGate' affair," *Vanity Fair*, November 2005.

60. Martin Lee and Norman Solomon, *Unreliable Sources: A Guide to Detecting Bias in the News Media* (NY: Carol Publishing Group, 1991), p. 98.

61. Dennis Mazzocco, *Networks of Power: Corporate TV's Threat to Democracy* (Boston: South End Press, 1994), p. 27.

62. Sandra Precop, from the transcript of an interview with Lanie Hurdle, Brad Milburn and Michelle Pisani, March 18, 1996.

63. Craig Pearson, from the transcript of an interview with Lanie Hurdle, Brad Milburn and Michelle Pisani, February, 1996.

64. Martin Lee and Norman Solomon, *Unreliable Sources*, p. 92.

65. Ibid.

66. Sandra Precop, interview, March 18, 1996.

67. Peter C. Newman, "Honderich full of phobias, but fair," *Toronto Star*, Nov. 12, 2005.

68. Quoted by Peter C. Newman, "The inexorable spread of the Black empire, " *Maclean's,* February 3, 1992, p. 68.

69. Martin Lee and Norman Solomon, *Unreliable Sources,* p. 93.

70. Allan Fotheringham, "Australian culture imperialism?" *Maclean's,* August 22, 1988, p. 48.

71. Quoted in Daniel Chomsky, "Mechanisms of Management Control at the *New York Times,*" *Media, Culture and Society,* 21: 580, 1999.

72. Craig Pearson, *Printing News and Money,* p. 186.

73. Ben Bagdikian, *The Media Monopoly,* 3rd Edition (Boston: Beacon Press, 1990), p. 47.

74. Quoted in James Winter, *Democracy's Oxygen: How Corporations Control the News,* Black Rose Books, Montreal, 1996, p.99.

75. David Altheide, *Creating Reality: How TV News Distorts Events,* (Beverly Hills, CA: Sage, 1974).

76. Winter, *Democracy's Oxygen,* p.98.

77. See also Warren Breed, "Social Control in the Newsroom," *Social Forces,* May, 1955, 33: 326-35; John Porter, *The Vertical Mosaic,* (Toronto: U. of T. Press, 1965); E.J. Epstein, *News From Nowhere,* (Toronto: Random House, 1973); David Altheide, *Creating Reality;* Wallace Clement, *The Canadian Corporate Elite,* (Ottawa: Carleton U. Press, 1975); Gaye Tuchman, *Making News: A Study in the Construction of Reality* (NY: Macmillan, 1978); Herbert Gans, *Deciding What's News* (NY: Vintage, 1980); Kent et al, *The Royal Commission on Newspapers,* (Ottawa: Ministry of Supply and Services, 1981). For a further contribution and overview of research, see R. Ericson, P. Baranek, J. Chan, *Visualizing Deviance,* (Toronto: U. of Toronto Press, 1987).

78. One of the earlier studies addressing this was, Leon Sigal, *Reporters and Officials: The Organization and Politics of Newsmaking,* D.C. Heath and Co., Lexington Mass, 1973. Sigal found that 81 percent of news sources were officials. A landmark FAIR study is reported in Martin Lee and Norman Solomon, *Unreliable Sources: A Guide to Detecting Bias in News Media,*" Carol Publishing, N.Y., 1991. A 40-month-long study of ABC's "Nightline" found that 89 percent of the U.S. guests on Nightline were men; 92 percent were white. On economic issues, corporate reps outnumbered labour reps by 7-to-1. Also see, Twange Kasoma, and Scott Maier, "Information as Good as its Source: Source Diversity and Accuracy at Nine Daily U.S. Newspapers," paper presented to the *International Communication Association* annual meetings, New York, 2005.

79. Kasoma and Maier, "Information…"

80. Reported in Lee and Solomon, *Unreliable Sources,* p.27.

81. Peter Mitchell and John Schoeffel, (Eds) *Understanding Power: The Indispensable Chomsky,* The New Press, N.Y., 2002, p.26, (emphasis added).

82. Claire Sibboney, "The Comeback of Kirke LaPointe," *The Ryerson Review of Journalism,* Summer, 2000.

83. David Olive, "In the end, Black amounts to little," *Toronto Star,* November 18, 2005.

Chapter Two

ECO-ZEALOTS, GREENWASHERS AND PARASITES

AFTER THE INTRODUCTORY LECTURE in my media literacy class each semester, I usually begin with a discussion of reporting on the environment. I use this as a means of easing students into the course with a topic I assume is near and dear to all of us. This contrasts with the way I began the course as recently as 2004, by figuratively hitting them over the head with the topics of corporate globalization, followed by U.S. foreign policy.

My first question to students is: "How many of you think of yourselves as environmentalists? Raise your hands." The results may surprise you: about ten or at the most fifteen students out of a class of 120 or 140 will raise their hands. I then put up on the overhead a dictionary definition of an environmentalist:

> Environmentalist: a. A person who seeks to protect the natural environment, as from air and water pollution, waste of natural resources, and excessive human encroachments. b. Someone who works to protect the environment from destruction or pollution.

After we read the definition, I ask the students if there is anyone *who does not* want to protect the environment? Now the situation is more than reversed, as at most only one or two students out of the whole class raise their hand. Obviously, we all should be—must be—concerned with protecting the environment. As David Suzuki points out in one of his wonderful books and a subsequent documentary film, we literally *are* the environment, so it is suicidal to be unconcerned.

Human bodies are composed of the water we drink (averaging 60 percent, by weight—a human baby is 75 percent water, by weight), food from the earth's soil, and the air we breathe. "In everyday life we absorb atoms from the air that were once a part of birds and trees and snakes and worms, because all aerobic forms of life share that same air...air is a matrix that joins all life together," Suzuki writes.[1]

> Even the crudest calculation reveals that each of us very quickly absorbs atoms into our bodies that were once an integral part of everyone else in the room, and vice versa. The eminent Harvard astronomer Harlow Shapley once performed another thought exercise about air. He pointed out that while 99 per cent of the air we breathe is highly active oxygen and mildly reactive nitrogen, about one per cent is made up of argon, an inert gas. Because it is inert, it is breathed in and out without becoming a part of our bodies or entering into metabolic transformations. Shapely calculated that each breath contains about 30,000,000,000,000,000,000, or 3.0×10^{19} atoms of argon plus quintillions of molecules of carbon dioxide. Suppose you exhale a single breath and follow those argon atoms. Within minutes, they have diffused through the air far beyond the spot where they were released, traveling into the neighbourhood. After a year, those argon atoms have been mixed up in the atmosphere and spread around the planet in such a way that each breath you take includes at least 15 atoms of argon released in that one breath a year earlier! All people over the age of twenty have taken at least 100 million breaths and have inhaled argon atoms that were emitted in the first breath of every child born in the world a year before! According to Shapley: "Your next breath will contain more than 400,000 of the argon atoms that [Mahatma] Ghandi breathed in his long life."

A brief perusal of news stories including the term "environmentalist" is enough to explain why many of us don't want to be associated with the term, despite its dictionary definition. News stories are filled with accounts of radicals who spout doom and gloom and worry the sky is falling. They report "angry" environmentalists who "clash" and "protest," "fume" and "worry." One *Globe and Mail* story depicted Canadian Green Party leader Elizabeth May as a "career environmentalist," while others are described as "ardent," or "militant," or "ideologues." When I did a Google news search for the term in September, 2005, I even found one commentary which stated: "Environmentalists Hate Black People," by someone named Ted Pierce of Virginia.

To use just a few examples from the summer of 2001, when the debate over the Kyoto Accord was 'heating up,' in June, the *Ottawa Citizen* described environmentalism as a sort of a cult:

> This environmental movement is firmly rooted in the favourite philosophers of most university professors—Kant and Marx. Consequently, environmentalists are passionately anti-capitalistic. From the beginning, environmentalism has attracted young university students, then young high school students, and now elementary school students. Unfortunately, they have been taught in school what to believe and how to be activists, rather than how to think (see note 125, this chapter).

By September, 2001, the *Citizen* was attacking proponents of the Kyoto Accord, for "the modern history of environmental scares. For while the jury is still out on 'global warming,' it is in for any number of the previous, expensive terrors the 'Friends of the Earth' have unleashed. Their batting average remains .000."[2]

That same summer, the *Vancouver Province* provided a backlash against what it called, "eco-zealots."

> It's comforting to know that, despite the flurry of interest in the Green Party in B.C. and a wave of anti-Bush sentiment in Europe, the global backlash against the environmental protest movement appears to be growing. Leading former Greenpeacers are amongst those now speaking out against the misinformation from the latter-day eco-zealots.[3]

To the news media, we are not all environmentalists, instead, these are militants who like to protest, and worry needlessly about saving ancient trees and rare owls. They chain themselves to trees and wind up being hauled away by police. This one-sided depiction is typical of news media bias, and aligns closely with the corporate perspective: after all, it's often corporate actions that are being criticized, from logging to pollution, from oil companies to automobile manufacturers. Indeed, if one makes the reasonable assumption that corporations involved in either gas and oil production and sales, or automobile production, are among the major environmental culprits, then eight of the ten largest corporations in the world fall into this category: Exxon Mobil, Royal Dutch Shell, BP, General Motors, Chevron, DaimlerChrysler, Toyota Motors, and the Ford Motor Corp.

TEN LARGEST GLOBAL CORPORATIONS, 2006, BY REVENUES

Rank	Company	Revenues ($ millions)	Profits ($ millions)
1.	Exxon Mobil	339,938.00	36,130.00
2.	Wal-Mart Stores	315,654.00	11,231.00
3.	Royal Dutch Shell	306,731.00	25,311.00
4.	BP	267,600.00	22,341.00
5.	General Motors	192,604.00	-10,567.00
6.	Chevron	189,481.00	14,099.00
7.	DaimlerChrysler	186,106.30	3,536.30
8.	Toyota Motor	185,805.00	12,119.60
9.	Ford Motor	177,210.00	2,024.00
10.	ConocoPhillips	166,683.00	13,529.00

Source: *Fortune 500 Magazine, Global 500,* 2006

So, you're a business owner who happens to publish newspapers. Your huge parent corporation is involved in everything from soup to nuts, as the saying goes. There is a "debate" over the environment going on. On the one side are the environmentalists, and on the other is Exxon Mobil and company. What side do you choose?

Does The Environment Matter?

Vanity Fair seems like an unlikely source for an answer to this question, but in September 2004, *This Magazine* ran an editorial by its Canadian-born editor, Graydon Carter. He used the third anniversary of the 9/11 World Trade Centre disaster to reflect on the role played by the U.S. Environmental Protection Agency (EPA), and the Bush Administration, in assessing air quality and public safety. Carter pointed out that the asbestos used in construction of the World Trade Centre buildings is lethal even in small doses. He noted that an EPA chemist found windowsill dust four blocks from ground zero contained 79,000 fibres of asbestos per square centimetre. The air also contained toxic PCBs, microscopic glass particles, mercury, concrete particles, toxic dioxin, and in short, dust "as caustic as liquid drain cleaner," according to a report in the *St. Louis Post-Dispatch*, on a study by a U.S. Geological Survey team. Carter reported that although the air surrounding Ground Zero was unsafe, the EPA's public statements were censored by the National Security Council, headed by the Bush administration's Condoleezza Rice, and mislead the public and agencies such as the police and firefighters, into thinking the air was safe to breathe.

Subsequently, a U.S. Congressional committee heard testimony that as many as 50 percent of workers at the site who have been screened, suffer from long-term health problems. A report by the Mount Sinai School of Medicine found that 78 percent of the workers at Ground Zero were suffering from respiratory or lung ailments. By late 2003, 2400 members of the New York Fire Department were on disability leave.[4] Only 30 percent of the firefighters working on the site in October, 2001, were wearing any protective equipment at all.[5] In 2006, the first deaths were officially attributed to workers breathing Ground Zero dust. According to the *New York Times*,

> Detective James Zadroga, 34, died in January [2006] when his badly scarred lungs weakened and his heart gave out. The coroner's report gave the cause of death as "granulomatous pneumonitis," and the autopsy found swirls throughout his lungs caused by foreign material consistent with dust. Detective Zadroga's death was the first to be officially linked by an autopsy report to exposure to the ground zero dust, although the electronmicroscope comparisons that could have proved the match beyond a reasonable doubt were not done by the coroner's office. The Uniformed Firefighters Association earlier this year linked the deaths of two firefighters and a battalion chief —from lung disease and respiratory ailments—to the air at ground zero, although the Fire Department itself has not formally acknowledged that those deaths were connected to ground zero work. And three young emergency medical technicians who worked in the dust and smoke at ground zero have died from pulmonary diseases and coronary problems aggravated by their battered lungs, according to the union that represented them.[6]

Two years earlier, Graydon Carter, an extremely unusual mainstream journalist, concluded in his *Vanity Fair* editorial that the White House was eager to reassure Wall Street employees that "the air around them was safe." Why? In his view it was, "So that the New York Stock Exchange could be reopened quickly." The EPA followed along with this by issuing "deceptively upbeat news." This is an interesting point. While George Bush and film makers and others have been praising the work by firefighters and police and other workers at Ground Zero, to the Bush Administration and the EPA, opening the Stock Exchange in a hurry, and the return of "normalcy" was more important than these workers' lives. Money trumped people.

The example provided by the toxic air surrounding Ground Zero illustrates that the environment is extremely important, that our air quality is crucial to our health, and that the mainstream media will work in concert with governments and/or corporations and their agencies and against the interest of citizens, despite the available evidence. There are many other examples which demonstrate this latter point.

Global Warming and Climate Change

The evidence that the world is getting warmer is becoming increasingly difficult to deny, even for the most fervent disbelievers. The ten warmest years on record have occurred since 1994. Heat waves and droughts have taken a huge toll, while winter's snows have been delayed, reduced, or extinguished altogether. There have been reports that some bears have stopped hibernating, as they can now forage year-round. As the oceans and seas have warmed, extreme weather has resulted, with more violent storms and hurricanes.

Global warming refers in part to the increased presence of so-called "greenhouse gas emissions," such as carbon dioxide, which prevent solar heat from radiating out into space. The heat from the sun would, to a great extent, bounce back into the universe leaving the earth cold, if it were not for that invisible layer of greenhouse gases. But the greater the buildup of these gases, the more heat is trapped and the more global warming. The greenhouse effect was first identified by French scientist Jean-Baptise-Joseph Fourier, in 1824.[7] Although this effect was seen as positive, historically, as it saves us from freezing, that began to change as early as the 1880s, when scientists began to predict that the burning of fossil fuels would increase carbon dioxide levels and impact on the world's climate. The first of these was Swedish Nobel Prize chemist Svante August Arrhenius.[8]

It was about a hundred years before this research really caught on, linking fossil fuels to global warming.

In 1988, the first scientific conference on the topic of global warming was held in Toronto, the World Conference on the Atmosphere, with delegates from 46 countries attending. In their closing statement, the scientists declared: "Humanity is conducting an unintended, uncontrolled, globally pervasive experiment whose ultimate consequences could be second only to a global nuclear war." They recommended a 20-percent reduction in CO_2 emissions, based on 1988 levels.[9] In 1990, at an international conference on the atmosphere in Geneva, Switzerland, 700 leading scientists from more than 100 countries signed a statement that, in their judgment, global warming is a real environmental threat demanding immediate action to reduce the risk.[10]

By November, 1992, about 1700 scientists released a document entitled, "World Scientists' Warning to Humanity." Among those signing the document were 92 Nobel laureates, over 50 percent of all living Nobel recipients in the sciences. These scientists decried various effects humans are having on the earth: ranging from ozone depletion, to water shortages, the collapse of fisheries, soil degradation, rainforest destruction, the loss of living species, deforestation, and unrestrained population growth. Their paper declared,

> No more than one or a few decades remain before the chance to avert the threats we now confront will be lost and the prospects for humanity immeasurably diminished...we must, for example, move away from fossil fuels to more benign, inexhaustible energy resources to cut greenhouse gas emissions.[11]

Few would argue with the perspective that such a serious warning by such eminent scholars is tremendously newsworthy. This is page one material, fit for the top of the newscast. It's a huge wakeup call. And yet, this warning by Nobel laureates went completely unreported by the *New York Times*, the *Washington Post*, the *Globe and Mail* or any of the national media. It wasn't covered by the major U.S. television networks, nor by the CBC. A computer search of Canadian newspapers turned up just one story, in one newspaper.[12] That newspaper hasn't run anything else since. A few months later, the *Toronto Star* ran a column by David Suzuki, pointing out that no one publicized the scientists' warning.[13] The *Star* hasn't run anything since. In 1994, the *Edmonton Journal* ran a letter which criticized one of their columnists for ignoring global warming. The letter made reference to the 1992 warning. Seven years later, in 1999, the *National Post* printed a letter in which the writer referred to the world scientists' warning, taking one of the *Post's* columnists to task over omission.[14] I was unable to find any other reference, in the Canadian media, to this significant warning.

In 2006, former U.S. Vice-President Al Gore released his film, *An Inconvenient Truth*, documenting in a popular venue the evidence and the dire consequences. The British government of Tony Blair promptly hired Gore as an advisor on global warming.

The Kyoto Accord

By far, the most important environmental debate in recent decades has centred on the Kyoto Accord. In 1997, representatives of 160 countries gathered in Kyoto, Japan, and signed "the Kyoto Protocol," described by the Canadian government as "the first global agreement that establishes binding targets for cutting greenhouse gas emissions."[15] Canada's target was set at a six percent reduction from 1990 levels by the year 2012.

Kyoto, or the Kyoto Accord, as it came to be known, was regarded as a minimal first step, by environmentalists. Indeed, as we will see, a good case has been made that the Accord is largely toothless: that is, it didn't go nearly far enough and it was virtually unenforceable. But the reaction it generated from the media and other big businesses made Kyoto seem like a plan hatched by a radical militant sect. Canadian Prime Minister Stephen Harper, then leader of the Canadian Alliance Party, said in 2002 that Kyoto, signed five years earlier by representatives of 160 countries, was a "socialist scheme to suck money out of wealth-producing nations."[16]

An underlying assumption behind capitalism is that there are simply no limits to growth. Anything short of this is heretical. Writing in the *Monthly Review*, John Bellamy Foster has noted that:

Capitalist economies are geared first and foremost to the growth of profits, and hence to economic growth at virtually any cost—including the exploitation and misery of the vast majority of the world's population. This rush to grow generally means rapid absorption of energy and materials and the dumping of more and more wastes into the environment—hence widening environmental degradation.[17]

This degradation, and any (rare) assessed fines are simply treated as a cost of doing business. But any attempts by governments to get serious about preventing environmental degradation would, predictably, meet with corporate wrath. Hence, one could have anticipated an adverse reaction to Kyoto, which at least initially for the first time established "legally binding" reductions in greenhouse gas emissions of 5.2 percent below 1990 levels, by 2008–2012, for all industrialized countries. The European Union (EU) under this agreement was required to reduce its greenhouse gas emissions by eight percent below 1990 levels, the United States by seven percent, and Canada and Japan by six percent.[18]

Negotiations on the implementation of Kyoto from 1997 to 2001 focused on two points: tradable emission permits, which would allow countries to comply by purchasing permits from other countries, and allowances for "carbon sinks," giving emission credits for forests and farmlands. The EU saw these proposals as disguising failures to meet emission targets. Support for the measures came from the United States, Japan, Canada, Australia, and New Zealand. Negotiations broke down in November 2000, with both sides refusing to give in.[19]

In March 2001, the Bush administration declared that Kyoto was "fatally flawed" and announced it was unilaterally pulling out. But, negotiations went forward in July 2001 in Bonn. For the treaty to come into effect it had to be ratified by countries with 55 percent of global greenhouse gas emissions. Without U.S. participation, at 25 percent, ratification by Japan, Canada, Australia, and Russia was essential. The EU was forced to concede in the negotiations—adopting the very positions the United States and others previously advanced at the Hague.[20]

Although Kyoto was kept alive in Bonn without the U.S., it was rendered toothless. Farmlands and forests became carbon sinks, resulting in credits for emission reduction. Countries would have "reduced emissions" just for "watching their trees grow." Tradable pollution permits enabled countries like Japan, Canada, and Australia, which increased greenhouse emissions substantially since 1990, to buy permits from countries like Russia which had dramatic declines in emissions beginning with its meltdown in 1990. The only penalty for a country failing to meet its targets would be that the targets would be increased in the next round by a certain percentage. A major concession to Japan meant the "legally binding" character of the original agreement was dropped in favor of the meaningless term, "politically binding."[21]

Virtually none of the above information could be learned from the mainstream news media, although it is vital context for any meaningful assessment of Kyoto: which of course was what the media were supposed to provide. But they hardly could admit the accord they were objecting too had been gutted. No matter that it was, there was a principle at stake here: North American corporations were not about to be pushed around by puny governments. Besides, weren't governments usually on their side? Isn't that what they paid them for? Well, the Bush administration did, as mentioned, quickly correct for the lapse of judgement under Bill Clinton in 1997. But what explains the Canadian government's position under Jean Chrétien?

In the next chapter we briefly discuss the role played by Chrétien's neoliberals in undermining social programs, including health care: so these were not flaming progressives who would balk at a little environmental destruction.

Yes, in the heat of the 9/11 moment Chrétien was onboard for the invasion of Afghanistan, but he demurred when it came to the Iraq invasion in 2003, refusing to sign up for Bush's Coalition of the Willing. It was eighteen months later, Chrétien was being hotly pursued—some would say hounded out of office—by his former lieutenant Paul Martin, in a strategic coup d'etat. Perhaps, under siege from Martin and the Quebec sponsorship scandal, and with the whiff of the 1999-2001 Shawinigate hotel/golf course scandal still in the air, Chrétien was looking back with nostalgia and wanted to leave some semblance of a progressive legacy. Or, perhaps it was just mean-spiritedness, a desire to exact revenge on Martin for pushing him out of the leadership, by locking him into policies Chrétien knew Martin wouldn't agree with. The two men hated each other with a passion, after all, although you'd never know it from the press.

Whatever the reason, it was out-of-character for Chrétien to stand up to the Americans on Iraq, no matter how much Canadians opposed joining in. And, it was surprising that he announced in spring, 2002 that he, Canada, would sign on to Kyoto. Or at least, that he would put it to a vote in the House. In Canada, when there's not a minority government, it's really the same thing.

How The Globe Reported Kyoto

University of Western Ontario professor Robert Babe analyzed the *Globe and Mail's* coverage of the Kyoto debate which followed Chrétien's announcement in September 3, 2002, that Canada would ratify the protocol in a December vote. Babe studied the *Globe*, which is still Canada's most influential newspaper, until December 11, the day after ratification in the House of Commons.

Dr. Babe found the *Globe's* coverage of Kyoto wasn't primarily "environmental." Instead, it was portrayed as a story of political conflict: the provinces vs. federal government; Alberta Premier Ralph Klein vs. Jean Chrétien; Prime Minister-in-waiting Paul Martin vs. Jean Chrétien; the energy and manufacturing sectors vs. the federal government. It was also a story of Chrétien "clinging to power," his change of focus after announcing his retirement, and whether he could control his MPs in the vote in the House. And it was a story of political uncertainty—who would Ontario Premier Ernie Eves support?[22]

In the *Globe*, Kyoto was also usually treated as an economics or business or financial story, about what ratifying it would do "to employment, profits, investment, balance of trade, innovation, and other economic/financial indicators." What it was not, primarily, for the *Globe*, was a story "on the impact of global warming on the capacity of the planet to sustain life," or the impact of the Kyoto Protocol on present and anticipated global warming.[23]

In Dr. Babe's content analysis of 137 items, almost twice as many headlines were negative (45 percent) as were positive towards Kyoto (25 percent). The same held for the content of items: opinion columns, editorials and news combined were twice as likely to be unfavourable (43 percent) as favourable (20 percent).

Kyoto Coverage in the Globe and Mail, Robert Babe

- The most commonly cited reasons for not favouring Kyoto were: it is divisive and unfair to energy-rich regions; it is too costly; it will cause dis-investment and unemployment; it is not proven that global warming is caused by humans; there is too much uncertainty and no plan for implementation; Canada is disadvantaged vis a vis the U.S.; Kyoto will be ineffective; it ignores population growth; Canada will have to buy carbon emission rights abroad (from Russia).

- The most frequently cited arguments in favour of Kyoto were: Canada assumes an international leadership role on global warming; the treaty will reduce global warming; Canadians are in favour of Kyoto; the majority of scientists agree that greenhouse gases cause global warming; new technologies and new opportunities will be spawned; there are negligible costs to implementing Kyoto; Kyoto will stimulate employment; Kyoto incorporates pollution in the price mechanism; ratification is needed before a plan will be developed; costs of global warming are seldom considered by economists and businesses; it is proven that reductions in emissions can take place; it is better to proceed internationally than nationally on a global issue.

Dr. Babe looked at the coverage of four specific issues, which we will briefly recount here.

1. Is Human-Induced Global Warming Real?
In several pieces, writers in the *Globe and Mail* queried whether global warming is real, and if real, whether humans are responsible. *Globe* columnist Margaret Wente, for example. Wente pronounced global warming to be a monumental scam. She charged that "science has been corrupted by the official doctrine; governments, including Canada's, hand out millions to people to conduct research into climate change—but only if the research confirms the central thesis."

2. Commissioning and Reporting Polls
The first poll during the period of intensive debate was taken by Ipsos-Reid for the *Globe and Mail*, and was reported on page one under the headline, "Albertans Turn Against Kyoto in Poll." The reporting alleged that support for Kyoto had dropped, especially in Alberta, but what's apparent, what the reporting neglected to point out, is that the poll's context and questions invalidated any comparisons. For example, 59 percent of respondents said they did not have enough information to assess the Kyoto Accord, yet in the very next question 74 percent said Kyoto should be implemented as "a first good step."

Approval and Disapproval of Kyoto

	Agree	Disagree
1. The government of Canada needs to spend more time in investigating the cost and impact of the Kyoto accord before implementing it.	78%	20%
2. I don't think I have enough information about the Kyoto accord to say whether I support or oppose it.	59%	40%
3. Even if there are some problems with the Kyoto accord, I think it should be implemented because it is a good first step.	74%	22%
4. It is possible for Canada to develop an alternative to the Kyoto accord that is just as effective but would cost the Canadian economy a lot less.	71%	22%
5. The government of Canada should ratify the Kyoto accord and implement it, even if it means significant costs to the economy and changes to the lifestyles of Canadians.	57%	39%

Source: Ipsos-Reid, *Globe and Mail*, Oct. 8, 2002, p. A4. from Babe, 2005

If anything, matters got even worse the next month, with publication of another poll by Ipsos-Reid, but this time commissioned by the Alberta government. Respondents were asked to choose one of the following: withdraw from the Kyoto Protocol and develop a made-in-Canada plan for reducing greenhouse-gas emissions (45 percent agreed), ratify the Kyoto Protocol (44 percent responded yes), or do nothing. The headline on the front page of the *Globe and Mail* claimed that support for Kyoto had "plunged"—from 75 percent to 45 percent! The *Globe* did print a letter to the editor four days later from the president of a rival polling firm, who pointed out that the first poll asked respondents if they favoured Kyoto, whereas the second asked them to choose among Kyoto, a "made-in-Canada solution," and doing nothing. Not surprisingly, "when provided with three rather than two choices, the incidence of support for ratification drops."

Dr. Babe commented,

Indeed, on the basis of the results published by the *Globe,* the proper conclusion would be that support for action against greenhouse gas emissions had increased substantially. In the October poll, almost thirty percent of Canadians felt no action was required, whereas in the November (Alberta government) poll, only about 10 percent either recommended no action or expressed no opinion.[24]

3. Trashing the Public
A number of stories trivialized Kyoto, and denigrated the public, indicating that people don't and can't understand such issues, and they should leave the decision-making to the experts. An elitist quote from the *Globe's* political affairs columnist Jeffrey Simpson is representative:

A big chunk of Canadians are ignorant or barely informed about anything in the public domain. They get most of their information from television, but what they take in doesn't inform them very much. Television, in general, entertains but does not inform. A corollary point: a chunk of the electorate is completely tuned out of everything beyond its immediate world. It doesn't matter what the media, interest groups, governments or political parties do.

4. Accepting Industry Statements as Fact
The *Globe* editorial of December 9, 2002 was headlined, "The Terms of Canada's Participation in Kyoto." Here the *Globe* charged that Chrétien's plan to pass the Protocol before Christmas was "precipitate" and "irresponsible." The editorial ended: "Canada, if it ratifies the Accord, will be the only nation in the Western Hemisphere to take on the international obligation to reduce greenhouse gases." This false statement, it would appear, was lifted directly from the pages of the *National Post* and the opinion piece appearing there by Imperial Oil's CEO.[25]

Dr. Babe concluded, in part, that "the great bulk of the *Globe's* coverage was negative towards Kyoto." Most of the coverage didn't concern the Accord, or even global warming and the environment, but rather political conflicts and alleged economic repercussions. Much of the coverage centred on personality. There were no attempts to quantify the benefits of Kyoto, only the alleged costs.[26]

From this analysis of the debate over the Kyoto Accord and its portrayal in the *Globe and Mail*, it's apparent that crucial background material was completely omitted. The perspective that Kyoto had been largely gutted beforehand was nowhere to be found in the Canadian debate. By leaving these facts out, the *Globe* was able to portray Kyoto, with its moderate goal of a six percent reduction in Canada's 1990 CO_2 emissions by 2012, as an extreme, radical position. This despite the fact that Canada and 159 other countries signed this agreement in 1997.

The *Globe and Mail* was so stubbornly oblivious to the environmental concerns which led to Kyoto, concerns which have been highlighted by the scientific community at least since 1988, that in 2002 it treated the Kyoto debate as mere politics. Largely due to the way the *Globe* and other news media have depicted the evidence for global warming, as a mere debate, and a specious one at that, in 2005 one commentator observed,

> Unhappily, a lot of people, including powerful and influential people, still doggedly dismiss the suggestion that global warming is even a real phenomenon—or if it is, that human activity has anything to do with it. They insist that the whole concept is a propaganda fantasy dreamed up by leftie environmentalists, as a stick to beat capitalism and industrial growth with. One wonders how many monster storms, melted ice caps, flooded coastal lowlands and so forth it will take to shake them out of denial.[27]

Hurricane Katrina

In late August, 2005, Hurricane Katrina struck New Orleans, La, causing massive flooding, deaths and destruction. About 2000 people were killed. Much has been written about these events, even including allegations of racism and classism in the treatment of people of colour in New Orleans by the Bush Administration and various levels of government, especially after the mayor of New Orleans spoke out.[28] What I'd like to examine here is the way the media resisted putting Katrina in the context of climate change and global warming. For this chapter, I conducted a full-text computer search of the three national Canadian newspapers, the *Toronto Star*, *Globe and Mail* and *National Post*, along with all the major dailies of the CanWest Global chain, stretching from Prince Edward Island to Vancouver. I searched all stories in the six weeks following Hurricane Katrina. While there were some letters to the editor which made the link, and some freelance columnists, there were hardly any news articles which did so. This despite the fact that an important scientific article was released on the topic of global warming and hurricanes, about two weeks after Katrina struck. Instead, some of these newspapers continued their attack on the concept of global warming, as well as on environmentalists and some politicians, for making these obvious connections.

Making these connections is child's play. For example, an elementary school student in Windsor, Ontario wrote a letter to the *Windsor Star* in October, 2005, in which he pointed out that scientists believe there is a direct connection between more frequent intense hurricanes such as Katrina, and global warming. He wrote, "They think this is because global warming is heating the Earth's surface and causing the water temperatures to rise. Since hurricanes thrive on warm water and global warming is making the water warmer, the hurricanes can get bigger and stronger."[29]

But what an elementary school child can see, the blinkered media cannot. Aside from two columns by scientist and environmentalist Dr. David Suzuki, which were each run in just two newspapers, there were just five articles or opinion columns in all these newspapers, over a period of six weeks, which made the connection. Two of these were written by freelancers, including one retired university professor, and were published in either The *Halifax Daily News*, or the *Guardian* of Charlottetown, PEI.[30] One of these was in the *Saskatoon Star-Phoenix*, in the lifestyle section, noting simply,

> [C]atastrophic storms like hurricane Katrina are hardly new. It would be unfair to blame them entirely on global warming or George W. Bush. On the other hand, catastrophes are increasing in frequency and severity, probably as a result of a warmer climate.[31]

Another, appearing five weeks after Katrina, was in the business section of the *Calgary Herald*, and indicated that investment corporations are beginning to tell clients that "global warming poses financial risks." Although this article reported the Sierra Club claims that "rising sea temperatures are causing more ferocious storms," it went on to quote a "climate professor" from the Massachusetts Institute of Technology as saying this was "absurd."[32] Unreported, except by Dr. David Suzuki, was the work of another MIT professor: an expert in hurricanes.

Kerry Emanuel of the Massachusetts Institute of Technology has conducted the most comprehensive analysis of hurricane power over the past 30 years. His paper, prophetically published pre-Katrina this August in the journal *Nature*, reports: "My results suggest that future warming may lead to an upward trend in tropical cyclone destructive potential, and—taking into account an increasing coastal population—a substantial increase in hurricane-related losses in the 21st century.[33]

The last article, reprinted in six of the CanWest Global newspapers, reported briefly on a study by the Georgia Institute of Technology and the U.S. National Center for Atmospheric Research published in the journal *Science*, September 16, 2005. "What we found was rather astonishing," said lead scientist Peter Webster.

In the 1970s, there was an average of about 10 Category 4 and 5 hurricanes per year globally. Since 1990, the number of Category 4 and 5 hurricanes has almost doubled, averaging 18 per year globally. The scientists said that warmer oceans are making disasters like this "the face of the future."[34]

So, out of twenty large daily newspapers, only a handful of articles were published—over a six week period—making this important connection. If the newspapers were not reporting on this obvious link, nor on the research results from the U.S. National Center for Atmospheric Research, then, on what were they reporting? Part of what the newspapers did was to use the occasion of Katrina to continue to bash the scientists and environmentalists who make these links, who provide evidence for climate change generally and global warming specifically.

This genre is represented by a lengthy article stretching to 1100 words, written for the conservative *National Post*. The writer referred to Robert F. Kennedy Jr., as an "enviro-predator."

Environmentalists and some media link Katrina to climate change, but there is no shred of scientific basis to the claim....the response of environmental extremists fills me with what only can be called disgust. They have decided to exploit the death and devastation to win support for the failed Kyoto Protocol, which requires massive cutbacks in energy use to reduce, by a few tenths of a degree, surface warming projected 100 years from now.[35]

Scientist David Suzuki's disagreement with this perspective was marinalized, run in only two newspapers. Suzuki wrote,

The world's most prestigious scientific bodies—the U.S. National Academy of Science, the Royal Society of the UK, the Royal Society of Canada and others—recently signed a declaration warning about the "clear and increasing" threat of climate change and urging our leaders to act. An analysis in [the journal] *Science* of all 928 peer-reviewed climate studies published between 1993 and 2003 found that not a single one disagreed with the general scientific consensus on climate change.[36]

We've seen how the news media's stubborn denial of climate change and global warming stretched from 1988, when the World Conference on the Atmosphere was held in Toronto, through to Kyoto, in 1997 and 2002, to Hurricane Katrina, in August, 2005. By the spring of 2007, a shift in coverage was becoming apparent. I'm not sure why. Perhaps it was in May, 2006, when Britain's most trusted celebrity, Sir David Attenborough, finally went on the record with his opinion. Attenborough, the highly-regarded nature documentary presenter, wrote an article for the *Independent* newspaper in London. Previously he had not publicly acknowledged the dangers of global warming in any of his popular documentaries. Even *Planet Earth*, about the extinction of the polar bears, in 2006, did not mention rising global temperatures as a cause. Now Sir David spoke out:

> I was skeptical about climate change. I was cautious about crying wolf. I am always cautious about crying wolf. I think conservationists have to be careful in saying things are catastrophic when, in fact, they are less than catastrophic... But I'm no longer skeptical. Now I do not have any doubt at all. I think climate change is the major challenge facing the world. I have waited until the proof was conclusive that it was humanity changing the climate.[37]

Attenborough, being a celebrity, got a lot of attention. And so too did former U.S. Vice President Al Gore. Perhaps it was Gore's film, *An Inconvenient Truth*, which played to mostly popular acclaim through the summer and fall of 2006, although there was the usual concerted attack in the news media, from the usual cast of characters. Because of Gore's stature and because climate scientists confirmed what Gore said in the film, it became increasingly difficult to maintain a complete state of denial. In Roger Ebert's June 2006 review of the film, he wrote: "In 39 years, I have never written these words in a movie review, but here they are: You owe it to yourself to see this film. If you do not, and you have grandchildren, you should explain to them why you decided not to."

AN INCONVENIENT TRUTH
Ebert Rating: ****

By Roger Ebert, Jun 2, 2006

I want to write this review so every reader will begin it and finish it. I am a liberal, but I do not intend this as a review reflecting any kind of politics. It reflects the truth as I understand it, and it represents, I believe, agreement among the world's experts.

Global warming is real. It is caused by human activity.

Mankind and its governments must begin immediate action to halt and reverse it.

If we do nothing, in about 10 years the planet may reach a "tipping point" and begin a slide toward destruction of our civilization and most of the other species on this planet.

After that point is reached, it would be too late for any action.

These facts are stated by Al Gore in the documentary "An Inconvenient Truth." Forget he ever ran for office. Consider him a concerned man speaking out on the approaching crisis. "There is no controversy about these facts," he says in the film. "Out of 925 recent articles in peer-review scientific journals about global warming, there was no disagreement. Zero."

He stands on a stage before a vast screen, in front of an audience. The documentary is based on a speech he has been developing for six years, and is supported by dramatic visuals. He shows the famous photograph "Earthrise," taken from space by the first American astronauts. Then he shows a series of later space photographs, clearly indicating that glaciers and lakes are shrinking, snows are melting, shorelines are retreating.

He provides statistics: The 10 warmest years in history were in the last 14 years. Last year South America experienced its first hurricane. Japan and the Pacific are setting records for typhoons. Hurricane Katrina passed over Florida, doubled back over the Gulf, picked up strength from unusually warm Gulf waters, and went from Category 3 to Category 5. There are changes in the Gulf Stream and the jet stream. Cores of polar ice show that carbon dioxide is much, much higher than ever before in a quarter of a million years. It was once thought that such things went in cycles. Gore stands in front of a graph showing the ups and downs of carbon dioxide over the centuries. Yes, there is a cyclical pattern. Then, in recent years, the graph turns up and keeps going up, higher and higher, off the chart.

continued

The primary man-made cause of global warming is the burning of fossil fuels. We are taking energy stored over hundreds of millions of years in the form of coal, gas and oil, and releasing it suddenly. This causes global warming, and there is a pass-along effect. Since glaciers and snow reflect sunlight but sea water absorbs it, the more the ice melts, the more of the sun's energy is retained by the sea.

Gore says that although there is "100 percent agreement" among scientists, a database search of newspaper and magazine articles shows that 57 percent question the fact of global warming, while 43 percent support it. These figures are the result, he says, of a disinformation campaign started in the 1990s by the energy industries to "reposition global warming as a debate." It is the same strategy used for years by the defenders of tobacco. My father was a Luckys smoker who died of lung cancer in 1960, and 20 years later it was still "debatable" that there was a link between smoking and lung cancer. Now we are talking about the death of the future, starting in the lives of those now living.

"The world won't 'end' overnight in 10 years," Gore says. "But a point will have been passed, and there will be an irreversible slide into destruction."

In England, Sir James Lovelock, the scientist who proposed the Gaia hypothesis (that the planet functions like a living organism), has published a new book saying that in 100 years mankind will be reduced to "a few breeding couples at the Poles." Gore thinks "that's too pessimistic, We can turn this around just as we reversed the hole in the ozone layer. But it takes action right now, and politicians in every nation must have the courage to do what is necessary. It is not a political issue. It is a moral issue."

When I said I was going to a press screening of "An Inconvenient Truth," a friend said, "Al Gore talking about the environment! Bor...ing!" This is not a boring film. The director, Davis Guggenheim, uses words, images and Gore's concise litany of facts to build a film that is fascinating and relentless. In 39 years, I have never written these words in a movie review, but here they are: You owe it to yourself to see this film. If you do not, and you have grandchildren, you should explain to them why you decided not to.

Am I acting as an advocate in this review? Yes, I am. I believe that to be "impartial" and "balanced" on global warming means one must take a position like Gore's. There is no other view that can be defended. Sen. James Inhofe (R-Okla.), chairman of the Senate Environment Committee, has said, "Global warming is the greatest hoax ever perpetrated on the American people."

continued

I hope he takes his job seriously enough to see this film. I think he has a responsibility to do that.

What can we do? Switch to and encourage the development of alternative energy sources: Solar, wind, tidal, and, yes, nuclear. Move quickly toward hybrid and electric cars. Pour money into public transit, and subsidize the fares. Save energy in our houses. I did a funny thing when I came home after seeing "An Inconvenient Truth." I went around the house turning off the lights.

Somehow, this film seemed to mark a sea change of sorts in the media coverage of global warming. *An Inconvenient Truth* may have done for environmentalism what Michael Moore's *Fahrenheit 911* did for, well, 9/11.

And, just as with Moore, Gore has his detractors. There was a backlash against the film. One example of this was a British ITV Channel 4 documentary, *The Great Global Warming Swindle*, broadcast in early March, 2007, and immediately thereafter available on Google video. One of the people interviewed in *Swindle*, Carl Wunsch, professor of physical oceanography at the Massachusetts Institute of Technology, said he was misrepresented, taken out of context, that *Swindle* was "grossly distorted" and "as close to pure propaganda as anything since World War Two." Wunsch said he was considering legal action.[38]

The UK media watch organization Medialens said eight of the scientists in the film: John Christy, Paul Reiter, Richard Lindzen, Paul Driessen, Roy Spencer, Patrick Michaels, Fred Singer and Tim Ball, "are linked to American neo-conservative and right-wing think-tanks, many of which have received tens of millions of dollars from Exxon."[39]

An Inconvenient Truth, Fahrenheit 911, and *Swindle* are all part of a new cinema or video activism which is contributing to the diversity of perspectives. I was somewhat surprised to read a positive account of this idea in the *National Post*, of all places, where reviewer Jay Stone wrote,

[W]e had known and talked about [global warming] for a decade or longer, but through a propitious collision of timing and mounting evidence, it took a documentary—not a sexy one, admittedly, but a movie nonetheless, a medium that uses images rather than the written argument everyone seemed to have been ignoring—to propel it to centre stage.[40]

Actually, that was mostly *denial* about global warming going on over those years. But now there is a certain amount of acceptance. *An Inconvenient Truth* had some help from elsewhere, including other cinema. A top box-office animated film released in fall, 2006, *Happy Feet*, is about human-made problems threatening emperor penguins at the South Pole, and the penguins struggling to survive with a depleted food supply.[41]

Film reviewers are artsie-types and newsroom outsiders who, because they are usually reviewing fiction, have more leeway than news journalists. Sometimes they can get away with a favourable review for a film or documentary which would be panned—or wouldn't appear—if the decision was left up to the news side.

On the other side of things from *Happy Feet* and Gore was *Jurassic Park* author Michael Crichton's 2004 novel *State of Fear*. The book is about eco-terrorists with the National Environmental Resource Fund (NERF), a fictitious environmental organization, who conspire to engineer four "natural disasters" including a tsunami, to sell the theory of human-induced global warming. The book has a two-fold message: first, the scientific evidence doesn't support global warming, and second the environmental movement has jumped on this bandwagon because that's where the government research money is. The only thing we have to fear in all of this, is fear itself. Although this is a novel, Crichton, an MD, presents it as historically accurate fiction, referencing his 'science' with articles. He went on a speaking tour with the book to promote his anti-global warming views. Watch for the film, but the time for this message appears to have passed, and it's likely to be viewed as simply entertainment.

Then, there was *The Day After Tomorrow*, a 2004 film starring Dennis Quaid as a paleoclimatologist who tries to save the world from an ice age resulting from global warming. Audiences might have asked: could this really happen?

The Stern Report

There were other events as well, such as the Stern Report of October, 2006. This was a study commissioned by the U.K. government and headed by Sir Nicholas Stern, once the chief economist with the World Bank. Global climate change will cost the world economy as much as $7-trillion in lost output and could force as many as 200 million people out of their homes because of flood or drought unless drastic action is taken, Stern said. This was beginning to sound a lot like Al Gore. Stern concluded that rising average temperatures are a serious global threat meriting immediate and drastic action. Otherwise, we face natural disasters of increasing ferocity, damage to food production, the spread of diseases and the destruction of ecosystems: "risks of major disruption to economic and social activity, later in this century and in the next, on a scale similar to those associated with the great wars and the economic depression of the first half of the 20th century," Stern wrote. Using data from the Intergovernmental Panel on Climate Change (IPCC), Stern estimated the world's countries may lose 5-20 percent of GDP annually, so, "the benefits over time of actions to shift the world onto a low-carbon path could be in the order of $2.5 trillion each year."[42]

Instead of the usual arguments that reducing CO_2 levels and global warming would cost governments billions, we now had a former chief economist with the World Bank saying that *it would cost us trillions of dollars not to act*. Of course, there was a reaction to this. Terrence Corcoran of the *National Post* referred to Stern's report as, "The new green totalitarianism." But Stern's reputation and his weighty 700-page report were not to be taken lightly, and their impact was considerable.

Following on this, we had the election of Stephane Dion as federal Liberal Party leader, in fall 2006, on an environmental platform. Part of the reason for Dion's victory was that he slipped up the middle between Bob Rae (Paul Desmarais' candidate) and Michael Ignatief, but his popularity also had something to do with Dion's emphasis on the environment.

The IPCC Weighs In

February 2007 brought the release of the Intergovernmental Panel on Climate Change (IPCC) AR4. Written by a weighty international group of scientists and approved by 113 countries, including the U.S., the report only served to back up Stern, Gore, and others. The IPCC said global warming is "very likely" caused by humans, its strongest conclusion to date. Concentrations of heat-trapping greenhouse gases in the planet's atmosphere, "have increased markedly as a result of human activities since 1750," mainly from the use of fossil fuels like oil, gas and coal, and because of agriculture, the report said.[43]

The reaction was swift. French President Jacques Chirac called for a new environmental body to slow "inevitable global warming" and protect the planet, perhaps with policing powers to punish violators. Chirac said "It is our responsibility. The future of humanity demands it." Without naming the U.S. which produces about one-quarter of the world's greenhouse gases, Chirac expressed frustration over "some large, rich countries...refusing to accept the consequences of their acts."[44] Forty-five nations responded almost immediately to Chirac's call, and signed up.

Articles began to run—even in the conservative CanWest Global *Calgary Herald*, which said, "Global warming 'denialists' grow scarce: Science finally wins over most holdouts."[45]

Now, it was those who were *against* the evidence for global warming, who were cast as being "in denial." At long last, the sheer weight of the evidence had begun to shift the balance of reporting. Because the results of the IPCC report had been bandied about amongst governments for months, everyone knew what was coming. And even though the report was inevitably a conservative statement, those in denial had been working on the backlash.

On the day the IPCC report was released, news broke that scientists and economists had been offered cash to write articles disagreeing with the results. The *Guardian* newspaper in Britain revealed that academics were offered $10,000 each and travel expenses, by a lobby group funded by one of the world's largest oil companies to undermine the IPCC report. Letters sent by the American Enterprise Institute (AEI), an ExxonMobil-funded think tank with close links to the Bush administration, offered the payments for articles that emphasized the shortcomings of the report.[46]

Suddenly, after years of denial about global warming and climate change generally, views began to change. For example, the elitist participants at the January 2007 World Economic Forum annual meetings in Davos, Switzerland voted for climate change as the issue that will have the greatest global impact in coming years, but also as the one for which the world is least prepared.[47] An Angus Reid poll published in the conservative *National Post* in March, 2007, indicated that, "most Canadian adults (77%) believe climate change is a reality. Another 21% think it may be happening and only two per cent flatly reject it."[48]

The momentum had shifted.

NAFTA, Chapter 11, and the Environment

In many of the cases brought before NAFTA Tribunals and the World Trade Organization (WTO) thus far, commercial interests have won, whether it was commercial shrimp fishing versus giant sea turtles, air quality versus oil interests, or U.S. cattle producers versus the European Union's ban on hormone-treated beef. Even in the area of Canadian protection of home-grown magazines from predatory American influences, the former lost out.[49] Two important (Canadian) exceptions to this are the Canadian government's failed appeal over France banning the import of Canadian asbestos, in 2001, and the 2005 decision on the Canadian-based Methanex Corporation vs. The State of California, under NAFTA's Chapter 11.

Methanex argued that California's ban on MTBE, the gasoline additive containing methanol made by Methanex, was an effective expropriation of Methanex, without compensation, which was prohibited under NAFTA's Article 1110. California argued that banning MTBE (methyl tertiary butyl ether) was necessary because it was contaminating drinking water supplies and risking public health and safety. In 1999, the State of California had asked that the octane enhancer MTBE be removed from gasoline by 2002. The case dragged on for six years, and was finally settled in 2005.

The Tribunal found the legislative process to be transparent, science-based, subject to due process and legitimate peer review, and conducted in a manner consistent with California practice. Hence, the NAFTA Tribunal ruled in favour of the State of California, upholding the ban on MTBE, without compensation.[50]

The Methanex decision was somewhat surprising, if welcomed, in view of an earlier decision in Metalclad v. Mexico. In 1994 the municipality of Guadalcazar, Mexico, ordered Metalclad, a California company, to cease construction on a hazardous waste transfer station. Metalclad paid for an environmental assessment, and continued construction, which was completed in 1995. The municipal government denied Metalclad's request for a permit. In 1996, Metalclad sued for $90 million under NAFTA's Chapter 11: alleging expropriation without compensation. The NAFTA Tribunal ruled in 2000 in favor of Metalclad, awarding about $17 million. Mexico challenged the ruling. In 2001, a Canadian court reduced the award to $15.6 million, but ordered Mexico to pay. The NAFTA Tribunal focused on economic considerations and appeared to dismiss environmental concerns. However, it refused to compensate Metalclad for future loss of business profits, which it said were speculative.[51]

According to Murray Dobbin, as of 2002 more than 70 Canadian municipalities demanded an exemption from the General Agreement on Trade in Services (GATS) being negotiated by the WTO.

The European Commission (which represents the European Union at the WTO) is asking Canada to completely open all "water collection, purification and distribution services through mains" to foreign competition. European water corporations dominate the global market for water treatment and distribution systems.[52]

Dobbin indicates that restrictions on the foreign ownership of farmland in the four Western provinces may be lifted, and public auto insurance in British Columbia, Manitoba and Saskatchewan, may be threatened, along with public liquor distribution in Ontario.[53] Additionally, Canada Post and its subsidiaries such as Purolator, and as we'll see in Chapter Three, ultimately even public health care and public education, may be threatened. More recently, Dobbin has argued that an interprovincial agreement, TILMA, The Trade, Investment and Labour Mobility Agreement, will use deregulation to do an end-run around Canada's provincial and municipal regulations, in the same way as NAFTA, only it's more draconian.[54]

The MMT Scandal

There's a Canadian equivalent to the Methanex and Metalclad NAFTA cases, only the Canadian government conceded, perhaps too hastily, in an out-of-court settlement. This happened prior to the Methanex case, a decision which calls into question the MMT settlement. Canadian gasoline companies began using MMT as a substitute for lead additives, in 1977. The additives were used to reduce engine knock or "pinging" and to boost octane and engine performance. In 1997 parliament passed a law, Bill C-29, otherwise known as the Manganese-Based Fuel Additive Act, restricting the import and interprovincial transport of MMT, a neurotoxic gasoline additive, which, like the lead additive it replaced, was harmful to people's health and the environment. The Minister of the Environment, Sergio Marchi, said the additive was a hazard to the public health and to the environment. In addition, the minister pointed out, automobile manufacturers believed the substance "damaged emissions control equipment" installed in their vehicles to monitor fuel performance, producing an increase in harmful tail-pipe pollutants.

Within days of the federal law in 1997, the U.S. multinational Ethyl Corporation (now Afton Chemical), the sole supplier of MMT in Canada, invoked the "expropriation" clause of the investment chapter of NAFTA to sue the government for $350 million for damages and lost income. With the NAFTA agreement in place, and in view of the Metalclad ruling, the federal government caved in, settling out-of-court on July 20, 1998, before the NAFTA arbitration panel could rule.[55]

According to Kenneth Traynor, a researcher with the Canadian Environmental Law Association, "In the final cruel irony, the $20 million compensation payment to Ethyl (one of this country's true environmental villains) for lost profits and legal costs, exceeds the total 1998 Environment Canada budget for Enforcement and Compliance programs, of $16.9 million."[56]

In 1998, when the Canadian government settled with Ethyl Corp. over MMT, neither the Metalclad nor Methanex decisions had been made. Metalclad, the first of these decisions in 2001, may have led the government to think it made the right decision, as Metalclad trumped the Mexican government. If Metalclad won against Mexico, couldn't Ethyl win against Canada? However, as we've seen, since that time Methanex lost against California. Might Ethyl have lost as well?

These questions are important as MMT is a deadly poison, and governments should take whatever expensive precautions necessary to prevent it from being burned in our gasoline and spewed into the air, from whence it enters our lungs. It has been nine years at this writing, since the Canadian government settled out of court with Ethyl/Afton. There has been lots of time to pursue other avenues to ban the additive. Why has the government not acted? As Dalton Camp wrote back in 1998, "So that we understand this bizarre episode in our own history: A government bill approved by the Parliament of Canada has been vetoed by Ethyl Corp. of Virginia."[57]

Originally, Canada was apparently unable to ban MMT on health grounds due to a 1994 Health Canada report stating it did not have evidence MMT posed a risk to health. Their research apparently was based on exposure assessments (i.e. measurements of the amount of airborne manganese inhaled by the typical individual) rather than epidemiological studies of population health effects. Similarly, the government was unable to ban MMT on the grounds of environmental protection because the environmental ministry took the position that sufficient studies to determine the effects of MMT on emission control systems had not been carried out.[58] Reportedly, however, the government took the step of banning MMT in part because of complaints from auto manufacturers that MMT was damaging catalytic converters, (pollution control devices) and hence this would harm the environment. (See the quote from Sergio Marchi above.) Perhaps more importantly for the government, the automakers wanted MMT out, to save on replacement costs. Some accounts indicate that it was GM which pressured Sheila Copps, Marchi's predecessor as environment minister, into introducing Bill C-29.[59]

For the past thirty years, Canadians have been lulled into thinking that fumes were safe from the "unleaded gas" they pumped into their cars and breathed at stop lights. A 2006 review article in the *Lancet* medical journal coauthored by a Harvard professor of medicine concluded:

> Community exposures to manganese released into the environment by combustion of MMT, exposures from a toxic waste site in the USA, and from contaminated drinking water in Bangladesh, have been associated with subclinical neurological impairment in children.[60]

The MMT combustion study the authors referenced was published in 1999.[61] Those authors found that higher blood levels of MMT led to poorer learning, recall, and performance in motor tasks such as pointing task functions, and arm movements. They concluded that MMT neurotoxicity, "can be viewed on a continuum of dysfunction, with early, subtle changes at lower exposure levels."

In a letter to a Tory government minister in 1991, then-Opposition Leader Jean Chrétien wrote:

> Some of our leading neurotoxic scientists, as well as studies and documents from medical schools and universities, in addition to other institutions, outline in detail the truly horrific effects that allowing the continued use of this neurotoxin [MMT] could have on the Canadian people.[62]

According to the U.S. Environmental Protection Agency, Chrétien was right. MMT "is a neurotoxin and can cause irreversible neurological disease."[63] However, at the rate it is allowed, 1/32 grams per gallon of gasoline, the EPA was unable to demonstrate harmful effects. The EPA is currently awaiting further research by Afton Chemical, (formerly Ethyl Corporation) expected by 2008.

In 2006, some news reports said MMT has been voluntarily replaced by ethanol, by manufacturers, and so we need not worry. "If you fill up your car in Canada today, there isn't much chance there will be MMT in the tank. Companies have voluntarily phased it out, probably as a result of pressure from car manufacturers and environmentalists," one Vancouver *Sun* columnist wrote, reassuringly. He concluded: "Social pressure can work. Consumers have to get smarter about toxic chemicals, and more aggressive in their spending decisions. Companies will change their practices if their bottom lines depend on it."[64] Perhaps, if you're willing to wait thirty years.

The Precautionary Principle

When an activity raises threats of harm to human health or the environment, precautionary measures should be taken even if some cause and effect relationships are not fully established scientifically. In this context the proponent of an activity, rather than the public, should bear the burden of proof. —www.rachel.org

Leaded Gasoline

That bit about substituting ethanol for MMT as an octane-booster is a nice segue into an incredible related story which I want to briefly recount: the story of leaded gasoline. One historian called it, "among the great environmental disasters of the 20th century, given the numbers of people killed or slowly poisoned."[65] This is a story I've been unable to find in the mainstream media, although it does appear in the alternative media, for example, Jamie Lincoln Kitman's article, "The Secret History of Lead," in the *Nation*.[66] Kitman himself later wrote an article for the Media Channel, describing his frustration over trying to get the story into the mainstream. Kitman wrote, "There were many remarkable things about the story of how General Motors, DuPont and Standard Oil of New Jersey (today Exxon-Mobil) got together to add lead to gasoline, not the least being that no one had ever written about it in the popular press." Kitman wrote that "no one in print journalism," picked up on his story, except for automotive columnist Lesley Hazleton, who wrote one column for the Detroit *Free Press*.[67]

When you pull up to the pumps and see "unleaded gasoline," you might think that lead occurs naturally in gas, and they remove it for our safety. Not so. The first thing to note is that lead is highly poisonous, a potent neurotoxin whose sickening and deadly effects have been known for nearly 3,000 years. Lead poisoning symptoms include blindness, brain damage, kidney disease, convulsions and cancer, often leading, of course, to death. In recent decades, parents have learned their children can die from nibbling on chipping paint made with a lead base, or from lead dust in metal window blinds.

If the ancient Egyptians were aware of this, then so-too was an engineer named Thomas Midgley Jr., working on the problem of engine-knock for General Motors in Dayton, Ohio, in 1921. Midgley discovered that tetraethyl lead, also called TEL, reduced engine knock or "ping." Earlier (here's the segue) he discovered that ethyl alcohol, also called grain alcohol (the kind you drink), or ethanol, worked too. Iodine worked as well, but it was corrosive and costly. It happens that Henry Ford built his very first car to run on what he called this "farm alcohol." Four years later, his Model A was an early hybrid, equipped with a dashboard knob to adjust its carburetor to run on gasoline or alcohol. As *Scientific American* reported in 1918, "It is now definitely established that alcohol can be blended with gasoline to produce a suitable motor fuel."[68]

There were two "problems" with using ethanol. First, any layabout could make it in his backyard: it wasn't a patentable process, so profits from it were minimal. Second, the big oil and gas companies didn't want to share their market with farmers who grew corn for ethanol. Unlike TEL, which required just four grams per gallon, ethanol would fill a portion of the tank, and that would detract from big oil's gas profits. (And, of course, conserve oil and gas resources.) Regarding the patents and profits, Midgley would write to his boss,

> The way I feel about the Ethyl Gas situation is about as follows: It looks as though we could count on a minimum of 20 percent of the gas sold in the country if we advertise and go after the business —this at three cent gross to us from each gallon sold. I think we ought to go after it as soon as we can without being too hasty.[69]

This turned out to be a conservative estimate. To produce and market the new TEL additive, General Motors, Du Pont and Standard Oil of New Jersey (known nowadays as Exxon-Mobil) formed a new company, the Ethyl Gas Corporation, in 1924. But a lack of adequate precautions in the manufacturing process led to sickness and poisoning from the deadly substance. Five workers died in quick succession at Standard Oil's plant in Bayway, New Jersey, "after wrenching fits of violent insanity." Thirty-five other workers experienced "tremors, hallucinations, severe palsies and other neurological symptoms of organic lead poisoning." In all, "more than 80 percent of Bayway staff would die or suffer severe poisoning."[70]

With grave sympathy, a Du Pont spokesperson commented, "we have a great deal of trouble inducing the men to be cautious. We have to protect them against themselves." Soon after these deaths, and the release of a report vetted by Ethyl Corp., the *New York Times* provided the company with a story and front page headline which was a dream: "No Peril to Public Seen in Ethyl Gas/Bureau of Mines Reports after Long Experiments with Motor Exhausts/More Deaths Unlikely." This was just one example of assistance from both media and government. But by far the government's greatest assistance, writes Kitman, was an act of omission: "a signal failure to arrange for independent examination of the effects of automotive lead emissions on the public health."[71]

The U.S. Surgeon General held a grand total of less than seven hours of hearings into what one observer called, "probably the greatest single question in the field of public health that has ever faced the American public," before handing the matter over to a special committee. In January 1926, the committee found "no good grounds" for prohibiting the sale of Ethyl gasoline:

> So far as the committee could ascertain all the reported cases of fatal-
> ities and serious injuries in connection with the use of tetraethyl lead
> [TEL] have occurred either in the process of manufacture of this sub-
> stance or in the procedures of blending and ethylizing.[72]

By 1936 Ethyl fluid would be added to 90 percent of gasoline sold in America —a resounding commercial success.

Dr. Robert Kehoe of the University of Cincinnati was Ethyl's chief medical consultant, and a member of the Surgeon General's special committee. Kehoe was appointed to the post in 1925 and remained until his retirement in 1958. His laboratory at the University of Cincinnati was founded with an initial grant of $130,000 from Ethyl Corp. Here, the lead industry paid Kehoe's salary for decades, and here he worked to promote TEL and defend it against its detractors. (His lab also certified the safety of the refrigerant Freon, another environmentally insensitive GM patent which earned hundreds of millions of dollars before it was banned.)[73]

Kehoe's central position, which was debunked initially by medical authorities from Yale, Harvard and Columbia and is thoroughly discredited today, was that lead appeared "naturally in the human body," and the high blood-lead levels his subjects evidenced were "normal and healthy."[74]

In recent years, Robert Kehoe is identified as the father of a paradigm governing American industry and its hazardous products for much of the twentieth century. Relying on "the cascading uncertainty rule" which holds that there is always uncertainty in a world of imperfect information, the lead industry and Ethyl argued in 1925: "You say it's dangerous. We say it's not. Prove us wrong."[75] Little has changed, and won't until some variation of the Precautionary Principle— summarized above—is adopted: the proponent, rather than the public, should bear the burden of proof. Tobacco, the chemical industry, pharmaceuticals, asbestos, all have applied similar strategies to that employed by Ethyl.

By 1963, Ethyl's annual report bragged that its additive was used in more than 98 percent of all gasoline sold in the U.S., and in increasing amounts around the world. But in 1965, a telling event occurred, when a California Institute of Technology geochemist, Dr. Clair Patterson, published his important work, "Contaminated and Natural Lead Environments of Man," in the Archives of Environmental Health. Here, finally, was bedrock evidence that high lead levels in industrial lands were man-made. Patterson detailed how industrial man had raised his own lead levels 100 times and levels of atmospheric lead 1,000 times. By analyzing 1,600-year-old bones of pre-Columbian humans, he showed that lead levels in 1965 were seriously elevated. His article earned the professor a visit from representatives of Ethyl, who, in Patterson's words, tried to "buy me out through research support that would yield results favourable to their cause."[76]

In January 1970, GM announced it would meet pending clean-air laws with catalytic converters, beginning in 1974. Kitman writes that,

> Attached to automotive exhaust systems, these devices trap many harmful emissions. However, the catalysts' active element, platinum, is expensive, a real problem when it is rendered instantly inoperative (and the car undrivable) by the lead in "ethylized" gasoline. Farewell, then, leaded gasoline.[77]

The EPA reported that between 1976 and 1980 the amount of lead consumed in gasoline dropped 50 percent. Meanwhile, blood-lead levels dropped 37 percent. The EPA estimated that the public benefits of the phase out, including reduced medical costs, exceeded costs by $700 million. Between 1975 and 1984 lead for gasoline consumption dropped 73 percent, while ambient air lead decreased 71 percent. The phasing out of lead which began in 1975 was largely completed by 1986, and entirely by 1989. So, the process still took 14 years! Based on data collected in more than sixty U.S. cities, the U.S. Department of Health and Human Services reported that blood-lead levels in Americans aged one to seventy-four had declined 78 percent between 1978 and 1991.[78] In 2006, Statistics Canada announced that it would begin testing a random sample of 5000 Canadians for lead and numerous other contaminants and poisons, including DDT.

Lead For the Poor

As lead was phased out in the U.S., Ethyl first reacted by raising its prices, making more money on fewer sales. The company's second reaction was to begin massive marketing abroad, especially in third-world countries, where the environmental standards lagged. By 1979, Ethyl observed, "It is worth noting that during the second half of 1979, for the first time, Ethyl's foreign sales of lead antiknock compounds exceeded domestic sales." In 1983, the *New Internationalist* magazine ran a feature story on this lead dumping.[79] By 1996, 93 percent of all gasoline sold in Africa contained lead, 94 percent in the Middle East, 30 percent in Asia and 35 percent in Latin America.

> I think if we argue anything at all, we say, [to developing countries] 'well, if you're going to go out of lead, fine, let's talk a bit, but there's no need, this is the lead in health information, there's no proven adverse health affect, and so there's no need for you to do it precipitously. You might not want to take twenty years [as in the European phase out] but really, there's no need to rush.' because if you replaced it with other components of petrol then there's a risk from anything...
> Petrol itself is a risk without lead (Ethyl Corp/Octel Spokesperson).[80]

In Canada, leaded gas was initially supposed to be banned late in the 1980s, but its sale was extended by the federal government into 1990 so as not to unduly harm the oil companies and the makers of TEL, the Ethyl Corporation, and the Associated Octel Company of Ellesmere Port, England. Long after it was banned for domestic use, it was manufactured at the Ethyl plant in Sarnia, Ontario, and exported to the Third World.

Although lead has finally been removed from gasoline in Canada and the U.S., after more than 65 years, leaded paint in housing still poses a risk to children. In 2005, The American Academy of Pediatrics issued a new policy statement urging the U.S. to eliminate toxic lead from all housing, to stop poisoning the nation's children. The Academy says 25 percent of children in the U.S. still, "live in housing with deteriorating lead-based paint and are at risk of lead exposure with resulting cognitive impairment and other sequelae [consequences]."[81]

> [TEL is] a colorless liquid of sweetish odor, very poisonous if absorbed through the skin, resulting in lead poisoning almost immediately. —Pierre Du Pont

Rachel vs. Bjorn

In some ways, the mainstream media record on environmental reporting may best be studied through a paired comparison case study, which is one of Noam Chomsky's preferred methods.[82] To this effect, I want to briefly summarize newspaper coverage of two books, published about forty years apart: first, the writings of the woman widely credited with founding the modern day environmental movement: Rachel Carson,[83] author of *Silent Spring*, published in 1962; and secondly that of Bjorn Lomborg, a Danish political scientist. Lomborg struck media gold in 2001, with the English-language publication of his book, *The Skeptical Environmentalist*. So much so that in April, 2004, he was named by *Time* magazine as one of the 100 most influential people in the world, although this book was virtually his only publication. I'll begin with an examination of Rachel Carson's book, and then turn to Bjorn Lomborg. These two books have been described as "polar opposites," by a reviewer for the *Washington Post*.[84] The way the corporate media reported on them is a reflection of their inherent biases. How did the press treat Rachel Carson, founder of the environmental movement, versus Bjorn Lomborg, skeptic?

Silent Spring

Rachel Carson earned bachelor's and master's degrees in zoology, the latter from Johns Hopkins University. For a time, she taught biology at university. In 1936 she became the first woman to take and pass the U.S. federal civil service test. She was hired as a junior marine biologist with the U.S. Bureau of Fisheries. Despite the sexism and glass ceiling, over the next 15 years, she rose in the ranks to become the chief editor of all publications for the U.S. Fish and Wildlife Service. Carson published an acclaimed best-selling trilogy of books on marine biology, *Under the Sea-Wind* (1941), *The Sea Around Us*, winner of the National Book Award (1951), and *The Edge of the Sea* (1955). Then, after five years of research and writing, Carson first published her startling allegations from *Silent Spring* in a three-part series of articles beginning in June, 1962, in the *New Yorker* magazine.

The series and book which followed led U.S. President John Kennedy to appoint a committee headed by his senior scientific adviser, to review the pesticide industry. The Committee's report in 1963 vindicated Carson, who had come under attack by the chemical industries, as the report called for the eventual "elimination of the use of persistent toxic pesticides," and for greatly augmented federal research. By 1965, the dangers of a deteriorating environment were acknowledged at the highest levels of government: this is when the President's Advisory Committee published *Restoring the Quality of our Environment*, a catalogue of pollution problems and their effects on human and environmental health. In 1969, the U.S. Congress passed the Environmental Policy Act, and in 1970 President Nixon created the Environmental Protection Agency (EPA) by executive order.[85] Carson's work ultimately led to the banning of the pesticide DDT in the U.S., in 1972, although DDT has recently been revived in some jurisdictions.[86] In 1992, a panel of distinguished Americans declared Rachel Carson's *Silent Spring* the most influential book of the past 50 years. In December, 2006, the popular science and technology magazine *Discover* ran an article on the 25 Greatest Science Books of All Time, which included *Silent Spring*.

> *Silent Spring* sparked a firestorm of public outrage. Officially published in September 1962, more than a quarter million copies were sold by the end of the year. A favorable review by Hermann J. Muller, a Nobel Prize-winning biologist, was seconded by Loren Eisely of the University of Pennsylvania, who described the book as a "devastating, heavily documented, relentless attack upon human carelessness, greed and irresponsibility..." United States Supreme Court Justice William O. Douglas called it "the most important chronicle of this century for the human race." The volume and fervor of the favorable reviews were matched by the intense attacks of the chemical industry and those it influenced. The president of the Montrose Chemical Corporation, the nation's largest producer of DDT, asserted that Carson had written not "as a scientist but rather as a fanatic defender of the balance of nature." She was labeled by critics a "food-faddist, nature nut, and fish-lover."[87]

For her part, Carson had written quite reasonably in the book, "It is not my contention that chemical insecticides must never be used. I do contend that we have put poisonous and biologically potent chemicals indiscriminately into the hands of persons largely or wholly ignorant of their potential for harm."[88]

To explore the Canadian media's treatment of Carson, I again selected the *Globe and Mail*, the most prestigious national daily. It wielded even more influence in the 1960s than it does today. The first notice readers of the *Globe and Mail* had of Ms. Carson's book back in 1962 was a business section article courtesy of the *New York Times* wire services. The headline on the story read: "Author Called Pest," and it carried a kicker headline: "We're Aghast"—the latter quoting a pesticide industry spokesman. The article noted that while Rachel Carson had been praised for the beauty and precision of her previous works such as *The Sea Around Us*, her latest work was "crass commercialism" or "idealistic flag waving," at least according to the industrial toxicologist who was quoted. The article went on to say, presciently,

Some agricultural-chemicals concerns have set their scientists to an-alyzing Miss Carson's work, line by line. Other companies are pre-paring briefs defending the use of the products. Meetings have been held in Washington and New York. Statements are being drafted and counterattacks plotted.[89]

These counterattacks bore fruit almost immediately. Surprisingly, however, two days after "The Pest" report, the *Globe* ran an editorial sounding a precau-tionary note.

If these miraculous chemicals damage the natural resources of Canada's land and water and wildlife and upset the delicate and essential balance of nature, if they threaten the health and the lives of the people who con-sume the products of the land, they are a black magic against which soci-ety must develop the protections of doubt and denial.[90]

Next came an article out of Washington on the *London Observer* wire service, September 6. The article described the early impact of the yet-to-be-published book, including the establishment of the Federal Government Committee, and outlined some of Ms. Carson's contentions. The article closed with a govern-ment denial which would do industry proud:

Government officials of the Food and Drug Administration, the Na-tional Cancer Institute and other relevant agencies to whom I talked concede in general the scientific accuracy of Miss Carson's book. But they consider she has deliberately assembled in the most striking form one-sided evidence. They point out that the chemicals she at-tacks have done a great deal of good in underdeveloped countries and in raising world food production. And they maintain that U.S. standards of control are already quite high.[91]

Later that month the real attack came, in the form of a book review written by the federal civil servant responsible for the government's research program on pesticides and their use. Dr. Henry Hurtig slammed Carson as a "crusader" who uses "poetic license" which is "abused by the distortion of facts." Her in-dictment of pesticides is based upon "well-publicized, unfortunate incidents" arising from "claims" in the U.S., he wrote, insinuating that they were few in number and questionable. According to Hurtig,

Industry is contributing to [her goal of moderate chemical controls combined with biological controls] by providing pesticides of low

mammalian toxicity, that governments are indeed supporting research aimed at an intelligent marriage of chemical and biological
control, and that never before have we been assured such an ample
supply of food of uniform quality and wholesomeness.[92]

While Ms. Carson quotes facts, Hurtig said, there is "nothing new in her accusations," and she is guilty of "premeditated" bias in her conclusions. "While
some of the observations of the authorities she quotes may be in part or in
whole correct, there are other equally authoritative positive results of research
that have established the safety of modern pesticides, if used properly." Having earlier quoted Carson to the effect that she was not calling for an outright
ban on pesticides, he then went on to chastise that, "We cannot produce and
protect our food supply without pesticides."

This indictment of Carson's book was the only review to run in the *Globe
and Mail* that year. It condemned Carson's book as a biased and distorted man-
ifesto, containing nothing that was new. Two letters to the editor were published in response to the book review. On October 4, John A. Livingston of
Toronto wrote that Hurtig "seems to have missed, or chosen to ignore, the fundamental point of the book," which is "a formidable indictment of the techno-
logical orientation of our society."

This is an orientation conceived by expediency and biological illiteracy, maintained by vested interests and their spokesmen, endorsed
or at least condoned at most levels of government, which does not
acknowledge the broad ecological picture of man in his environment: That man, like any other organism, is subject to immutable
natural controls, and that he disrupts natural interrelationships at
his peril. The philosophy that accepts the chemical pesticide as a
panacea for all that ails field and forest, that accepts technology as a
substitute for ecology, can only lead us to disaster.[93]

A subsequent letter from Eva Moudry of Toronto agreed with Livingston, and
also took Hurtig to task, for writing a review "bordering on the supercilious
and condescending." Contrary to Hurtig's implication, the damages and dangers of pesticides are documented in the book, not just in a few incidents, but
"by a wealth of factual evidence encompassing the whole content and the past
decade." Moudry wrote that Hurtig's reference to "flashes of Miss Carson's old
poetic style," implies "that the whole thing has more to do with imagination
than with science," and objected to his "derisive" and "patronizing" tone, especially as emanating from a government scientist.[94]

As forceful as these letters were, it is questionable whether they could undo the damage to the book and Ms. Carson, done by the review itself, which employs a number of the devices used by the chemical companies to discredit *Silent Spring*, and which have been used against environmentalists ever since.

In October 1962, the *Globe's* science writer David Spurgeon cited support for one of Carson's contentions: not only are chemical pesticides dangerous to plant and animal life generally, but they are sometimes not effective, or not as effective as is believed. Research by biologist Roy Edwards at the University of Saskatchewan found that significant numbers of grasshoppers are not killed when sprayed with insecticides. "They simply move out of the sprayed area, and later return."[95]

Perhaps more importantly, in the same column Spurgeon queried what the "frantic activity on the part of the pesticide makers" in response to Carson's books, would lead to. "Are they going to launch a counter-attack with great fanfare at a carefully chosen moment, or have they decided that, discretion being the better part of valor, they would profit most by just keeping quiet in the hope that the indignation Miss Carson aroused will just go away?"

This is a vital question, and Spurgeon is to be congratulated for bringing it out into the open. It does appear that although there wasn't any great fanfare, the industry steadily worked through the media to turn around public opinion. Spurgeon revisited the question in a Report on Science article four months later, in February 1963. He noted that few books have caused "more furor" than *Silent Spring*, in recent years. On the positive side, he noted that the House of Commons committee on drugs was examining pesticides, thanks to the book. On the negative side, he quoted Dr. George Decker, entomologist for the Illinois Natural History Survey, who said, "I regard it as science fiction, to be read in the same way that the TV program 'Twilight Zone' is to be watched."[96]

Spurgeon next discussed some of the harsher reactions to the book from industry, including a parody of the book written by Thomas Jukes of American Cyanamid Co., and published in *Chemical Week*. Jukes described a nation beset by disease and pestilence, barely able to subsist, because of a lack of chemical pesticides. Spurgeon doesn't mention that chemical giant Monsanto also published a parody of Carson's work, called "The Desolate Year," in the October 1962 issue of *Monsanto Magazine*, and 5000 copies were mailed out to journalists across the U.S.[97] There was also a kit distributed by The Nutrition Foundation Inc., of New York, containing "much more sophisticated material

designed to discredit Miss Carson's book." Spurgeon stated that it isn't difficult to understand the hostility of the chemical and pesticide industries, but
it's more difficult to understand why outstanding scientists also "would heap
scorn on her and try to discredit her as a scientist." He wrote, "What annoys
these scientists most is what Miss Carson wrote."

> And rightly so. *Silent Spring* is not scientifically objective in its ap-
> proach. It is as its critics say, highly selective... The book is anything
> but impartial, and it is written with an undercurrent of compassion-
> ate emotion.

Nevertheless, Spurgeon states that "not all scientists" agree the book should
be condemned because of this. "Some believe it has performed a valuable service if it has drawn attention to a danger, however overstated."

Although this author displays some agreement with some of the points
raised by Carson in her book, and invites some sympathy over her treatment by
corporations, his own characterizations of her work tend to support the contentions made by industry, for example that Carson is biased and emotional,
characteristics which are the antithesis of cold, hard, science.

In April, 1963, the *Globe* reported that a federal government probe on pesticide residue in wildlife was being urged, following the testing of an Atlantic
tuna which had 200 ppm of DDT. The "safe maximum" was thought to be 7
ppm. Regional laboratories were urgently needed to study pesticide residues, a
federal-provincial wildlife conference in Ottawa was told.[98]

In June, the *Globe* ran a *New York Times* wire story headlined, "Refuses
Comment on Book," in which Carson was described as, "shy, very feminine,"
and someone who refuses to be drawn into retaliatory comments about those
attacking her book. Most of the article is a fairly straightforward background
to Ms. Carson's career and books. The article did say, in the second last paragraph, that the author was "equipped by academic training" and by her "professional work as a biologist, to tackle the subject of pesticides."[99]

Later that same month a CP story ran in the business section on how a
conference of forestry experts was told that in the U.S., "public resentment"
against chemical insect controls is "forcing" the U.S. Forest Service into "a
crash program of research on biological control." The public resentment was
directly linked to Ms. Carson's book, and was described as growing rather
than diminishing.[100]

"A Few Horrible Examples"

In September, 1963, *Globe* science reporter David Spurgeon wrote about a symposium in New York, at which Rachel Carson was criticized. Participants at a symposium on food processing and pesticide residues at the American Chemical Society's annual meetings in New York "couldn't seem to avoid making references to the author of *Silent Spring*, the book that stirred up a hornet's nest over pesticides."[101] The chairman of the dairy industry's technical advisory committee referred to "outbursts of demagoguery like *Silent Spring*." He went on to say that "pesticides are a two-edged sword: They are necessary and desirable for the production of high-quality foods in quantity, but they also can have undesirable toxic effects." The *Globe's* David Spurgeon, concluded that despite the "somewhat slighting tone of the asides," the controversy begun by Carson "has had, over all, a generally beneficial effect," as both government and industry are now more "residue-conscious than ever..." and it has led to more research.

Within about two weeks of the story about the "Rachel Carson cloud" hanging over chemists, another story had "a Canadian expert" who was quoted in Rachel Carson's book, attacking her as well. Professor A.W. Brown, head of the zoology department at the University of Western Ontario, had recently been a biologist with the World Health Organization, engaged in "large-scale insecticide programs," in work which had taken him to 60 countries.

> Although conceding some parts of *Silent Spring* were accurate, Dr. Brown labeled the book the work of an extremist. "She took a few horrible examples and built them up into a very lucrative book," he said." "Miss Carson," he added, allowed herself to be pressured by persons who had a vested interest in opposing insecticides.[102]

He went on to indicate that Ms. Carson's book "had made competent public servants pay for the sins of occasional gross misuse of insecticides by others."

> Dr. Brown indicated that emotionalism could have no place in determining the extent to which insecticides should be used. He said officials must weigh the loss of Canada's whole pulpwood supply, if forests were not sprayed, against the advantages to be gained from safeguarding fish for U.S. anglers.

So, here Rachel Carson is denounced as an "extremist," who is guilty of "emotionalism," who is being manipulated by others with "vested interests," and as someone who has unfairly victimized competent public servants. Her cause is reduced to safeguarding fish for American anglers, and her extremism is said to threaten the supply of Canada's whole pulpwood industry.

These ludicrous charges were made, and allowed to stand unchallenged in the article, because they came from a Canadian "expert," despite the fact that he himself has been in the employ, indirectly, of the pesticide industry. As he was now a university professor, his own ulterior motives and vested interests went unquestioned.

The next article on the controversy appeared the following month, when a "U.S. expert" testified before the House of Commons food and drug committee. The headline reported, "Pest Sprays No Peril, U.S. Expert Declares." The first paragraph began, "The public need not worry about the immediate effects of eating foods sprayed with insecticides, a U.S. expert on poison" said. The next paragraph quoted the expert, Dr. J.M. Coon, head of pharmacology at Jefferson Medical College, Philadelphia: "As far as pesticide residues in foods are concerned, things appear to be under good control and we have reason to be optimistic about the future."[103]

But contrary to the headline and carefully constructed opening, Dr. Coon in fact raised some serious concerns, even as reported in the article, written by the Canadian Press wire service. He asked:

Is the population being slowly poisoned? Is there some insidious unrecognized toxic action? Will cancer develop in large numbers of people, or has it developed already from eating pesticides? Is there another thalidomide episode lurking among our pesticides?

Here, the editors at the *Globe* were downplaying the concerns of this expert, through their choice of headline and introductory paragraphs. As a result, to the casual reader the expert would be contradicting Carson's work, rather than asking similar questions and hence being supportive.

It is interesting that the news articles about *Silent Spring*, especially in the business section, were negative, as was the book review, and yet the editorial representing the views of management at the newspaper was supportive and mildly favorable. This compares favorably with the current state of affairs at Canadian daily newspapers, where the editorial stance is almost invariably —perhaps inevitably—corporate. With the spate of media mergers and acquisitions in recent decades has come a merging of another kind: the melding of the business and news/editorial functions of the press, previously regarded as a "church vs. state" distinction. By way of example, if we turn briefly to the more recent coverage of Rachel Carson and *Silent Spring* in the neocon *National Post*, we find that virtually any mention in the newspaper is dismissive. In a 1900-word book review on another book in 2000, for example, we read that Carson's was an "apocalyptic doomsday book."

> Last month [Maurice] Strong also released his new book *Where on Earth are We Going?*, which follows in the great tradition of apocalyptic doomsday books on the environment. The genre was started by Rachel Carson's *Silent Spring* that condemned the use of DDT.[104]

With the arrival of the West Nile virus in 2003, the *National Post* editorialized that DDT and malathion should be re-introduced, claiming that harmful effects have never been "confirmed."

> The claims made in Rachel Carson's infamously romanticized 1962 book *Silent Spring*, that DDT thinned wild bird's egg shells and disrupted their breeding, and that it caused cancer in humans, were never confirmed in laboratories.[105]

Finally, in a *National Post* business column proclaiming "Junk Science Week," in 2002, we are told:

> Rachel Carson inflamed the public against DDT with her book *Silent Spring*. She claimed DDT harmed bird reproduction and caused cancer. But Carson misrepresented the then-existing science on bird reproduction and was dead wrong about DDT causing cancer.[106]

These examples illustrate that with mergers in Canada, the editorials, book reviews, business pages and even the news pages have all become one. As discussed in Chapter One, this situation was brought home to working journalists by the CanWest Global empire in 2002, when a memo was issued indicating that content elsewhere in the newspapers was not to contradict regular head office editorials issued from once to thrice weekly.[107]

The Skeptical Environmentalist

In contrast to many scientists from relevant disciplines in the natural and physical sciences who went before him, including Rachel Carson, Bjorn Lomborg argued that scare stories in the media have promoted environmentalists who twist the scientific truth, exaggerating the state of the world environment, and promoting irrational fears. One reviewer summed up his arguments this way:

The world is cleaner, and people are healthier and more prosperous than ever before. More progress is coming. Problems such as waste disposal, contaminants, food scarcity and acid rain are far less serious than is widely believed. Cures for problems like climate change may be worse than the disease. New technologies such as genetic engineering promise large benefits, but risk rejection because of irrational fears.[108]

Here is how Lomborg put it, in his own words, in 2003:

I am Danish, liberal, vegetarian, a former member of Greenpeace; and I used to believe in the litany of our ever-deteriorating environment. You know, the doomsday message repeated by the media, as when *Time* magazine tells us that "everyone knows the planet is in bad shape." We're defiling our Earth, we're told. Our resources are running out. Our air and water are more and more polluted. The planet's species are becoming extinct, we're paving over nature, decimating the biosphere. The problem is that this litany doesn't seem to be backed up by facts.[109]

Lomborg also argued, for example, that "the data do not support" any link between PCBs and cancer.

How did the media portrayal of Lomborg contrast with that afforded to Rachel Carson's ground-breaking work? When it was first published in 1998 in Denmark, Lomborg's book attracted a lot of controversy and negative reviews from the scientific community, but was welcomed with open arms by the corporate media. The editor-in-chief of *Politiken*, a Danish national daily, took the highly unusual step of running four long commentary articles by Lomborg in one month, and eventually assigned him a regular column. With the English-language publication in 2001, in Britain, the *Economist* magazine and *Daily Telegraph* made him a *cause celebre*. In the U.S., the *New York Times*, *Washington Post* and *Wall Street Journal* all ran very positive reviews. The *Post*, for example, said Lomborg's book was, "the most significant work on the environment since the appearance of its polar opposite, Rachel Carson's *Silent Spring*, in 1962. It's a magnificent achievement." In Canada, the *National Post* put him on the front page and eventually ran a series of lengthy commentaries written by him.

According to Danish biologist Kåre Fog:

> The reviews were very positive in the *Daily Telegraph,* the *Economist,* the *Wall Street Journal, Washington Post,* and *New York Times.* Lomborg has obtained an especially close connection with the editors of the *Economist,* similar to that with *Politiken* in Denmark.[110]

It's hard to imagine a greater contrast between the reaction in the popular media and that of the scientific communities involved. Here's Kåre Fog again:

> In the scientific world, on the other hand, the reactions were almost uniformly negative. The World Resources Institute, based in Washington DC, published a list of "Nine things journalists should know about *The Skeptical Environmentalist.* The "Union of Concerned Scientists" in [the] USA gathered on their web site contributions from experts in a wide range of fields with harsh criticism of Lomborg. *Science* had a rather negative review, and *Nature* an unusually negative review. Most remarkable, however, was the role played by *Scientific American.*[111]

In its January 2002 issue, *Scientific American* gathered reviews from experts in four different fields, who concluded that Lomborg's work was "a clever polemic," that it was "superficial, muddled, often plain wrong and filled with misreadings and misunderstandings of data," that it was "simply wrong," filled with "factual errors, poor research and poor understanding of basic values."[112]

Biologist Fog notes that, "It is very unusual that a book receives an 11-page unreserved, merciless slating by respected scientists in one of the world´s most widely read journals, and it is small wonder that this slating made a great impact everywhere."

Indeed, by January, 2002, Dr. Peter Raven, the president of the American Association for the Advancement of Science, singled out Lomborg in his speech opening the association's annual meetings. Raven said he was distressed by the skeptics who deliver good news about the environment. "They basically win fame by telling people what they want to hear," he said, singling out Lomborg as a case in point.[113]

In November 2001, Lomborg had been selected Global Leader for Tomorrow by the conservative World Economic Forum. In June 2002, Lomborg was named one of the "50 stars of Europe" (as one of the nine "agenda setters" in Europe) in *Business Week* (June 17). In April 2004, Lomborg (listed amongst scientists, but described as an "author,") was named one of the world's 100 most influential people by *Time Magazine.*

By way of contrast, in December 2001 *Grist* magazine published a special issue with a range of experts in various environmental fields publishing their critiques of Lomborg's theories. The experts were: Norman Myers (Biodiversity), and David Nemtzow (Energy), Emily Matthews (Forests), Lester R. Brown (Population), Stephen H. Schneider (Climate), E.O. Wilson (Extinction), Devra Davis (Human Health), and Allen Hammond (Statistics). To just provide one example, biologist Edward O. Wilson has been a Harvard professor for four decades, has written 20 books, won two Pulitzer prizes, and discovered hundreds of new species. He is considered by some, to be one of the world's greatest living scientists. He dismissed Lomborg as "a parasite."

> My greatest regret about the Lomborg scam is the extraordinary amount of scientific talent that has to be expended to combat it in the media. We will always have contrarians like Lomborg whose sallies are characterized by willful ignorance, selective quotations, disregard for communication with genuine experts, and destructive campaigning to attract the attention of the media rather than scientists. They are the parasite load on scholars who earn success through the slow process of peer review and approval. The question is: How much load should be tolerated before a response is necessary? Lomborg is evidently over the threshold.[114]

Lomborg's training is in political science, specifically in game theory. According to the biography on his web site, (www.lomborg.com) in addition to writing *The Skeptical Environmentalist*, he has published just one peer-reviewed journal article, on "the prisoner's dilemma," in the *American Sociological Review,* (1996), and an unpublished article on election voting behaviour. An online computer search for his name turned up just two articles, both critiques of his book in economics journals. The first of these was by one of his colleagues, noted below. The second was by a British scholar who concluded that: "Lomborg's analysis suffers from several problems, including selective use of data, over-simplification of issues, posing the wrong questions and lack of objectivity in his quest for optimistic trends."[115]

Lomborg describes himself as a reformed environmentalist who says he began by intending to debunk the views of American right-wing economist Julian Simon, who similarly argued in his books (*The Ultimate Resource*, 1981; *The Resourceful Earth*, 1984) that the "prophecies of doom" issued by environmentalists are completely unwarranted, and that in fact the environment is improving. Anti-environmentalist books have been published by others as well, for example, Ronald Bailey's edited book, *The True State of the Planet*, 1995, and so this is not a new phenomenon. Indeed, this latter title bears a striking resemblance to the Danish title of Lomborg's book, *Verdens sande tilstand*, or *The True State of the World*.[116]

The academic reviews of Lomborg's book generally have not been favorable. In one, Mikael Skou Andersen, one of Lomborg's former colleagues in the political science department at the University of Aarhus, notes an interesting parallel:

> A comparison of Lomborg's pesticide section with chapter five in Bruce Ames's contribution to *The True State of The Planet*, reveals that the argumentation is largely parallel and several of the references are identical...a reference to Ames's chapter would have been appropriate. Not least because the publisher Ronald Bailey is associated with Fred Singer's Competitive Enterprise Institute, one of the flag ships of the American anti-environmental movement, which also advertises the book and its arguments on their website (www.cei.org).[117]

By way of context, Ronald Bailey edited the 1995 book, *The True State of The Planet*, and more recently, *Global Warming and Other Eco Myths* (2002) published by the right-wing Competitive Enterprise Institute.[118] He is listed as the science correspondent for *Reason* magazine, whose motto is: "Free minds, free markets." The magazine is supported by the Reason Foundation, a right-wing libertarian advocacy group. Its mission statement says that: "The mission of the Reason Foundation is to advance a free society by developing, applying, and promoting libertarian principles, including free markets, individual liberty, and the rule of law. We use journalism and public policy to change the frameworks and actions of policymakers, journalists, and opinion leaders."[119]

What's increasingly apparent is that corporate America is funding these foundations and institutes, in order to promote what they have termed, "free market environmentalism," and to attack what they euphemistically label as "ideological environmentalism." Here is an example from the web pages of the Competitive Enterprise Institute, promoting the idea of *Global Warming and Other Eco Myths*:

> The modern environmentalist movement began with the publication of three seminal works: Rachel Carson's *Silent Spring*, Paul Ehrlich's *The Population Bomb*, and the Club of Rome's *The Limits of Growth*.

These books' dismal vision of a poisoned, overpopulated, polluted, resource-depleted world spiraling downward toward environmental collapse, are today's conventional wisdom. According to a number of respected scientists, however, leaders of the environmental movement are guilty of twisting—and sometimes manufacturing—facts in an effort to frighten people into joining their cause.[120]

According to John Stauber and Sheldon Rampton in their work on the public relations industry, by 1995, "a virulent, pro-industry, *anti*-environmentalism is on the rise…U.S. businesses spend an estimated $1 billion a year on the services of anti-environmental PR professionals and on 'greenwashing' their corporate image."[121]

What sets Lomborg's work apart is the amount of attention it has received, and the fact that it was not published by a right-wing institute, but by the prestigious Cambridge University Press.[122] But in addition to employing their own stable of neocon writers, greenwashers are willing to promote others who agree with their perspective, just as the right promoted the views of Katie Roiphe and Camille Paglia, as part of the backlash against feminism.[123]

The response to Lomborg's work from the Canadian media specifically, was extremely positive. I concentrated my search on the CanWest Global publications, (formerly the Hollinger and Southam chains) as they are the predominant newspaper publisher in Canada, publishing a national daily in Toronto (the *National Post*), and a chain of 11 large daily newspapers in cities across much of the country, from Vancouver, to Calgary, Edmonton, and Winnipeg, from Ottawa to Montreal.

The main venue for the pro-Lomborg material was the *National Post*, but the other newspapers in the chain were all onboard. For example, the *Calgary Herald* wrote in January 2002 about how Lomborg, "has been branded a traitor" by "the nabobs of the international environmental movement," because "he debunked almost all of its claims about the earth's perilous state."[124]

In the quotation earlier in this chapter, I noted how the *Ottawa Citizen* described environmentalism as a sort of a cult: rooted in Kant and Marx, taught by cradle-robbing professors to "young university students," learning how to be activists rather than how to think. This led into its favorable discussion of Lomborg, in June, 2001.[125] By September, 2001, the *Citizen* was using Lomborg as a cudgel with which to beat proponents of the Kyoto Accord. It said Lomborg's book,

...serves as a useful reference for the modern history of environmental scares. For while the jury is still out on 'global warming,' it is in for any number of the previous, expensive terrors the 'friends of the Earth' have unleashed. Their batting average remains .000."[126]

The *Vancouver Province* took comfort in Lomborg's backlash against what it called, "eco-zealots."[127] Describing Lomborg as an "environmental statistician," (he is not), the *Edmonton Journal* used him as an authority to describe Kyoto as "a waste of money." Instead of wasting money on Kyoto, Lomborg says, "the world would do better to invest much more than at present in research into renewable forms of energy, such as solar power and nuclear fusion."[128]

As indicated above, the main promotion of Lomborg came from the flagship national daily, the *National Post*. A favorable review in June, 2001, described him as a "Greenpeace exile," which he is not. In fact, he allegedly contributed money to Greenpeace, but was not active.

Mr. Lomborg's book, which is bolstered by statistics from internationally recognized research institutes and 2,500 footnotes, is a direct attack on what he says are environmental organizations selectively twisting scientific evidence and statistics to cultivate public support for their causes.[129]

In September, 2001, the *Post* ran a four-part series by Lomborg, just one of which ran to 2100 words, about three times the length of a normal column or commentary.[130] For its part, the *Vancouver Sun* ran an interview with him which stretched to 2500 words.[131]

Rotten In The State Of Denmark

Perhaps the most incredible aspect of the coverage of Lomborg was still to come, however. In November 2001, the right-wing Danish Liberal Party under Prime Minister Anders Fogh Rasmussen, was elected. Soon after, it cut all funding to the Danish Ecological Council, which had organized the opposition against Lomborg. Rasmussen, a graduate of Aarhus University where Lomborg taught, previously promised Lomborg that if he was elected, an Environmental Assessment Institute would be established. It was, and under Ole P. Kristensen, as Chairman of the board. Kristensen was also Lomborg's former dissertation adviser and friend. Soon, Kristensen had hired Lomborg as director of the institute. The government also dismissed the Nature Council, which was critical of Lomborg, and its office in central Copenhagen was instead given to Lomborg´s institute. In a parallel development, a number of complaints about Lomborg were made by scientists to a standing academic committee under the Danish Ministry for Science called the Danish Committees for Scientific Dishonesty.[132]

As per their mandate, the committees (in their entirety) investigated the complaints against Lomborg and reported in January, 2003, concluding that what Lomborg had written in *The Skeptical Environmentalist* was "contrary to the standards of good scientific practice."

> [The book was] misleading. [The committee described Lomborg] as 'objectively dishonest', that is, dishonest when evaluated by an external standard. They also judged that he was guilty of systematic bias in his choice of data and line of argument, thereby acting at variance with what they call 'good scientific practice.' On the other hand, they did not feel able to prove that his bias was deliberate, and therefore do not describe him as 'subjectively dishonest'.[133]

Lomborg lodged a complaint about the committee to the Minister of Research, Helge Sander, whose Ministry issued a political decision in December, 2003, declaring the scientific committee's decision invalid. Furthermore, in the view of the Ministry, the scientific committees had not documented that *The Skeptical Environmentalist* was a scientific publication, and thus said it is doubtful whether they were allowed to evaluate it at all!

Hence, Lomborg was evaluated by a scientific committee of his peers, and found to have been intellectually dishonest in virtually his sole publication. On appeal, this decision was nullified by a political body.

How did the media portray these events? Well, the original investigation by the science committees was treated as though it was a scene out of George Orwell, with a crazed group of environmental terrorists torturing the poor author. The political decision by the ministry was portrayed as a return to sanity. University of Calgary neoconservative Barry Cooper, wrote in the *National Post*,

> Lomborg had the temerity to challenge a gaggle of radical environmentalists on their own turf. In his book and in his response to its reception, Lomborg showed beyond question that his critics were mostly ideological fanatics hiding behind their professional credentials as biologists and health scientists.[134]

Terence Corcoran wrote in the *Post* that the decision was a vindication for Lomborg, and a victory for "science."

> For two years, environmental activists had sought to discredit Mr. Lomborg, whose brilliant book valiantly demolished much of the junk science and fabricated alarmism that drives the global environmental movement... It's been a rough year for environmental extremists... The attacks on Mr. Lomborg were vicious, personal and extreme... The real issue here is the politicization of the process to discredit Mr. Lomborg...[135]

Finally, weighing in for CBC and the *Globe and Mail* in April, 2004, was commentator Rex Murphy.

> An even more recent and telling example is that of the Danish author and statistician Bjorn Lomborg, who offered a critique of the doctrine of global warming. The fury of the environmental establishment toward Mr. Lomborg was prodigious, and the coarseness of some of the attacks on him and his well-tempered book, *The Skeptical Environmentalist*, exceptional, except by the unhappy example of the [Spanish] Inquisition.[136]

Not *absolutely everything* written about Lomborg in the press was positive. For example, an unusual journalist with a pro-environment bent, Stephen Hume, wrote an article referenced above, which ran in Vancouver and Edmonton.[137] And, there was a 500-word hard news story reporting criticism from scientists at a conference, which ran in the *National Post*.[138] Indeed, one daily, the *St. John's Telegram* in Newfoundland, (then, but not now, owned by CanWest Global) ran a negative column on Lomborg's book by David Suzuki![139] But the amount of criticism afforded to Lomborg was infinitesimal in comparison to the copious amounts of praise, and promotion for his book and ideas. The contrast with the reaction from the bulk of the scientific community is also quite telling.

If this was the way the CanWest newspapers saw Lomborg, what of the *Globe and Mail*? The first time his name appeared in the *Globe* was in an October 2001 book review by Andrew Nikiforuk, a freelance Calgary journalist and author. The review said some positive things, but it was a negative review. While he described Lomborg as a "tall, charming Dane with a gift for gab and a mind for numbers," and said "it's important to acknowledge what is true in Lomborg's argument," (i.e., many environmentalists are "guilty of crying wolf,") he also went on to dissect "Lomborg's shallow analyses, inaccurate science, selective sources and bogus claims." Nikiforuk also wrote that Lomborg, "like many greens, omits the facts that don't fit his own particular litany..." and asked: "Should the media be as skeptical of green exaggerators as it is of statisticians, liars and politicians? You bet." He pointed to problems with Lomborg's positive take on water pollution, and his dismissal of acid rain, pointing out that David Schindler, "the world's most highly regarded water ecologist," disagrees. He wrote, "Lomborg's selective use of data discolours every chapter in this anti-intellectual work." Regarding fisheries, "The ill-informed Dane hasn't heard of cod or salmon declines and doesn't care." Still, in some respects the reviewer staked out a middle ground by writing "Lomborg's litany is as dangerously inaccurate as that of the doomsayers."[140]

Although this was the only formal review of Lomborg's work in the *Globe*, the story doesn't end here. In the next mention of him the following spring, a book reviewer for Harvard biologist Edward O. Wilson's *The Future of Life* slags Wilson's work as "the announcement of Armageddon," while asserting that "most of his arguments have been gravely challenged by a Danish statistician, Bjorn Lomborg, in his recent book *The Skeptical Environmentalist*." Reviewer Richard Lubbock sides with Lomborg.[141]

Next, in May, columnist Margaret Wente described Lomborg as the notorious "Heretic of Kyoto," and "Public Enemy No. 1 among environmental groups." Her sympathetic account painted Lomborg as a statistician with "no axe to grind," and "a boyish 37-year-old professor who used to write cheques to Greenpeace." Unlike "his attackers, Mr. Lomborg's tone is mild and moderate. So are his conclusions." Wente went on to quote the conservative British magazine the *Economist*, which called his book "one of the most valuable books on public policy in the last decade," and she said "many leading scientists defend it," without naming any. She did name Patrick Moore, whom she described as "the Canadian who helped found Greenpeace," now "an environmental moderate."[142] Moore praised Lomborg, but what would you expect from a man who farms fish and shills for the forest industry and nuclear industry and genetically modified foods, et cetera? Moore is a favorite with the media. They love people like him and Lomborg, former Greenpeace "extremists" who now see the light.

Next, like CanWest and the British press such as the *Guardian*, the *Globe* gave Lomborg his own forum, a 1000-plus word column in August 2002. Here, he decried the "worrying" about such things as: fossil fuels leading to air pollution, because "in richer Western" cities, "almost every type of air pollution has diminished significantly." He then went on to dismiss the Kyoto Protocol as too expensive.[143]

About a week later, columnist Marcus Gee from the *Globe* wrote that "development is good for the environment," because "people in poor countries denude hillsides for cooking wood, graze cattle in rain forests and dump their garbage and waste into rivers." To resolve this, we have "to pull people out of poverty as quickly as possible," he wrote. Then he quoted Lomborg, favourably, calling him a "dissident environmentalist."[144] Like Wente, Gee's work is quoted liberally herein, as it was in *MediaThink*, where he was disparaging towards the people of East Timor.

Next, as part of the anti-Kyoto coverage, Ian Brown wrote a huge *Focus* piece in the *Globe*, almost 5000 words, which in part discussed Lomborg and approvingly noted that The Fraser Institute brought him to Calgary where 400 people paid $250 to listen to him. Partly because of these efforts, support for Kyoto in Alberta, which was 72 percent, is now 21 percent, Brown wrote. Brown helped to promote Lomborg's book.[145]

Then, it was Margaret Wente again, promoting Lomborg's book and his web site, in an article attacking Kyoto and the "global warming scare," and promoting *Taken By Storm*, a book written by "a serious player in the world of climate science," one professor Chris Essex. Wente says Essex's work will "effectively demolish most of what you think you know," for example, about "global temperature." What Wente didn't mention is that Essex is a professor at the University of Western Ontario in London, a *mathematician* who teaches in *theoretical physics* (not climatology).[146]

There was a hiatus of about 15 months, and then in April 2004, it was Rex Murphy from CBC, moonlighting at the *Globe* long enough to disparage the "evangelical" environmental movement, with its "irresistible instinct to proselytize and convert" and to impugn its "heretics," such as Patrick Moore and Bjorn Lomborg. I've quoted Murphy above.[147]

Next came the relentless Margaret Wente again, (could I get her to promote my books?) She attacked what is actually an excellent documentary outing the scientists paid by Exxon-Mobil and others to help deny global warming, *The Denial Machine* on CBC's "Fifth Estate." And along the way, plugged Lomborg as "one of the smart people [who] have questions about climate change." Wente argued, "It's hard to believe they've all been bought off."[148] Really? Remember the $10,000 and expenses offered by the Exxon-Mobil-funded *American Enterprise Institute* to those who would critique the IPCC Report?

Aside from this, there were four letters to the editor of the *Globe* mentioning Lomborg: two in favour and two opposed. Which only goes to show that letters usually are more balanced than anything else you'll find in the news.

Disparate Results

It's difficult to imagine more disparate results than these. The media were critical of an author and scientist who issued dire warnings about the deleterious effects of man-made chemicals on ourselves and nature generally, although she was highly qualified, and has been subsequently proven to be correct. As *Time* magazine noted in 2003, "When the book appeared, industry critics assailed 'the hysterical woman,' but it became an instant best seller with lasting impact. It spurred the banning of DDT in the U.S., the passage of major environmental laws and eventually a global treaty to phase out 12 pesticides known as 'the dirty dozen'."[149] For its part, by 1966 the *Globe and Mail* was editorializing about Carson, "Alarmist? Some people thought so in 1962. But researchers have been reinforcing her case ever since."[150]

On the other hand, the media did everything in their power to promote the work of a man who had no relevant expertise, whose assertions were contradicted by bona fide experts in the field, and who came under intense criticism from the scientific community. Was it just coincidence that Rachel Carson's work threatened corporate profits, while Bjorn Lomborg's work protected and enhanced them (temporarily) by reassuring people that all is well?

In his critical analysis in the *Columbia Journalism Review* of the news media's glowing portrayal of Lomborg, Russ Baker concluded that the culprit was journalists, who are too easily influenced by "contrarian" views. Journalists, he wrote, "may be too easily...enamored of contrarian insights. The news business loves personality pieces about the new star who has emerged to shake up this or that piece of conventional wisdom."[151]

But this explanation only holds up if the other constellations are aligned. The media loved Lomborg's contrarian views, but rejected Carson's, in favor of the conventional wisdom. The deeper explanation lies in the corporate and industrial vested interests and common goals shared with their media siblings.

Radical Ecology

The *Globe and Mail* and other media dismissed Rachel Carson's argument that chemicals are harming the ecosystem. But this was only a portion of what she had to say: they *entirely omitted* her more sophisticated, important, and radical position. According to historian Gary Kroll, Carson's work promoted ecology as a "subversive subject," in that it "cut against the grain of materialism, scientism, and the technologically engineered control of nature."

Carson speaks as the critic of science; she did this in two ways. First, she takes aim at the overly mechanical and reductive sciences—economic entomology and organic chemistry in this instance—that isolate nature to the neglect of interconnections. Secondly, she critiques the wider—and perhaps more nebulous—*cultural authority of science and technology to control nature* (emphasis added).[152]

Carson pointed to our alarming misfortune that "so primitive a science" in its incredibly arrogant belief that "nature exists for the convenience of man," has turned its terrible weapons not only on insects, but "against the earth" itself. The two come together in the often-quoted final paragraph of *Silent Spring:*

The 'control of nature' is a phrase conceived in arrogance, born of the Neanderthal age of biology and philosophy, when it was supposed that nature exists for the convenience of man... It is our alarming misfortune that so primitive a science has armed itself with the most modern and terrible weapons, and that in turning them against the insects it has also turned them against the earth.

Kroll notes that, "there is an element of critical theory in *Silent Spring* that begins to contemplate a wholly new relationship between humans and nature." Carson called for humility on the part of humans, and noted that we would be faced with fundamental choices, the "Other Road." She wrote of the interconnectedness of the world which made the threat of toxins so dire.

In popular accounts including the news media, Carson's work was simply an "anti-pesticide tract." But it was more than this, it was radical ecology, an essay written to awaken people to the techno-scientific control of the world. It questioned the fundamental values of scientific sovereignty, economics, and consumerism. But in the popular press, Carson's book, like the ecology movement itself, became co-opted by capitalism, as Herbert Marcuse notes in his essay on *Ecology and Revolution.*[153] The social and cultural problems of waste, pollution, population and toxicity, in this "engineering mentality," could be solved scientifically.

NOTES

1. David Suzuki, *The Sacred Balance*, Greystone Books, Vancouver, 1997, p. 38. See also, *Suzuki Speaks*, Avanti Pictures, 2004.

2. David Warren, "Global warming and green hot air," *Ottawa Citizen*, Sept. 11, 2001.

3. Jon Ferry, "Dire warnings of environmental doom overblown," *Province*, June 12, 2001.

4. Graydon Carter, "The Air at Ground Zero," Editor's Letter, *Vanity Fair*, September, 2004.

5. Steve Watson, "Ground Zero Toxic Death Fumes Covered Up From Day One: Government Officials and agencies knowingly exposed 9/11 rescuers to deadly air and then tried to cover it up," *Infowars*, September 8, 2006. Http://infowars.net/articles/September2006/080906toxic.htm.

6. Anthony DePalma, "Tracing Lung Ailments That Rose With 9-11 Dust," *New York Times*, May 13, 2006.

7. See Gale Christianson, Greenhouse: The 200-Year Story of Global Warming, Vancouver, GreyStone Books, 1999, p. 12. Cited in Robert Babe, "Newspaper Discourses on Environment," in Jeffery Klaehn, Ed., *Filtering the News: Essays on Herman and Chomsky's Propaganda Model*, Black Rose Books, Montreal, 2005. p. 195.

8. For an interesting account of this, see Linda McQuaig, *It's the Crude, Dude: War, Big Oil, and the Fight for the Planet*, DoubleDay Canada, Toronto, 2004, Chapter Five.

9. Babe, "Newspaper Discourses..." p. 196.

10. Reported in David Suzuki, "Media ignored unprecedented warning by scientists," *Toronto Star*, January 23, 1993.

11. This document is cited in Babe, "Newspaper Discourses..." P. 188. It may be found on a web site of the Union of Concerned Scientists, http://www.ucsusa.org/ucs/about/1992-world-scientists-warning-to-humanity.html.

12. " 'Great movement' needed to save Earth from doom," Scripps Howard Service. *Windsor Star*, Nov. 19, 1992.

13. David Suzuki, "Media ignored unprecedented warning by scientists," *Toronto Star*, January 23, 1993.

14. Tom Sandborn, "Global warming," *National Post*, January 4, 1999. Andrew Macpherson, Ostriches remain to be convinced," *Edmonton Journal*, August 6, 1994.

15. Canada, Department of Foreign Affairs and International Trade, "Taking Action on Climate Change," 7 Feb., 2003; Cited in Babe, "Newspaper Discourses," p. 196. http://www.dfait-maeci.gc.ca/department/focus/kyotoporotocol-en.asp.

16. Canadian Press, "Harper letter called Kyoto 'socialist scheme.'" *Toronto Star*, January 30, 2007. Harper's comments were contained in a 2002 fundraising letter.

17. John Bellamy Foster, "Ecology Against Capitalism," *Monthly Review*, October, 2001.

18. My assessment of Kyoto relies heavily on Foster, "Ecology Against Capitalism."

19. Foster, "Ecology Against Capitalism."

20. Ibid.

21. Ibid.

22. Robert Babe, "Newspaper Discourses on Environment," in Jeffrey Klaehn (Ed), *Filtering The News: Essays on Herman and Chomsky's Propaganda Model,* Black Rose Books, Montreal, 2005, pp. 187-222.

23. Babe, "Newspaper Discourses," p. 199.

24. Ibid, p. 211.

25. Ibid, p. 215.

26. Ibid, p. 217.

27. Charles Moore, "Global warming a heated debate," *Daily News*, Halifax, September 12, 2005. A freelance commentary.

28. cf. CBS News, "Race an issue in Katrina Response, September 3, 2005. www.cbsnews.com.

29. Jacob Jacques, "Hurricanes will intensify unless pollution is curbed," *Windsor Star*, Oct. 12, 2005.

30. Nagarajan Palanisamy, "Katrina, soaring oil prices prove the need to reduce reliance on fossil fuels," *Guardian*, PEI, September 12, 2005; Charles Moore, "Global warming a heated debate," *Halifax Daily News*, September 12, 2005.

31. Paul Hanley, "Natural disasters all too common," *Star-Phoenix*, September 20, 2005.

32. Kim Chipman, "The heat is on," *Calgary Herald*, October 9, 2005. This article was also run in the *Montreal Gazette*.

33. Dr. David Suzuki, "Heat adds power to storms," *Telegram*, St. John's Nfld, Sept. 18, 2005.

34. Tom Spears, "Scientists link severe hurricanes to global warming of oceans," *Edmonton Journal*, September 16, 2005. About 450 words. Reprinted in five other CanWest Global newspapers.

35. James Glassman, "Exploiting Disaster," *National Post*, Sept. 2, 2005.

36 David Suzuki, "Extreme elements likely to increase," *Calgary Herald*, Sept. 18, 2005.

37. David Attenborough, "Attenborough: Climate change is the major challenge facing the world," *The Independent*, May 24, 2006; See also, Bonnie Alter, "Sir David Attenborough Condemns Climate Change," in www.oneworld.ca, and www.treehugger.com, http://www.oneworld.ca/external/?url=http%3A%2F%2Fwww.treehugger.com%2Ffiles %2F2006%2F05%2Fsir_david_atten_1.php.

38. Ben Goldacre and David Adam, "Climate scientist 'duped to deny global warming'," *The Observer*, Mar 11, 2007. http://observer.guardian.co.uk/uk_news/story/0,,2031455,00.html.

39. "Pure Propaganda—The Great Global Warming Swindle: The Scientists Are The Bad Guys," *MediaLens*, March 13, 2007. http://www.medialens.org/alerts/07/0313pure_propaganda_the.php.

40. Jay Stone, "How movies can change the world: New cinema activism," *National Post*, March 23, 2007.

41. John Donnelly, "Some happy that a family film flaunts dire facts," *Boston Globe*, December 6, 2006.

42. Partially summarized in, Ernesto Zedillo, "Debating the Price of Global Warming," *Forbes*, Current Events, Commentary, March 26, 2007. Http://members.forbes.com/forbes/2007/0326/035.html.

43. "Climate change report's main findings," *Telegraph Journal*, New Brunswick, February 3, 2007.

44. AP, "46 nations back action on climate," *Toronto Star*, February 4, 2007.

45. Andrew Thomson. "Global warming 'denialists' grow scarce: Science finally wins over most holdouts," *Calgary Herald*, February 3, 2007.

46. Ian Sample, "Scientists offered cash to dispute climate study," *Guardian,* February 2, 2007.

47. Ernesto Zedillo, "Debating the Price of Global Warming."

48. "Climate change real to most: poll," *National Post*, March 23, 2007.

49. One exception is the 2001 Asbestos Case, where the WTO Appellate Body affirmed the rights of members (in this case France) to take whatever measures they deem necessary to protect health. See Lawrence L. Herman, "WTO has Far-Reaching Impact on Domestic Law," *Lawyers Weekly*, June 29, 2001 page 14. http://www.casselsbrock.com/publication detail.asp?aid=205&printthis=1&x=68&y=8.

50. Howard Mann, "The Final Decision in Methanex v. United States: Some New Wine in Some New Bottles," International Institute for Sustainable Development (IISD), August 2005. http://www.iisd.org/.

51. "Issue Profile: International Panel Rules Investor Can Obtain Damages from NAFTA Government," Davies, Ward and Beck, Barristers & Solicitors, Toronto. www.dwb.com. http://www.envireform.utoronto.ca/pdf/Soloway/Nov10.pdf.

52. Murray Dobbin, 'The view from the West: Europe has its eye on Canadian water—and more.' *Winnipeg Free Press* online, May 2, 2002.

53. Ibid.

54. Murray Dobbin, "Corporate Rights Deal to Make Us April Fools," TILMA will strip our ability to set local limits, TheTyee.ca, January 24, 2007. View full article and comments here http://thetyee.ca/Views/2007/01/24/TILMA/.

55. George Monbiot, "The Multilateral Agreement on Investments will force governments to poison their citizens," *Guardian*, August 13, 1998. Http://www.monbiot.com/archives/1998/08/13/running-on-mmt/.

56. Ken Traynor, "MMT fuel additive scandal?" *Briarpatch*, September, 1998.

57. Quoted in Traynor, "MMT fuel."

58. "MMT Fact Sheet," Global Lead Network, http://www.globalleadnet.org/pdf/MMT factSheet.pdf.

59. See Shawn McCarthy, "Gas war: the fall and rise of MMT When the car and oil firms went to battle, Ottawa lost," *Globe and Mail,* July 24, 1998.

60. P. Granjean and P. Landrigan, "Developmental neurotoxicity of industrial chemicals," *Lancet*, Vol. 368, Issue 9553, 16 December 2006, Pages 2167-2178.

61. D. Mergler, M. Baldwin, S. Belanger et al., "Manganese Neurotoxicity, a Continuum of Dysfunction: Results From a Community Based Study," *Neurotoxicology* 1999, 20:327-42.

62. Quoted in, Dalton Camp, "We can thank free trade," *Guardian*, Charlottetown, PEI: July 30, 1998.

63. "Comments on the Gasoline Additive MMT (methylcyclopentadienyl manganese tricarbonyl)," the U.S. EPA, http://www.epa.gov/otaq/regs/fuels/additive/mmt_cmts.htm.

64. Brian Turner, "Don't worry about MMT in Canada: Fuel companies have turned to ethanol to boost octane," *Vancouver Sun,* August 4, 2006.

65. See Bill Kovarik, "Overview: Leaded Gasoline History and Current Situation," http://www.runet.edu/~wkovarik/ethylwar/overview.html.

66. Jamie Lincoln Kitman, "The Secret History of Lead," *Nation*, March 20, 2000. www.thenation.com; see also Ken Traynor, "MMT fuel additive scandal?" I am greatly indebted to Kitman's far more detailed account of these events, which I have summarized very briefly here. Mr. Kitman has written, "I don't own this story. A lot of better writers and better historians than I have already helped push this ball forward to where I picked it up."

67. Jamie Lincoln Kitman, "Leading With Lead," The Media Channel, April 5, 2000. www.mediachannel.org.

68. Kitman, "The Secret History."

69. Ibid.

70. Ibid.

71. Ibid.

72. Quoted in Kitman, "The Secret History."

73. Kitman, "The Secret History."

74. Ibid.

75. Ibid.

76. Ibid.

77. Ibid.

78. Ibid.

79. "Dumping Lead in gasoline: The Leaden Proletariat," *New Internationalist*, No. 129, November 1983.

80. Associated Octel's public affairs spokesman Bob Larbey, since retired, quoted in Kitman, "The Secret History." The British firm Octel now manufactures TEL, Ethyl markets it.

81. See "Pediatricians Urge A Precautionary Approach to Toxic Lead, *Rachel's Environment & Health News*, No. 827, September 29, 2005. www.rachel.org.

82. Cf. Ed Herman and Noam Chomsky, *Manufacturing Consent: The Political Economy of the Media*, Pantheon Books, N.Y., 1988. An earlier version of this Carson-Bjorn analysis was published in Robert Babe and James Winter, "Canadian Critical Communication," in David Berry and John Theobald, (Eds) *Radical Mass Media Criticism*, Black Rose Books, Montreal, 2006, pp. 140-160.

83. I would be remiss if I did not mention Murray Bookchin, who died in August, 2006, at 85. He wrote *Our Synthetic Environment* under the pseudonym Lewis Herber, in 1962, in which he called for alternative energy supplies among other environmental proposals. It was in that book—which predated by five months the better known work by Rachel Carson —that Mr. Bookchin introduced the notion of social ecology.

84. Cited in Richard C. Bell, "Skeptical Environmentalist, Media Sheep: How did The Skeptical Environmentalist pull the wool over the eyes of so many editors?" *Worldwatch Institute*, July 2, 2002.

85. Described by Peter Montague, "Environmental Trends," *Rachel's Environment & Health Weekly*, #613, August 27, 1998.

87. See Margaret Wente, "DDT's return is a good thing. Really," *Globe and Mail*, September 23, 2006.

87. Lisa Budwig, "Breaking Nature's Silence: Pennyslvania's Rachel Carson. From Pennsylvania's Environmental Heritage, homepage. http://www.dep.state.pa.us/dep/PA_Env-Her/rachel.htm.

88. Rachel Carson, *Silent Spring*, Fawcett Crest Books, N.Y., 1964, p. 22.

89. NYT News Service, "'We're Aghast' Author Called Pest," *Globe and Mail*, July 24, 1962.

90. Editorial, "Miracle or Mischief?" *Globe and Mail*, July 26, 1962.

91. Godfrey Hodson, "Insecticide Fear: 'Guests of the Borgias'," *Globe and Mail*, September 6, 1962.

92. Henry Hurtig, "Are Insecticides Stealthily Endangering Man's Future?", Review of Books, *Globe and Mail*, September 29, 1962.

93. John A. Livingston, "Silent Spring," letter, *Globe and Mail*, October 4, 1962.

94. Eva Moudry, "Silent Spring," letter, *Globe and Mail*, October 15, 1962.

95. David Spurgeon, "Report on Science: Shifty Grasshoppers," *Globe and Mail*, October 16, 1962.

96. David Spurgeon, "Report on Science: The Pesticide Controversy," *Globe and Mail*, February 11, 1963.

97. "The Story of Silent Spring," Natural Resources Defense Council, http://www.nrdc.org/health/pesticides/hcarson.asp.

98. Robin Green, "Federal Probe Urged of Pesticide Residue in Wildlife," *Globe and Mail*, April 20, 1963.

99. NYT Service, "Refuses Comment On Book," *Globe and Mail*, June 10, 1963.

100. CP, "Forest Service Seeks New Way to Kill Insects," *Globe and Mail*, ROB, June 18, 1963.

101. David Spurgeon, "Author Criticized by Industry: Rachel Carson Cloud Hangs Over Chemists," *Globe and Mail*, September 12, 1963.

102. No author, "Killing Confidence: Expert Berates Book on Insect Spraying," *Globe and Mail*, October 3, 1963.

103. CP, "Pest Sprays No Peril, U.S. Expert Declares," *Globe and Mail*, November 20, 1963.

104. Patrick Luciani, "Environmental crisis? What rot!: The apocalyptic views of today's environmentalists aren't as accurate as people have believed," *National Post*, July 15, 2000. pg. B.3.

105. Editorial, "Let God sort 'em out," *National Post*, May 12, 2003. pg. A.15.

106. Stephen Milloy, "The DDT ban, 30 years later Series: Junk Science Week, *National Post*, June 22, 2002. pg. FP.11.

107. Cf. Keith Damsell, "Former Southam brass slams CanWest editorial policy, National editorials menace 'free speech, democracy and pluralism,' statement says," *Toronto Star*, Jun. 5, 2002; also http://www.diversityofvoices.ca/DOV_declaration.htm.

108. As summarized by Stephen Bocking, "The skeptical con," *Alternatives Journal*, Waterloo: Summer 2002. Vol. 28, Issue 3; pg. 9.

109. Bjorn Lomborg. "Something Is Rotten in the State of Denmark," *Wall Street Journal*, January 23, 2003. pg. A.14 .

110. The Lomborg Story: An Account of the Lomborg Case as understood by biologist Kåre Fog, Denmark, http://www.lomborg-errors.dk/.

111. The Lomborg Story. The Scientific American article, along with Lomborg's response, is reproduced on the website of anti-environmentalist Patrick Moore, at: http://www.greenspirit.com/lomborg/.

112. Summarized by Canadian journalist Stephen Hume, in, "Iffy theory keeps anti-greens warm: The World According To Bjorn," *Edmonton Journal*, Jan 19, 2003. pg. D.8.

113. Quoted in, Margaret Munro, "Earth's woes are real, lead scientist says: Environmental skeptics 'tell people what they want to hear'," *National Post*, Feb 15, 2002. pg. A.21.

114. Edward O. Wilson, "Vanishing Point: On Bjorn Lomborg and extinction," *Grist* Magazine, December 12, 2001.

115. Matthew A. Cole, "Environmental Optimists, Environmental Pessimists and the Real State of the World—An Article Examining *The Skeptical Environmentalist*: Measuring the Real State of the World by Bjorn Lomborg," *Economic Journal*, vol. 113, no. 488, June 2003, pp. F362-80.

116. This analogy is drawn by Danish biologist Kåre Fog, in The Lomborg Story.

117. Mikael Skou Andersen, Book Review, "Bjørn Lomborg: The True State of the World," Viby: Centrum, 1998, 322 pages. *Politica*, No. 1, 1999. Andersen is an associate professor, Department of Political Science, University of Aarhus.

118. The CEI's Mission Statement on their web site reads, in part, "The Competitive Enterprise Institute is a non-profit public policy organization dedicated to the principles of free enterprise and limited government." It describes itself as "one of the leading proponents of free market environmentalism." www.cei.org.

119. www.reason.org.

120. Taken from the CEI web pages, at: http://www.cei.org/gencon/026,03198.cfm.

121. John Stauber and Sheldon Rampton, "Silencing Spring," in *Toxic Sludge is Good for You: Lies, Damn Lies and the Public Relations Industry,* Common Courage Press, Monroe Maine, 1995, p. 125.

122. A number of sources indicated that the book was reviewed by the social sciences division at the press, rather than the biological sciences, because Lomborg is a political scientist, and thus the reviews were not as stringent as they otherwise would have been. Cf. Richard C. Bell, "Skeptical Environmentalist, Media Sheep: How did The Skeptical Environmentalist pull the wool over the eyes of so many editors?" *Worldwatch Institute,* July 2, 2002.

123. I discussed these examples in "Feminism Did It," in *MediaThink*, Black Rose Books, Montreal, 2002.

124. David Thomas, "Green Rebel: Bjorn Lomborg, a former member of Greenpeace, has been branded a traitor by the international environmental movement. His crime? He debunked almost all of its claims about the earth's perilous state. Now, he is a marked man." *Calgary Herald,* Jan 26, 2002.

125. Fred Ford, "How do you like those apples?: The green lobby gets a rare, and deserved, shot from inside," *Ottawa Citizen,* Jun 14, 2001.

126. David Warren, "Global warming and green hot air," *Ottawa Citizen,* Sept. 11, 2001.

127. Jon Ferry, "Dire warnings of environmental doom overblown," *The Province,* June 12, 2001.

128. No author, "Kyoto treaty a waste of money, environmentalist says: Fighting poverty, famine better move, new book suggests," *Edmonton Journal,* June 11, 2001.

129. Mary Vallis, "Greens preaching 'phantom problems': Planet is healthy, Greenpeace exile argues in new book," *National Post,* June 11, 2001.

130. Cf. Bjorn Lomborg, "Driven to extinction: a specious theory," *National Post,* Sept. 3, 2001; Bjorn Lomborg, "Global warming? So what?: As world leaders debate the best way to curb emissions and stop Earth's rising temperature, they ignore one clear reality: The trillions it would cost would be far better spent improving Third World economies," *National Post,* Sept. 5, 2001.

131. Bjorn Lomborg, "The sky is not falling: Author argues global warming is not the end of the world, but pollution in the Third World is a worry," *Vancouver Sun,* April 1, 2002.

132. Danish biologist Kåre Fog, The Lomborg Story.

133. Kåre Fog, The Lomborg Story.

134. Barry Cooper, "Reality trumps enviro fantasies," *National Post,* Dec. 30, 2003.

135. Terence Corcoran, "Science wins," *National Post,* Dec 19, 2003.

136. Rex Murphy, "Praise the green god from whom all blessings flow," *Globe and Mail*, April 24, 2004.

137. Stephen Hume, "Iffy theory keeps anti-greens warm: The World According To Bjorn," *Edmonton Journal,* Jan 19, 2003. pg. D.8.

138. Margaret Munro, "Earth's woes are real, lead scientist says: Environmental skeptics 'tell people what they want to hear'," *National Post*, Feb. 15, 2002.

139. David Suzuki, "Skepticism: the good, the bad and the ugly," *The Telegram*, Nov 18, 2001.

140. Andrew Nikiforuk, "Crying eco-wolf," *Globe and Mail*, October 6, 2001.

141. Richard Lubbock, "Can biophilia save the planet?" *Globe and Mail*, March 23, 2002.

142. Margaret Wente, "Global warming: a heretic's view," *Globe and Mail*, May 23, 2002.

143. Bjorn Lomborg, "Earth's a tough mother," *Globe and Mail*, August 23, 2002.

144. Marcus Gee, "Sad facts to recall at the summit," *Globe and Mail*, August 31, 2002.

145. Ian Brown, "The Kyoto Stampede," *Globe and Mail*, October 26, 2002.

146. Margaret Wente, "The Kyoto-speak brainwashers," *Globe and Mail*, December 7, 2002.

147. Rex Murphy, "Praise the green god from whom all blessings flow," *Globe and Mail*, April 24, 2004.

148. Margaret Wente, "Denying the new realists," *Globe and Mail*, November 14, 2006.

149. Charles Alexander, "Breaking the silence on DDT," *Time*, March 31, 2003.

150. Editorial, "The poisons that threaten the riches of the seas," *Globe and Mail*, February 14, 1966.

151. Russ Baker, "The Lomborg File: When the Press is Lured By a Contrarian's Tale," *Columbia Journalism Review*, March/April, 2002.

152. Gary Kroll, "A Brief History of Ecology as a Subversive Subject," Online Ethics Center: Rachel Carson and Silent Spring, The Online Ethics Center for Engineering and Science at Case Western Reserve University. www.onlineethics.org.

153. Ibid. Also, see Douglas Kellner, "Marcuse, Liberation, and Radical Ecology," *Illuminations*, undated, University of Texas, Austin, http://www.uta.edu/huma/illuminations/kell11.htm.

Chapter Three
BIG PHARMA

IT'S WITH GREAT PLEASURE THAT I announce to the world that my students and I have discovered the cure for the common cold. We should probably do this in an academic journal of sorts, like the *New England Journal of Medicine*, and then we'd be on our way to becoming rich and famous. Instead, we usually do this in a lecture class, as we did again early in 2007. It's a simple process, and I go through it every semester with different classes. We begin by discussing how "science" has long sought a cure, and then I simply ask students what they see as a cure, and then take a number of answers until they come up with garlic. This semester a student got it right away. In years of doing this, they've never failed to discover the cure.

Garlic has been used for colds and the heart and circulation system for thousands of years, and there is scads of anecdotal evidence—and even some academic research—indicating its curative powers. The ancient Egyptians gave it to the slaves building the pyramids, to keep them healthy. The Romans fed it to their soldiers before battle. About 15 or 20 years ago, I began taking garlic, raw, cooked, or in pill form, to ward off and cure colds. It works. Right now I'm using an odorless, coated pill made by Kwai, which you can pick up in most drug stores. The main thing to look for is a high Allicin count. For me, my family, friends, and former students, it is indeed a cure. Unlike the antibiotics mistakenly prescribed at times, garlic is both anti-viral and anti-bacterial. There is an article on the topic, on my media literacy course web site, under the health lecture topic [www.uwindsor.ca/medialiteracy].

Herbal cures have been around on this continent for thousands of years. When the Iroquois living around the St. Lawrence River discovered Jacques

Cartier and his men on their shores, around 1534, the Europeans were deathly ill with scurvy. European civilization was so advanced at the time, that they believed scurvy was caused by the "bad air" encountered on voyages. One of their cures for this and any other ailment at the time was bleeding. The medical doctors just cut people open until enough bad blood flowed out. It either killed you or it cured you. Fortunately for old Jacques and the remainder of his men, the Iroquoian people knew that if you drank a tea made with white pine bark, it would cure scurvy. This is because white pine bark is rich in vitamin C.

The question that occurs is, if indeed garlic is a cure for colds and other ailments, why do drug manufacturers ignore this and continue to seek a pharmacological cure? And, why do they promote other non-effective "cures?" It's really the same answer to the question about farm alcohol in the last chapter. Just as anyone can produce gasohol, anyone can grow garlic in their kitchen or backyard. So, it can't be patented. Herbal manufacturers can make a good profit, but there's no captive and exclusive market, no MDs prescribing it, no drug plans to pay for it, and no billions of dollars in profits.[1]

Big Pharma

On the other hand, Big Pharma makes huge profits, using patents, captive and sometimes exclusive markets, MDs, and drug plans. The pharmaceutical industry is a dirty business. They falsify research, risk people's health and lives, use celebrities to push drugs, use medical doctors to push drugs, manufacture nonexistent diseases they can then "cure," and try to enlist lifelong patients. Big Pharma revised the cholesterol level guidelines so they could create a "high cholesterol epidemic," and profit from Statin drugs which have serious side effects. But it doesn't stop there. They "educate" medical students and doctors, provide freebie incentives or bribes such as free vacations to those who prescribe their drugs; they control the release of research results with big bucks and tight contracts. Then, they try to ruin the careers and reputations of MD whistleblowers who defend public safety.

That still isn't the end of the corruption. Big Pharma "ghostwrites" articles for well-known medical researchers, who put their names on the articles —sometimes without ever seeing the data—in return for payoffs. Of course, these ostensibly "objective, scientific" articles are published in academic medical journals, and serve to play up the benefits of company drugs, and downplay their problems.

Any student who has ever been warned about avoiding plagiarism should take note: these professors are plagiarizing, using other people's work as their own, and making a bundle in the process. We'll look at some concrete case studies of these unethical, immoral and sometimes illegal actions in this chapter.

As a result of drug company efforts, we have become pill popping nations. Americans alone consume about 40 percent of all the drugs prescribed annually, throughout the world. It's now at the point where we are getting pharmaceutical drugs through our drinking water, because there are so many of them out there. In Germany, where prescription levels are much lower than North America, researchers have found from 30-60 drugs in a typical drinking water sample.

The Pfizer Example

Let's begin with the example of Pfizer Inc. In January 2007, Pfizer announced it was slashing 10,000 jobs to save annual costs of $2 billion, "amid fierce competition from generic drugs."[2] Pfizer blamed generic drugs, as its U.S. sales of Lipitor, one of the statin drugs for treating high cholesterol, slipped 6 percent to $1.9 billion (U.S.), according to an article in the *Toronto Star*. Globally, Pfizer sells about $12 billion worth of Lipitor annually. The company's after-tax profit in 2006 was $7.9 billion (U.S.).

In 2002, the top 10 American drug companies had a median profit margin of 17 percent, compared with less than 3.1 percent for the other *Fortune 500* industries.[3] For most of the 1990s and the early part of this decade, the pharmaceutical industry was the most profitable business sector in the U.S. According to the nonprofit watchdog group *Public Citizen*, the combined profits of the top ten pharmaceutical companies in the Fortune 500 exceeded the combined profits of the other 490 companies.[4]

When Pfizer blamed generics, the popular media merely echoed the company's claim, but that's not the real story.

Spin Doctoring

In common parlance, "spin doctoring" refers to the way politicians spin their own account of events, using public relations. But there is another type of spin doctoring going on.

Pfizer is the largest drug manufacturer in the world, with $50 billion U.S. in annual sales, and familiar names such as Lipitor, Viagra, and antidepressant

Zoloft (which admittedly did lose its patent protection in 2006). Every week-day, about 38,000 Pfizer sales reps whistle their way to work around the globe. The sales reps cost Pfizer $170,000 U.S. per year, including their company car, personal computers and benefits. Pfizer can afford it. In 2004, the company generated $45 billion in gross profits, or $1.2 million per sales rep.[5] With their briefcases full of free drug samples and lavish expense accounts for wining and dining their prey, the sales reps head into hospitals, clinics, pharmacies and medical doctors' offices. In some cases they buy lists of MDs' prescribed drugs from pharmacies, so they know whom to target. One 2001 report in the *Journal of the American Medical Association* indicated that drug companies such as Pfizer spend as much as $13,000 (U.S.) annually, on every MD targeted.[6] The goal is to get Pfizer drugs prescribed by the MDs. And it works.

> How does a drug company find its target doctor? It begins in a drug-store when you fill a prescription and the data is stored. The pharmacy then erases your personal information and sells your doctor's name and billing number and your list of meds to an intermediary like IMS, which processes 165 billion pharmacy records a month, capturing 70% of prescriptions worldwide, and sells the information to drug firms. Then reps from these firms get a target list, and start selling. Among the tactics used is the dash-and-dine. Unaware of be-ing followed, a doctor dashes out for some take-away. A sales rep then unexpectedly swoops in, takes the opportunity to pitch the lat-est drug and foots the bill. There are the many freebies—small stuff like clocks, pens, mouse pads with the company's insignia, and big-ticket items like trips, cash and World Series tickets—and great con-troversy over their influence on doctors' prescription-writing habits.[7]

Phyllis Adams, a former drug rep in Canada, was told by a doctor that he would not prescribe her product unless her company made him a consultant. For another doctor, she arranged a $35,000 "unrestricted educational grant" for him to use for a swimming pool in his back yard.[8] Another U.S. example in-volves a drug rep paying $50,000 for a consulting accountant to turn around a failing medical clinic with about 50 MDs who didn't know how to run a busi-ness. He turned the practice into a smoothly running financial machine, all the while promoting the drug rep's company, and its prescriptions and profits soared. Why? The MDs were grateful for the economic bonanza.

Drug giant GlaxoSmithKline has been accused of using exotic holidays, stereos, World Cup soccer tickets and cash to bribe thousands of Italian and German doctors into prescribing its products. In the U.S., AstraZeneca paid a $355 million court settlement for a kickback scheme in 2003, where doctors billed insurance providers for drugs they received free from the company. TAP Pharmaceutical Products pulled the same stunt and settled for $875 million in 2001.[9]

Some MDs avoid reps like the plague. But, it must be difficult. The reps are young, good-looking, and frequently women. They have large expense accounts. Writes one American MD,

> Many reps are so friendly, so easygoing, so much fun to flirt with that it is virtually impossible to demonize them. How can you demonize someone who brings you lunch and touches your arm and remembers your birthday and knows the names of all your children? After awhile even the most steel-willed doctors may look forward to visits by a rep, if only in the self-interested way that they look forward to the UPS truck pulling up in their driveway. A rep at the door means a delivery has arrived: take-out for the staff; trinkets for the kids, and, most indispensably, drug samples on the house. Although samples are the single largest marketing expense for the drug industry, they pay handsome dividends: doctors who accept samples of a drug are far more likely to prescribe that drug later on.[10]

MDs who accept gifts deny that it influences the prescriptions they write, but the evidence shows otherwise: gifts turn into script. As one former rep noted, "If you could get ten minutes with a doctor, your market share would go through the roof." These bribes are changing MDs' prescribing habits. For example, a review paper by Ashley Wazana, then a resident at Montreal's McGill University, found that doctors who attended pharma-sponsored CME, received free drug samples or accepted pharma funds for travel expenses, were more likely to prescribe the sponsor's drug. The Canadian company Biovail paid American MDs $1,000 for signing up 11 patients each, in 2003.[11] This is another form of spin doctoring. Indeed, the *Journal of the American Medical Association* admitted in their February 2, 2002 issue that 87% of their medical experts formulating the practice guidelines with which doctors must comply, are tied financially to the pharmaceutical companies.[12]

A Marketing Blitz

In addition, of course, for Pfizer and other pharma companies, there are the other elements of a vast marketing blitz: such as more than $3 billion in annual advertising, placing Pfizer, for example, fourth amongst all American companies in 2003, behind only General Motors, Proctor & Gamble, and Time Warner. And it doesn't matter that these are prescription drugs being advertised. The commercials coax us to "ask your doctor" if this pill is for you. Consequently, MDs are bombarded by patients as well as drug reps. Apparently, it works. As a recent Health Canada/*British Medical Journal* study reported, "physicians often prescribe drugs requested by patients, even when the doctors aren't convinced the advertised medication is better than older, often cheaper pills."[13] By one estimate, Americans consume 40 percent of all the drugs prescribed around the world every year. In 2004, Americans averaged 12 prescriptions each. Developing countries bear a disproportionate part of the world's disease burden. But with 80 per cent of the world's population they account for only 10 per cent of global drug sales. The drug bill for the whole continent of Africa is just one per cent of the world total.[14]

Advertising expands the market, promoting diseases to fit drugs. Thus, "millions of normal people come to believe that they have dubious or exaggerated aliments such as 'generalized anxiety disorder,' 'erectile dysfunction,' 'premenstrual dysphoric disorder,' and GERD (gastroesophageal reflux disease)."[15]

As American MD and bioethics professor Carl Elliott points out, Americans have become reliant on pill popping. Baseball players in the U.S. take drugs to improve their performance; college students take Ritalin to improve their academic performance; musicians take beta blockers to improve their on-stage performance; middle-aged men take Viagra to improve their sexual performance; shy people take Paxil to improve their social performance.[16]

This incredible drug use impacts on all of us: as it shows up in our drinking water. Drugs given to people and animals have been showing up in water samples: surface water, groundwater, and tap drinking water, dating back to the early 1990s. Researchers have found antibiotics, hormones, strong pain killers, tranquilizers and chemotherapy chemicals given to cancer patients, for example. German scientists report that between 30 and 60 drugs can be measured in a typical water sample.[17]

THE KILLING OF WOODY BY BIG PHARMA

Statement of Kim Witczak of Minneapolis, Minnesota

On behalf of Woodymatters before the Senate Committee on Health, Education, Labour, and Pensions hearing on Drug User Fees: Enhancing Patient Access and Drug Safety

March 14, 2007

Mr. Chairman, Senator Enzi, Members of the Committee:

Thank you for inviting me to testify today.

I am here today to represent the voice of thousands of families who live every day with the consequences of the current drug safety system. Unfortunately, I know first hand what it feels like to lose someone because of unsafe drugs. On August 6th, 2003, my life changed forever. I became a widow.

My husband of almost 10 years was found dead hanging from the rafters of our garage of Zoloft-induced suicide at age 37. Tim Witczak, known to most as Woody, was not depressed nor did he have a history of depression or any other so-called mental illness. Woody had just started his dream job as Vice President of Sales with a start up energy efficient lighting company a couple months prior and was having difficulty sleeping which is not uncommon for new entrepreneurs. So Woody went to see his general physician and was given Zoloft for an insomnia diagnosis. Five weeks later, Woody took his own life. His doctor gave him a 3-week Pfizer-supplied sample pack that automatically doubled the dose after week one. No cautionary warning was given to him or me about the need to be closely monitored when first going on drug or dosage changes. In fact, I was out of the country on business for the first 3 weeks he was on Zoloft. When I returned, I found Woody one night in fetal position on our kitchen floor with his hands wrapped around his head like a vise, crying, "Help me, help me. I don't know what is happening to me. I am losing my mind. It's like my head is outside my body looking in."

Never once did we question the drug. Why would we? It was FDA approved, heavily advertised as safe and effective, AND it was given by Woody's doctor that he has seen for years and trusted...[18]

As for big Pharma's much-vaunted research and development, far more money is spent on marketing than on research. According to Dr. Marcia Angell, a Harvard professor of medicine and former editor of the prestigious *New England Journal of Medicine,* from 1998 through 2003, 487 drugs were approved by the U.S. Food and Drug Administration (FDA). Of those, 379 (78%) were classified by the agency as "appear[ing] to have therapeutic qualities similar to those of one or more already marketed drugs," and 333 (68%) weren't even new compounds (what the FDA calls "new molecular entities"), but instead were formulations or combinations of old ones. Only 67 (14% of the 487) were actually new compounds considered likely to be improvements over older drugs.[19] Fourteen percent.

Most marketing is aimed at persuading doctors and patients to choose one of these "me-too" drugs over another, without any scientific basis. So most free samples are recently patented me-too drugs. Says Dr. Marcia Angell, "AstraZenica was reported to have spent a half-billion dollars in a year to switch Prilosec users to Nexium." That may explain why we were suddenly bombarded with ads for "the purple pill." There's another danger with new drugs, in that they are tested on relatively few people so less frequent side effects aren't detected. If you test a drug on 5000 people, and one death occurs as a result, that's not significant and may be ignored. But if 5 million people subsequently go on that drug, this translates into 1000 people who will die from it.

The next blockbuster drug in the Pfizer lineup was called by the chemical name of Torcetrapid. In clinical trials, it was found to raise HDL or "good cholesterol" levels. Pfizer was three years into 100 clinical trials involving 15,000 patients, on three continents. The company reportedly invested between $1 billion and $2.1 billion on the drug, with hopes of a very high payoff. "If it works, it will be the biggest blockbuster ever," CEO Hank McKinnell Jr. told the business press in 2005.[20]

Suddenly, the wheel fell off. In early December, 2006, the company learned from independent monitors that the drug was increasing people's risk of dying by an alarming 161 percent. It was also causing other problems, related to heart failure, *et cetera,* for people who had not died in the trials. In all, 82 people died taking the drug in the trials, versus 51 who were not taking it. These were very scary numbers, and Pfizer pulled the plug on the drug tests. The discontinuation of Torcetrapid was the second major failure in the Pfizer development program in less than a week. Earlier, Pfizer said it would no longer collaborate with Akzo Nobel, a European company, on Asenapine, a drug for schizophrenia.[21]

Although to the media—and even in my wording above—this incident was seen as a "failure," in reality it is a success story, as the problems with the drug were divulged before the testing was completed, and before the drug was sold to the public. We're not always so lucky. For example, Vioxx. By the time it was withdrawn in September, 2004, Merck & Co. Inc.'s anti-inflamatory painkiller Vioxx had been taken by an estimated 80 million people, and its sales reached $2.5 billion (U.S.) in 2003.

According to a report in the *New Scientist*, Cox-2 inhibitors such as Vioxx were licensed for the treatment of chronic inflammation as a safer alternative to traditional anti-inflammatory drugs such as ibuprofen, for people at high risk for specific side-effects. Ibuprofen can cause gastrointestinal bleeding and stomach ulcers in some people, such as those over 65 years of age. In September 2004, Merck's Vioxx was voluntarily withdrawn amid revelations that its long term use might double the risk of heart attack and stroke amongst users.

Soon after, in December 2004, it emerged that another Cox-2 inhibitor —Pfizer's Celebrex—might triple the risk of heart attacks and stroke, although other studies found no additional risk and the drug was not withdrawn. And a previous study suggested that Vioxx increased the risk of coronary heart disease compared with a traditional NSAID called Naproxen, which may have actually protected the heart.[22] A study published in 2005 suggested that huge numbers of people may have been put at risk by taking Cox-2 inhibitors. The *Lancet* suggested Vioxx could have caused between 88,000 and 140,000 extra cases of serious coronary heart disease in the U.S., by not withdrawing the drug sooner.[23]

As was eventually reported even in the popular press, "When a study found that patients on Vioxx were three times more likely to have heart attacks than patients on Naproxen, Merck-funded scientists decided it was because Naproxen prevented heart attacks. It wasn't until four years later that Merck pulled Vioxx off the market because of concerns it increased the risk of heart attacks."[24]

Researchers at the British medical journal, the *Lancet* looked at the studies conducted between 1999 and 2004, concluding,

If Merck's statement in their recent press release that 'given the availability of alternative therapies, and the questions raised by the data, we concluded that a voluntary withdrawal is the responsible course to take,' was appropriate in September, 2004, then the same statement could and should have been made several years earlier, when the data summarised here first became available. Instead, Merck continued to market the safety of [Vioxx].[25]

Vioxx and Merck are not alone. As one pharmaceutical watchdog summed things up, in 2004:

> Fen-Phen, the popular weight-loss drug that was linked to pulmonary hypertension and heart disease, has killed and harmed so many people that Wyeth, its manufacturer, has put aside more than $16 billion to compensate victims. Hormone replacement therapy, promoted in the 1960's as an anti-aging drug for women, has been linked to an increased risk of heart disease, strokes, pulmonary emboli and breast cancer. Antidepressants like Prozac, Paxil and Zoloft were described as "cosmetic psychopharmacology" a decade ago; today they are embroiled in a public controversy over their links to suicide and homicide.[26]

In 1975, Canadians spent an average of $46.50 on drugs. By 1985, this had risen to $4 billion, averaging about $150 each. By 2005, drug spending was forecast to be up by more than 600 percent, to over $24 billion. Per capita, we're now spending almost $800, instead of $46.50. Prescription drugs account for $20 billion, or 83 percent.[27] This latter amount was more than we paid for all of the physicians' services in the country, combined, annually. The *Canadian Medical Association Journal* reports that the annual increase in prescription drug spending alone—now $1.5 billion—could pay for 3500 more MDs, annually.[28]

Championing Cholesterol

For the last couple of years, my own wonderful medical doctor has been urging me to go on a statin drug, for reducing cholesterol. I've resisted, because I'm a firm believer that exercise and weight loss will accomplish the same thing—once I get around to it. I'm particularly wary of statins, however, since reading a *Toronto Star* series, which I'll come to shortly. Not everyone feels the same way that I do, however. More than 23.6 million prescriptions for cholesterol reducers were dispensed from Canadian retail drug stores for the 12-month period ending Sept. 30, 2006, according to the drug-tracking firm IMS Health. In Canada alone, statins are a $2-billion market. There were more than 12.3 million prescriptions over the same period for Pfizer's Lipitor, the No. 1-selling drug in the country. It can be sold in subtle ways.

> Perched on a stool under television camera lights and surrounded by a crowd of reporters, Maple Leafs hockey coach Pat Quinn spoke of his own heart scare two years earlier, and the need for eight million Canadians to get tested for high cholesterol. It was the summer of 2004. Quinn praised his own cholesterol medication at a media brunch at Toronto's Hockey Hall of Fame. Pfizer paid for the event. Quinn later acknowledged he got a "modest" fee for his appearance.[29]

Quinn is part of a select group of celebrity drug pushers, including actors Olympia Dukakis, the "West Wing's" Rob Lowe, and pop singer Carnie Wilson. U.S. presidential candidate Bob Dole promoted Viagra for Pfizer. Wyeth hired supermodel Lauren Hutton to hawk hormone replacement therapy for menopause. Gymnast Bart Connor, Olympic figure skater Dorothy Hamill, who promoted Merck's Vioxx, jockey Julie Krone, former NFL coach Bill Parcells, San Francisco 49er legend Joe Montana, actors Rita Moreno, Bob Uecker and Debbie Reynolds—all are celebrity pill pushers. Joan Lunden promoted Claritin. Kathleen Turner apparently suffers from rheumatoid arthritis, and has appeared on "Good Morning America" to quietly plug Wyeth's Enbrel, a drug for arthritis sufferers.

Wayne Gretsky touted Tylenol arthritis formula, even though he didn't have osteoarthritis, but this was openly paid advertising. This was part of a long tradition of celebrity endorsements: the star's connection to the company was obvious; the pitch was straightforward promotion. It was like Ricardo Montalban pushing coffee, or Mean Joe Green touting Coke. But with drugs there were controversies, and the pitches weren't as effective as they could be, so the drug companies went underground. They gave us celebrity-driven public awareness campaigns which completely obscured the financial relationship between the star and the drug company, allowing both parties to avoid any talk of side effects or potential problems with the drug. With all hints of drugs and money hidden, celebrities were again willing to sign up, taking fees as high as $1 million to do a series of television and newspaper interviews in which they speak about a particular illness and urge sufferers to seek treatment. Sometimes the celebrities don't mention their sponsor or its product by name, instead urging people to see their doctors about the latest treatments, or, in the case of Kathleen Turner, suggest that viewers or readers visit a specific Web site that offers information about a condition.[30] When "Frasier" star Kelsey Grammar and his wife were promoting irritable bowel syndrome on top-rated TV shows, viewers thought the pair was speaking on behalf of an independent foundation. In fact their fee came from GSK, which was at that time preparing the market for Alosetron (lotronex), a controversial new drug that carried modest benefits and "severe side effects, including possible death."[31]

These awareness campaigns also happen to be a way for the drug companies to avoid the remaining U.S. FDA regulations on TV advertising of prescription drugs. In a straightforward television commercial for a drug, viewers must be told about the drug's major side effects or be directed to another source—a web site, or 800 number, for example—where they can get more information. Awareness campaigns are exempt from these restrictions because the FDA doesn't consider them to be advertisements.[32]

What Pat Quinn didn't mention—likely didn't know—was that statins can cause muscle damage or myopathy, which can lead to muscle pain and weakness, and can be a sign of a rare, potentially fatal muscle-wasting disease called rhabdomyolysis. In its worse form patients can die due to muscle breakdown leading to kidney damage. As well, doctors are seeing more cases of statin-induced peripheral neuropathy, where the long nerves in the body die off, causing numbness and pain in the feet. A number of studies and case histories have reported memory loss due to statins, with recovery after the drug use was halted. In August, 2001, Bayer's Baycol was pulled from the market because of dozens of cases worldwide involving rhabdomyolysis, the muscle-wasting disease. As of October, 2004, Health Canada reports for statins on the market showed that there were 62 reports of rhabdomyolysis in patients taking Lipitor, 18 for Zocor, 12 for Merck's Mevacor, five for Pravachol, made by Bristol-Myers Squibb, and 11 for AstraZeneca's Crestor.[33]

Have A Nap Instead

What one has to weigh against these risks, is the benefit of using a cholesterol drug. One 2004 study indicated, for example, that a 42-year-old man with high cholesterol who took statins for 10 years would reduce his risk of a heart attack or stroke by only 2 per cent.[34] Let's compare this to what you can do naturally, by exercising, eating a low-cholesterol diet, or even snoozing. Yes, I said snoozing. The Toronto Star reported in February, 2007:

In the largest study to date on the health effects of napping, researchers tracked 23,681 healthy Greek adults for an average of about six years. Those who napped at least three times weekly for about half an hour had a 37 percent lower risk of dying from heart attacks or other heart problems than those who did not nap.[35]

My own doctor tells me not to worry about side effects, as they only affect "older patients." But my brother-in-law Rod, an outdoors type who's not much older than me, went on a statin recently and experienced muscle pain, weakness, and possible damage. Researchers now have found that patients who don't have evidence of occlusive vascular disease, which leads to clogged arteries, should not be taking the drugs. Yet, only one quarter of statin users fall into this category. Statins have also been found to be ineffective on women.[36]

So part of the problem is that statins are prescribed so broadly, where they may not be appropriate, or as a—perhaps costly—preventative measure. The cure could be worse than the disease, as they say. But why all of the sudden concern about high cholesterol? Was it junk food bingeing, a lack of exercise? What created the problems which resulted in skyrocketing high cholesterol levels and soaring prescription drugs? Was it really well-intentioned physicians recognizing an international epidemic and trying to make people healthy again? Or was it something else?

Revising Cholesterol Guidelines

Even some physicians may not be aware that the definition of just what constitutes "high cholesterol" is regularly revised. As with other conditions, the definition can be broadened in ways that describe more and more healthy people as "at risk," and hence requiring prescriptions. A minor scandal erupted in the U.S. in 2003, when it was learned that eight of the nine experts who wrote the 2003 cholesterol guidelines also served as paid speakers, consultants or researchers for the world's major drug companies. Some of the members had multiple ties to companies and one "expert" had taken money from 10 of them.[37] In 2005, the *Canadian Medical Association Journal* reported that the "new Canadian guidelines have so changed the threshold for 'high' cholesterol that an additional 500,000 Canadians should be getting statin medication," at a cost of another $250 million.[38] This may or may not be good for us, but it's undoubtedly good for the drug companies.

Dr. Jacques Genest, a cardiologist at the Royal Victoria Hospital at Montreal's McGill University, acknowledged in an interview that he and the other doctors involved in revising the Canadian guidelines for prescribing statins have all worked as consultants for at least some of the six pharmaceutical giants that make statins. Genest himself has worked for four of them, including Pfizer.[39]

As the Big Pharma companies do studies to demonstrate the value of their drugs, miraculously, these cut-off points for high cholesterol have gradually lowered. "Once it was reserved for blood cholesterol levels over 280mm per deciliter," says Dr. Marcia Angell. "Then it fell to 240. Now most doctors try to knock it down to below 100."[40]

These seemingly distant events are ultimately played out in my own doctor's office, and in my brother-in-law's health problems. Recently a colleague and friend whose brother is a Seattle MD, was, like my doctor, telling me about a cholesterol epidemic. "You should get on a statin," he advised.

Of course, the problem is not restricted to just cholesterol levels or statin drugs. 'Abnormal' levels of blood pressure, obesity and bone density have all changed over the years to expand the markets for disease. High blood pressure (hypertension) was once defined as blood pressure above 140/90. An expert panel then introduced something called prehypertension in 2003, which embraces readings between (120/80 and 140/90). "Overnight, people with blood pressure in this range found they had a medical condition," says Dr. Angell.[41] Bipolar disorder, irritable bowel syndrome, male and female sexual dysfunction, and attention deficit hyperactivity disorder (ADHD) which has become pandemic, are all part of what has been called "disease mongering" on the part of Big Pharma and the medical establishment. So-called "disease awareness campaigns" are underwritten by pharmaceuticals. Of course, there will be some individuals who suffer severe forms of these problems, who will benefit from treatments and from the publicity given to the disorders. But there is a difference between legitimate public education about an under diagnosed disease, and turning us all into patients, with crude attempts to build markets for potentially dangerous drugs.[42]

The Eli Lilly-sponsored promotion of premenstrual dysphoric disorder to help sell a re-branded version of fluoxetine (re-branded from Prozac to Sarafem) is a case in point, according to some medical doctors. "Considered by some as a serious psychiatric illness, premenstrual dysphoric disorder is regarded by others as a condition which does not exist."[43]

Until Death Do Us Part

In his analysis of the selling of "bipolar disorder," Dr. David Healy notes that the whole concept of "mood stabilizer" drugs was invented around 1995, and by 2001, around a hundred scientific articles a year featured this term.[44] Although the academic psychiatric community hasn't come to a consensus about what the term means, many physicians are convinced that bipolar disorders must be detected and treated with these mood stabilizers. Bipolar disorders entered the literature in 1980, and involved acute cases of manic-depression, involving hospitalization. Since 1995, the definition has been expanded to include other disorders, and estimates for their prevalence has risen from 0.1 percent of the population, to 5 percent or more. While treatment of the acute manic states of bipolar disorders has been effected using antipsychotic drugs, no drugs have been successfully scientifically tested for the prevention of the broadened definition of "bipolar disorder." Despite this, a whole new industry has cropped up, with the company producing Zyprexa advertising, reminiscent of Nurse Ratchet in *One Flew Over the Cuckoos' Nest*, that:

> Bipolar disorder is often a lifelong illness needing lifelong treatment; symptoms come and go, but the illness stays; people feel better because the medication is working; almost everyone who stops taking the medication will get ill again and the more episodes you have, the more difficult they are to treat.

Clearly, this is a blatant attempt to create lifelong patients. But, based on what scientific research? Janssen, which makes Risperdal, states that:

> Medicines are crucially important in the treatment of bipolar disorders. Studies over the past twenty years have shown beyond the shadow of doubt that people who receive the appropriate drugs are better off in the long term than those who receive no medicine.

But what is beyond "the shadow of doubt" to Janseen is completely fabricated, according to Dr. David Healy, who writes that "With the possible exception of lithium for bipolar I disorder, there are no randomized controlled trials to show that patients with bipolar disorders in general who receive psychotropic drugs are better in the long term than those who receive no medicine."[45]

Healy notes that any slight evidence of benefits for these drugs must be weighed against a consistent body of evidence that regular treatments with antipsychotic drugs in the long run may increase *mortality*, through suicide and for other reasons.

In 2002, the *British Medical Journal* reported the text of a secret, internal memo obtained through a whistleblower at GlaxoSmithKline (GSK). GSK was working on a three-year program (2000-2003) to "create a new perception of irritable bowl syndrome as a concrete disease [which] must be established in the minds of doctors as a significant and discrete disease. Patients also need to be convinced that [it] is a...medical disorder." Commented University of British Columbia medical researcher, Barbara Mintzes: "Not content with providing a pill for every ill, the drug companies now push an ill for every pill."[46]

Disease-Mongering

In her book, *Disease-Mongers: How doctors, drug companies and insurers are making you feel sick*, Lynn Payer describes it as "trying to convince essentially well people that they are sick, or slightly sick people that they are very ill." She lists the ten major Disease-Mongering Tactics, reproduced below. These include: identifying an "abnormality," imputing suffering to people, identifying a (large) population of potential sufferers, defining new diseases, spin doctoring, framing the issues, selective use of statistics, using the wrong end point, promoting technology as risk-free magic, and calling a common ambiguous symptom a disease.[47]

One example of disease-mongering is the Hormone Replacement Therapy (HRT) scandal. Professor of medicine at Harvard University, Dr. JoAnn Manson, recently cited the 20 million women on HRT in the U.S. alone. She blamed the rise of HRT on patients and doctors both swallowing the industry propaganda which began in 1966 with Dr. Robert Wilson's book *Feminine Forever*. Financed in its entirety by the pharmaceutical company Wyeth-Ayerst, the manufacturers of Premarin, this book promised: "Breasts and genital organs will not shrivel. Such women [on HRT] will be much more pleasant to live with and will not become dull and unattractive." Dr. Manson added that rather than conducting proper trials, "it was just assumed that there would be an overall favorable benefit-to-risk ratio."[48]

A study of 16,608 postmenopausal women in a U.S. nationwide study reported in the July, 2002 issue of the *Journal of the American Medical Association* (*JAMA*) reported that women taking the dual-hormone therapy for five years had 26 percent more cases of breast cancer than women receiving a placebo. Moreover, compared with the placebo, the hormones doubled the incidence of blood clots, hiked stroke incidence by 41 percent, and upped the occurrence of heart disease by 29 percent.[49]

The *Journal of the American Medical Association* announced recently that estrogen/progesterone combined synthetic HRT doesn't protect you from anything much and increases your risk of getting breast cancer by 60–80%. In some circumstances, it also seems to trigger ovarian cancer. The study known as the Women's Health Initiative, was halted as the evidence became undeniable.[50]

By 2003, with millions of women on HRT, the mainstream began to report problems. One Canadian Press story reported that HRT was previously "believed to protect women against heart disease, colon cancer, age-related mental decline and osteoporosis," however, based on recent research, the story said "women were actually at greater risk of having a heart attack, stroke or life-threatening blood clot." While reporting this—even belatedly—is a good thing, such articles continued to present mixed reports, which would be confusing for the public. For example, this article went on to quote Dr. Robert Reid, a medical professor at Queen's University who said, "Hormone replacement therapy is still, by far, the best treatment for symptomatic women with hot flashes and…night sweats."[51] Well, which would you rather have, hot flashes or a heart attack or stroke, or cancer?

Another example of disease-mongering is male and female "sexual dysfunction." Leonore Tiefer has reviewed this history, concluding that, "…the pharmaceutical industry has taken an aggressive interest in sex, using public relations, direct-to-consumer advertising, promotion of off-label prescribing, and other tactics to create a sense of widespread sexual inadequacy and interest in drug treatments."[52] Tiefer writes that in the 1980s and 1990s, urologists created organizations, journals, and "sexual health clinics" focusing on men's erection problems. The creation of "erectile dysfunction" as a serious, prevalent, and treatable medical disorder was firmly in place by the time Viagra was launched in 1998 with an unprecedented global public relations campaign, as Joel Lexchin has described. Lexchin wrote, "Pfizer's well-financed campaign was aimed at raising awareness of the problem of ED, while at the same time narrowing the treatment possibilities to just a single option: medication."[53] Though journalists began calling for a "female Viagra" only days after the US Food and Drug Administration (FDA) approved Viagra in March 1998 (examples of journalists' calling for a "pink Viagra" are collected on http://www.fsd-alert.org/press.html), it was "far from clear what medical condition Viagra was supposed to treat in women."[54]

In the early years, key players in the medicalization of women's sexual problems were a small group of urologists who, capitalizing on their relationships with industry, recruited many sex researchers and therapists. Irwin Goldstein of Boston University, an active erectile dysfunction researcher, opened the first Women's Sexual Health clinic in 1998. Goldstein convened the first conference on female sexual function in October 1999 in Boston. Goldstein is the editor of a journal which was launched in 2004—the *Journal of Sexual Medicine* (http://jsm.issir.org)—which has already published an industry-supported supplement on FSD.[55]

Pfizer was the main promoter of FSD from 1997 to 2004, when its attempts to have Viagra approved to treat "female sexual arousal disorder" ended due to consistently poor clinical trial results. In a public statement, Pfizer said that several large-scale, placebo-controlled studies including about 3,000 women with female sexual arousal disorder, showed inconclusive results.[56]

The Major Disease-Mongering Tactics Identified by Lynn Payer

- Taking a normal function and implying that there's something wrong with it and it should be treated
- Imputing suffering that isn't necessarily there
- Defining as large a proportion of the population as possible as suffering from the 'disease'
- Defining a [condition] as a deficiency disease or disease of hormonal imbalance
- Getting the right spin doctors
- Framing the issues in a particular way
- Selective use of statistics to exaggerate the benefits of treatment
- Using the wrong end point
- Promoting technology as risk-free magic
- Taking a common symptom that could mean anything and making it sound as if it is a sign of a serious disease

Drug Co's Educate Medical Students, Faculty

One of the ways in which disease mongering is advanced, is through medical education. Although most of us tend to think of the academic community as

being largely independent of outside business, this independence is under attack. Cutbacks to government spending on education mean educators and administrators increasingly look to corporations to replace lost funding. But such
funding doesn't come without a cost.

The medical profession has largely abandoned its responsibility to educate medical students and doctors in the use of prescription drugs. Instead, it's
the drug companies themselves that support continuing medical education,
medical conferences, professional association meetings, and even university
classroom education. The billions of dollars to do this with comes out of Big
Pharma's marketing budgets.[57] In an *Atlantic Monthly* article entitled "The Drug
Pushers," American academic Dr. Carl Elliott described what this can mean,
for medical students.

> Last spring [2005] a small group of first-year medical students at the
> University of Minnesota spoke to me about a lecture on erectile dys-
> function that had just been given by a member of the urology depart-
> ment. The doctor's PowerPoint slides had a large, watermarked logo
> in the corner. At one point during the lecture a student raised his
> hand and, somewhat disingenuously, asked the urologist to explain
> the logo. The urologist, caught off-guard, stumbled for a moment
> and then said that it was the logo for Cialis, a drug for erectile dys-
> function that is manufactured by Eli Lilly. Another student asked if
> he had a special relationship with Eli Lilly. The urologist replied that
> yes, he was on the advisory board for the company, which had sup-
> plied the slides. But he quickly added that nobody needed to worry
> about the objectivity of his lecture because he was also on the advi-
> sory boards of the makers of the competing drugs Viagra and Levitra.
> The second student told me, "A lot of people agreed that it was a
> pharm lecture and that we should have gotten a free breakfast."[58]

According to two medical educators, psychiatry residents may be particularly
susceptible to the influences of pharmaceutical marketing practices, because,
"the residents have assumed the dual roles of learners and practicing physicians." Consequently, "their prescribing preferences have yet to be established
and their fund of knowledge, though developing, is limited."[59]

As one commentator has pointed out,[60] it's perfectly reasonable to require
teaching faculty to disclose a conflict of interest to students and residents.
Meaningful disclosure would include research grants and honoraria received

from industry, and any other significant relationship between the faculty member and the pharmaceutical company, including stock ownership and work as a company speaker, adviser, or consultant. Any other legal or business relationship between the company and the faculty member which might exert influence over the faculty member's teaching activities should be disclosed, as well as the specific relevancy of the conflict to the subject matter.

But simply disclosing conflicts of interest doesn't resolve them. Key opinion leaders list relationships with Big Pharma when presenting at medical conferences and publishing in peer-reviewed journals. But the process of disclosing conflicts reveals nothing about how they're actually managed, which is a crucial point. When a person has disclosed a relationship, or ended it, any associated conflict of interest may be resolved, but it's naive to believe that clinician-researchers will permanently sever ties to industry, and even if they do, prior interactions with industry may still influence future behavior.[61]

What's necessary is that the medical community, including its educators, replace its apparent lackadaisical acceptance of Big Pharma's PR with—at a minimum—healthy skepticism, and even outright rejection. But given the money involved, this won't happen anytime soon.

As bad as this situation is in the developed west, it's worse for the under-funded nations of the south. According to Dr. Dennis Ross-Degnan, a Harvard professor who studies pharmaceutical policy, "The only people providing meaningful education for doctors in developing countries are the drug companies. The problem is it is biased education."[62]

Who Does The Research? The Whistleblowers

There is also the related impact drug companies have had on research. Professors of medicine not only teach students, but conduct research for drug companies, in return for funding for themselves and their universities. Ideally, of course, this research should be conducted by independent, government-funded third parties. But with cutbacks to government departments, and an explosion of drugs awaiting testing, the research is conducted by the industry itself. Although it may nominally involve independent medical educators, the reality of the situation is that frequently, "he who pays the piper calls the tune." One example of this, involving Dr. Aubrey Blumsohn, is elaborated by Dr. Carl Elliott.

Ethicists looking for textbook examples of how universities ought *not* to behave in the face of pharmaceutical industry muscle-flexing might be interested in the case of Dr. Aubrey Blumsohn, who was until recently a senior lecturer in the Bone Metabolism Unit at Sheffield University. Among Sheffield's pharmaceutical funders was Proctor & Gamble. Blumsohn performed clinical research that contributed to the FDA approval of P&G's osteoporosis drug, Actonel (risedronate). But when Blumsohn asked P&G for the raw data upon which the Actonel research was based, the company refused—even though it was generating ghostwritten abstracts and manuscripts in Blumsohn's name. When Blumsohn was finally allowed to see the data, he says he found evidence of fraud. After lodging formal complaints over a period of 18 months with Sheffield administrators and getting no result, he turned to the press. For this, Sheffield fired him.[63]

Unfortunately, what happened to Blumsohn isn't an isolated case. Many will be familiar with the true story of Dr. Jeffrey Wigand, made famous in the 1999 film, *The Insider*. Wigand was a former VP for research with the giant tobacco company Brown & Williamson. Wigand became a famous whistle-blower by telling his story to Mike Wallace of CBS's "60 Minutes." Wigand revealed that Big Tobacco knew about the addictive powers of nicotine, despite testimony to the contrary by tobacco company executives. The film documents how Brown & Williamson attempted to silence Wigand, now working as a high school science teacher, through intimidation, death threats, lawsuits, and a smear campaign. *Vanity Fair* described it as "a multi-million-dollar campaign to destroy him." And of course, it shows how CBS was influenced by its own corporate interests, in initially refusing to run the Wigand interview, because it could have jeopardized a potential merger. In this, CBS producer Lowell Bergman became a whistleblower at "60 Minutes," in his own right.[64]

Since this all happened in the 1990s, and was first written about in 1996, it's not news. Big Tobacco, as John Grisham indicated in his novel *The Runaway Jury*, also published that year, is guilty of high crimes as well as mere misdemeanors. But what we *are* finding out about more recently is the culpability of Big Pharma, about whom no-one has, as yet, made a blockbuster thriller, although there are a number of documentaries and books.[65] Perhaps it's just that the case against the tobacco companies is so clear-cut, whereas, as we will see, Big Pharma continues to be able to muddy the waters of popular opinion. We'll just explore a few case studies, on the topic of medical whistleblowers, to demonstrate how Big Pharma and Big Education are in cahoots when it comes to medical research.

Nancy Olivieri

Today, at least on the surface, Dr. Nancy Olivieri of the University of Toronto is a celebrated academic who receives honourary degrees from universities and is feted as a champion of academic freedom. But things didn't always look so bright for her, especially—as for Jeffrey Wigand—back in the mid-nineties. Professor Arthur Schafer, Director of the Centre for Professional and Applied Ethics at the University of Manitoba, has called the Olivieri case "the greatest academic scandal of our era."[66]

Dr. Olivieri was employed by the University of Toronto and Sick Children's Hospital, which are affiliated. In 1993 she was conducting research supported by the Toronto drug company Apotex. At the time, the University of Toronto was in the process of negotiating a donation of from $20-30 million from Apotex, for a new medical building. Olivieri headed the hospital's treatment program for patients with sickle cell disease and thalassemia. She is a full professor at the University of Toronto, with more than $1 million in research funds from the Medical Research Council of Canada, the National Institute of Health, and elsewhere. Apotex, meanwhile, is one of Canada's leading producers of generic drugs. Its owner, Barry Sherman, has a reputation as a successful entrepreneur and he also heads one of Canada's ten biggest private charitable bodies, the Apotex Foundation.

Apotex was primarily a generic drug producer, but wanted to get into the discovery of new drugs. In 1993, Apotex began sponsoring Olivieri's clinical trials of Deferiprone, which would be their first new drug. In 1995, Olivieri published a favorable report in the *New England Journal of Medicine*. But within months of that report, Olivieri began to worry. She thought there "had been an increase in hepatic iron in some patients taking the new pill. In them, the drug seemed to become ineffective after prolonged use. A rise in iron puts thalassemia patients at risk of early death."[67]

When these findings first began to emerge, Olivieri wanted to tell the Research Ethics Board at the hospital, but Apotex objected. "We took a look at the data and we said we're sorry...we disagree," a researcher with the hospital explained in an interview.[68]

But Olivieri did go to the ethics board, which suggested a revised consent form be developed for the clinical trial. Instead, the company stopped the hospital trial and removed Olivieri as head of the European trials for the drug. Olivieri informed her Research Ethics Board, her patients, and the federal regulatory bodies. She also published her new findings in the *New England Journal of Medicine*. Olivieri hired a lawyer and then alerted Health Canada and the U.S. Food and Drug Administration about her concerns.

In response, Apotex Inc. threatened her with legal action, and sued her for $20 million in 2000, because her contract contained a confidentiality clause. Dr. Olivieri appealed to the hospital and the university for help, for legal and professional assistance: they provided neither. The hospital did establish a review process, headed by Arnold Naimark, former President of the University of Manitoba. Dr. Olivieri subsequently refused to cooperate because Naimark had a previous relationship with the drug company, Apotex, and because Naimark was empowered to choose the other members of the review committee, rather than having them independently appointed.

In January 1999, the hospital fired Olivieri as Director of its Haemoglobinopathy program. Of course, Olivieri was a tenured professor of medicine and retained that position. But, there was considerable hardship and negative publicity related to the case, which dragged on for six years. She did receive support from the Canadian Association of University Teachers, with her case. In 2002, Olivieri reached an out-of-court settlement with U of T and the hospital, and although the terms of the agreement are confidential, she says she was vindicated.

According to Dr. Olivieri, what happened to her in terms of a pharmaceutical company interfering with a doctor providing information to patients, has been repeated several times since her case. The broader issue here is one of protecting academic freedom and patient safety, in a milieu where "pharmaceutical companies control 95 percent of clinical trials." Olivieri says the government can fund these clinical trials instead. They can fund an agency which conducts clinical trials independently of drug companies. Even if drug companies supported the research, it would have to be at arm's length, so "there is no connection between a certain trial, a certain company, and a certain outcome."[69]

DRUG MONEY ON CAMPUS

Editorial, *Gazette*, Montreal, PQ: Nov 24, 2002

An ugly six-year battle ended last week when Dr. Nancy Olivieri and four colleagues reached a settlement with the University of Toronto and its affiliated Hospital for Sick Children. The case echoed that of Dr. David Healy and the same university's Centre for Addictions and Mental Health, which also ended in an out-of-court settlement. The two cases serve to remind us that Canada needs meaningful, well-thought out rules on how much control pharmaceutical companies should have over medical research they help to fund.

The out-of-court settlements mean the justice system gave no definitive answers to some important questions. But a number of concerned organizations are working on the issue, and new policy is beginning to take shape.

The two cases, in brief:

• Dr. Olivieri, a hematologist, was conducting trials of the drug deferiprone when she discovered a potential risk to patients with thalassemia, a rare blood disorder. A one-year confidentiality clause in her contract banned her from making any results public, even to trial participants. When she made moves to do so anyway, the drug's maker, Apotex Inc., which was funding the trials, aborted them and threatened legal action. The publication of her findings in the *New England Journal of Medicine* in 1998 brought workplace repercussions for Dr. Olivieri and four fellow researchers.

• Dr. Healy's job offer from the U of T's Centre for Addictions and Mental Health was revoked after he gave a speech linking risks of suicide with the antidepressant Prozac. That drug's maker, Eli Lilly, is a significant financial contributor to the university and the centre.

The terms of both settlements are confidential, but a Canadian Association of University Teachers inquiry into the Olivieri case produced a 500-page report with enough disturbing details to warrant serious concern about the way industry-sponsored research is conducted at universities.

Statistics Canada reports that in 2000, Canadian universities and teaching hospitals received $161 million from industry for medical research and development, most of it from drug companies. This exceeded the total contribution from all provincial governments combined and was more than half the amount received from federal sources.

continued

With government funding dropping, it is unrealistic to expect an absolute separation of academia and industry. But it is imperative for universities to stand their ground and not sacrifice the public interest and the integrity of their institutions.

The primary aim of drug companies, which worldwide invest $40 billion U.S. annually in R&D, is to sell drugs. That can mean that clinical trials that show little or no improvement over existing drugs, or even point to adverse effects, can go unreported; tests can also be designed to produce positive results. This is unacceptable if the public and doctors, not to mention policy- makers, are to have any faith in this research, which directs everything from the treatment we receive at our local doctor's office to the government's health-care priorities. Too often, clinical trials become vehicles for drug approval rather than tools for genuine scientific inquiry.

Universities should be left to oversee their contractual relationships through their own research ethics boards, which must be vigilant in vetting contracts. But universities across Canada should agree—perhaps by way of the Association of Universities and Colleges—on basic standards that will not be compromised.

A good place to start would be the ethics guidelines drawn up last year by the editors of 12 leading medical journals—partly in response to the Healy and Olivieri cases. In them, the editors stress the need for researchers' independence in experiment design, access to data and publication of results—the three areas particularly vulnerable to interference from industry sponsors.

Government will also have to get involved if clinical trials that fall outside academia are to be subject to the same rigorous standards—as they should be. Funding and regulatory bodies such as Health Canada and the Canadian Institutes for Health Research can do their part by making funding and drug approval contingent on compliance with scientifically and ethically sound guidelines.

An Association of University Teachers task force is currently conducting a survey of all of Canada's medical schools and teaching hospitals, examining how they conduct their research. It is due to report in a year and a half; at that time, we hope this issue will get the full airing out it desperately needs.

But that wasn't the end of things, as they say. In 2005 a book was published about Olivieri, written by Dr. Miriam Shuchman, who lives in Toronto and teaches in the Department of Psychiatry at the University of Toronto. Shuchman's husband is Dr. Donald Redelmeier, a member of the editorial board of the Canadian Medical Association Journal. The book, *The Drug Trial: Nancy Olivieri and the Science Scandal that Rocked the Hospital for Sick Children*, won the Writers' Trust of Canada's $15,000 Shaughnessy Cohen Prize in 2006, receiving considerable publicity. One reviewer summed up the book's premise as follows: "As Shuchman tells the story, the real scandal is not that a wealthy drug company attempted to suppress negative data but that Olivieri's scientific doubts about Deferiprone are not well-founded."[70]

Another reviewer continues,

> On this account, Nancy Olivieri in all likelihood got the science wrong, and her claims to be a heroine are based not on the science but on a stunning public relations coup that has fooled almost everyone, except a few executives in the Hospital for Sick Kids, whose efforts to put the record straight have been thwarted at every turn.[71]

Reviews of the book were good, and Nancy Olivieri came under harsh criticism in the book and in the press. For example, the *Globe and Mail* reviewer wrote, "Shuchman does an excellent job... All in all, the book is a great cautionary tale." The *Toronto Star* reviewer wrote that,

> Apotex, is not as black as it has been painted; Olivieri's supervisors did not hang her out to dry; and Olivieri herself is presented in the book as much sinning as sinned against. In fact, almost no one in this tangled tale can claim to have behaved well.[72]

The CanWest Global reviewer, published in the Ottawa *Citizen*, the *Montreal Gazette*, and elsewhere, wrote that "Far from the victim of a conspiracy by the drug company, Olivieri is portrayed as calculating, scheming and quick to turn on any colleague who held an opposing view on her research."[73]

So, the media have muddied the waters. Now there are two sides to the story, and Olivieri has fallen from her saintly status. "She says—she says," so to speak. Cat fight. More backlash against the brave whistleblower. But wherein lies the truth? And is there any such thing? Well, one can turn to the scientific community for answers, which of course the media are not wont to do.

I looked at two academic reviews of the book, published in bioethics journals by knowledgeable and reputable academics. These both provided scathing indictments of Shuchman's book, which should be sufficient to thoroughly embarrass the Cohen Book Award committee members, and have them retract Shuchman's award. One review pointed out that, "The veritable cornucopia of discredit which Shuchman heaps on Nancy Olivieri is, I'm sorry to say, standard punishment for those who have the temerity to challenge powerful vested interests." He continued,

> To persuade us that Olivieri got the science disastrously wrong, which is the main thesis of her book, Shuchman quotes a large number of Apotex-funded scientists, who claim that deferiprone is safe and effective. However, Shuchman omits to inform readers of her book that the published results upon which she relies have been criticized in the scientific literature… Reading *The Drug Trial* I was repeatedly struck by how often Shuchman's account of events is contradicted by the findings of a series of independent inquiries—all public documents, all easily obtainable.[74]

Shuchman's book, for whatever reason, the reviewer writes, "attempts to demonstrate that Olivieri is a bad scientist, a bad doctor and a bad person to boot." Perhaps because of this focus, the book missed the whole point of the controversy, according to this professor. "Put quite simply: patient safety is a value which trumps all others. Olivieri fulfilled her duty to warn her patients of possible risks. She did so in the face of company threats and hospital harassment. For this she is rightly honoured," the review notes.

This reviewer pointed out that Olivieri's principled stand and the resulting scandal, "led universities to offer researchers some protection against illegitimate drug company pressure." In addition, medical journals "changed their publication rules," while research hospitals "changed their policies." Olivieri became "an international icon."[75]

The second academic review comes to similar conclusions. The author implies that this is a hatchet job, a personal attack with ulterior political or personal, or possibly economic motivations. He writes, Olivieri is caught in a double bind, "criticized for not recognizing the hazards that others suspected before she used the drug and criticized for her later conviction there were hazards when others were less certain."[76]

Like the first academic reviewer, he notes that the key issue here is whether, faced with ambiguous clinical trial data, "one should err on the side of the patient or on the side of the corporation that hopes to make money out of future patients." Apotex wanted to delay, resisted warnings and proposed a panel of experts. But, the reviewer notes, "it has always been possible to convene panels of experts who will come up with other explanations for inconvenient data, and will dismiss safety concerns as premature." In conclusion, the reviewer states, "I'd like to know more about the ethics and motives behind an *ad hominem* academic mugging of this sort and what bioethicists plan to do about it."

These two solid academic reviews leave little doubt that Shuchman's award-winning book is no more than a scurrilous personal attack, conveniently emanating from the side of her employer (the University of Toronto), the generous Apotex Foundation, and its wealthy owner Barry Sherman.

Dr. David Healy

Coincidentally, the second academic review of Shuchman's book I relied upon was written by Dr. David Healy, the internationally-renowned psychiatrist and prolific author. His own story bears some similarity to Dr. Olivieri's. Healy is director of the North Wales dept. of psychological medicine, part of the University of Wales College of Medicine, UK. He is known as one of the foremost historians of psychopharmacology. In August, 2000, he was offered a position at the Centre for Addiction and Mental Health, (CAMH), affiliated with the University of Toronto. Dr. Healy had been courted by the centre for more than a year to direct its mood and anxiety disorders program. The offer included a professorship at the U. of T. These positions were to be taken up the following spring.

That November, Dr. Healy gave a lecture at CAMH, which was very well received by the audience, as it was again a few days later at Cornell University in Ithaca, New York, and later at the Centre for National Research in Health, in Paris. The talk also was a synopsis of *The Creation of Psychopharmacology*, subsequently published by Harvard University Press. The lecture was a review of the history of psychiatric drugs. He reviewed the material on the SSRIs or Selective Seratonin Re-uptake Inhibitors. The best known of these is Prozac, the most widely prescribed anti-depressant in the world. Healy also raised some concerns about new anti-psychotic drugs. And, one of his main themes was conflict of interest with drug companies and the increasing challenges faced by doctors in avoiding it. Reportedly, audience evaluations ranked Healy's lecture as the best given at the symposium that day.

Part of Healy's concern is what the U.S. Federal Drug Administration calls the public health multiplier, which means that "a small hazard distributed among millions of people becomes a big problem."[77] So, for example, if Prozac causes one in a thousand people to commit suicide, that doesn't seem too bad, but if 50 million people are on the drug, that means 50,000 suicides, and you obviously have a problem. In fact, in one study Dr. Healy supervised, two of twenty healthy volunteer patients became suicidal, during a clinical trial involving SSRIs. Healy argues that SSRIs are suitable for some patients but in fact can be very harmful for others.

In the evening following his lecture, Dr. Healy met with his future boss, Dr. David Goldbloom, physician-in-chief at CAMH. Healy told the CBC:

> When I met Dr. Goldbloom that evening after the lecture, my guts told me that there was a much more serious problem than my head said that there could be. I saw a man who was more worked up than I've seen almost anyone else before ever. He seemed to me to be at risk of a stroke he was so worked up. It's an extraordinary switch to have happened just during the course of a few hours.[78]

This was on November 30th. By December 7th, Dr. Goldbloom emailed Dr. Healy, telling him the job offer had been withdrawn. Goldbloom wrote,

> [W]e believe that it is not a good fit between you and the role as leader of an academic program... This view was solidified by your recent appearance at the Centre in the context of an academic lecture. While you are held in high regard as a scholar of the history of modern psychiatry, we do not feel your approach is compatible with the goals for development of the academic and clinical resource that we have.[79]

Goldbloom refused to be interviewed, but CAMH CEO Paul Garfinkle later said that the problem was, "the extreme nature" of Dr. Healy's views, who was making "extraordinary extrapolations." Garfinkle said, "If he says that these medications cause suicide, our view of this is that this isn't about Prozac. This is about sweeping statements based on inadequate science."

Healy seems to think something else was going on. He says there was nothing in his lecture that day that he hadn't already published in his previous book, *The Anti-Depressant Era,* or said in previous speeches. He told CBC TV's "The National,"

> Well I can't see that there's anything in the actual lecture per se that would cause them to bite the contract. They had heard all of the stuff before. Other audiences have heard exactly the same lecture and the response has been extremely enthusiastic. It has not been hostile in any way at all.[80]

James Turk from the Canadian Association of University Teachers told the CBC, "I think they took away the job because they didn't want someone asking probing questions about the role of pharmaceutical companies in shaping medical research." Well, perhaps that's it. After all, Eli Lilly, the manufacturer of Prozac did donate over $1.5 million to the CAMH in 2000. In *Let them Eat Prozac* Healy presented evidence that Eli Lilly knew in 1986 that patients on Prozac attempted more suicides than patients on different anti-depressants and placebos. Clinical trial results showed that patients on Prozac had a suicide attempt rate of 10 per 1000, but those patients randomized to other anti-depressants had a rate of only 1.5/1000.[81]

But David Healy has also testified as an expert witness in a number of trials where families say drugs have caused people to kill and commit suicide. For example, in June 2001, six months after his Toronto job was rescinded, an American jury agreed with him that Paxil, an SSRI manufactured by GlaxoSmithKline, caused Donald Schell to kill his wife, daughter, granddaughter and himself and awarded the remaining family members $4.2 million (U.S.) in compensation.[82] And, for obvious reasons, Dr. Healy is one of the very few MDs who is willing to testify in such cases. The question is, why would Big Pharma, with all its money, *not* retaliate? As Chomsky would say, this is not conspiracy theory, it's modern capitalism. The big drug companies would see Dr. Healy as a problem to be dealt with, possibly even as some kind of lunatic. Why should he be hired by universities and medical centres reliant on their funding? Why should this type of activity be indirectly condoned?

What about the charges that Dr. Healy is simply a radical, making extreme allegations based on inadequate science? Well, in an unusual development, the medical science community intervened in his case. In September, 2001, 27 experts in the field of neuropsychopharmacology, including two Nobel laureates in medicine, wrote condemning the University of Toronto's decision to withdraw his job offer.[83] According to a news item in the *British Medical Journal,*

In a letter to the university president, an international group of renowned scientists accused the university of violating academic freedom for fear of losing research funds, saying the decision to rescind Dr. Healy's offer "besmirched" the name of the university and "poisoned the reputation" of the centre. It called the affair "an affront to the standards of free speech and academic freedom."[84]

Dr. Healy filed a lawsuit against the University of Toronto in 2001. After the intervention of these academics, and all of the negative publicity, the University needed to make this controversy disappear. The lawsuit was settled out-of-court in May, 2002. As part of the settlement, Dr. Healy was appointed to a visiting professorship at U. of T., for a three-year period.

An interesting post-script to the Healy affair concerns Dr. Charles Nemeroff, once described as "the most powerful man in psychiatry." Nemeroff was Chair of the Dept. of Psychiatry at Atlanta's Emory University, and editor of the influential journal, *Neuropsychopharmacology*. In summer, 2000, Healy had a run-in with Nemeroff at Cambridge University in England, where they had some differing views. According to Healy, Nemeroff, who is closely tied to numerous drug firms,

> ...came up to me in the course of the meeting in what was a very scary meeting between him and me and told me that my career would be destroyed if I kept on showing results like the ones that I'd just shown: that I had no right to bring out hazards of the pills like these.[85]

Nemeroff had re-surfaced at the CAMH Conference in Toronto where Healy gave his 'controversial' talk. Later, some alleged that Nemeroff had influenced what happened to Healy's U. of T. appointment. Nemeroff did make derogatory comments about Healy, in public.

In July, 2006, the *Wall Street Journal* ran a story disclosing that Dr. Charles Nemeroff wrote a favourable review for a new device for treating depression, without disclosing his financial ties to the device's maker, Cyberonics Inc., of Houston. The next month, Nemeroff resigned as editor of the journal *Neuropsychopharmacology*, because of adverse publicity.[86] A similar controversy arose in 2003, when Nemeroff was reprimanded for conflict-of-interest in not disclosing about $1 million (U.S.) in shares he held in a company producing a drug he promoted in a journal article, referring to "impressive studies" with Mifepristone, and indicating that it "is very effective in the treatment of psychotic depression." Nemeroff also promoted a device for which he held the patent, without disclosing this.[87]

In January 2007, secret emails revealed that GlaxoSmithKline (GSK), the UK's biggest drug company, distorted trial results of an anti-depressant, covering up a link with suicide in teenagers. BBC One's "Panorama," an investigative program, revealed that GSK tried to show that Seroxat worked for depressed children despite failed clinical trials.[88] It looks like David Healy was right.

Government Whistleblowers

Not only has academia been corrupted by Big Pharma, but so too have supposedly independent government agencies which review, test and approve drugs in the public interest: such as Health Canada. In July, 2004, three Health Canada scientists: Drs. Shiv Chopra, Margaret Haydon and Gerard Lambert, were fired for insubordination on the same day. The researchers were fired a few months after federal legislation to protect whistleblowers died on the order paper with the previous, 2003 federal election.

The scientists, from the government office that tests new drugs used on animals raised for food, said publicly they were being pressured to approve drugs despite human safety concerns. In the late 1990s, they publicly opposed bovine growth hormone, a Monsanto product that enhances milk production in cows. Two of the scientists who complained about pressure to approve the hormone, Dr. Haydon and Dr. Chopra, were reprimanded by Health Canada for going public with their concerns on national television. A Federal Court judge later overturned the reprimand. Their criticism led to a Senate inquiry and a decision not to approve the drug.

Chopra and Haydon warned in 2003 that measures to prevent mad cow disease were inadequate, that too little was being done by the food industry and its regulators in the Canadian Food Inspection Agency to prevent remains of dead cattle being used as feed for other cows. Subsequently a case of the disease was identified in Alberta, with disastrous results for the beef industry. The three veterinarians were part of a group of four scientists in Health Canada's veterinary drugs directorate who wrote directly to then-health minister Anne McLellan in May, 2003, urging a total ban on animal feeds containing rendered materials of other animals. The fourth scientist, Dr. Cris Basudde, died in December, 2003, while on sick leave.[89]

Health Canada initiated numerous disciplinary proceedings against the scientists, who in turn filed grievances in a complicated tangle of cases, most of which they won. The substance of the issue was the ability of the powerful food and pharmaceutical lobbies to pressure Ottawa to bypass scientific concerns about the introduction of suspected cancer-causing hormones and the excessive use of antibiotics in animals. "The pharmaceutical companies openly for years kept on going to the Privy Council (and saying) that there are problems within veterinary drugs at Health Canada; they have backlogs of drugs that are not being passed. When we ask (the drug companies) for data, they don't produce any," Chopra said.[90]

In 1998 the standing Senate Committee on Agriculture and Forestry promised Health Canada scientists that in exchange for testimony on the safety of Canada's food, their jobs would not be jeopardized. "They told us, 'anytime, if anything happens to you, come to us'," said Chopra.[91]

According to reports, the story the scientists told to the Senate was incredible. Stolen scientific files, critical data gone missing, an alleged bribe by a giant multinational drug company, all intended to pressure the scientists into approving bovine growth hormone. Dr. Haydon told the senators that, "officials from Monsanto offered her department one million dollars in research funding in 1990—an offer she interpreted as an attempted bribe to obtain approval of growth hormone." Haydon also testified that her files on BGH had gone missing from her Ottawa office in 1994.[92]

More recently, Chopra and Lambert complained when the department approved a new method of use for the antibiotic Tylosin, marketed by the Canadian animal health division of Eli Lilly and Co., despite their concerns that it could lead to antibiotic-resistant bacteria.

One editorial commented:

Reporters who have worked with federal access to information legislation know full well that the department charged with protecting Canadians' health regularly seems to view the need to protect corporations' commercial information as paramount. It is, without a doubt, a federal department where the letter of the law is far more important than the spirit of legislation, and one where the health of Canadians seems to lag behind the imperatives of protocol and process.[93]

Drs. Chopra and Haydon are mentioned in the compelling 2005 documentary film, *The Corporation*, which contains a segment about two former Florida Fox news investigative reporters, Steve Wilson and Jane Akre, fired in 1998 over a TV news item they tried to air about Monsanto's (now Solutia Inc.) bovine growth hormone.[94] The news item, which never aired, relied on research from Dr. Chopra and Dr. Haydon that claimed a bovine growth hormone approved by the U.S. FDA may cause cancer. That same year, both scientists were reprimanded for repeating their concerns about the controversial bovine growth hormone, rBST, on CTV's "Canada AM." They said their warnings were being ignored and they had been punished by the department. Two years later, a Federal Court ruled Dr. Chopra and Dr. Haydon were justified in going to the media and should not have been reprimanded because they "were bringing up a legitimate health and safety concern."[95]

In 2000, Dr. Chopra outlined his concerns to a Senate committee, claiming he was later reprimanded for doing so. At the time, he told the *Ottawa Citizen* that a supervisor told him he could be "sent to a place where you'll never be heard again," and that he and his colleagues were "troublemakers."[96]

In 2005, the Federal Court criticized the federal public services' integrity officer for failing to investigate complaints from Health Canada scientists who said they were under pressure to approve unsafe drugs. The court ordered Edward Keyserlingk to reconsider his investigation of complaints laid by scientists Shiv Chopra, Margaret Haydon, Gerard Lambert and the late Cris Bassude. The verdict could help their campaign for reinstatement.[97]

> "How does this conflict with my interest?" —Joe Staszak (a state senator and tavern owner in Baltimore, on being asked whether a bill he sponsored benefiting taverns constituted a conflict of interest)

Playing The Game

If this is what happens to whistleblowers, what happens to you if you play along with the game? Well, there's Dr. Bruce Pollock. Pollock used to be on the faculty at the University of Pittsburgh, but in 2005, he was appointed to the Sandra A. Rotman Chair in Neuropsychiatry and Head of the Division of Geriatric Psychiatry at the University of Toronto. In 2004, the U.S. Congress was holding hearings on the question of whether GlaxoSmithKline had suppressed studies unfavorable to Paxil, and the New York attorney general had charged GlaxoSmithKline with consumer fraud. (GlaxoSmithKline settled the lawsuit without admitting wrongdoing, but paid a $2.5 million fine.) Dr. Carl Elliot commented on these events in the *Bioethics Forum*.

How To Get a Chair at U. of T.

When the FDA's Psychopharmacologic Drugs Advisory Committee holds its public hearing on December 13 [2006] to consider yet again the possible links between suicide and the SSRI/SNRI antidepressants, one distinguished member of the advisory committee will be Dr. Bruce Pollock. Pollock used to be on the faculty at the University of Pittsburgh, but last year he was appointed to the Sandra A. Rotman Chair in Neuropsychiatry and Head of the Division of Geriatric Psychiatry at the University of Toronto. Pollock is also one of three committee members with extensive financial ties to antidepressant manufacturers.

continued

Pollock will not be allowed to vote, but his expertise was deemed so important by the FDA that his conflicts of interests were waived so that he could be included on the committee. Pollock's name may be familiar to scandal watchers. Two years ago, Congress was holding hearings on the question of whether GlaxoSmithKline had suppressed studies unfavorable to Paxil, and the New York attorney general had charged GlaxoSmithKline with consumer fraud. (GlaxoSmithKline settled the lawsuit without admitting wrongdoing, but paid a $2.5 million fine.)

In December 2004, ABC News aired an investigative report on GlaxoSmithKline titled "Drug Maker Withheld Paxil Study Data: ABC News Uncovers Documents Unknown to Regulators and Many Study Doctors." One of those documents concerned Pollock's work for GlaxoSmithKline. In the late 1990s, worries had emerged that patients might become dependent on the SSRIs. To combat the perception that people who stopped using Paxil might experience withdrawal symptoms—or "discontinuation" symptoms, as they were often called—GlaxoSmithKline (then still known as SmithKline Beecham) hired a public relations agency called Ruder Finn. Ruder Finn drafted letters that they planned to submit to scientific journals and that downplayed the idea that Paxil was associated with discontinuation symptoms. According to internal memos, Pollock was one of four psychiatrists whom they planned to invite to "author" the letters. A letter from Pollock eventually appeared in the *Journal of Clinical Psychiatry*. Although the wording of Pollock's letter was somewhat different from the draft written by Ruder Finn, it made all the same points. It even made them in the same order. But there was no disclosure, no mention of industry funding, no mention of "editorial assistance," and no mention of Ruder Finn. Pollock concluded his letter by saying, "Rather than directing our efforts towards the relatively infrequent, minor and transient discontinuation symptoms associated with SSRI therapy, clinicians may be well advised to focus their energies on the greater issues of efficacy, safety, and patient outcome." The bottom line: concerns about discontinuation symptoms were overblown. Pollock was on the GlaxoSmithKline advisory board at the time, but he told ABC News that he had written the letter to the *Journal of Clinical Psychiatry* himself and had no knowledge of the draft letter prepared by the PR firm with his name on it. He did admit, however, that he "could imagine a scenario where a representative from the makers of Paxil said, 'Could you make this point?' "

continued

According to ABC News, Pollock's letter later appeared in an internal business plan guide prepared for GlaxoSmithKline sales reps. It cited Pollock's letter as "an effective tool for addressing discontinuation." Writing about the Paxil fraud case last year in the Hastings Center Report, Leemon McHenry described today's pharmaceutical company marketing strategy as "defending the molecule." Rather than drawing conclusions from the evidence, wrote McHenry, the strategy is to select the data that promote the drugs, ignore the unfavorable data, pay a prominent academic to sign onto ghostwritten articles about the positive data, and publish the ghostwritten article in the best journals. Then you complete the circle by citing the ghostwritten articles in your marketing literature. Actually, McHenry left out one crucial part of the circle. If you are the person who signs the ghosted article, you just may get a seat on an FDA advisory committee and a named chair at the University of Toronto.[98]

Getting The Laws They Need

The big drug companies don't just work around and against the laws: they *actually make them*. Billions of dollars in profits means they can afford to hire political lobbyists, who in turn pressure legislators to pass favourable laws. In 2003, the big drug companies employed an army of 675 lobbyists in Washington D.C., more than one for every member of Congress. Coincidentally, in that year the U.S. Congress passed a law which explicitly prohibits Medicare from using its purchasing power to bargain for low prices or discounts, which is done by every other large insurer, including the U.S. Department of Defense.

In 1992 the U.S. Congress passed the Prescription Drug User Fee Act, which allows drug companies to pay a variety of fees to the FDA, to speed up drug approval. This makes the drug industry a major funding resource of the agency which was set up to regulate it. In 1997, the FDA dropped most restrictions on direct-to-consumer advertising of prescription drugs.[99] All these laws help the drug companies.

In June, 2006, the FDA approved a Merck vaccine named Gardasil, for treatment of two kinds of human papilloma virus, or HPV, that cause 70 percent of cervical cancer cases. Some 11,000 women a year in the U.S. are diagnosed with cervical cancer; nearly 4,000 die.

Merck wanted to make sure Gardasil would be as widely used as possible. Even before the FDA approved Gardasil, Merck was lobbying State governments to make the vaccine mandatory for school girls. At the same time, it was making donations to State legislators. For example, California Assemblyman Ed Hernandez introduced a bill mandating the vaccine in California. He also received a $5,000 campaign donation from Merck.[100]

Ghostwriting Or Falsifying Medical Research

"No man but a blockhead ever wrote, except for money."
—Samuel Johnson, 1709–1784

In a recent article in the *Bioethics Forum*, Dr. Kate Jirik asked, "What kind of fraud could possibly involve academic researchers and universities?"[101] The answer, as I noted above, is that Big Pharma "ghostwrites" articles for well-known medical researchers, who put their names on the articles—sometimes without ever seeing the data—in return for payoffs. Ghostwritten articles are by someone working directly or indirectly for a pharmaceutical company. A second person, frequently a well-known academic researcher, is paid for letting their name appear as the author of the article. This conceals the article's origin, and of course is highly unethical. Dr. Jirik writes,

> According to recent studies in *JAMA* and the *British Journal of Psychiatry*, somewhere between 11% and 50% of articles on pharmaceuticals that appear in the major medical journals are thought to be ghostwritten.[102]

The people selling their names are some of the best and brightest because "the pharmaceutical companies want the support of key opinion leaders." Unfortunately, the articles are anything but impartial analyses. According to a study in *JAMA*, "the industry sponsored articles report more favorably on a drug than those done by independent researchers by an 8:1 margin." And yet, the ghostwritten articles appear in more prestigious journals and are more often cited by other researchers.[103]

Dr. Adriane Fugh-Berman was approached in the summer of 2004 by a medical education company, to write a review article on Warfarin, a blood-thinner (and rodent poison!).[104] The article's sponsor was a pharmaceutical company which manufactured neither herbal products nor Warfarin. On August 24, 2004, she was sent a draft article with a title, her name and institution, and suggestions for potential journals. The medical education company asked for a one-week turnaround. The ghostwritten article didn't name any pharmaceuticals manufactured by the drug company sponsoring the article: it just described numerous problems with Warfarin. Coincidentally, the pharmaceutical company had developed a competitor to Warfarin. Dr. Fugh-Berman refused to sign off as author of the paper. Just by chance, a few months later she was asked to peer-review the ghostwritten article when it was submitted to the *Journal of General Internal Medicine* by a different researcher.[105]

> The drug industry has even managed to turn peer-reviewed scientific literature into a sophisticated marketing device. It has long been known that corporate-funded research studies are more likely than impartial studies to favor the products of their corporate sponsor. But only recently has evidence emerged to suggest how many "scientific" studies have actually been ghostwritten by specialized PR firms—"medical communications" agencies—that represent the drug industry. These firms then pay well-known academic researchers to sign on as authors. Often these academic researchers are not even allowed to see the raw data upon which the published studies are based. A recent article in the *British Journal of Psychiatry* examined articles on Pfizer's antidepressant Zoloft (sertraline) whose authorship had been coordinated by the communications agency Current Medical Directions. When checked against the raw data, which had come to light in a lawsuit, it became clear that the studies authored by Current Medical Directions omitted or greatly minimized Zoloft's side effects, including the risk of suicidal acts. Yet these studies outnumbered "traditionally authored" articles, were published in more prestigious journals, and were cited by other researchers at a much higher rate.[106]

In "Ghostly Data," a commentary on a web site, Dr. David Healy lists a number of concrete instances, where it can be certain that some ghost-writing happened.[107] In one of these, Healy was approached by the pharmaceutical company Pierre Fabre, which provided a ghost written Healy article called "Bridging the Gap." Healy writes, "This was subsequently published with the apparent author as Siegfried Kasper."

In 2005, an anonymous MD noted that "Several years ago, editors at the New England Journal of Medicine lamented that they were almost unable to find an expert academic psychiatrist without industry links who could review a clinical trial involving anti-depressants."[108] In June that year, the editor of the *Cleveland Clinical Journal of Medicine* decided to stop publishing articles from private (non-academic) researchers. The editor wrote, "We and others have noted an increase in submissions produced by medical education companies at the behest of pharmaceutical companies, with an academician's name appended as author."

Dr. Betty Dong, a professor of clinical pharmacology at the University of California, was approached by Flint Pharmaceuticals (later acquired by Boots Pharmaceuticals) because she had published a small study in 1988 which suggested that Flint's premium-priced thyroid medication Synthroid might have the upper hand over competing drugs. Anxious for more, Flint gave Dong $250,000 to conduct a trial comparing the drug with three generic competitors. Flint's scientists also helpfully designed the protocols for her research. But when Dong's study concluded that Synthroid was actually no better than the others, Boots reminded the scientist that her contract contained a clause allowing them final say over her right to publish. A seven-year campaign ensued to discredit Dong and to stop her publishing the results. In 1995, she withdrew a paper from the *Journal of the American Medical Association* after being threatened with legal action. That same year Boots was gobbled up by Knoll Pharmaceuticals (a division of the German chemical giant BASF) who then published an 'interpretation' of Dong's data by a doctor in their pay. After further legal wrangles and media exposés, Dong finally managed in 1997 to publish her work. Knoll was promptly sued on behalf of Synthroid users who had paid out an estimated extra $365 million per year for a drug that they had been misled into believing was superior. Knoll settled out of court for $98 million – but seven years of gagging Dong had earned the makers of Synthroid an estimated $2.45 billion.[109]

Obviously, if you have megabucks at your disposal the way Big Pharma does, then you can mount pretty serious public relations campaigns. When problems arise with their drugs or allegations surface, whether from a David Healy, Nancy Olivieri, or Betty Dong, Big Pharma trots out the heavy duty PR artillery. Aside from the usual smear campaign such as that which was unleashed on Dr. Jeffrey Wigand by Big Tobacco, there are a number of methods employed.[110] A special issue of the *New Internationalist* reviewed these, amongst other related matters (see five points below). The fightback strategies are as follows: Denial, Shutdown, Extrication, Purging, and Compensation. In some respects, this differs little from the Crisis Management strategies long propagated by the public relations industry, in crises ranging from the Union Carbide gas leak in Bhopal India, to the Dalkon Shield UID, Dow Corning's leaky silicone breast implants, the cyanide-laced Extra Strength Tylenol incident, the selling of the Gulf War, or the Exxon Valdez oil spill, to name a few.[111] Another aspect of this is the way pharmaceutical companies can muddy the waters of just about any debate, by using their own high-priced academic talent. Virtually any research may be criticized for shortcomings in one fashion or another. This would probably fall under the first stage of reactions: Denial.

How Big Pharma Reacts When a Drug Scandal Breaks
1) Denial: Side-effects and unforeseen deaths are part of the deal when you're pushing drugs. It's when the media and the activists start snooping around that the problems start.
   Fightback strategies
      Deny everything.
      Take the high road. Accuse the media of sensationalism.
      Attack the accuracy of their reporting.

2) Shutdown: As evidence mounts that problems are serious, politicians get in on the act, mouthing off to the media and threatening to call in the regulators.
   Fightback strategies
      Boycott the media and starve the rat pack.
      Claim there's a conspiracy—rival companies, lefty journos and other vested interests are out to get you.

3) Extrication: What a pain! Here come the regulators, poking and prying.
   Fightback strategy
      Call in the high-priced lawyers to search for an escape route.

4) Purging: Things are getting a bit too hot – there are stiffs all around and the threat of 'incontrovertible evidence' looms. The regulators are recalling the drug.
   Fightback strategies
      Find a fall guy—preferably some old fogey in R&D who oversees trials and tests and is about to retire anyway.
      Pay them to take the rap and then say it was all their fault.

5) Compensation: With the fall guy behind bars, the company escapes un-scathed and it's back to business as usual. Except for those pesky victims' families and their lawsuits.

Fightback strategy

> Settle— offer big bucks as compensation, but only if they agree there was no malpractice. Now everything's running smoothly again, put it down to experience and move on—there's money to be made.[112]

The Media Role

Obviously, public relations and crisis management, as with sales generally, have a lot to do with the media. The news media are instrumental as a means of delivering audiences to advertisers, for example. They also cooperate in the marketing blitzes, and their uncritical—indeed promotional—coverage of new drugs is virtually another form of advertising. One extensive study of newspaper reporting, for example, found 68 percent of articles examined mentioned a drug's benefits but made no mention of possible harm or side effects. No articles failed to mention a drug's benefits. Overall, there were five times as many benefits as harm, reported. Financial links to pharmaceutical companies were mentioned for only three percent of all non-government, non-industry spokespeople.[113]

Because the drug industry is so predominant in the area of research, and because news media love to report on medical studies, their reporting can amount to a PR arm for the industry. And, because pharma spokespersons are influential MDs, professors and opinion leaders, they warrant positive coverage by news media, by default.

Another way to examine news media coverage is to look at what they leave out. There have been a number of books written in recent years which are critical of Big Pharma: from Lynn Payer's *Disease-Mongers* in the early 90s through to John Abramson's best-seller, *Overdosed America*, in 2005. I put six of these into a computer full text data search of Canadian daily newspapers, to see how many reviews and how much attention they warranted. They ranged from zero articles for *Disease-Mongers*, to six for *Selling Sickness*. There was a total of 14 reviews for the six books, or an average of about two reviews per book. That's amongst 20 newspapers, stretching from Victoria's *Daily Colonist* to the St. John's *Evening Telegram* in Newfoundland. So, another way to look at it is that for each book, there was an average of one book review in every ten news-papers.[114] Here's how they fared:

Selling Sickness (6)

The Truth About Drug Companies (3)

Generation Rx (2)

Prescription Games (2)

Overdosed America (1)

Disease-Mongers (0)

So, criticism of Big Pharma doesn't exactly find a receptive audience in Canadian daily newspapers. Contrast this with the way they received skeptical environmentalist Bjorn Lomborg, discussed in Chapter Two.

If the critical message is missing from the news, what about the drug companies' side of things? Here's an example of another way drug companies respond to the charges against them—by hiring someone to write a column defending them: in this case, Kevin Hassett of the corporate-sponsored American Enterprise Institute.

THE MISGUIDED ASSAULT ON THE U.S. DRUG INDUSTRY

By Kevin Hassett, Bloomberg, Aug. 29, 2005

If you have a disease that has yet to be cured, your best hope is the U.S. pharmaceutical industry.

U.S. drug manufacturers are leading the fight against deadly diseases by designing safer and ever more effective treatments for the world's leading killers. Between 1998 and 2002, U.S. firms introduced more new drugs than all of Europe combined.

If trial lawyers and politicians have their way, though, your hopes will be dashed with the flick of a pen or the rap of a gavel. The U.S. drug industry is under unprecedented assault.

The $253 million verdict against Merck & Co. on Aug. 19 is the first strike by the trial lawyers in what is likely to be a long war against the embattled Vioxx maker. After the verdict, Credit Suisse First Boston analyst Catherine Arnold raised her estimate of Merck's liability to $10 billion, based on the assumption that 48,000 Americans would sue.

continued

The bad news about Vioxx, which Merck withdrew from the market in September, has crushed the company's stock; it's down almost 40 percent in the past year. Pharmaceuticals in general have been hit hard, with the Standard and Poor's 500 Pharmaceuticals Index down more than 8 percent in the same period.

Two Flanks

While litigation is spinning out of control on one flank, politicians are mobilizing on another. At the federal level, two bills are making their way through Congress that would allow U.S. consumers to import drugs from abroad, effectively eliminating the ability of firms to set prices in the most important market on earth. Since foreign governments often dictate low prices to U.S. firms, reimportation is akin to allowing the French government to set prices in the U.S.

The importation fight has been launched because, it seems, U.S. drug companies make too much money. Barry Piatt, a spokesman for Democratic Senator Byron Dorgan of North Dakota, sponsor of one of the misguided importation bills, recently told the *Los Angeles Times*, "The fact remains they overcharge American consumers for prescriptions to the tune of billions of dollars a year."

One hears a steady drumbeat of such accusations on Capitol Hill. We shouldn't be surprised if juries ignore scientific evidence and hammer companies in an environment like this.

At the state level, the attacks have also begun. Most recently, California announced last week that it was suing drug firms for charging prices that were too high.

How It Works

If the money is so good, why is the drugmakers' stock index down more than 8 percent? The problems stem from the industry's unusual economics.

It costs hundreds of millions of dollars to investigate a new drug, and many potential products fail before they hit the market. Once a company has a successful product, it has a relatively short patent window in which it has exclusive rights to market the drug. During that period, the cost of manufacturing is much lower than the price charged to consumers. Cash flow can be darn impressive. Companies then look like profiteers. But that's only if you ignore all of the hard work of planting (and the failed crops) that went before the harvest.

continued

Politicians promise senior citizens generous drug benefits, but can't deliver on their promises if prices of patented medicines are set in the marketplace.

Why Bother?

So, forgetting their economics, they seek ways to force "greedy" companies to lower prices. "Since their wallets are so fat," the politicians reason, "there is no harm if I take a little away."

Trial lawyers also see the large piles of cash, and dream up clever ways to take their slice of it. Since virtually every drug has some low-probability side effect, and since drugs by definition are taken by sick individuals, it's inevitable that an entrepreneurial attorney can find something to sue over.

Cutting prices through drug reimportation and cutting profits through litigation both discourage future activity. Why would anyone bother to go to the trouble of discovering a new drug if he can't keep the profits? Imagine the outrage if a politician proposed a heavy tax on any profits from a future cancer drug. The reimportation bills and the runaway trial lawyers have the same effect. If we wouldn't accept the tax, we shouldn't accept them either.

Why It Matters

But effects are hard to see in a year or two. They take time to accumulate into real harm. This may not matter to a politician who wants to be elected next year, or a trial lawyer who will retire on his riches, but it should matter to us.

Most of the advances in medicine that have occurred during my lifetime have been the result of new drug discoveries. Without new drugs, progress will slow to a crawl or even stop.

Instead of piling on with populist rhetoric and economically illiterate reimportation bills, Congress should seek ways to shelter firms from excessive litigation. Protections such as those in place to guard against vaccination lawsuits should be extended to all FDA-approved drugs.

After the war on terror, the war against the drug companies may be the single biggest issue in our country today. If the enemies of innovation have their way, many maladies that could have been cured will continue to plague us.

To contact the writer of this column: Kevin Hassett at khassett@aei.org.Kevin Hassett is director of economic policy studies at the American Enterprise Institute. He was chief economic adviser to Republican Senator John McCain of Arizona during the 2000 primaries. The opinions expressed are his own. Last Updated: August 29, 2005 00:01 EDT

The ratings chart below from mediadoctor.ca indicates that the news media get a failing or barely passing grade for articles about new medical drugs and treatments, ranging from 22 percent to 53 percent. The worst offender in this bad lot was the *Times Colonist*, and *Montreal Gazette*, the "best," with bare passing grades, were the *Globe and Mail* and *Ottawa Citizen*. But overall, the differences are small and may well not be statistically or socially significant. No statistical test was reported.[115]

	Article	Count Average Rating
CBC.CA	23	48%
CTV.CA	17	47%
Calgary Herald	10	39%
Edmonton Journal	11	41%
Globe and Mail	31	53%
Medical Post	13	45%
Montreal Gazette	5	36%
National Post	3	45%
Ottawa Citizen	3	52%
Toronto Star	10	49%
Vancouver Sun	10	43%
Victoria Times Colonist	4	22%

If the *Globe and Mail* is indeed at the high end of the reporting, we're really in trouble. The following story, reporting on academic research near Love Canal, New York, indicates that the researchers found "No link between cancer and Pesticide." The *Globe's* editors liked the story so much that they ran a front page paragraph pointing to the story inside. Unfortunately, the *Globe and Mail* has gravely distorted the study's findings. An accurate headline would read, "Breast-feeding reduces risk of cancer from pesticides." Two very different conclusions. The researchers found that breast feeding flushed carcinogens such as DDT and PCBs from women's breasts. Unfortunately, the story was picked up and run in the same way by other newspapers as well.[116] Pay close attention to the sentence in italics in the article.

NO LINK BETWEEN CANCER, PESTICIDE
Breast cancer target of study

By Wallace Immen, *Globe and Mail*, Toronto, ON: Aug 21, 1997. pg. A.12

A new study concludes that there is no direct link between high levels of pesticides or PCBs in the body and breast cancer, but that breast feeding might decrease cancer risk.

In general, women with breast cancer were found to have no higher levels of pesticide compounds or PCBs (polychlorinated biphenyls) than women who do not, Kirsten Moysich of the State University of New York at Buffalo reported yesterday at an environmental meeting in Taiwan.

The study involved women from two counties in western New York who lived near a number of chemical factories as well as several toxic waste dumps, including the infamous Love Canal.

"These results suggest that higher blood levels of organochlorides [such as DDT, Mirex and PCBs] were a risk factor for breast cancer only for women with no history of breast feeding," said Dr. Moysich, a specialist in preventive medicine who was chief of the study team.

Women who had not breast fed had significantly higher levels of DDE, a residue from DDT, in their blood and twice the rate of breast cancers as women of similar age and habits who breast fed.

The study included 154 women with breast cancer and 192 healthy women of similar age and background.

The link between cancer and pesticides was a major issue at last month's World Conference on Breast Cancer held in Kingston, Ont. Speakers at the meeting urged that more research be done, and the findings reported yesterday suggest that it will not be easy getting the answers.

"We're learning it's not how much you're exposed to but how your body responds to it. It appears there is a complex chain of events in how it might affect breast-cancer risk," said John Vena, a specialist at the Buffalo University's environmental-health program who was co-investigator in the study.

Studies on animals have shown that organochlorides can have effects similar to estrogen, the female hormone. Even though they were banned in the 1970s, the substances persist in soil and water for years and get into the body through vegetables, meats or fish that absorb them.

"They are fat-loving substances and they collect in the fatter parts of the body, including breasts," Dr. Vena said.

continued

While the body has processes that break down the substances over a period of weeks or months, some of them remain stored long term in fat. Cancer risk appears to rise only if the body is not efficient at eliminating them.

"The chief mechanism for eliminating them from breast tissue is lactation, which flushes them from the system," Dr. Moysich concluded.

She noted that while the baby is exposed to the substances, the benefits of breast feeding appear to outweigh any potential risks associated with organochlorides.

"But our study, and others, don't show an adverse effect for the general population," Dr. Moysich added in an interview. "It is tempting to blame environmental exposure to potential carcinogens for causing breast cancer. Because there is little to be done about it, it eliminates the responsibility for changing one's lifestyle or habits."

How much effect toxic substances that remain stored in fat have on cancer formation is still a question. A recent study by the U.S. National Cancer Institute indicated that pesticides stored in fat may pose a cancer risk only if they are released from fat during dieting.

Dr. Vena noted that this first part of the Buffalo study found that postmenopausal women who are obese tended to have higher levels of pesticide residues in their blood, and a higher cancer risk.

However, a second part of the study that examined premenopausal women is finding a higher risk of cancer among the thinnest women. That study will not be complete until next year, Dr. Vena said.

The research is being conducted by staff of the Buffalo Department of Social and Preventive Medicine, the Toxicology Research Center and the National Cancer Institute.

Selling Private Medicine

The impact of selling Big Pharma and indiscriminate pill popping is horrid, as we have seen from the impact of these drugs on the lives and deaths of patients. It's painful to read Kim Witczak's account of her husband Tim's suicide after taking Zoloft, for example, without an emotional reaction. When you multiply this problem by the number of drugs and the number of serious side effects and deaths, you have a health care crisis. But there is another way the news media are promoting problems, potentially on an even larger scale, and that is their consistent promotion of privatized health care.

As Linda McQuaig documented in *Shooting the Hippo*, in the early 1990s, manufactured hysteria in the press about government deficits and accumulated debt, credit ratings and the "debt wall" paved the way for drastic cuts to social program spending in Canada. The neoliberals or "business liberals" of the Chrétien Liberal government and finance minister Paul Martin cut health and education transfer payments to the provinces from $17.3 billion in 1995, to $12.9 billion in 1996, and then $10.3 billion in 1997—a 40 percent cut in two years. Murray Dobbin notes, "Mulroney had cut Ottawa's contribution to health, education and welfare programs from 20 percent to 15 percent of provincial spending in nine years; Martin would cut it to nine percent in four years."[117]

These deliberate and unnecessary actions manufactured a crisis in Canada's health care system, which was the best health system in the world. It's still a very good system, especially compared to its American counterpart, but problems related to MD shortages, and long waits for surgery and emergency room treatment have been greatly exacerbated. And why not? The 1996 cuts alone meant that Quebec, for example, lost $1.1 billion, *equivalent to half of its payments for all MD's services*.[118]

I have intentionally called this a manufactured crisis, for two reasons. First of all, the cuts were unnecessary, as McQuaig and a host of economists have pointed out. The ballooning debt was the result of interest payments related to the Bank of Canada's obsession with inflation, rather than social program spending. Secondly, the Chrétien/Martin Liberal governments fatally undermined the "most important core principle of Canadian social democracy," the philosophy of universality, the principle that everyone, regardless of income would receive key public services, paid for through progressive taxation.[119] I'll return to this topic momentarily, but first, a comparative analysis.

The Canadian single-provider health care system is still demonstrably more cost efficient and effective than its American counterpart, as we will see. On a per capita basis, the Canadian system costs 48 percent less, with 100 percent coverage. In the U.S., approximately 47 million people, perhaps one in six people, are without health care insurance, although they pay 91 percent more for their system. The U.S. system is based on the ability to pay, rather than need, and Canada's system compares quite favorably, according to Marcia Angell, a Harvard professor and the former editor of the *New England Journal of Medicine*.[120] All Canada's system requires is a cash infusion, to return it to its former speedy efficiency, while the U.S. system must be totally revamped.

Let's explore the figures. In Canada, health care spending comprised 10.3 percent of Gross Domestic Product in 2006.[121] In the U.S., this was about 55 percent higher, at 16 percent of GDP. U.S. expenditures are higher, both per capita and as a percentage of GDP, than for any other major industrialized country. Despite this, sixteen percent of Americans, or 47 million, lack health care coverage altogether.[122] This is more than the aggregate population of 24 States, plus Washington D.C. One out of three Americans below age 65—85 million people—lacked private or public health insurance for all or part of 2003-2004. Millions more are underinsured, lacking adequate coverage for medical expenses.[123] As of 2003, Canadian per capita spending on health care was $2989 versus $5711 for Americans, a difference of 91 percent.

The U.S. does not have guaranteed universal health care. Most Americans have health insurance which is paid for through their employment, or which they purchase directly from private insurers. There are some publicly funded health care programs for the elderly, disabled, and the poor, and U.S. federal law is supposed to guarantee public access to emergency services regardless of ability to pay. A number of free clinics also provide free or low-cost care for poor, uninsured patients, in non-emergency situations. However, according to Ron Pollack, founding executive director of Families USA, "In 42 states a childless adult can be literally penniless but not fit a 'deserving' category and therefore be ineligible for assistance."[124]

A *New York Times*/CBS poll in January 2006 found that 90 percent of respondents said the U.S. health care system needs fundamental changes or to be completely rebuilt (56 percent and 34 percent, respectively).[125] This finding has been fairly consistent over the past 15 years. However, the Employee Benefit Research Institute's annual Health Confidence Survey has found from 1998 to 2004 that the percent of respondents rating the U.S. health care system as "poor" has doubled from 15 percent to 30 percent.[126]

In the words of Dr. Christopher Murray of the World Health Organization (WHO), "Basically, you die earlier and spend more time disabled if you're an American rather than a member of most other advanced countries."

Well, how well are we doing? Below is the World Health Organization's 2006 comparison of health statistics for Canadians and Americans. The report was published in 2006, but relies on data from 2002-2004.

World Health Organization Statistics

	U.S.	Canada
Total population:	298,213,000	32,268,000
GDP per capita (Intl $, 2004):	39,901	31,389
Life expectancy at birth m/f (years):	75.0/80.0	78.0/83.0
Healthy life expectancy at birth m/f (years, 2002):	67.2/71.3	70.1/74.0
Child mortality m/f (per 1000):	8/7	6/5
Adult mortality m/f (per 1000):	137/81	91/57
Total health expenditure per capita (Intl $, 2003):	5,711	2,989
Total health expenditure as % of GDP (2003):	15.2	9.9

Source: World Health Report, WHO, 2006. Figures are for 2004 unless indicated.

What we see from these statistics is that although Canada has a smaller population and lower gross domestic product, per capita, it leads everywhere else. Life expectancy is three years longer, child mortality is 25 percent lower, adult mortality is 66 percent lower for men, and 70 percent lower for women. Health expenditure per capita in Canada is only 52 percent of what it is in the U.S., and as a percentage of GDP it is only 65 percent of the U.S. proportion in Canada. In short, using these admittedly broad measures, Canada's universal health care system compares quite favourably, despite serious cutbacks in the last ten years or so.

In spite of this, powerful forces in Canada consistently have been pushing hard in the direction of a private health care system similar to that in the U.S. This is ironic given that opinion polls show Americans are in favour of a single-payer, "Canadian style" health care system. So, if the Canadian system is better, why is there this push for privatization? The answer is profits. Although the system of multiple private providers is less efficient and more costly, it is very profitable for the insurers and other corporations involved. Canadian insurance companies want some of these profits, and their chums in government who make the laws want their friends in business to profit greatly, even if it means adopting an inferior system.

In writing this, I don't have the "smoking gun," which might consist of an email from Paul Martin to his (and Chrétien's, Bob Rae's, and Mulroney's) mentor at *Power Corporation*, Paul Desmarais Sr. But, as I pointed out in *Democracy's Oxygen*, the family ties are very close, and it doesn't take a huge stretch of the imagination to think of them sharing thoughts about policy initiatives over dinner. Chrétien's daughter France is married to Paul Desmarais' son Andre; Paul Desmarais Sr. sold Canada Steamship Lines for $195 million to his then-employee Paul Martin, in 1981. Desmarais also hired Brian Mulroney as a lawyer to help settle a strike at his Montreal newspaper, *La Presse*, in 1972. Four years later, Desmarais was Mulroney's biggest backer in the latter's first bid for the leadership of the Progressive Conservative Party. It was Mulroney who started us down the path of the first Free Trade Agreement, and then Chrétien with NAFTA, and in part these agreements have opened up Canada's public enterprise to privatization.[127]

As Peter C. Newman noted, "No businessman in Canadian history has ever had more intimate and more extended influence with Canadian prime ministers than Desmarais."[128]

Multi-billionaire Desmarais' group of companies includes Great West Life Assurance Co., Canada Life Assurance Co., London Life Insurance Co., Great-West Lifeco Inc., Great-West Life & Annuity Assurance Co., London Reinsurance Group, and others, which stand to benefit enormously from privatization of medical care and medical insurance in Canada. Indeed, the Power Financial subsidiary Great-West Life & Annuity Assurance Co. is already a provider of self-funded employee health plans for businesses in the U.S., with 2 million health plan members and 2005 revenues of $3.3 billion (U.S.).

Through Gesca Ltee., and Power Communications, Desmarais has also been a significant news media owner over the decades. In the 1990s, he partnered with Conrad Black in controlling the Southam newspaper chain, the largest in the country. Today, Gesca controls seven daily newspapers in Quebec and Ontario. This media ownership did not harm Desmarais or Black when it came to promoting their shared belief in private enterprise. And it may go some of the way toward explaining the news media's steady criticism of public health care, and advocacy of private health care.

A recent editorial in the *Montreal Gazette* was headed, "Two-tier medicine is here—live with it." Over at the *Globe and Mail*, columnist Jeffrey Simpson wrote, "Canadians are warming to private health-care delivery," while an editorial chastised the provincial government over "Ontario's dismissal of privately provided care." At the *National Post*, William Watson concluded, "Canadians ready to change medicare." On the west coast at the Vancouver *Province*, subscribers could read that, "Private care is a growing field: Public system is over-stressed."[129] The columnists and editorialists representing the news media and the Desmarais' of Corporate Canada, are more than ready for privatization.

NOTES

1. The best resource for environment and health news that I'm aware of is: Rachel's Environment and Health Weekly, at www.rachel.org.

2. Theresa Agovino, "Drug maker Pfizer to cut 10,000," *Toronto Star*, January 23, 2007.

3. Arnold S Relman, Marcia Angell, "A Prescription for Controlling Drug Costs," *Newsweek*, December 6, 2004, p. 74.

4. Carl Elliott, "The Drug Pushers," *Atlantic Monthly*, April, 2006.

5. Amy Barrett, "Pfizer's Funk," *BusinessWeek* online, February 28, 2005.

6. Karen Van Kampen, "Triumph of the Pill: A story of health, wealth and stealth," *National Post Business* Magazine, September, 2002.

7. Van Kampen, "Triumph of the Pill…"

8. Carl Elliott, "The Drug Pushers," *Atlantic Monthly*, April, 2006.

9. Tamar Wilner, "Freemarket Freebies," *New Internationalist*, #362, Nov. 2003.

10. Elliot, "The Drug Pushers."

11. Gregory Zuckerman, "Biovail's tactics on marketing heart medicine focus of probe," *Wall Street Journal*, August 24, 2003.

12. Cited in, Helke Ferrie, "The HRT Scandal," KOS Publishing, Toronto, undated, http://www.kospublishing.com/html/hrt.html.

13. Van Kampen, "Triumph of the Pill…"

14. Martin Foreman, Patents, pills and public health: Can TRIPS deliver? (The Panos Institute 2002). Cited in, Adriane Fugh-Berman, "The Corporate Coauthor," *Journal of General Internal Medicine*, 20(6), June, 2005, 546-548.

15. Marcia Angell, "Excess in the pharmaceutical industry," *Canadian Medical Association Journal*, December 7, 2004.

16. Carl Elliott, "This Is Your Country on Drugs," *New York Times*, December 14, 2004.

17. "Drugs In The Water," *Rachel's Environment and Health Weekly*, #614, September 03, 1998.

18. Kim Witczak, "The Killing of Woody by Big Pharma," statement before the Senate Committee on Health, Education, Labour, and Pensions hearing on Drug User Fees: Enhancing Patient Access and Drug Safety, March 14, 2007. *Psychiatric News*: A chronicle of human rights violations and crimes by the psychiatric industry, http://psychiatricnews.wordpress.com/2007/03/14/the-killing-of-woody-by-big-pharma/.

19. Marcia Angell, "Excess in the pharmaceutical…"

20. Amy Barrett, "Pfizer's Funk," *BusinessWeek* online, February 28, 2005.

21. Alex Berenson, "End of Drug Trial Is a Big Loss for Pfizer," *New York Times*, December 4, 2006.

22. Shaoni Bhattacharya, "Up to 140,000 heart attacks linked to Vioxx," *New Scientist*, January 25, 2005, www.newscientist.com.

23. Cited in Shaoni Bhattacharya, "Up to 140,000."

24. Kris Hundley, "Win-win partnership," *St. Petersburg Times*, February 2, 2007.

25. Peter Jüni, Linda Nartey, Stephan Reichenbach, Rebekka Sterchi, Paul A Dieppe and Matthias Egger, "Risk of cardiovascular events and rofecoxib: cumulative meta-analysis," *Lancet*, 2004; 364:2021-2029.

26. Carl Elliott, "This Is Your Country on Drugs," *New York Times*, December 14, 2004.

27. Canadian Institute for Health Information, statistical information, 2007. The statistical graphs contain actual figures up to and including 2003, with projections for 2004 and 2005, as of January 2007.

28. Judy Gerstel, "Pushing pills down our throats," *Toronto Star*, September 2, 2005.

29. Rita Daly and Karen Palmer, "Side effects; Drugs called statins can lower cholesterol levels, a risk factor for heart disease. But they can also cause serious problems," *Toronto Star*, December 4, 2004.

30. Cf. Lawrence Goodman, "Celebrity pill pushers," *Salon*, July 11, 2002. Lawrence Goodman, "Well, if Kathleen Turner says it works: Celebrities in the pay of the drug companies," *Guardian*, July 23, 2002.

3.1 Ray Moynihan, "The intangible magic of celebrity marketing," *PLoS Med* 1(2): 2004, e42.

32. Lawrence Goodman, "Celebrity pill pushers."

33. Daly and Palmer, "Side effects."

34. Elaine Carey, "Cholesterol drug spending may soar; Guidelines say 27% more patients need statins But few benefits for low-risk patients, study says," *Toronto Star*, April 12, 2005.

35. Lindsey Tanner, "Midday snooze helps the heart: Study," *Toronto Star*, February 12, 2007.

36. Sharon Kirkey, "Cholesterol drugs don't help 'bulk' of takers," *National Post*, Jan. 23, 2007.

37. Alan Cassels, "Selling sickness to the masses," *Toronto Star*, Sep. 21, 2005.

38. Cassels, "Selling sickness."

39. Elaine Carey, "Cholesterol drug spending..."

40. Jacky Law, "It's a medical scandal. The pharmaceutical giants are making billions by persuading us we have illnesses that only their products can cure. This is the real Drug Abuse," *Daily Mail*, April 13, 2006. http://campaignfortruth.com/Eclub/080506/CTM%20 -%20drug%20abuse.htm.

41. Jacky Law, "It's a medical scandal."

42. Ray Moynihan and David Henry, "The fight against disease mongering: Generating knowledge for action, PLoS Med 3(4):e191, April, 2006.

43. Moynihan and Henry, "The fight." See also Ray Moynihan and Allan Cassells, *Selling sickness: How the worlds biggest pharmaceutical companies are turning us all into patients*, Nation Books, New York, 2005, p. 99-118.

44. David Healy, "The latest Mania: selling Bipolar Disorder," *PLoS Med* 3(4): e185.

45. David Healy, "The latest Mania."

46. Helke Ferrie, "The HRT Scandal," http://www.kospublishing.com/html/hrt.html.

47. Lynn Payer, *Disease-Mongers: How Doctors, Drug Companies, and Insurers are Making You Feel Sick*, New York, Wiley & Sons, 1992.

48. See Helke Ferrie, "The HRT Scandal," KOS Publishing, undated, http://www.kospublish ing.com/html/hrt.html; "Conference Updates Hormone Replacement Therapy," *Focus*, a Harvard Medical School Newsletter, November 8, 2002. http://focus.hms.harvard.edu /2002/Nov8_2002/womens_health.html.

49. Nathan Seppa, "Hormone therapy falls out of favor," *Science News Online*, 162:4, www. sciencenews.org.

50. Helke Ferrie, "The HRT Scandal."

51. Helen Branswell, "Study shows HRT of no use," *Windsor Star*, March 18, 2003.

52. Leonore Tiefer, Female Sexual Dysfunction: A Case Study of Disease Mongering and Activist Resistance. *PLoS Med* 3(4): e178, 2006. doi:10.1371/journal.pmed.0030178.

53. Joel Lexchin, "Bigger and better: How Pfizer redefined erectile dysfunction," *PLoS Med*, 3(4): e132, 2006, http://medicine.plosjournals.org/perlserv/?request=get-document &doi=10.1371/journal.pmed.0030132. Lexchin writes, "Pfizer's well-financed campaign was aimed at raising awareness for the problem of ED, while at the same time narrowing the treatment possibilities to just a single option: medication."

54. Tiefer, "Female Sexual Dysfunction."

55. Ibid.

56. Ibid.

57. Relman, A. "Separating continuing medical education from pharmaceutical marketing," *Journal of the American Medical Association*, 2001; 285:2009-12. Cited in Angell, "Excess…".

58. Carl Elliott, "The Drug Pushers," *Atlantic Monthly*, April, 2006. Dr. Elliott is a professor in the Centre for Bioethics at the University of Minnesota.

59. Richard C. Christensen and Michael J. Tueth, "Commentary: Pharmaceutical Companies and Academic Departments of Psychiatry: A Call for Ethics Education," *Academic Psychiatry* 22:135-137, June 1998.

60. Arthur Lazarus, "Commentary: The Role of the Pharmaceutical Industry in Medical Education in Psychiatry," *Academic Psychiatry* 30:40-44, February 2006.

61. Arthur Lazarus, "Commentary."

62. Quoted in, Tamar Wilner, "Freemarket Freebies," *New Internationalist*, #362, Nov. 2003.

63. Carl Elliott, "How Not to Deal With Pharma," *Bioethics Forum*, June 7, 2006.

64. See *The Insider*, a 1999 film starring Al Pacino and Russell Crowe. Also, the article the film was based on: Marie Brenner, "The Man Who Knew Too Much," *Vanity Fair*, May 1996.

65. Cf. Lynn Payer, *Disease-Mongers: How doctors, drug companies and insurers are making you feel sick*, N.Y. Wiley & Sons, 1992; Ray Moynihan and Alan Cassels, *Selling Sickness: How The World's Biggest Pharmaceutical Companies Are Turning Us All Into Patients*, Greystone Books, 2005; Marcia Angell, *The Truth About the Drug Companies: How They Deceive Us and What To Do About It*, Random House, N.Y., 2005; John Abramson, *Overdo$ed America: The Broken Prom-*

ise of American Medicine, HarperCollins, N.Y., 2004; Greg Critser, *Generation Rx: How prescription drugs are altering American lives, minds and bodies*, Houghton-Mifflin, Boston, 2005; Jeffrey Robinson, *Prescription Games*, Simon & Schuster, N.Y., 2001.

66. Quoted in an article in the University of Toronto Faculty Association Newsletter, "Nancy Olivieri and the Scandal at Sick Kids Hospital," February 11, 1999. Some of this account of the case is taken from this newsletter. http://www.utfa.org/newsletters/feb111999/#historic.

67. See Dr. Miriam Shuchman, "Potential for conflicts in drug research," *Toronto Star*, October 27, 1998. pg. 1. Some of the description of these events comes from this article.

68. Dr. Miriam Shuchman, "Potential for conflicts."

69. Quoted in, Laura Stradiotoo, "MD still battling system: Dr. Nancy Olivieri put her patients ahead of a drug company," *Sudbury Star*, October 4, 2005.

70. Dr. David Healy, "Review Article: Miriam Shuchman, *The Drug Trial. Nancy Olivieri and the Science Scandal that Rocked the Hospital for Sick Children*, Random House, Canada, 2005, *Monash Bioethics Review*, Vol. 24:4, October 2005.

71. Arthur Schafer, "Commentary: Science Scandal or Ethics Scandal?" *Bioethics*, Vol. 21:2, 2007, pp 111-115. http://www.umanitoba.ca/centres/ethics/articles/article%2043.pdf.

72. Michael Smith, "Soap opera science; An unflattering portrayal of Nancy Olivieri reopens wounds," *Toronto Star*, May 15, 2005.

73. Aaron Derfel, "Martyr, schemer—something in between?," *Ottawa Citizen*, May 22, 2005.

74. Arthur Schafer, "Commentary: Science Scandal or Ethics Scandal?" *Bioethics*, Vol. 21:2, 2007, pp 111-115.

75. Schafer, "Commentary…"

76. Dr. David Healy, "Review Article: Miriam Shuchman, *The Drug Trial. Nancy Olivieri and the Science Scandal that Rocked the Hospital for Sick Children*, Random House, Canada, 2005, *Monash Bioethics Review*, Vol. 24:4, October 2005.

77. A quote by Dr. David Healy, interviewed by Darrow MacIntyre, on "The National" with Peter Mansbridge, CBC News and Current Affairs, June 12, 2001.

78. CBC News, June 12, 2001.

79. Karen Birmingham, "Dark clouds over Toronto psychiatry research," *Nature Medicine*, News Section, Vol. 7, p. 643, 2001. http://www.nature.com/nm/journal/v7/n6/full/nm0601_643.html#top Karen Birmingham.

80. CBC News, "The National," June 12, 2001.

81. Taken from the entry for David Healy, in Wikipedia, http://en.wikipedia.org/wiki/David_Healy_(psychiatrist).

82. Anne McIlroy, "Prozac scandal 'besmirches' Canadian University," *Guardian*, Sept 10, 2001.

83. McIlroy, "Prozac…"

84. David Spurgeon, "Psychiatrist settles dispute with Toronto University," *British Medical Journal*, May 18, 2002 324(7347):1177 http://www.pubmedcentral.nih.gov/articlerender.fcgi?artid=1174757.

85. CBC TV News, "The National," June 12, 2001.

86. David Armstrong, "Charles Nemeroff Steps Down Over Undisclosed Ties," *Wall Street Journal*, August 28, 2006.

87. Melody Petersen, "Undisclosed Financial Ties Prompt Reproval of Doctor," *New York Times*, August 3, 2003.

88. "Secrets of the drug trials," Panorama, BBC One, January 29, 2007. http://news.bbc.co.uk/2/hi/programmes/panorama/6291773.stm.

89. Bill Curry, "Health Canada fires whistleblowers, Insubordination cited: Three scientists criticized department for failing to protect safety of food chain," *National Post*, July 15, 2004.

90. Paul Weinberg, "Fired Scientists Spoke Out on Drug Approvals," Inter Press Service: August 5, 2004, Toronto, IPS.

91. Ibid.

92. Quoted in Murrary Dobbin, *Paul Martin: CEO For Canada?* James Lorimer & Co. Ltd., Toronto, 2003, p.111.

93. Editorial, "Again, Health Canada Misses the Point," *Toronto Star*, July 22, 2004, Comment Page, Worth Repeating, from an editorial in the St. John's *Telegram*.

94. See Liane Casten, "Journalists, not Activists: Steve Wilson, Jane Akre & Fox News, *In These Times*, July 2005. Http://www.thirdworldtraveler.com/Broadcast_Media/Wilson_Akre_FoxNews.html. Also see www.foxbghsuit.com, and Jeannette Batz, "Hormonal Rage: Monsanto spikes a Florida TV story about its bovine growth hormone. Reporters refused to be cowed," http://www.purefood.org/rBGH/foxBgh.htm.

95. Bill Curry, "Health Canada fires whistleblowers."

96. Ibid.

97. "Court blasts federal investigation into drug complaints," *Edmonton Journal*, May 3, 2005. pg. A.10.

98. Carl Elliott, "Paxil's Ghost," *Bioethics Forum*, December 12, 2006.

99. Carl Elliott, "The Drug Pushers," *Atlantic Monthly*, April, 2006.

100. "On guard against big pharma's lobbying efforts," *Marketplace*, National Public Radio, Monday, March 19, 2007, http://marketplace.publicradio.org/shows/2007/03/19/PM200703195.html.

101. Kate Jirik, "How Great Researchers Get By-lines, Get Paid, and Get Medicine in Trouble," *Bioethics Forum*, December 28, 2006.

102. Kate Jirik, "How Great Researchers."

103. Ibid.

104. Ibid. See also, Adriane Fugh-Berman, "The Corporate Coauthor," *Journal of General Internal Medicine*, June, 2005: 20(6): 546–548.

105. Kate Jirik, "How Great Researchers;" Adriane Fugh-Berman, "The Corporate Co-author."

106. Carl Elliott, "Not-So-Public Relations: How the drug industry is branding itself with bioethics," *Slate,* December 15, 2003. http://www.slate.com/id/2092442/.

107. David Healy, "Ghostly Data," in Let Them Eat Prozac, (web site) http://www.healy prozac.com/GhostlyData/default.htm.

108. Anonymous, "Industry involvement in preparation of articles," *Cleveland Clinical Journal of Medicine,* Vol. 72:6, June, 2005. His/her reference is: Marcia Angell, "Is academic medicine for sale?" *New England Journal of Medicine,* 2000, 342:1516-1518.

109. From, "Health Hazard: Case Studies of Big Pharma's Sharp Practice," *New Internationalist,* No. 362, November 2003. Additional sources: Jeffrey Robinson, *Prescription Games,* Simon & Schuster, N.Y., 2001; Sheldon Rampton and John Stauber, *Trust Us We're Experts,* Tarcher/Putnam, N.Y., 2001.

110. On Wigand, see Marie Brenner, "The Man Who Knew Too Much," *Vanity Fair,* May 1996.

111. See John Staube and Sheldon Rampton, *Toxic Sludge is Good For You!,* Common Courage Press, Monroe, Maine, 1995. Also, The Center For Media and Democracy, www.prwatch.org.

112. From, "Pressure points: how Big Pharma reacts when a drug scandal breaks," *New Internationalist,* #362, November, 2003.

113. Alan Cassels, "Canada's newspapers get failing grade for coverage of new prescription drugs," editorial, Canadian Centre for Policy Alternatives, http://policyalternatives.ca/index.cfm?act=news&call=622&do=article&pA=BB736455; Alan Cassels, Merrilee Atina Hughes, Carol Cole, Barbara Mintzes, Joel Lexchin and James McCormack, "Drugs in the News: How well do Canadian newspapers report the good, the bad and the ugly of new prescription drugs?" The Canadian Centre for Policy Alternatives April, 2003.

114. If the book was merely mentioned in a list, or in passing in an article, I didn't count this: I was looking for book reviews. Cf. Lynn Payer, *Disease-Mongers: How Doctors, Drug Companies and Insurers Are Making You Feel Sick,* N.Y. Wiley & Sons, 1992; Ray Moynihan and Alan Cassels, *Selling Sickness: How The World's Biggest Pharmaceutical Companies Are Turning Us All Into Patients,* Greystone Books, 2005; Marcia Angell, *The Truth About the Drug Companies: How They Deceive Us and What To Do About It,* Random House, N.Y., 2005; John Abramson, *Overdosed America: The Broken Promise of American Medicine,* Harper Perennial, N.Y., 2005; Greg Critser, *Generation Rx: How Prescription Drugs Are Altering American Lives, Minds and Bodies,* Houghton-Mifflin, Boston, 2005; Jeffrey Robinson, *Prescription Games,* Simon & Schuster, N.Y., 2001.

115. Mediadoctor.ca is published by the Institute for Media, Policy and Civil Society, a group of academics and clinicians from the University of British Columbia, York University and the University of Victoria. The goal of Media Doctor Canada is to improve Canadian media coverage of new medical drugs and treatments.

116. Cf. "Study finds no link between cancer, pesticides," *Kingston Whig–Standard,* August 21, 1997.

117. See Linda McQuaig, *Shooting The Hippo: Death by Deficit and Other Canadian Myths,* Viking, Toronto, 1996; Murray Dobbin, *Paul Martin: CEO For Canada?* James Lorimer & Company,

Toronto, 2003; Maude Barlow and Bruce Campbell, *Straight Through the Heart: How the Liberals Abandoned the Just Society and What Canadians Can Do About It,* HarperCollins Canada, Toronto, 1996.

118. Dobbin, *Paul Martin*, p. 77-78.

119. Ibid.

120. Quoted in, "Canadian health care system makes U.S. system look insane: editor," *Canadian Press NewsWire,* Toronto: July 4, 2000.

121. Canadian Institute for Health Information, 2007. Total expenditures in 2006 were $148 billion, or $4548 per capita. http://secure.cihi.ca/cihiweb/dispPage.jsp?cw_page=media_05dec2006_e#1.

122. Plunkett Research, Ltd. Industry Statistics, Trends and In-depth Analysis of Top Companies. Health Care Trends. 1) Introduction to the Health Care Industry, Health Expenditures and Services in the U.S.: http://www.plunkettresearch.com/HealthCare/HealthCareTrends/tabid/294/Default.aspx.

123. Holly Sklar, "Time For Health Care For All On Medicare's 40th Anniversary," *ZNet* Daily Commentary, August 13, 2005, www.zmag.org.

124. "Universal health care advocate speaks," The University of Pittsburgh, *University Times*, Vol. 39:5, Oct. 26, 2006. Ron Pollack, founding executive director of Families USA. The Oct. 19, 2006 lecture was part of the Rubash Distinguished Lecture Series, co-sponsored by the School of Law and School of Social Work.

125. The *New York Times*/CBS News Poll of 1,229 adults, conducted January 20-25, 2006.

126. Employee Benefit Research Institute and Mathew Greenwald & Associates, Inc. 1998-2004 Health Confidence Surveys. "Public Attitudes on the U.S. Health Care System: Findings from the Health Confidence Survey" EBRI Issue Brief No. 275. November 2004.

127. See Jim Grieshaber-Otto and Scott Sinclair, *Bad Medicine: Trade treaties, privatization and health care reform in Canada,* The Canadian Centre for Policy Alternatives, Ottawa, 2004.

128. Peter C. Newman, "Epitaph for the two-party state," *Maclean's*, November 1, 1993, p. 14.

129. See editorial, "Two-tier medicine is here—live with it," *Gazette,* February 2, 2007; Jeffrey Simpson, "Canadians are warming to private health-care delivery," *Globe and Mail*, February 21, 2007; William Watson, "Canadians ready to change medicare," *National Post*, March 8, 2007; editorial, Ontario's dismissal of privately provided care, *Globe and Mail,* Mar 19, 2007; "Private care is a growing field: Public system is over-stressed," *Province,* January 14, 2007.

Chapter Four

CANADA JOINS THE IMPERIALISTS

WE CANADIANS HAVE LONG thought of ourselves as international peace-keepers, at least since former Prime Minister Lester Pearson won a Nobel Peace Prize in 1957. Since the Vietnam war, we have taken great delight in ridiculing U.S. foreign policy, with an air of smugness and self-satisfaction. Canadians, who evolved seamlessly from a British colony to an American outpost, seemingly without a breath of independence in between, might be expected to side, reflexively, with other colonies. Imagine our surprise, then, as we find ourselves up to our necks in the service of imperialism.

One must acknowledge that beneath the thin veneer of Canada's social conscience lies the dirty little secret of armament manufacturing: while our soldiers were not officially participating in U.S. invasions since before the Vietnam débâcle, our businesses were profiting handsomely. The veneer began to pull away in earnest, however, with Canadian troop participation in three U.S.-led invasions of the 1990s, in the Persian Gulf, Somalia and the Balkans. But these were primarily tactical supporting roles.

The Thatcher-Reagan-Mulroney years of the 1980s begat free trade agreements which saw Canada hitching its wagon ever more closely behind the American locomotive. As our economies became more closely entwined, we turned over our oil and water reserves to the Americans, and simultaneously began to adapt our foreign policies.

Prime Minister Trudeau's dalliance with Cuba's Fidel Castro in the 1970s became Brian Mulroney's tap dance with Ronald Reagan in the 1980s. The FTA of the 1980s became the NAFTA of the 1990s and the FTAA of 2000. By the time the World Trade Center in New York was struck in 2001, Liberal PM

Jean Chrétien would rashly commit Canada to help defend the U.S. against terrorism, leading to our partnership in the illegal invasion of Afghanistan.

Strong public opposition contributed to Canada's refusal to join the invasion of Iraq in 2003. But successive Canadian governments under Liberals Jean Chrétien and Paul Martin, and then Stephen Harper's Conservatives, have sent troops to join in the occupations of Afghanistan and Haiti. Canadian troops also helped to oust Haiti's former president Jean-Bertrand Aristide, in 2004, while the government supported the repressive and murderous client dictatorship of Gérard LaTortue, a former Miami talk show host.

By February 2006, newly-elected Conservative PM Stephen Harper was glad-handing the Canadian troops in Afghanistan, decked out in military fatigues, mimicking George Bush. Later in 2006, Harper's Minister of Defense Gordon O'Connor explained that the Canadian "mission" in Afghanistan was undertaken to deprive "Osama bin Laden's al Qaeda of its base' following the 9/11 attacks. The Taliban government gave shelter to al Qaeda, forced women to wear burkas and kept them from working outside the home. Finally, he said, Canada's focus in Afghanistan was on 'reconstruction and development."[1]

Media Salute "War: Canadian Style"

The Canadian media have not simply reported O'Connor's stated rationale, but have adopted it as their own from the outset. Afghanistan, as the mainstream media proudly tell us, is 'War: Canadian Style'. That is, when they are not disguising the war by calling it a 'conflict' or a 'mission'. It is the first war with Canadian troops officially involved since Korea.

Mergers and takeovers in media industries over the past twenty years have led to huge conglomerates, with accompanying debt loads and a focus on the bottom line. The penny-pinching of Lord Thomson gave way to the ruthless swindling of Lord Black, who in turn was bought out by the broadcast empire of CanWest Global. Cutting a swath through the ranks of journalists meant closing foreign bureaus and turning increasingly to international wire services for news. Gradually and covertly, then, Canada's news of the world has been increasingly written by the *Associated Press* or the *New York Times* News Service.

Today's mainstream coverage of Afghanistan almost entirely assumes that Canada's war efforts are noble and purely motivated. In this, we have adopted what American media critic Norman Solomon calls "American exceptionalism" or "the belief that unlike other great powers, the United

States is motivated not by the self-interest of some set of elites but by benevolence—which allows policy-makers to sell wars that are designed to extend and deepen U.S. power as a kind of international community service."[2]

On the (visible) "far left wing" of Canadian politics, New Democratic Party leader Jack Layton called in September 2006 for the immediate withdrawal of Canadian troops from Afghanistan, but apparently more because the war was unwinnable than because it was immoral and illegal. Layton wrote in the *Toronto Star* that the mission was "ill-defined, unbalanced" and with "no exit strategy." As Canadian journalist Linda McQuaig wrote recently, in the context of the Iraq war, the problem is not the incompetence of the invading forces. "The real problem is that it is illegal for one country to invade another country." McQuaig's lone voice aside, this perspective is beyond the pale of Canadian journalism, and even Jack Layton's protests were met with scorn by the press. The *Vancouver Sun*, for example, editorialized that when "Layton calls for Canada to pull out of Afghanistan, he is handing victory to these [drug] criminals and the Taliban."[3]

A Close Look at *Toronto Star* Coverage

Just as it is difficult to distinguish Conservative PM Stephen Harper from his American counterpart, decked out in army fatigues, visiting the troops, so too has it been hard to discern a difference between Canadian news media cheerleading for the Afghanistan war effort, and American media support for the invasions of Afghanistan and Iraq. In spring, 2006, while the erstwhile progressive *Toronto Star* had sycophantic columnist Rosie Dimanno abroad, drooling after the troops, I studied their special report news coverage, headlined, "Canada's War." Nowhere to be found was reference to the simple question of *why* Canadian troops were in Afghanistan.

Very briefly, let's return to the events of 2001. Allegedly, a group of terrorist hijackers brought down the World Trade Center's twin towers in New York, resulting in about 2500 deaths. Within two hours, the U.S. Administration identified the culprit as Osama bin Laden. Eventually, it was determined by the U.S. that 15 of the 19 hijackers were from Saudi Arabia, with the others from the United Arab Emirates (2), Lebanon (1), and Egypt (1). However, George W. Bush immediately targeted the Taliban government of Afghanistan, as sheltering bin Laden, and threatened reprisals unless he was turned over immediately. The Taliban, a despotic government, replied quite reasonably according to media reports that it would turn over bin Laden to an international court of law, in exchange for evidence of his involvement in 9/11. Bush responded that this was unreasonable, and as with Kosovo, using NATO as a vehicle, invaded Afghanistan, bombing that country's rubble into even smaller pieces and installing an interim government.[4] According to Noam Chomsky,

> A week after the bombing began, the President reiterated that U.S. forces would attack Afghanistan 'for as long as it takes' to destroy the al Qaeda terrorist network of Osama bin Laden, but he offered to reconsider the military assault on Afghanistan if the country's ruling Taliban would surrender Mr. bin Laden: 'If you cough him up and his people today, then we'll reconsider what we are doing to your country,' the President declared: 'You still have a second chance.'[5]

Ironically, with all its resources the U.S. has been unable to locate bin Laden, proving itself incapable of complying with its own demands on the Taliban, which resulted in the invasion. Instead, the U.S. government turned to its next target, Iraq. Failing to obtain UN sanctions for an invasion of Iraq, the U.S. acted unilaterally, and again illegally, with its "coalition of the willing," including Britain but this time not Canada.

War—Canadian Style

In the horror immediately following 9/11, Jean Chretien's Canadian government offered whatever assistance it could, landing American aircraft at Canadian airports, housing American passengers, and effectively offering to assist in any reprisals. This is how Canada became involved in Afghanistan, and eventually assumed a leadership role in the NATO "mission" there, in 2006.

So, for Canadians, there are serious questions to ask about our involvement there, a fact which is reflected in the very divided public opinion on our involvement.[6] I think the reason why people are skeptical about Afghanistan is that they remember these events which I have described, as they unfolded. Everything I have written here was initially reported in the mainstream media, but the reporters and columnists and editorial writers are not interested in remembering these facts or questioning our involvement in the war, despite these events, which were immediately forgotten. Instead, they've readily adopted the mantra of the U.S. administration, and the Canadian governments, about liberating people and despotic governments, and coming to the aid of Afghani women, who are now reportedly as oppressed as ever. The media have become cheerleaders for an illegal invasion and war. I'll come back to the reasons for this, after reviewing some of the evidence for it.

The first thing to note is that the reasons for the invasion and Canadian troop involvement, are omitted, replaced with a bare bones and meaningless factual account, such as, "the Taliban [was] toppled by the post-9/11 invasion of coalition forces in 2001."[7]

I've chosen to examine some of the coverage of Afghanistan in Canada's largest and most "progressive" daily newspaper, the *Toronto Star*, since it is usually the best of a rather poor lot. The *Star* published a special report, an eight-part series in March, 2006, written by journalist Mitch Potter. The report was during the time when Canada was assuming a more prominent role with the NATO forces in Afghanistan, and while Canadian soldiers were on a mission named, "Operation Peacemaker." The series was captioned, "War—Canadian Style," and beneath this heading on the features page on the web, there was the brief explanation: "Canada's soldiers are fighting a battle in Afghanistan that few of their countrymen yet understand." This seemed to imply that the *Star* intended that its series would help to explain Canada's involvement in Afghanistan to its readers.

'Medieval Religious Dogma'

The first part of the series ("Bringing the War Home: Drugs, Dogma and Insurgents") described how Canadian soldiers in Afghanistan were up against "Drugs and Dogma" which was the headline. We're told the soldiers are well-trained, in readiness for Canada's first real combat mission since the Korean War. They were confronted by a "stone age" civilization, with little more than poppies for opium, and Mosques. Clearly, the implication is these people are in need of some form of intervention. We are told that, "Here, mud-walled homes stand in clustered communities that lack virtually everything one associates with modernity. They have no electricity, no teachers, no doctors, no roads worthy of the name, no means with which to rise from the ashes of a quarter century of conflict."

The article continued, juxtaposing calls to prayer at mosques and the crowing of roosters, (itself offensive) then, unbelievably dismissing Islam as "medieval religious dogma."

What these villages do have are mosques, with calls to prayer five times a day the only sound that carries apart from the crowing of roosters. And…what will become a new poppy harvest…. Drugs and medieval religious dogma, an unholy alliance…is what the Canadians find themselves up against.

Dismissing and de-humanizing the enemy is a common tactic in war propaganda, and a means of justifying massive intervention in their lives. If they are medieval—if not stone aged—then they obviously need our help. As for their condition—mired in "a quarter century of conflict"—it is they who bear the responsibility, in a classic case of blaming the victims, who actually have long been pawns in a war of the superpowers.[8]

The second part in the series ("A Fruitful Meeting"), describes how Canadian soldiers gain grudging acceptance from Kudalan villagers, after making promises about building schools. The troops inform the villagers, "You must understand that these are not Canadian problems, these are Afghanistan's problems. We are only here temporarily to help get your government back on its feet." These military statements are presented by the reporter as factual, and there are no qualifications, contradictions, or alternative perspectives. It is a story about how helpful Canadian soldiers are to the locals, and how it is their role to help the people.

The third part of the series ("The Birthplace of Dust"), describes the hardships suffered by the Canadian troops, living without running water or showers, in all the dust. The perspective on the enemy insurgents is revealing: in his own words the reporter describes how, in an earlier period under U.S. infantry occupation, "The valleys were allowed to fester unchecked with an ever more emboldened insurgency, eager to test the will of the coalition forces." So here, Afghani resistance fighters are compared to infectious bacteria, which "fester unchecked."

Part Four in the series ("LAVs and Luck—the 'Ratpicker' "), is one part advertisement, one part ode-to-technology. It is about the "LAV III" a Canadian-made light armoured troop carrier, a $3.5 million vehicle which we are told can withstand a direct hit from explosives beneath it. The reporter writes, "The LAV's top-mounted 24mm canon is the biggest gun—it fires a supersonic round whose shockwave alone can be fatal within one metre of its target." The effect here is to celebrate superior technology and accomplishments, and again, implicityly, to contrast these with the "stone age" inhabitants of Afghanistan.

Abandoning Neutrality

Part Five of the series ("Fathers and Sons—True Confessions"), is about family traditions, generations of soldiering, which gets into the blood. The story starts with the perspective of a 55 year-old soldier, who describes soldiering as the hardest work, harder even than jack hammering, because when you're finished there's no hot tub or cold beer. We learn that he has a 25-year-old son in the same unit, whose grandfather also fought in World War I. This is about dedication to tradition and to your country. Another soldier says what they have is "not just a peacekeeping army, but a peacemaking army," reflecting the way in which the motto for the military operation has been internalized by the troops.

In part six of the series ("Axe Attack—Backup Arrives—We're Okay"), a Canadian lieutenant sitting in a circle with tribal elders is suddenly attacked by a 16-year-old youth with an axe, who delivers a head blow and then meets swift "justice": "Seconds later [he was] cut down by 14 bullets from three Canadian guns."

For the embedded journalists, this brutal attack led them to openly abandon any principles of objectivity. No questions were asked about the propriety of putting 14 rounds in a teenager with an axe, in fact, these actions are justified by the reporter. That evening, the embedded journalists drew back, out of respect for the soldiers.

> Photographer Rick Madonik and I found a quiet corner far out of earshot as the 1st Platoon closed ranks to make sense of the incomprehensible. They huddled at the firepit, a private murmur of voices whose words will never be known. Eventually, they came to us. And came to realize that, *under the circumstances, their wound was in some way our wound as well.* This is dangerous terrain, we knew. The business of news papering is built upon practiced detachment. But *there was no detachment on this night*, as Trevor Greene lay prone in the hospital at Kandahar Airfield. He was—he is—simply too likeable a man *to now revert back to the neutrality* with which we joined the Red Devils (emphasis added).

So, for the journalists, when a Canadian soldier was attacked and wounded in a war zone, his wounding was theirs as well, grounds for abandoning their "neutrality," and closing ranks.

In part seven ("One Soldier's Week—A Chance to Fight"), one of the soldiers who shot the teenager is interviewed about his thoughts.

> What troubles him is that *killing was the only available option* in those fleeting moments after the axe came down. [Captain] Schamuhn saw the "pure poison hatred" in the young Afghan's eyes. It was *a look that sought death, for his victim, for himself.* And all the Canadians on the ground could do was oblige (emphasis added).

The journalist continues, regarding the Captain.

> The impulse to do more comes naturally to the soft-spoken Schamuhn, who commands his platoon with a maturity and nuance beyond his 26 years. On one hand, the Regina-born commander is a pastor's son, *spiritually committed to the humanitarian mission of changing lives for the better half-a-world away.* Another part of him is a warrior's son, dedicated to the belief that there is no greater honour than leading men into battle and getting everyone out alive.

So, here is a justification not just for this shooting itself, but for the military presence as a whole, seamlessly inserted into the story. The soldier's thoughts, the journalist's thoughts—what we all should think—is quite apparent. But of course, this is all heavily value-laden. First of all, the teenage insurgent's motives are as easily dismissed as his life. He was crazy. Possessed by irrational, "pure, poison hatred." The captain sees "honour" in the soldiers' killing of the teen. The boy wanted death for those around him and for himself. The soldier and the journalist know the intentions of the dead youth. All the Canadian soldiers were doing was obliging him. One wonders, would the Canadian account differ if this was a French teenager, during WWII resistance, axing a German Lieutenant, and being shot by German soldiers? Would Germans merely be obliging such a crazed youth by killing him? We next learn that the soldier is a pastor's son who is "spiritually committed to the humanitarian mission of changing lives for the better half-a world away." And so this, for the soldier, reporter and the *Toronto Star* itself, is what the invasion of Afghanistan is all about: *changing lives for the better.*

The next part of the story dismisses pacifists, those who object to the invasion, as being out of touch with reality. You have to be there, and to fight, to understand the "reality." Then, and only then, will your opinions have some merit.

As a student of military history, the young captain also has something to say about the Canadian tendency to take its peace for
granted. The sheer lack of fighting on our own soil, he says, has damaged the Canadian perception of what really goes on in the world and
fostered a culture of blithe pacifism. It is one thing for someone to
come back from seeing reality in a place like this and to say, 'I'm a
pacifist. I don't want Canada to have an army.' 'I can respect that,
even if I don't agree,' says Schamuhn. 'But if you're born in Canada
and that's all you've ever known, your words mean nothing to me.
Because you haven't seen the other side of the world. You haven't
seen the necessity of conflict. There are people who are fighting
against peace, against stable government. And Canada, whether
they want to know it or not, has a very strong warrior class. I guess
that is what the front-line soldiers really want Canadians to understand. *We want Canadians to get on board*, to realize we are out here and
to allow us to do what we are prepared to do' (emphasis added).

According to this view, the insurgents are irrational, "fighting against peace,
against stable government." Nowhere to be found are the facts: their country
was invaded, illegally, by a foreign occupational force, which deposed the government, bombed the countryside, and is now attempting to quash opposition
and impose a client regime. The message is simple: "We want Canadians to get
on board, support our troops." It's not surprising that this message should
come from the military; what's shocking is that it should come so forcefully
from the news media.

Helping 'Ungrateful Locals'

In the final part of the series ("Frustrations—Back Over the Wire—Small Vic-
tories"), we are told how Canadian soldiers give toys and gifts to the young
children in the area near their encampment, but this ends after the attack on
the lieutenant, for security reasons. "Helping Ungrateful Locals" could be the
title of the series, it is certainly a theme running through it. The soldiers' challenge is fighting insurgents who are merely shadows, "shadows that hide behind a dirt-poor civilian population who must be brought onside if
Afghanistan is to stand whole again." It is a common theme in imperialist propaganda: the ignorant, savage locals who stubbornly refuse help, and in so doing reject a better way of life. This is the story told by the French missionaries
who came to Canada to convert native peoples to Christianity. It is the story

told by American historians about the people of South Vietnam. And this paternalistic, bigoted language has been adopted by Canadian armed forces, and Canadian news media, in Afghanistan. Sergeant Scott Proctor is quoted:

> "We were dealing with fairly educated populations in the past," he said. "You could say to them, 'Come on, you actually know better than this.' And they would say, 'Well, yeah. We do.' That's not the case with Afghanistan, and that's part of what makes this such a big task. But it is doable," he said. "And we're trying to go about it the right way with the support for the new Afghan government. We need to get them used to having a government and to get them to see that their police are actually police and not just another extortionist group. Right now, the people around here don't have anything Canadians would even consider a lifestyle. They live in a mud hut and have a little patch of dirt on which they grow a meagre existence. Right now they probably just want us to leave, along with Taliban and other opposing military forces. But we can't leave until [the Taliban] leave and the government gets up and running."

Finally, the reporter sums up the series and the war effort. Again, we have the image of Afghanis as ignorant, helpless children, battered by (their own) warring factions.

> You may call the Afghan villagers of Gombad and places like it helpless. The lingering paradox now is that they may also be unhelpable —altogether too shredded by successive generations of conflict and decline to accept the hand within reach. It is a question Capt. Schamuhn has been pondering for months, even before he came to Kandahar. He went to his father, the pastor, for answers. "I was struggling with the problem that we can't help everybody. We could be here for the rest of our lives and we still won't be able to solve Afghanistan, it is such a complex and deeply rooted problem," he says. "But my dad's advice was, 'Don't worry about changing the world. Just change individual people's worlds, one at a time." "There will always be war, there will always be bad guys," says Schamuhn. "It is the nature of humanity. But just to smile at the kids as we go through these villages, to see their faces light up, you are touching a life on the other side of the planet. "That's what we have to focus on: the individual victories."

Adopting American Exceptionalism

Saving the world one country at a time. These are the same platitudes used by successive U.S. Administrations and foisted on their citizens and the world over the past century, to justify wholesale slaughter and exploitation. The reporter is explaining away any potential failures: these people may be beyond help, no matter how noble our intentions. It's all about benevolence, helping, educating, liberating, restoring (or introducing) democracy. There is no other way to look at this, other than through the crazed eyes of a teenager with a death wish, or the festering insurgents as a whole.

So, just as Canadian political leaders have adopted the U.S. political economic mantra about "free trade," resulting in exported jobs and manufacturing, so too has the Canadian State adopted the U.S. mantra which portrays empire building as benevolent. It's apparent that the *Toronto Star*, as an effective arm of the Canadian State, is promoting Canadian exceptionalism. This is why John Pilger has called the media, "weapons of war." The series I've examined is little more than public relations puffery, which couldn't have been more effectively written by the armed forces themselves. It is a value-laden narrative which has entirely adopted the army mantras about "peacemaking," and determination to "change lives for the better," no matter how unpopular these changes might be, in the invaded country. For their part, the embedded journalists are "sharing the wounds" suffered by the soldiers and openly abandoning any neutrality which might be called for by (easily discarded) professional standards. Events leading up to the invasion, and all historical context is omitted, such as the 1980s U.S. support for Osama bin Laden and the Mujahadeen in their war against another imperialist aggressor—the Soviet Union. Censoring this information avoids having to ask messy questions such as: if the Soviets were invaders, why aren't we?

One irony in all of this is that a series such as this is quite capable of winning a National Newspaper Award, bestowed by the industry itself. Time will tell.

During Wars, the Media Should Question Everything

Because of the huge stakes, and because truth is the first casualty, in a time of war the news media must be most skeptical, most adversarial: they should accept nothing and question everything. Instead, like their American counterparts, the mainstream Canadian media have adopted the role of stenographers to power, and cheerleaders for the war team. Although this performance has served the establishment well, it is a disservice to the public, the troops, and to the victims in Afghanistan.

Canadian media, like our political leadership, have shamed us. By joining the U.S. Administration in its century-long campaign of privileging empire and profits over human rights and lives, this nexus of politics and propaganda has left us with the blood of innocent victims on our hands. What's more, despite their contention that they are saving the world from terrorism, they have further endangered lives in Canada, by exposing us to retaliatory terrorist attacks.

The Incredible Example of Cuba

Canada has a reputation for having a "kinder, gentler" society than the U.S., with a mixed economy including public as well as private economic initiatives, and where we value "peace, order and good government." Unlike the U.S., with its historical emphasis on "life, liberty and the pursuit of [individual] happiness," Canadians have had a more interventionist economy, which has traditionally meant relatively less disparity between rich and poor, and stronger social programs. When these social programs were at their zenith, in the years of the Trudeau government, there might possibly have been more appreciation for the accomplishments of Cuban society, with its lack of homelessness and poverty, its superior and free health care and education systems, *et cetera*. It may have been possible, within that context, to emphasize these accomplishments. The era of corporate globalization and its free trade agreements, along with the advent of the International Monetary Fund and World Trade Organization, have served to undermine these historic differences, under the successive Liberal/Conservative governments of Brian Mulroney, Jean Chrétien and Paul Martin. Especially under the corporate-like fiscal management of Liberal finance minister Paul Martin, Canada's health care and education systems and budget deficits were pruned in favour of increased corporate profits, budget surpluses, and debt reduction. These developments may be viewed within the broader context of, not only corporate globalization, but Thatcherism and Tony Blair's New Labour in Britain, and Reaganomics and its successors, the Clinton and Bush administrations, in the U.S. As NDP strategist Robin Sears noted,

> The United States is placing inexorable pressure on our freedom of decision-making in immigration, agricultural, maritime, cultural and even fiscal policy. Sometimes, it's an intentional flexing of imperial

muscles; sometimes, as in the case of the presidential dismissiveness to Canadian war deaths, it's just insensitivity to one small ally in a burgeoning empire.[9]

In this neoliberal context, while it is still possible for the Canadian news media to present an alternative perspective to the American take on Cuban government and society, it is increasingly unlikely that they will do so, owing to the triumph of corporatism within the media and internationally.

As we have seen above, with the process of corporate globalization promoted by neoliberalism, Canadian government policies, ruefully, have become increasingly aligned with those of the U.S. Gone are the cool relations between former Prime Minister John Diefenbaker or Pierre Trudeau, and their U.S. counterparts. Like Paul Martin before him, Stephen Harper is bent on closer ties with the U.S. The latter entertained involvement in the U.S. 'Star Wars' Missile Defense project, only ultimately abandoning it, faced with public opposition and his minority government status. Entangled in economic trade deals such as the FTA, NAFTA, and FTAA, Canadian governments now seem reluctant to extract themselves from U.S. foreign policy, global pariah though it is.

Historically, Cuba has perhaps represented the most significant departure in foreign policy between Canada and the U.S. Canada has never recognized the American trade embargo, and has maintained relatively close diplomatic and trade relations with Cuba. In 1996, Canada objected to the Helms-Burton Act, whose provisions penalize Canadian companies and others who invest in Cuba. Provisions in the bill bar executives of foreign companies which invest in Cuba and their families from entering the U.S. Of course, relations have not been consistently warm. Shamefully, Canada did suspend aid to Cuba in 1978, when the latter sent troops to Angola, only resuming aid in 1994.

The Trudeau family made a memorable and highly publicized visit to Cuba in 1976, which reflected the evidently close relationship between Pierre Trudeau and Fidel Castro. Relations were somewhat cooler when Jean Chretien visited for two days in 1998. Indeed, the news about that visit was leaked by the Clinton administration, and the trip was reported to have ruffled American feathers.[10] On the other hand, no American president has visited Cuba since Calvin Coolidge, in 1928. That is, not until May, 2002, when former U.S. president Jimmy Carter undertook his own rapprochement with Cuba.

At a time when U.S. policies toward Cuba may be on a path towards softening, given corporate and congressional pressures and despite George W.

Bush's own hard line stance, Canadian media appear to be calcifying, in keeping with their own shift to the right reflecting the influence of (former) media mogul Conrad Black and the Asper family of CanWest Global.

Here, I assess Canadian media coverage of Carter's 2002 trip, to compare and contrast their perspective with Canadian and U.S. foreign policies.[11] As Hackett *et al.* have indicated, "…a great deal of reputable research suggests that mainstream media tend to amplify official definitions of reality and to marginalize and delegitimize fundamental opposition."[12] Certainly this has been abundantly documented by U.S. researchers such as Noam Chomsky and Ed Herman, supporting their Propaganda Model of media.[13] If this is so, and if —as it appears—Canadian policy is increasingly aligned with the U.S. orbit, then one would expect Canadian media to trumpet a hard-line *American* position, instead of a (traditionally) more pacifist Canadian one.

Trotting Out the Clichés

I reviewed a total of 36 texts that appeared in May, 2002 in the five different major Canadian media outlets (three national newspapers, one weekly magazine and one public broadcaster). Nine of these 36 texts, or one in four, were foreign, drawn from among the *New York Times*, *Associated Press* wire service, and the British *Reuters* wire service. Seven stories were filed from Havana; most of these (4) were carried by the *Toronto Star*. The five Canadian stories from abroad were carried by CBC (2) and Torstar (3), suggesting an undertaking by them of greater expense in order to bring their audiences a Canadian perspective on international issues.

Jimmy Carter's trip to Cuba provided an opportunity for the corporate media to trot out all of their clichés about Cuba and Fidel Castro, and to display their deep-seated ideological biases. These biases centered primarily around the lack of democracy in Cuba, the communist if not totalitarian nature of Castro's dictatorship, and the natural right of the Bush administration to interfere openly in the affairs of Cuba, even to the point of funding and fomenting the overthrow of a government which does not have Bush's approval. Although there was a certain amount of bluster about how the American embargo of Cuba should be ended, the coverage generally portrayed Carter as taking a more *radical* perspective, and to my surprise, overall the media tended to support George Bush's ostensibly more hard-line stance.

Jimmy Carter

Jimmy Carter was portrayed in the press as an elder statesman who wanted to broker the Cuban transition to democracy. His credentials were enumerated, he was described as a human rights advocate, even as "the activist former president," in a Reuters story in the *National Post*. A *Toronto Star* article summed things up this way:

> Carter, 77, is one of the world's most experienced and respected statesmen, spending the past two decades involved in human rights issues, elections and conflict mediation in the world's most troubled spots. Many historians now regard Carter's presidential experience as a progressive time in relations with Cuba. In 1977 Carter lifted travel prohibitions, which were reimposed by Reagan. Carter also negotiated agreements on fishing rights and maritime boundaries and secured Castro's release of 3,600 political prisoners. The two governments opened "interest sections"—a step short of embassies—in each other's capitals for the first time since relations were cut in 1961.[14]

There is another very different perspective on Jimmy Carter, which we will explore. But nonetheless, Carter was treated respectfully by the Cuban people, including by Castro, and by the media in both Cuba and Canada. With regard to the former, this respect was afforded to Carter despite his own strong ideological biases toward, and naïvete about, Cuba. For example, Carter began his speech at the University of Havana by commenting that relations between the two countries are complex, and that we must reject overly simplistic solutions. He said that:

> There are some in Cuba who think the simple answer is for the United States to lift the embargo, and there are some in my country who believe the answer is for your president to step down from power and allow free elections. There is no doubt that the question deserves a more comprehensive assessment.

Hence, it was clear from the outset of Carter's speech that he was not going to call for the embargo to be lifted, without some *quid pro quo*. What's also interesting is his juxtaposition between, and equating of, these two "simple" positions, a) the U.S. lifts its embargo, and b) Castro resigns and allows "free elections." In other words, to Carter it is equally simplistic for Cubans to call for the end of the embargo as it is for Bush to call for Castro's resignation and "free elections," i.e. the complete overhaul of the Cuban constitution and electoral system. Fidel Castro and the Cuban people in general displayed restraint in listening politely to these comments.

As for the Canadian media reaction, well, they thought Carter was fabulous. Paul Knox of the *Globe and Mail*, for example, wrote that: "The former U.S. president won't win any gold stars for his Spanish, but he packed a lot into his 1,400 words. If there were any justice, the [Communist] party would be debating it in study sessions for months."[15] This demeaning and paternalistic perspective displays ignorance about Cuban politics.

Carter went on to say he hoped that as the superpower in the relationship the U.S. Congress would take the first step and end the embargo, but he fully expected the Cubans to reciprocate by taking measures to "democratize" their elections and open their country to free market capitalism. "Democracy is a framework that permits a people to accommodate changing times and correct past mistakes," Carter said, listing some accomplishments in the U.S. In contrast, he lectured,

> Cuba has adopted a socialist government where one political party dominates, and people are not permitted to organize any opposition movements. Your Constitution recognizes freedom of speech and association, but other laws deny these freedoms to those who disagree with the government.

Carter, and the media reporting him, repeatedly take advantage of a technique called *presupposition*, in Critical Discourse Analysis terms, in which their particular perspective is privileged and alternative views are precluded.[16] The "one party domination" presupposition is a case in point. In fact, the Communist Party is prohibited from taking part in elections, under the Cuban constitution.[17] To the Cuban government opposition and "disagreement with the government" does not present a problem: it is those who are actively working in the hire of a foreign power to overthrow the Cuban government whose actions are prohibited and subject to Cuban laws.

The FLQ as Context

To provide some perspective, think about the Canadian government's reaction to the FLQ crisis in October 1970, for example, when the War Measures Act was invoked nationally, in response to two kidnappings and some bombings by a few dozen people in Quebec. British Trade Commissioner James Cross and Quebec Labour Minister Pierre Laporte were kidnapped by two separate groups. Laporte was killed a week later, and eventually Cross was released in return for safe conduct to Cuba for the kidnappers and their families. In the interim, on October 15th, 1970, the federal cabinet invoked the War Measures Act, which gave the police sweeping powers to arrest people and search homes without warrants, and to hold people without charging them for 90 days. Almost overnight, 468 people were arrested, including FLQ members but also many nationalists. About 408 were eventually released without charges. Only ten of those arrested were ever convicted of anything.

Parti Québècois leader René Levesque later commented that: "This was a manipulation of the people of Quebec, and Trudeau behaved like a fascist manipulator." NDP leader Tommy Douglas said:

> We are not prepared to use the preservation of law and order as a smoke screen to destroy the liberties and the freedom of the people of Canada... The government, I submit, is using a sledgehammer to crack a peanut.[18]

For his part, Trudeau responded to his critics as follows:

> [T]here are a lot of bleeding hearts around who just don't like to see people with helmets and guns. All I can say is, go on and bleed, but it is more important to keep law and order in the society than to be worried about weak-kneed people.

In a review article about the FLQ crisis when Trudeau died in 2000, John Gray of the *Globe and Mail* effectively admitted that Tommy Douglas was right, but managed to side with Trudeau anyway. Gray wrote, "Later, it became clear that the FLQ, as an organization, was a laughable threat. It was more than anything else a broad community of young nationalist radicals, sometimes friends, who found each other and made common cause." Obviously, if the FLQ turned out to be "a laughable threat," then imposing the War Measures Act and arresting 468 people for 10 convictions was indeed "using a sledgehammer to crack a peanut," as Douglas had said. And yet, John Gray and others in the media applauded Trudeau for what the *Toronto Star* called, his "steely determination" in the crisis. The *Globe and Mail* sub-head read, "How Trudeau halted the reign of terror/Thirty years later, the clearest image remains/that of a defiant prime minister standing his ground." A *Toronto Star* headline described him as "The Most Memorable Canadian of the 20th Century," in part because of his "steely determination" to "crush the FLQ."[19] Gray's conclusion read:

After the first shock of those extraordinary measures and those extraordinary events, October, 1970, seems to have had remarkably little impact on Canadian public life... It is troubling to shrug off the obvious injustice to more than 400 people, troubling to argue ends over means. But the legacy of that October 30 years ago is the bittersweet recognition that the War Measures Act worked. After seven years of bombs and deaths, there has not been a single resort to violence to achieve political ends since 1970. Perhaps we will never entirely understand the real cost to Canada's political system, but perhaps in the end there was no cost.[20]

So, when a Canadian Prime Minister imposed the draconian War Measures Act over what was later conceded to be "a laughable threat" posed by the FLQ, he is lauded by the Canadian media and celebrated—in part for this—as the "most memorable Canadian," and we are told that "it worked," and there "is no cost." And yet when Cuban president Fidel Castro and his government bring the rule of law to bear on those accused of sedition in their country, Castro and company are roundly condemned. What about Castro's "steely determination?"

Imagine how the Canadian government would react if it were subjected to the concerted campaign by the U.S. government and Miami Cuban-Americans against Cuba over the past 47 years, replete with dozens of documented assassination attempts, bombings, and so forth. Indeed, since Helms-Burton, it is official U.S. policy to overthrow the Cuban government. USAID alone provided $6 million (U.S.) to foster "opposition" in Cuba, in 2003. The U.S. government provided $9 million (U.S.) in 2002.[21] As Castro has put it, "For forty years you try to strangle us. And then you criticize us for the way we breathe."[22]

The Canadian media are seemingly incapable of this simple exercise in logic, and apparently unaware of these historical facts. And they are guilty of hypocrisy, amongst other things. As for democracy in Cuba, there is considerable evidence and quite a cogent argument for the seemingly absurd notion that Cuban democracy is far more advanced, more representative, indeed more "democratic" than the tremendously flawed Canadian or American variants.[23] Although space does not permit extensive elaboration of these matters, perhaps one example will illustrate. Returning once again to the relatively more progressive Trudeau era in Canada, as we did for the War Measures Act, we look at the subject of taxes and controls on wages.

Controlling Wages: The Cuban and Canadian Approaches

In December 1993, still reeling under the impact of the collapse of the Soviet Union, the Cuban Ministry of Finance proposed to the National Assembly a business and personal tax system, including a tax on wages.[24] This proposal was vigorously opposed by the unions, as it had not been previously discussed. As a result, the National Assembly voted to delay a decision pending a national debate. From January to March 1994, more than 80,000 meetings were held, involving more than three million workers (85% of the workforce). The consensus of these meetings was against the proposal for a tax on wages. Consequently, in May 1994 the National Assembly passed a resolution calling for study of a tax on income, "excluding wages." In August 1994 the National Assembly adopted an income tax law on self-employed rather than waged workers, which is still in effect. This example reflects the way in which changes in the Cuban economy involve the "broad and active participation of the population," according to professor Isaac Saney.

By comparison, in the 1974 Canadian federal election campaign Conservative leader Robert Stanfield proposed introducing wage and price controls, as a means of controlling inflation. In response, incumbent Prime Minister Pierre Trudeau ridiculed Stanfield, saying the whole idea was ridiculous. How do you freeze wages, Trudeau asked? "Zap, you're frozen!" Trudeau said, sarcastically, pointing his finger in ridicule. He said, "they didn't work in the U.S., [and] they didn't work in Britain."[25] Trudeau won the election, yet just 15 months later he imposed wage controls, introducing as policy what he'd condemned on the way to winning a federal election. The law was so unpopular that one million workers mobilized for a one-day protest strike on October 14, 1976. Trudeau ignored the protests and kept the freeze intact until the federal Anti-Inflation Act expired in 1978. In 1979, Trudeau lost an election to Conservative leader Joe Clark.

One is left to wonder which approach is more "democratic," and although the blatant public flip-flop by Trudeau's Liberal government is a relatively unusual occurrence, (Brian Mulroney's flip-flop on free trade agreements would be another example), the lack of consultation in policy formulation and implementation is quite typical in Canada.

Continuing with the reporting on Carter's speech, in a bizarre but not atypical reading appropriately entitled "Carter's Cuban Coup," the *Globe and Mail's* Marcus Gee wrote that the thrust of the speech was about the Cuban government's denial of human rights. Of course, Carter did mention this topic, but it was hardly the thrust of a speech which largely concerned restoring relations, which is what the trip was all about. Gee praised Carter for his gentlemanly conduct and for his deft handling of Castro, with his "excuses and evasions," and his "dodges."

> Like the southern gentleman that he is, Mr. Carter was careful to praise Cuba for things he considered praiseworthy—its schools, its health care, its music, its baseball… But the thrust of his speech was Cuba's denial of human rights…Mr. Carter neatly punctured the excuses and evasions that Mr. Castro uses when his dictatorship comes under attack…Mr. Carter was just as deft with another of Mr. Castro's dodges. For years, the Cuban leader has blamed the U.S. trade embargo for his country's poverty… Whether all this plain talk will change things in Cuba is impossible to say. But truth is poison to tyrants, and Mr. Carter's speech may one day be seen as a tipping point in the fall of the Castro regime.[26]

Gee also claimed that "Cubans have never seen anything like it," in terms of a nationally-broadcast speech which contained criticisms of the Cuban government. Well, of course, this is a startling presupposition by Gee, who is not fluent in Spanish and whose commentary was written from Toronto. Even Carter's own speeches and articles undermine the extremely speculative positions advanced by Gee. "Mr. Carter's speech may one day be seen as a tipping point in the fall of the Castro regime," Gee wrote. Gee ended his column with:

> The smiling Mr. Carter struck a tougher deal. 'If you want pictures of me shaking your hand,' he must have said, 'I want my speech broadcast untouched.' Mr. Castro agreed and Cubans got a taste of openness that they will not soon forget.

Note how Gee's initial speculative "he must have said" shifts into an assertive claim of action, "Mr. Castro agreed." For an account of the event from someone who was actually there, let us see what Carter had to say on the matter: "Surprisingly and without my requesting it, the entire text of my speech was broadcast on television and radio and printed in *Granma*, the official newspaper."

Similar presuppositions riddled the reports of others, such as *Globe* reporter Paul Knox, who began his report on Carter's speech as follows: "Cubans are among the best-educated people in Latin America, and among the worst informed. That's why Jimmy Carter's speech in Havana on Tuesday night was such a landmark."[27] Well, how does Knox know the extent to which Cubans are "informed?" A brief conversation with one or two Cubans would disprove this wild allegation. Having personally travelled across Cuba, and having spoken at length to dozens of Cubans, I would venture that they are informed. To be "informed" according to Knox apparently means having views which parrot American propaganda.

In his speech Carter also misrepresented the Cuban constitution, and in so doing promoted the "Varela Project," a petition campaign funded by the U.S. which focused on bringing to Cuba the American style democracy of a Nicaragua or Mexico, Guatamala or El Salvador (see below). Carter went on to chastise the Cubans over human rights, ignoring the deplorable U.S. record in that regard,[28] also ignoring the U.S. naval base at Guantanamo Bay, which Amnesty International has since described as "An icon of lawlessness," and "a human rights scandal,"[29] and where human rights transgressions are extreme, documented, publicized, and admitted,[30] none of which is true about Cuban human rights violations.

In a fairly blatant example of "backgrounding,"[31] in the form of omission, none of the media reports mention that the U.S. is illegally occupying Guantanamo Bay, over the longstanding objections of the Cuban government.

Carter's erstwhile *progressive* and even *leftist* position was that the U.S. should remove the embargo on the understanding that Cuba would respond with "free elections" and go on to negotiate property settlements and all of the outstanding U.S. "grievances" such as the human rights "abuses" inflicted on alleged "dissidents" hired by the U.S. government to overthrow the Cuban government. The difference between Carter's position and Bush's position was that Bush wanted Castro to act first, while Carter said the U.S. should go first as a sign of good faith. The eventual outcome was to be the same: the return of Cuba to the sphere of U.S. influence, in line with the disastrous Batista dictatorship of the 1950s.

George W. Bush

U.S. President George W. Bush was treated with deference by the media. Even when his administration, on the eve of the Carter trip and in the person of U.S. Undersecretary of State for arms control John Bolton, (subsequently Bush's controversial nomination as U.S. ambassador to the U.N.) wildly accused Cuba of engaging in bioterrorism, this was duly reported and treated in a serious fashion. Almost without exception the media failed to label this for the blatant propaganda that it was. Similarly, when Bush announced the results of the White House Cuba Review, headed up by Undersecretary of State for Western Hemisphere affairs, Otto Reich, described by Reuters as "an anti-Castro Cuban American," the media reported the news with alacrity.[32]

The CBC's online coverage was *somewhat* more balanced, describing Bush as "hard-line," for example, in his response to Carter, along with reference to "Cuba's communist regime." The implication is that both sides are entrenched, while Carter represents a progressive viewpoint. But the bulk of the coverage was focused on Bush and his spokesperson Ari Fleischer, who described Castro as a "tyrant," and said trade "only benefits the repressive government" rather than the people of Cuba. Just one line of response was given to the Democratic Senate Majority Leader, representing another side of things. No Cubans were consulted. Carter's criticisms of Cuba were included, but not his criticism of his own country, or any of the rapprochement which took up the bulk of his speech. To be fair of course, this was a story about Bush's response to Carter, so let's take a look at the CBC Online story reporting on Carter's speech.

JIMMY CARTER CRITICIZES CUBA IN UNCENSORED SPEECH
CBC News Online, 14 May 2002

HAVANA, CUBA: Former U.S. president Jimmy Carter delivered an unprecedented and uncensored speech to the Cuban public Tuesday, calling for a referendum on civil rights reforms in the country.

Carter told the public to support the Varela Project, a dissident plan to force a referendum that would ask Cubans if they favour human rights, electoral reform, an amnesty for political prisoners and the right to have a business."

Cuba has adopted a socialist government where one political party dominates, and people are not permitted to organize any opposition movements," Carter said. "Your constitution recognizes freedom of speech and association, but other laws deny these freedoms to those who disagree with the government."

Carter also criticized the United States government, urging Congress to lift a trade embargo imposed on Cuba 40 years ago.

It is time "to change our relationship and the way we think and talk about each other," Carter said. "Because the United States is the most powerful nation, we should take the first step."

continued

Carter spoke of his desire for Cuba to have freedom of travel and trade and "a massive student exchange between our universities."

"I want the people of the United States and Cuba to share more than a love of baseball and wonderful music. I want us to be friends, and to respect each other."

Cuban authorities claim the Varela Project was "imported" from the United States. They insist their political system is better than Western-styled democracy, and guarantees citizens free access to healthcare and education.

Organizers of the Varela Project insist their campaign was organized only by Cubans. They have given the legislature a petition of more than 11,000 signatures, asking for a referendum on civil liberties.

The Varela Project was named after Rev. Felix Varela, a Roman Catholic priest and revered independence hero whose remains are kept in an urn in the University of Havana's Aula Magna, or great hall.

Carter delivered his speech in the same hall.

Noting that Carter had mentioned the Varela Project, the CBC said, "It was the first time many Cubans had heard of a democracy effort in the one-party communist state." Some of the presuppositions are quite questionable: for example, how would the reporter know whether or not most Cubans had heard of the Varela Project? The article stated that "Cuban authorities claim" the Varela Project was "imported" from the U.S., and a response to this claim is provided. It is not leaders, or the government, but "authorities," with its implicit meaning of functionaries, autocrats, or authoritarians. Carter's assertions, on the other hand, are not "claims" but are simply factual: "one party dominates," and "people are not permitted to organize any opposition movements," and "other laws deny these freedoms," *et cetera*. Two sentences were given in response by Cuban authorities, first the "claim" of Varela as imported, above, and secondly "they *insist* their political system is better than Western-style democracy" (emphasis added). The use of "insist" is telling, as it implies that they continue to insist despite evidence to the contrary, or that they stubbornly insist, or they simply insist and fail to offer any evidence or arguments. Here we also find an example of what Chomsky describes as "concision," where the alternative perspective is rendered so brief as to be meaningless.[33] For example, we are given no clue as to what "their political system" is, although we immediately know that when contrasted with "Western-style democracy"—a wonderfully positive term that we hear repeatedly—the Cuban system must fall short. And of course we know from ample exposure that their system is a one-party dictatorship, without real elections, is socialist if not communist, *et cetera*. The Varela Project is given tremendous prominence in this report, although it received just a single mention in one paragraph of Carter's speech. We will discuss this project in detail below.

The CBC online stories were relatively more critical of Bush, for example with a headline stating that "Bush's new Cuba policy [is] just like the old policy." And the report below includes mention of the Florida connection with Jeb Bush and the political basis for Bush's policies. But aside from equating them there is no criticism of the new or old policy, nor of the political pork barrelling. And the bulk of the report simply reiterates Bush's views about Cuban political prisoners, elections, and democracy, and Bush's bald assertion that Cuban elections are all "a fraud and a sham" goes unquestioned. What's more, the blatant fraud and sham of Bush's own election in 2000 is unmentioned, leaving the stone of hypocrisy unturned.

Globe reporter Barrie McKenna began his report on Bush's response to Carter, as follows:

> U.S. President George W. Bush dismissed calls yesterday to soften his hard line on Cuba, calling Cuban leader Fidel Castro a tyrannical prison warden and setting tough new conditions for lifting a 42-year-old U.S. trade embargo. Just a week after former president Jimmy Carter called for an end to the embargo during a historic trip to the Communist island state, Mr. Bush made it clear that his administration isn't about to give an inch while Mr. Castro rules Cuba.

There was no rejoinder to the characterization of Castro as "a tyrannical prison warden," which was factually reported. The phrases "Communist island state" and "while Mr. Castro rules Cuba," are easily insinuated into what is ostensibly a factual news report. What passes for 'the other side' of things was *backgrounded*, in an example of *news framing*, in the final sentences of the report. "Critics on Capitol Hill called the new Cuba policy more of the same bad medicine that has failed to democratize Cuba for four decades," McKenna wrote. So, from the reported Democrats' perspective, the embargo is a failure only because it hasn't succeeded in pressuring Cubans to depose Fidel Castro. (See the embargo section below.)

An AP story in the *Toronto Star* reported Bush's speeches in Washington and to the Miami Cuban community in a straight-laced manner. Bush's "Initiative for a new Cuba" reportedly "set out a list of tough conditions for lifting" the embargo.[34] Bush said Castro must: Allow opposition parties to speak freely and organize; allow independent trade unions; free all political prisoners; allow human rights organizations to visit Cuba to ensure the conditions for free elections are being created; allow outside observers to monitor 2003 elections. Each of these "conditions" is in fact a questionable presupposition which is instrumental to the U.S. administration's propaganda campaign against Cuba. The fact that they are accepted unquestioningly by the media and listed as "conditions" for the removal of the embargo is a remarkable public relations coup, the result of 45 years of relentless and one-dimensional propaganda. This matter will be addressed further in the section on "Democracy" below.

Fidel Castro

Only glimpses, fleeting references are made to Fidel Castro, which may be plugged into the previously-formulated social construction of a man who has been demonized perhaps more than any other for almost half a century. For example, the above description of him as a "prison warden." No evidence or explanation is offered, nor is one required. These are simply truths, spoken by respected leaders and duly reported. They are presuppositions, promoted as taken-for-granted truths, but in reality untrue or at least highly debatable. When Marcus Gee reported on Carter's speech, for example, Castro was mentioned, in passing.

> Jimmy Carter's speech to students at the University of Havana was broadcast live and uncensored, something without precedent in a country where all media is [sic] strictly controlled and no criticism of the Castro regime is allowed. Mr. Carter spoke in Spanish, so everyone who tuned in could understand what he said (including Mr. Castro, who sat silently in the front row). And what he said was devastating.

So, it is "the Castro regime" where there is strict control and no criticism. Castro himself "sat silently," a description which uses *insinuation* to imply disapproval. It's not clear what Gee expected Castro to do during the speech, other than to sit quietly. Dance? Applaud? Stand and cheer? And, was he sitting *quietly* or was he sitting *politely*? How does Gee, who himself was sitting quietly in Toronto, know the difference? CBC news online wrote that: "Castro offered polite applause to the speech on Tuesday night." One is left to infer that Castro's applause was less than enthusiastic: he was merely being "polite." The insinuation is that Castro disapproved, that perhaps he only grudgingly allowed Carter to speak or to be broadcast. In a one-paragraph story, *Maclean's* magazine quoted George W. Bush to the effect that, "Fidel Castro is a dictator." CBC news Online quoted Bush saying, "Trade with Cuba would do nothing more than line the pockets of Castro and his cronies," and simply said, "Fidel Castro came to power in a 1959 revolution." Nothing of the real, U.S.-supported dictatorship beforehand.

The *Globe's* Marcus Gee referred to "the Castro regime," a synonym for dictatorship. Later on, he wrote, "Mr. Carter neatly punctured the excuses and evasions that Mr. Castro uses when his dictatorship comes under attack." Later still he refers to blaming the embargo for economic ills as "another of Mr. Castro's dodges." Later still, Castro is "a tyrant" and again, "a dictator." Gee refers to an earlier occasion,

> When Jean Chrétien visited Mr. Castro in 1998, he used his public appearances to mumble platitudes about Canada-Cuba relations, while Mr. Castro launched a diatribe about U.S. "genocide." The trip was a disaster, handing Mr. Castro a propaganda gift and securing nothing in return.

The quotes around "genocide" are to tell us that the U.S. has not committed any such thing, and that it is a wild allegation, part of a meaningless "diatribe." Others would disagree.

Paul Knox of the *Globe* also referred to "Fidel Castro's regime." He went on to say, "The lone national daily, *Granma,* is an eight-page tabloid that generally runs less than a page of world news and devotes vast acreage to Mr. Castro's pronouncements." This characterization reinforces the notion of a dictatorship, which issues *pronouncements*. Could they not be more accurately described as "speeches" in *Granma*? Knox says Castro "forbids dissent." He continues, "True, the media are starved for resources. But that is Mr. Castro's policy. He himself has a voracious appetite for information; it's of a piece with his penchant for micromanagement." Here, Cuban policies are the personal purview of Castro. His "micromanagement" is legion, a truism, with no need for evidence or example. Knox concludes,

Will Mr. Carter's visit kick off a Cuban perestroika? I doubt it. For Mr. Castro, its principal value lay in embarrassing George W. Bush and strengthening the forces in U.S. politics who believe in a steady improvement of economic ties with Cuba. He might even take some calculated action in the next few days to remind the world and Cubans that he's no Mikhail Gorbachev.

To Knox, Castro is the type who takes "calculated action." Whatever that is, we know it's sinister.

Barrie McKenna of the *Globe* quoted Bush saying Castro is "a tyrannical prison warden," and said Bush "isn't about to give an inch while Castro rules Cuba." McKenna wrote, "In a typically anti-Castro speech at the White House, Mr. Bush accused the Cuban President of being a brutal tyrant 'who turned a beautiful island into a prison.' McKenna went on to quote Bush: "In a career of oppression, Mr. Castro has imported nuclear-armed ballistic missiles, and he has exported his military forces to encourage civil war abroad. He is a dictator who jails and tortures and exiles his political opponents."

Virtually the only favorable context in which Castro was mentioned was in a letter to the editor of the *Globe and Mail* from a writer in Knowlton, Quebec. Here, Castro was favorably compared to his predecessor, Fulgencio Batista. "When U.S. President George W. Bush rants about a free and democratic Cuba, he really means a Cuba that will serve as a Caribbean Las Vegas for U.S. businessmen, as was the case during the reign of Fidel Castro's predecessor, Fulgencio Batista."[35] As usual, leave it to a letter writer to point out what is invisible to the journalist.

In an editorial, the *Toronto Star* slammed Castro in discussing Bush's 100th birthday wish for Cubans, and generalized Bush's views to most Canadians. "U.S. President George Bush wished 11 million Cubans nothing but the best Monday on the 100th anniversary of their independence. His appeal to President Fidel Castro to relax his one-party Communist grip is one that most Canadians can heartily endorse."[36] An AP story in the *Toronto Star* reported on Bush's White House speech about Cuba, and his reference to Castro. "Bush said Castro will have a chance to establish democratic credentials next year when voters elect members of the National Assembly. As a rule, only loyal members of the Communist party are eligible to run."[37] This is untrue, as Cuban elections are open to all citizens, and the Communist Party is prohibited under the constitution from taking part in elections. Membership in the Communist Party and its youth wing comprises just 1.5 million people, or 15 percent of the population.[38]

The article also stated that Castro should ease his "stranglehold" over Cuban economic activity. And, in an editorial headlined, "The old foe in Havana," the *Globe and Mail* referred to Castro as a "(non-elected) ruler," as a "dictator," and in an example of guilt-by-association, as an "old chum" to Saddam Hussein.[39]

These caricatures of Castro do not even pass minimal standards for reasoning and logic. For example, Carter and occasionally the media would admit that Cuba has excellent educational standards, with a high literacy rate, free university, and an educated population, and indeed Cuba trains medical students from around the world, including the United States. On the rare occasion when Castro is granted any prolonged exposure in the North American media, such as Oliver Stone's 2003 documentary film, *El Commandante*, it puts the lie to these many claims about him. Just to use one example, Stone demonstrates how, unannounced, Castro can go into the streets or any setting and he is a) unguarded, and b) greeted like a rock star by the Cuban people. Well, how does that square with the notion of him as a prison warden? What would happen to George W. Bush if he were to wander the streets of New York without body guards?

By listening to Castro at length, any but the most indoctrinated observers may see for themselves that Castro is rational in his defense of Cuban policies. One can rely on that vastly underrated human sense of *intuition* to assess whether Castro is a demon or not. Many will be uncomfortable with this alone, but as one among many means of assessing the Cuban leadership, it is a valuable tool. Of course, Castro could be a skilled pathological liar. So, in addition to using intuition we can examine the Cuban legal system and constitution, observe their regular elections process, study historical and current documents related to Cuban and U.S. policies and actions, i.e. the factual record, interview Cubans, *et cetera*. At least some of those who have done this, such as Professor Isaac Saney, or Arnold August, offer considerable evidence in support of the Cuban perspective, and refuting the American one.

Western-Style 'Democracy'

It's already clear that the media portray the Cuban political system as the antithesis of democracy, contrasting it with what we 'know' to be attainable, i.e. "western-style democracies" which we have in Canada, the U.S., etc. Despite what we have seen, for example, regarding the implementation of wage and price controls in Canada, versus the much more democratic Cuban approach, the notion that Cuba is a dictatorship is always treated as a presupposition, and the Cuban system is never described beyond oblique references to the "one-party state." Well, if we are to be reasonable and not simply react on the basis of dogmatism, the first thing we must ask ourselves is, "just how democratic are we?" We know for example that in the 2000 U.S. presidential election, George W. Bush used the Republican majority on the Supreme Court to steal that election from Democratic candidate Al Gore. It's not just that Gore received more popular votes, he actually won more Electoral College votes, or he would have if the Supreme Court allowed the votes to be formally counted in Florida, instead of simply awarding that State to Bush.[40] How democratic was that? But this was an unusual state of affairs. Normally, it's enough to simply allow things to take their course, whereby large corporations fund two candidates, one from each party, and they duke it out to see who wins. As Noam Chomsky put it, this means Americans have "corporate party one" squaring off against "corporate party two." Michael Lind, senior editor at *Harper's* magazine summed things up as follows: "Because the same economic oligarchy subsidizes almost all of our politicians, our political fights are as inconsequential as TV wrestling."[41] Lest we be too smug as Canadians, although technically there are six or more parties running federally, they are running in an anachronistic two-party system which has helped to ensure that the Liberal Party rules Canada, with brief interruptions by the even more corporate Conservative Party. Since 1960, there has been only one federal Canadian government elected with a majority of the votes cast: the 1984 Mulroney government. In the Province of Ontario, there has not been a true majority government of this sort since 1937.[42] According to former Trudeau Cabinet Minister Jim Fleming, "It's a bit scary. People are so proud to think that we have such a democracy. But relatively few people control the economic levers. They're not bad guys, they're just taking care of their interests," he said. "We're back to the Old Boys' Club."[43]

Numerous observers, from *Globe and Mail* columnist Jeffrey Simpson to Liberal backroom strategist-cum academic Donald Savoie, to the *Toronto Star's* Richard Gwyn or Thomas Walkom, have documented the extreme power vested in the Prime Minister or Premiers' Offices, in Canada, which approaches true dictatorial powers. Gwyn begins by quoting approvingly from the British weekly, the *Spectator*, in 2002:

The *Spectator's* editorial frames the issue pretty well. "We do not live in a democracy at all," it declares. "We live in an oligarchy, the only improvement (over the centuries, that's to say) being that it is now an elective oligarchy." In his contribution to the issue, philosopher Roger Scruton argues that this oligarchy, which once was composed of aristocrats, is now made up of "big business and pressure groups." What is known as "the general will" of the mass of citizens has been made largely irrelevant, politically... On the one hand, therefore, the governments we elect have less and less power. On the other hand, such power as they still possess is effectively exercised, not by MPs, but by corporations (which provide the money to the po- litical parties) and by special interest groups (often, again, repre- senting corporations).[44]

And of course it's not just at the level of federal politics. The *Star's* Tom Walkom described the dictatorial rule by Ontario Premier Ernie Eves, succes- sor to Mike Harris, after Eves was defeated by the Liberals in 2003.

Cabinet was rarely consulted about decisions. Indeed, the inner cab- inet, the powerful planning and priorities board, never met at all after Eves took the helm. "Ernie hated debating things in cabinet," ex- plained one Queen's Park insider. "He preferred making these deci- sions with one or two close advisers over steak at Bigliardi's," a Church St. restaurant. In some cases, ministers found out only through the press that they had agreed to spend millions of dollars on this or that project... "There was at least one case where cabinet had to approve something after he'd announced it," said one cabinet source." And there were others when it had just an hour or two to okay something before the announcement was made." As the elec- tion drew nearer, Eves' tendency to run a one-man show is said to have grown more pronounced. He crisscrossed the province an- nouncing such things as local highway improvements that had never been approved in cabinet and never accounted for in the finance ministry's budget plans.[45]

I have elaborated these points elsewhere and will not repeat all of the argu- ments here.[46] However, the first thing is, it's abundantly clear to even the ca- sual observer that our "western-style democracies" are anything but. What we have, in fact, more closely approximates an oligarchy or plutocracy (rule by the few and the rich, respectively) rather than a democracy. Even the basic requisite for a democracy—majority rule—is seldom attained, as a cursory examination of the popular vote in recent decades demonstrates. Additionally, the unsavory characteristics of "western-style democracies" are the very reason for their rejection by Cubans, who have ample knowledge of them, historically. For example, as professor Isaac Saney notes,

> While in other countries, economic wherewithal [wealth] is necessary for—and does lead to—political power, in Cuba this is not the case. Those who have the most money do not have political power, as they have no support among the masses and, thus, do not offer up candidates in the elections.[47]

What Cubans know is that so-called "multiparty elections" are the Trojan horse of politics, or, the "democracy of exploiters," as Castro has put it, allowing the U.S. government to bribe and buy its way into office through one power-hungry accomplice or another. In Third World elections the U.S. has openly or covertly run a favoured candidate, directed massive funding toward its preferred candidate, and threatened economic or military repercussions if its candidate is not elected. Once elected the candidate and his or her party run a client government at the beck and call of its American sponsors, just as the domestic equivalent is at the behest of his or her corporate backers. It's patently ridiculous to debate this point, since it is a matter of open historical record throughout the Third World over much of the past century.

As law professor Isaac Saney has indicated in elaborate detail, contrary to conventional wisdom, Cubans have developed an elaborate level of voluntary participation.[48] The media simply are not open to these points of view, choosing instead to parrot exclusively the views of the U.S. Administration, with its distorted perspectives and cold war caricatures.

The Varela Project

According to the media, the silver lining in the Cuban cloud was "the Varela Project," a petition project which was presented as a popular-based mass movement ostensibly culminating in a petition to have aspects of (Western-style) democracy implemented, through a referendum. Within the context we have already seen, this is, *prima facie*, an absurd concept. From Jimmy Carter through to the western press, much was made of numerous presuppositions, such as:

1. Western-style "open elections" would be democratic and a good thing.

2. Cuba is not a democracy, it is a dictatorship.

3. The Cuban constitution allows for such petitions, calling for a referendum, which would consequently, automatically become law.

4. 11,000 signatures on a petition was a phenomenal feat, given the repressive nature of the Cuban "police state."

5. These brave signatories were a clear indication of overwhelming dissatisfaction with Fidel Castro, amongst the approximately 14 million Cuban people.

6. Ignoring Varela was another black mark on the record of the Cuban government.

With impeccable timing, Osvaldo Paya, representing the Cuban Christian Liberation Movement, submitted a petition with apparently about 11,000 signatures, to the Cuban National Assembly on May 10, 2002, just before Carter's arrival. The petition "contained twenty points that ostensibly called for broader freedom of statement and association, amnesty for political prisoners, property rights, free enterprise and changes in the electoral system. In short, it solicited a dramatic change to the political, economic and social systems."[49]

The first thing to note is that even if the signatures on this petition were all legitimate, this represented about one in every 1300 Cubans. For comparison purposes, during the Canadian federal election in 2000 about one in every 23 Canadians apparently signed the petition sponsored by Rick Mercer and the CBC comedy program, "This Hour Has 22 Minutes," calling for Reform Party leader Stockwell Day to change his first name to "Doris."[50]

This aside, there were a number of crucial facts which were either omitted altogether, or backgrounded and dismissed by the media in their coverage of the Varela Project. For example, none of the media asked the simple question, "what would happen if a similar petition was presented in Canada or the U.S.?" The answer is that, like Cuba, neither the Canadian nor American constitutions allow for citizens to present petitions which automatically result in a referendum—nor for that matter would they automatically even be considered by the government. In Cuba, as in the rest of North America, citizens may present petitions to governments and the latter will perhaps take them under consideration, or not. Again, for comparison purposes even when Canadian Members of Parliament sponsor private member's bills, these have a notorious failure rate as they do not emanate from the legislation-generating apparatus within the government. This happens even if the MP is a member of the government. So, the position advanced by the media in their coverage of the Varela Project, implicitly and explicitly was: these reasonable petitioners are asking for something, why should the Castro dictatorship refuse them? The reality is that the petition was duly discussed and debated in the Cuban National Assembly, in a way which would very probably not happen in Canada or the U.S. or Mexico.

The petitioners stated that they had the right to present their demands and request a referendum as guaranteed under articles 63 and 88(g) of the Cuban Constitution. This was duly and uncritically reported by the media. None of the media reported that these articles of the constitution do not even discuss the matter of a referendum, let alone guarantee one to petitioners. Under Article 75 of the Constitution, only the National Assembly is authorized to call a referendum.[51] Even Carter, in his speech at the University of Havana, misrepresented the facts:

> That fundamental right is also guaranteed to Cubans. It is gratifying to note that Articles 63 and 88 of your constitution allows [sic] citizens to petition the National Assembly to permit a referendum to change laws if 10,000 or more citizens sign it. I am informed that such an effort, called the Varela Project, has gathered sufficient signatures and has presented such a petition to the National Assembly. When Cubans exercise this freedom to change laws peacefully by a direct vote, the world will see that Cubans, and not foreigners, will decide the future of this country.[52]

The media and Carter failed to ask questions about the legal status of the petition in Cuba. According to Saney, "As the modification of a constitution, by definition, is an extraordinary legal act, all countries require very specific and special means and methods by which these changes can be made. In legal terms, the Varela Project was *ab initio*, that is, invalid from the beginning," because it attempted to achieve an objective through an inappropriate avenue.[53] The Varela petition called for constitutional changes, which under Cuban laws can only be brought about or initiated by the National Assembly. This is not unusual. In Canada, Constitutional changes can be effected only with the consent of the federal government as well as most of the provinces, with most of the population of the country. It's not something that can be accomplished by petitioners, or even for that matter by the federal government alone, or the federal government and just some of the provinces. Constitutional changes are not brought about overnight, as the Trudeau government in Canada found out when there was an immense struggle to repatriate the British North America Act and reform the Canadian constitution in the 1970s and 1980s.

The Cuban constitution does, under 88(g), allow for (10,000+) petitioners to propose laws to the National Assembly, and were this done then they would be debated. Varela was indeed debated at length by the National Assembly, as in June, 2002, more than eight million Cubans mobilized around a petition in response to Varela, declaring the socialist foundations of Cuba "untouchable." In a special sitting in July 2002 the National Assembly discussed the petition for three days, voting to declare "the socialist system to be 'irrevocable'," and also that "Cuba would not return to capitalism."[54]

The media virtually ignored the massive mobilization of Cubans in support of their constitution, and in response to the Varela Project. Where it was reported, it was portrayed as an example of Castro forcing Cubans to defend his own, personal system. In keeping with their ideological biases the media narrowly focused on Varela, with its 11,000 signatures. An AP story run by the *Globe and Mail* framed the Cuban response to Varela through the eyes of the U.S. State Department.

> Opposition activists say the effort is Mr. Castro's answer to their own civil liberties campaign, known as the Varela Project. Most Cubans first heard of Varela last month in a speech by former President Jimmy Carter, who was visiting the island. In Washington, State Department spokesman Phil Reeker said Mr. Castro's proposal is obviously a reaction to the Varela Project's success. "Instead of addressing this peaceful plea for change, Mr. Castro has chosen to manufacture an alternative petition supporting the current constitution and to intimidate the population into signing it," Mr. Reeker said.[55]

The media simply reported Carter's assertions about Varela as fact. For example, the CBC reported,

> It was the first time many Cubans had heard of a democracy effort in the one-party communist state. Carter told the public to support the Varela Project, a dissident plan to force a referendum that would ask Cubans if they favour human rights, electoral reform, an amnesty for political prisoners and the right to have a business.[56]

"Backgrounded," later in the story, was a brief response, a "claim" by "Cuban authorities," with a response.

> Cuban authorities claim the Varela Project was "imported" from the United States. They insist their political system is better than West-ern-styled democracy, and guarantees citizens free access to healthcare and education. Organizers of the Varela Project insist their campaign was organized only by Cubans. They have given the legislature a petition of more than 11,000 signatures, asking for a ref-erendum on civil liberties.

Most of the references were even more unquestioning, and oblique. For exam-ple, Paul Knox, in the *Globe and Mail*, simply wrote: "[Carter] told Cubans the U.S. trade embargo isn't the source of all their economic woes. He told them about Project Varela, the quixotic effort by Cuban dissidents to force a national referendum on freedom of speech, freedom of association and the right to start a private business."[57]

The Embargo

First of all, in the coverage of Carter and Cuba the embargo was not described in any meaningful fashion, which is a serious omission. No historical context was provided, in any of the news coverage. There was no mention of how, un-der the American Torricelli and Helms-Burton Laws, the embargo has been in-tensified to the point where these are the harshest sanctions in the world today,[58] and extend beyond bilateral relations to involve any country trading with Cuba. For example, Ian Delaney, CEO of the Canadian company Sherritt, along with all company officers and directors have been blacklisted and barred from entering the U.S. because of Sherritt's joint ventures in Cuba, a fact which received some media attention in 1997.[59] However, this was not tied into any of the coverage of the embargo and Carter's visit. The media also downplayed the effects of the embargo when they reported on Carter's naive and unsubstanti-ated assertion that the embargo is not the problem. Carter said,

> My hope is that the Congress will soon act to permit unrestricted travel between the United States and Cuba, establish open trading relationships, and repeal the embargo. I should add that these re-straints are not the source of Cuba's economic problems. Cuba can trade with more than 100 countries, and buy medicines, for example, more cheaply in Mexico than in the United States.[60]

Carter did not elaborate on these views, failing to indicate just what, precisely, the problem is. One is left to conclude, as the media apparently did, that the problem is Fidel Castro. No mention was made, for example, of the collapse of the Soviet Union, which was Cuba's largest (almost exclusive) trading partner, accounting for 85 percent of trade, up until 1989. Russia provided 95% of Cuban oil imports, for example. Cubans' per capita income dropped by 39 percent following the Soviet collapse.[61]

In the 2002 media coverage there were those who supported the embargo, inasmuch as they supported it as long as the Cubans *continue to fail to meet* President Bush's conditions for its removal. This was the editorial position taken by the *National Post*, for example. Although it initially editorialized that Carter was right and the embargo was "a pointless anachronism, and Mr. Bush should end it," (May 14), the *Post* flip-flopped a week or so later, after Bush responded to Carter with his own policy statement. In keeping with Bush, the *Post* now argued that the onus is actually on Castro to see that the embargo is removed, by acceding to the U.S. demand for "democratic" elections, along with freeing prisoners, providing financial compensation for private property, *et cetera*. The *Post* said,

> Now, with what is really no more than a deft and forceful reiteration of Washington's longstanding position, Mr. Bush has put the onus on Mr. Castro in fact, not just in theory. The President has managed to restate existing policy but turn it into a new departure. It is now up to Mr. Castro to ensure the embargo is lifted, but he can do so only if he agrees to hold free and fair elections. This is as it should be: Even though the embargo is an anachronistic relic of the Cold War, so is Mr. Castro's dictatorship.[62]

Even for those who, like Carter, wanted the embargo removed, the leading rationale was that it "hasn't worked," in the sense that it hasn't gotten rid of Castro, and hence after 40-plus years it should be abandoned. This position was exemplified by the *Toronto Star*, in an Associated Press story which stated, "Critics on Capitol Hill said Bush maintained the status quo, including the trade embargo that had failed to bring democracy to Cuba."[63] Nowhere to be seen was the argument that the embargo violates international law, owing to its extra-territorial measures. Very little attention was given to the fact that it is inhumane in its impact on the Cuban people. Its downside was largely that it was ineffective, politically. Another criticism of the embargo was that it serves to provide a "scapegoat" for Castro, both abroad and with his own people, allowing him to point the finger at the U.S. for his economic woes. Implicitly, for the media, instead of doing this, he should—or will if the embargo is removed—look at his own failed policies which themselves are simply due to the inherent failures rooted in socialism. The *Globe and Mail* editorialized, "As with Iraq, the embargo against Cuba chiefly serves to punish the country's impoverished ordinary citizens rather than its (non-elected) rulers. As well, it provides those rulers with a handy scapegoat for every social ill that confronts the country, real or perceived."[64]

Barrie McKenna of the *Globe and Mail* reported that the onus is on Castro. "Mr. Bush marked the 100th Cuban Independence Day with speeches in Miami and Washington yesterday that laid out what Mr. Castro must do to see the strict embargo lifted."

In its editorial, to its credit the *Toronto Star* pointed out the hypocrisy in Bush's policies towards Cuba, given that his country does $6 billion (U.S.) in two-way trade with the "axis of evil:" Iran, Iraq, and North Korea. It did $120 billion (U.S.) in trade with China, and $19 billion (U.S.) in trade with Saudi Arabia. Why is trade okay with these countries, which are not "western-style democracies" either? This is an excellent question, especially in light of recent publicized information from Amnesty International that China, for example, executed almost 3400 people in 2004 alone.[65] The *Star* asked the question and answered it: "Why continue to impoverish Cubans with a trade embargo? For defying Washington for 41 years. And for Miami votes in a U.S. election year." The *Star* gets part marks for asking the right question, (which eluded everyone else in the media) but coming up with the wrong answer. "Defying Washington," although the *Star* does not explain how, is not the reason: if it was, then Washington wouldn't trade with China or Iran or Iraq or Korea either, all of which have defied Washington. It's quite all right to 'defy' Washington, if you do so in a brutal and repressive manner. And contrary to popular mythology, Bush didn't need the Miami Cuban vote to lose in 2000, or to win, if win he did, in 2004.

The Reason For the Embargo

The real reason for the embargo is so shocking, so unspeakable, that it must never be broached in the corporate media, except perhaps in a brief account or statement from someone who can be dismissed as a demented conspiracy theorist.

The real reason the U.S. continues its merciless punishment of Cuba, is because of what Noam Chomsky calls, "the threat of a good example." It's also called the "rotten apple theory," or in a distorted version for more popular consumption: "the Domino theory." If a country whether great or small starts to get along outside the U.S. sphere of influence, outside of the so-called "western-style democracies," where the U.S. cannot use its money and power to directly or indirectly subjugate the people and extort their labour and raw materials, then that country is a rotten apple which must be gotten rid of, before it spoils the rest of the barrel. When the people of a country take matters into their own hands and revolt against hierarchy and inequality and the abject squalor and poverty to which the American Empire has reduced them, they must be beaten down again. When a leader—a Fidel Castro or a Hugo Chavez—tries to do something for the poor and downtrodden of his country, instead of serving Washington and the IMF and other powers that be, there will be demonizing and economic squeezes and coup attempts. If all else fails, the U.S. invades. It is worth quoting Chomsky at length on this because he cites U.S. policy makers themselves, who are a trifle difficult to dismiss as mere conspiracy theorists.

> No country is exempt from U.S. intervention, no matter how unimportant. In fact, it's the weakest, poorest countries that often arouse the greatest hysteria… The weaker and poorer a country is, the more dangerous it is as an example. If a tiny, poor country like Grenada can succeed in bringing about a better life for its people, some other place that has more resources will ask, "why not us?"… If you want a global system that's subordinated to the needs of U.S. investors, you can't let pieces of it wander off. It's striking how clearly this is stated in the documentary record—even in the public record at times. Take Chile under Allende. Chile is a fairly big place, with a lot of natural resources, but again, the United States wasn't going to collapse if Chile became independent. Why were we so concerned about it? According to Kissinger, Chile was a "virus" that would "infect" the region with effects all the way to Italy… This "rotten apple theory" is called the domino theory for public consumption… Sometimes the point is explained with great clarity. When the U.S. was planning to overthrow Guatemalan democracy in 1954, a State Department official pointed out that "Guatemala has become an increasing threat to the stability of Honduras and El Salvador. Its

agrarian reform is a powerful propaganda weapon: its broad social program of aiding the workers and peasants in a victorious struggle against the upper classes and large foreign enterprises has a strong appeal to the populations of Central American neighbors where similar conditions prevail." In other words, what the U.S. wants is "stability," meaning security for the "upper classes and large foreign enterprises." If that can be achieved with formal democratic devices, OK. If not, the "threat to stability" posed by a good example has to be destroyed before the virus infects others. That's why even the tiniest speck poses such a threat, and may have to be crushed.[66]

At various intervals the U.S. government and its agencies have openly admitted to the real reasons for punishing Cuba. As Chomsky notes,

In July 1961 the CIA warned that "the extensive influence of 'Castroism' is not a function of Cuban power... Castro's shadow looms large because social and economic conditions throughout Latin America invite opposition to ruling authority and encourage agitation for radical change," for which Castro's Cuba provided a model. Earlier, Arthur Schlesinger had transmitted to the incoming President Kennedy his Latin American Mission report, which warned of the susceptibility of Latin Americans to "the Castro idea of taking matters into one's own hands."... The dangers of the "Castro idea" are particularly grave, Schlesinger later elaborated, when "the distribution of land and other forms of national wealth greatly favors the propertied classes" and "the poor and underprivileged, stimulated by the example of the Cuban revolution, are now demanding opportunities for a decent living." In early 1964, the State Department Policy Planning Council expanded on these concerns: "The primary danger we face in Castro is...in the impact the very existence of his regime has upon the leftist movement in many Latin American countries... The simple fact is that Castro represents a successful defiance of the US, a negation of our whole hemispheric policy of almost a century and a half."[67]

As noted above, American journalism professor Robert Jensen writes that the U.S. administration is able to spin and promote "absurd" interpretations of what is really going on, because of the American public's deep-seated belief in the mythology of America as a "fair and noble" superpower: American exceptionalism.

Returning to the *Globe and Mail* story above which concerned the Helms-Burton Act, for example, Dan Burton, Republican co-sponsor of the act is quoted as follows: "Only the United States is prepared to forgo economic opportunities in favour of human rights in Cuba." This is reported straight-up, with no criticism or contrary views, and presents the U.S. as the centre of benign benevolence.

Let's just take two further examples of viral control, in Chomsky's terms, which are a part of the public record. In Nicaragua, the U.S. Administration under Ronald Reagan illegally sold arms in return for cash which was used to bypass Congress to fund the Contra mercenaries, the armed resistance to the democratically elected Sandinista government of Daniel Ortega. This all came out eventually in the mainstream: how Reagan lied, how he and Oliver North broke the law and defied Congress. All of this was aimed at destabilizing and overthrowing a democratic government which they viewed as socialist. There was no oil involved. They also spent millions funding the opposition, and on an economic blockade, and mining the harbours to "discourage" other countries from doing business with Nicaragua. This happened in the latter half of the eighties, and they succeeded in pounding the people into submission and in driving the Sandinistas from government. (An apparently-reformed Daniel Ortega was re-elected in 2006, much to the chagrin of media commentators and government spokespersons alike.) North and Poindexter and everyone involved eventually received pardons in 1992 by George Bush. You can read about all of this in an encyclopedia. A documentary broadcast on the Discovery Channel, *Secret Warriors: The Brotherhood*, interviewed former CIA agents and officials who gloated about their involvement in these events. So, this is in the mainstream, but you really have to dig for it.

Another example is Panama, which of course the U.S. invaded in 1989, on the pretext that General Manuel Noriega was a drug lord. Of course he was one, under Carter and Reagan, and including the time when George Bush Sr. put him back on the CIA payroll, at $100,000 plus per year, as an ally, informer (and drug lord). "In 1979, for example, senior officials in the Carter administration blocked federal prosecutors from bringing drug-trafficking and arms-smuggling indictments against Noriega, because they preferred to continue receiving the intelligence information he was providing them."[68] Noriega allowed the Contras to train and to be based in Panama, for example. Noriega's mistake was a mixture of arrogance and inconsistency: he outlived his usefulness. Eventually his brutal, murderous past caught up to him, and as economic sanctions and a coup d'etat failed, the U.S. invaded. Much of this is recounted in detail in *The Panama Deception*, which won the Oscar for best documentary film in 1993. Or, you can read what William Blum, Noam Chomsky and others say about it, in books and on the Internet. The truth of the matter is that the U.S. invaded, kidnapping Noriega because he was no longer controllable.

As for the media role in all this, we can return to the comments made in the Iraq context by Karen DeYoung, a *Washington Post* reporter and former assistant managing editor, in an August 12, 2004 *Post* story examining that newspaper's failures leading up to the Iraq War: "We are inevitably the mouthpiece for whatever administration is in power. If the president stands up and says something, we report what the president said."[69] So, if the American president says Sandinistas are socialists, or Noriega is a drug lord who has to be taken out, or Fidel Castro is a dictator: that's what the media report.

American Terrorism Against Cuba

Under the category of sins of omission, we should briefly recount some of the terrorist attacks against Cuba by the U.S. government, or by Cuban Americans with the tacit approval of their government, since 1959. One could reasonably argue that these events are relevant to any discussion of Cuban-U.S. relations. The CIA-organized 1961 Bay of Pigs invasion and attempted coup is the most visible of these, but there are many others. Contrary to American and international law, the CIA established an operations headquarters in Miami, "with a staff of several hundred Americans and a budget in excess of $50 million yearly."[70] Bombing and strafing attacks on Cuba began in 1959, and have been supplemented with such actions as: 'pirate' attacks on Cuban fishing boats, shelling of a theatre, commando raids on oil refineries, chemical plants, bridges, cane fields, sugar mills; a bombing attack on a baseball stadium, blowing up ships, orchestrating ship collisions, and the use of chemical and biological weapons.[71] Cuban turkeys have been infected with viruses, rain clouds have been seeded with crystals producing torrential rains and killer floods. In 1971 the CIA provided Cuban exiles with a virus causing African swine fever, and within six weeks an outbreak forced the slaughter of 500,000 Cuban pigs. In 1984 a Cuban exile on trial in New York testified that he participated in biological warfare against Cuba, which may have resulted in an epidemic of Dengue fever which swept Cuba in 1981, infecting over 300,000 people and causing 158 fatalities, two-thirds of whom were children. In 1976 a Cubana airlines flight leaving Barbados was blown up, killing 73 people.[72] Chomsky writes,

> On the thirtieth anniversary of the missile crisis, Cuba protested a machine-gun attack against a Spanish-Cuban tourist hotel; responsibility was claimed by a group in Miami. Bombings in Cuba in 1997, which killed an Italian tourist, were traced back to Miami. The perpetrators were Salvadoran criminals operating under the direction of Luis Posada Carriles and financed in Miami.[73]

Regarding assassination attempts on Fidel Castro, there have been literally dozens of attempts documented, and the U.S. Senate Investigation into the CIA chaired by Senator Frank Church in 1975 concluded, "We have found concrete evidence of at least eight plots involving the CIA to assassinate Fidel Castro, from 1960 to 1965...the proposed assassination devices ran the gamut from high-powered rifles, to poison pills, poisoned pens, deadly bacterial powders, and other devices which strain the imagination."[74] This is a report by the U.S. Senate, and it only covered a five-year period in a history of more than 45 years!

It should be stressed that absolutely none of the above events rated mention in the coverage of Cuba by the Canadian media. This speaks volumes about the bias, selectivity, framing and sins of omission by the media. To do otherwise would be to abandon their role as an arm of the U.S. State Department.

Conclusions

This case study of Jimmy Carter's trip to Cuba provided an opportunity for the corporate media to trot out all of their clichés about Cuba and Fidel Castro, and to display their ideological biases. These biases centered primarily around the natural right of the Bush administration to interfere openly in the affairs of Cuba, even to the point of funding and fomenting the overthrow of a government which does not have Bush's approval. The editorial, opinion and news perspectives advanced by Canadian media outlets openly displayed the effects of 45 years of relentless propaganda by successive American administrations, to the point where one would be hard- pressed to differentiate between media content and State Department news releases, other than nuances. The framing of issues by the media presupposed American viewpoints and automatically censored Cuban perspectives.

The portrayal of Fidel Castro was a caricature drawn from a Cold War comic book, and contrasted sharply with the deferential coverage provided to Jimmy Carter and George W. Bush. The illegal U.S. embargo of Cuba was either defended or narrowly criticized. Cuban history, its political system generally, American atrocities against Cuba: nothing about any of this was written. In sum, the media coverage was positively shameful.

In the Canadian media, as with their American counterparts, the range of debate or what Chomsky calls "the bounds of the expressible," ran from Carter's position, which was that the U.S. should end the embargo and then Castro would hold 'free and democratic' Cuban elections, to Bush's position, which was that Castro would have to "democratize" Cuban elections and free political prisoners as a precondition to the lifting of the U.S. economic embargo. As Carter wrote in the *Washington Post*, after his trip, "...the ultimate goals of the White House and the Carter Center are the same: to see complete freedom come to Cuba and, in the meantime, to have friendly relations between the people of our two nations."[75] What remained beyond the pale to policy makers and journalists was the simple fact that the U.S. has no right to interfere in Cuban internal matters, or that the notion of U.S. electoral "freedom and democracy" as applied to Cuba, in the form of multiparty elections, would amount to American manipulation of Cuban elections and subsequently, control of the Cuban economy, as has happened historically in Nicaragua and elsewhere throughout Latin America and around the world.[76]

As for Jimmy Carter, elder statesman and "activist president," William Blum recently wrote that Carter may have been "closer to a decent human being than any post-World War Two president." But he continued,

> One could wax cynical about Jimmy Carter as well; for example, while in the White House he tried hard to sabotage the Sandinista revolution in Nicaragua; even worse, Carter supported the Islamic opposition to the leftist Afghanistan government in 1979, *which led to a decade of very bloody civil war, the Taliban, and anti-American terrorism in the United States and elsewhere* (emphasis added).[77]

Media content such as that examined above is indicative of the increasingly close relationship between the foreign policy of the American and Canadian governments. Sadly, it also predicts—in as much as media content is reflective of the elite agenda as well as influencing both public opinion and policy making—an even greater emerging symbiosis between the two.

NOTES

1. Kevin Dougherty, "PR Boost Sought for Afghan Mission," *Edmonton Journal*, November 18, 2006.

2. Norman Solomon, *War Made Easy: How Presidents and Pundits Keep Spinning Us to Death*, John Wiley & Sons, N.Y., 2005. Cited in a review by Robert Jensen, "It's the Empire, Stupid," ZNet Commentary, July 29, 2005.

3. Editorial, "Freeing Afghans from fanatics is a long-term, but necessary mission," *Vancouver Sun*, September 27, 2006.

4. John Pilger, "This War is a Fraud," *Mirror*, November 1, 2001. Pilger, John. "The Betrayal of Afghanistan," *Guardian*, Sept. 20, 2003.

5. Noam Chomsky, "The War in Afghanistan," Excerpted from Lakdawala lecture, New Delhi Online version with notes, prepared Dec. 30, 2001.

6. *Toronto Star*. "Voices: Canada's Troops in Afghanistan," TheStar.com, May 18, 2006.

7. Rosie Dimanno, "Taliban Targets Our Troops," *Toronto Star*, March 20, 2006.

8. Mitch Potter, "War: Canadian-style Bringing the war home | A special report," *Toronto Star*, March 12, 2006.

9. Robin Sears, "With sovereignty, less is more: It is a paradox that Canada must surrender much of its autonomy to best preserve what it values most," *Toronto Star*, May 4, 2002.

10. Cf. Linda Diebel, "Chretien Trip to Cuba Sparks Row With U.S.," *Toronto Star*, April 19, 1998.

11. For an elaboration of these ideas, see James Winter and Robert Everton, "How Jimmy Carter Spent his Cuban Vacation: Media Coverage and Ideological Bias," in Jeffrey Klaehn (Ed) *Bound By Power: Intended Consequences*, Black Rose Books, Montreal, 2005, pp. 150-187.

12. Hackett et al., "News Balance..." p. 17.

13. Cf. Ed Herman and Noam Chomsky, *Manufacturing Consent: The Political Economy of the Media*, Pantheon, N.Y., 1988; Robert McChesney, *Rich Media, Poor Democracy: Communication Politics in Dubious Times*, New Press, New York, 2000; James Winter, *Democracy's Oxygen: How Corporations Control the News*, Black Rose Books, Montreal, 1997.

14. Kevin Sullivan, "Open doors greet Carter in Cuba: Highest level U.S. encounter since 1959," *Toronto Star*, May 13, 2002.

15. Paul Knox, "Carter Shakes up Cuba," *Globe and Mail*, May 17, 2002.

16. Cf. Thomas Huckin, "Critical Discourse Analysis," in Thomas Miller (Ed), *Functional Approaches to Written Text: Social Approaches*, Ch. 6, A publication of the U.S. State Department, ESL program. http://exchanges.state.gov/education/engteaching/pubs/BR/functionalsec3_6.htm. Teun van Dijk writes, "In discourse analysis, and especially in critical discourse analysis, presupposition analysis especially focuses on those presuppositions that suggest that some proposition is (accepted to be) true, but in fact is not true at all, or at least controversial. Thus, if police or media report that energetic action is being undertaken against the 'rising crime among

minorities,' such an expression may falsely presuppose (or indirectly assert) that the crime rate among minorities is indeed rising." Teun van Dijk, "Cognitive Discourse Analysis: An introduction. Version 1.0. October 25, 2000. http://www.discourse-in-society.org/cogn-dis-anal.htm

17. Isaac Saney, *Cuba: A Revolution in Motion*,Fernwood, Halifax, 2004, p. 64.

18. Quoted in John Gray, "The War Measures Act was drastic, but it worked, John Gray concludes," *Globe and Mail*, September 30, 2000.

19. Warren Gerard, "He changed us as a Nation," *Toronto Star*, Sept. 29, 2000, p. B1.

20. Gray, "The War Measures Act."

21. *Prensa Latina*, "Cuba Will Confront Internal Subversion Financed by the U.S.," April 10, 2003. Cited in Saney, *Revolution*, p. 77.

22. Quoted in Cliff Durand, *Cuban National Identity and Socialism*, Chicago, Red Feather Institute. Cited in Saney, *Revolution*, p. 79.

23. Cf. Isaac Saney, *Revolution*, pp. 41-89; and Arnold August, *Democracy in Cuba*.

24. This case study is drawn from Saney, *Revolution*, pp. 51-52.

25. Quoted in Richard Gwyn, "Here I go sticking my neck out again," *Toronto Star*, January 1, 1976.

26. Marcus Gee, "Carter's Cuban Coup," *Globe and Mail*, May 18, 2002.

27. Paul Knox, "Carter Shakes up Cuba," *Globe and Mail*, May 17, 2002.

28. Cf. William Blum, *Killing Hope: U.S. Military and CIA Interventions Since WWII*, Black Rose Books, Montreal, 1998.

29. http://web.amnesty.org/pages/guantanamobay-index-eng.

30. AFX News Ltd., "U.S. acknowledges torture at Guantanamo; in Iraq, Afghanistan B UN," *Forbes Magazine*, June 24, 2005.   http://www.forbes.com/work/feeds/afx/2005/06/24/afx2110 388.html .

31. Thomas Huckin, "Critical Discourse Analysis."

32. John Whitesides, "Bush likely to tighten embargo against Cuba," *Reuters*, *National Post*, May 20, 2002.

33. Noam Chomsky, *Chronicles of Dissent: Interviews with David Barsamian*, Common Courage Press, Monroe, Maine, 1992.

34. George Gedda, Associated Press, Miami: "Cuba embargo stays: Bush, U.S. president lays out tough conditions for lifting sanctions," *Toronto Star*, May 21, 2002

35. Ross Gordon, "Cuba won't go back," letter, *Globe and Mail*, May 22, 2002.

36. Editorial, "Happy Birthday, Cuba," *Toronto Star*, May 22, 2002.

37. George Gedda, (AP) "Cuba embargo stays: Bush U.S. president lays out tough conditions for lifting sanctions," *Toronto Star*, May 21, 2002.

38. Saney, *Revolution*, p.65.

39. Editorial, "The old foe in Havana," *Globe and Mail*, May 16, 2002.

40. Cf. Vincent Bugliosi, "None Dare Call it Treason," *Nation*, February 5, 2001; Vincent Bugliosi, *The Betrayal of America: How the Supreme Court Undermined the Constitution and Chose our President*, Avalon Publishing, NY, 2001.

41. Michael Lind, "To Have and Have Not," *Harper's*, June, 1995, pp. 43-44.

42. Ian Urquhart, "Radical voting proposal gains steam," *Toronto Star*, February 22, 2007.

43. Jim Fleming, personal interview, May, 1996. This was in the context of a discussion about corporate Canada's influence over policy-making.

44. Richard Gwyn, "No wonder democracy is in trouble: Studies show scandal rarely affects a party's election chances," *Toronto Star*, May 26, 2002. See also, Donald Savoie, *Governing from the Centre: The Concentration of Power in Canadian Politics*, University of Toronto Press, Toronto, 1999; and Jeffrey Simpson, *The Friendly Dictatorship*, McLelland and Stewart, Toronto, 2001.

45. Thomas Walkom, "How Eves' empire collapsed: Cabinet was rarely consulted, top Conservatives recall, Insiders cite disorganization, dithering on crucial issues," *Toronto Star*, Nov. 2, 2003.

46. Cf. James Winter, *Democracy's Oxygen: How Corporations Control the News*, Black Rose Books, Montreal, 1997.

47. Saney, *Revolution*, p. 89.

48. Saney, *Revolution*, pp 54-55.

49. Saney, *Revolution*, p. 84.

50. "This Hour Has 22 Minutes" eventually claimed that more than 1.2 million Canadians signed their online petition, which called for Stockwell Day to change his first name to "Doris," in order to poke fun at the Reform Party's 2000 campaign promise to hold referenda in response to petitions.

51. Saney, *Revolution*, pp. 84-87.

52. Jimmy Carter, "The United States and Cuba: A Vision for the 21st Century," Remarks by Jimmy Carter at the University of Havana, Cuba, Web posted by the Carter Center, 14 May 2002.

53. Saney, *Revolution*, pp. 85-86.

54. Saney, *Revolution*, pp. 86-87.

55. AP, "Cubans asked to sign petition in support of Castro," *Globe and Mail*, June 14, 2002.

56. CBC News Online, "Jimmy Carter criticizes Cuba in uncensored speech," May 14, 2002.

57. Paul Knox, "Carter shakes up Cuba," *Globe and Mail*, May 17, 2002.

58. Noam Chomsky, *Rogue States: The Rule of Force in World Affairs*, South End Press, Cambridge Mass., 2000. p. 82. Cited in Isaac Saney, *Cuba: A Revolution in Motion*, Fernwood, 2004, p.168.

59. Saney, *Revolution*, p. 170.

60. Jimmy Carter, "The United States and Cuba: A Vision for the 21st Century," An Address given at the University of Havana, May 14, 2002. Web posted by the Carter Center. For reporting on this aspect, see for example, Marcus Gee, "Carter's Cuban coup," *Globe and Mail*, May 18, 2002.

61. Isaac Saney, *Revolution*, p. 21.

62. Editorial, "Bush puts Onus on Castro," *National Post*, May 22, 2002.

63. George Gedda, "Cuba embargo stays: Bush U.S. president lays out tough conditions for lifting sanctions," Associated Press, *Toronto Star*, May 21, 2002. On line.

64. Editorial, "The old foe in Havana," *Globe and Mail*, May 16, 2002.

65. "Death Penalty," Upfront World section, *Maclean's* magazine, April 18, 2005, p. 15.

66. Noam Chomsky, *What Uncle Sam Really Wants*, Odonian Press, Tucson, 1993.

67. Noam Chomsky, "Cuba in the Cross-Hairs: A Near Half-Century of Terror," October 24, 2003, www.commondreams.com, excerpted with permission from Noam Chomsky, *Hegemony or Survival: America's Quest for Global Dominance*, Metropolitan Books, N.Y., 2003.

68. Eytan Gilboa, "The Panama Invasion Revisited: Lessons for the Use of Force in the Post Cold War Era," *Political Science Quarterly*, (v110 n4), 1995, p539.

69. Quoted in Jensen, "It's The Empire, Stupid."

70. William Blum, *Killing Hope: U.S. Military and CIA Interventions Since World War II*, Black Rose Books, Montreal, 1998, p. 187.

71. Blum, *Killing Hope*, p. 187-188.

72. Blum, *Killing Hope*, p. 188-189.

73. Chomsky, *Cuba in the Cross-Hairs*, op. cit.

74. Frank Church, Chair, "Senate Select Committee to Study Governmental Operations with Respect to Intelligence Activities," U.S. Congress, 1976, p. 71.

75. Jimmy Carter, "Openings to Cuba: We must find a common ground," *Washington Post*, May 24, 2002.

76. Saney, *Revolution*, p. 89.

77. William Blum, "The Anti-Empire Report: Some things you need to know before the world ends," February 3, 2007, http://members.aol.com/bblum6/aer42.htm, retrieved March 1, 2007.

Chapter Five

GLOBAL VILLAGE, OR GLOBAL PILLAGE?[1]

IN A BROAD SURVEY COURSE covering lies the media tell us—or media literacy—it's really not possible to go into much depth on any of the topics, such as economics. For most of us, our eyes tend to glaze over when conversations or lecture material turns to economics. A research methods book I read as a graduate student offered the view that most of us recoil from mathematics and formulae because students who were good at this in high school were mostly geeks: who wants to be one of those? Whatever the reason, many of us avoid this topic. In the brief time I have, I try to impress on students that economics is easier to understand than we are (intentionally) led to believe, and that some knowledge is crucial to comprehending our situation and the prospects for change. One key to this understanding is an awareness of trade agreements and their impact on our society. This opens up the broader topic of "corporate globalization," and a discussion of the way international bodies hamstring national governments, such as the way NAFTA prevented the Canadian government from protecting the health of its citizens by banning MMT, discussed in Chapter Two. Hence, we can't understand or protect our environment and health, without knowing something about the economics of trade agreements. The same thing applies to jobs: a topic which is very much on the minds of university students.

If we rely solely on mainstream media to inform us about corporate globalization, we are likely to develop the mindset that: 1) it's inevitable 2) it's good for everyone and 3) youthful protesters are misguided, if not outright dangerous.

When organized global protests developed in the late 1990s, bringing together a broad coalition of students and pensioners, environmentalists and human rights advocates, the reaction on the part of the mainstream media was predictable. After all, the media are no less interested in order and social control than are the police—or educators. The media portrayed the protesters as mentally unstable, as mostly violent youth who, for no good reasons, were hell bent on destruction. While a few of the protesters were depicted as naïve and quixotic: idealistic individuals in search of a better world, these "types" were greatly outnumbered in news stories and even popular entertainment programs, by the seemingly crazed anarchists.

Readers and viewers could search in vain for sensible motivations or explanations. Why were these (mostly) young people out in the streets? The answer seemed to be that they just like violence. Was that it?

The roots of the anti-corporate globalization movement possibly lie in the opposition to free trade agreements, such as the FTA between the Canadian and U.S. governments in 1988, or the North American agreement including Mexico in 1994, or the FTAA, the Free Trade Agreement of the Americas, currently being negotiated. In the wake of the final vote on NAFTA in the U.S. Congress, environmental activist Jerry Mander invited people involved in social movements around the world to share what they had learned about economic globalization. This gathering called itself the International Forum on Globalization.[2] By 1995, when the Paris-based Organization for Economic Cooperation and Development (OECD) and the newly-formed World Trade Organization began to negotiate the Multilateral Agreement on Investment (MAI), a coalition of international non-governmental groups had developed to provide strong, unified opposition. With good reason. The MAI is, just in part, an international commercial treaty empowering corporations and investors to sue governments directly for cash compensation in retaliation for almost any government policy or action that undermines profits. We've seen how problematical this could be when it came to banning MMT, which the U.S. EPA admits is a dangerous neurotoxin, as a fuel additive.[3]

The anti-corporate globalization demonstrations perhaps began in 1997, with protests against the brutal Indonesian dictator, General Suharto, at the Asia-Pacific Economic Co-operation (APEC) meetings in Vancouver, B.C. Suharto was responsible for Indonesia's invasion of the tiny, pastoral island nation of East Timor, in the 1970s. Hundreds of thousands of Timorese were subsequently slaughtered, as Suharto brutally suppressed Timorese nationalists who opposed the occupation, while the international community turned a blind eye. Gradually, human rights activists in North America and elsewhere began to take up the cause of the people of East Timor. The East Timor Alert Network was founded. Noam Chomsky and others pointed to the atrocities. In *Manufacturing Consent*, a documentary film produced with support from the National Film Board of Canada, the producers confronted editors at the *New York Times*, over their distorted sense of news judgment, in ignoring East Timor. Elaine Briere made a haunting and evocative film about the invasion and its aftermath, *Bitter Paradise*.[4]

In advance of the APEC meetings, General Suharto sought assurances from Canadian Prime Minister Jean Chrétien that he would not be troubled by the sight of protesters. Suharto inquired whether his body guards could carry weapons and if they would be allowed to shoot protesters. Chrétien reassured Suharto that order would be maintained—but as it turned out, not without costs. When APEC began, the Royal Canadian Mounted Police followed orders from Chrétien's office. Peaceful protesters holding signs and exercising freedom of speech on public property at the University of British Columbia were roughed up, pepper-sprayed, arrested and strip-searched. All this, lest they offend a murderous dictator with their choice of words on their placards.

Documents revealing Chrétien's involvement were released during a subsequent hearing into RCMP actions, in 1998.[5] The hearing and the documents received national publicity, in part, because of the efforts of veteran Canadian Broadcasting Corporation reporter Terry Milewski. In October, 1998, the Prime Minister's Office successfully pressured the CBC into removing Milewski from the story. Milewski tenaciously and almost alone, worked with students to bring the APEC story to light. Chrétien's office demanded that the CBC investigate the reporter's actions, simply because Milewski (accurately) referred to the government as "the Forces of Darkness" in an e-mail message to a student, and offered the students advice on how to advance their case in the press. "Milewski is almost solely responsible for helping push [APEC] to the top of the news a year later, through his dogged release of leaked documents and continuing attention to the political and policing issues raised by the APEC protest," wrote Susan Delacourt of the *Globe and Mail* on October 17, 1998. After an investigation, the CBC rejected government claims that its reporting was biased, although it removed Milewski from the story and admonished him for getting too close to his student sources.

Virtually absent from the coverage of this was a crucial concern over the way the Government of Canada demonstrated police-state tactics by erasing the fundamental line between politicians and police. Jean Chrétien's office gave orders to the RCMP which were followed, orders which violated the rights of Canadian citizens who happened to be students and protesters.

If this marked the beginning of these protests, they continued in Seattle, Washington. Biased media coverage of the demonstrations at the 1999 World Trade Organization (WTO) meetings in Seattle has been the focus of some analysis and research. For example, just after tens of thousands of protestors rallied in Seattle to virtually close down the opening conference of the WTO meeting in November 1999, the *New York Times'* Thomas Friedman wrote that "knaves like Pat Buchanan" had "duped" the demonstrators—"a Noah's ark of flat-earth advocates, protectionist trade union yuppies looking for their 1960s fix"—into protesting the WTO.[6] Corporate media coverage of these demonstrations was so ideologically biased that Seattle organizers set up an Independent Media Centre (www.indymedia.org) to get an alternative message out. To illustrate the nature of the coverage in detail, in the Canadian context, we will look at a case study of press coverage of the meetings and protests surrounding the Organization of American States, (OAS) in Windsor, Ontario, Canada, from the summer of 2000. First, however, we will provide some historical context.

The IMF and the World Bank

The IMF and World Bank were established in 1944 at a conference held in Bretton Woods, a ski resort in New Hampshire. The IMF was to further global trade, and stabilize currencies and global financial disruptions. According to Michael Albert of ZNET, "The World Bank was intended to facilitate long-term investment in underdeveloped countries, to expand and strengthen economies."[7] In recent decades, according to Joseph Stiglitz, the 2001 Nobel economist and former chief economist of the World Bank, it has developed a "country assistance strategy" for each emerging market nation. In articles, interviews and now books, Stiglitz has shed considerable light on the operations of the World Bank, and IMF. His criticisms are telling because he was once the ultimate insider, and he is a conservative, although a highly critical one. Stiglitz is the equivalent of a medical whistleblower, but instead of revealing the secrets of the pharmaceutical industry, he is telling those of international finance. He writes,

> The IMF is pursuing not just the objectives set out in its original mandate, of enhancing global stability and ensuring that there are funds for countries facing a threat of recession to pursue expansionary policies. It is also pursuing the interests of the financial community... Simplistic free market ideology provided the curtain behind which the real business of the "new" mandate could be transacted... The change in mandate and objectives, while it may have been quiet, was hardly subtle: from serving global *economic* interests to serving the interests of global *finance*.[8]

Stiglitz reveals that these international economic institutions are not democratically responsible. IMF membership is composed of member countries' finance ministers and central bank governors. At the WTO, it is trade ministers. The leadership, chosen behind closed doors, comes from Europe for the former, and the U.S. for the latter, although they make decisions for developing nations. He disparages the way dogmatic zealotry has gripped these bankers, as they cling blindly to what he terms, "market fundamentalism." He writes, "the IMF simply assumed that markets arise quickly to meet every need, when in fact, many government activities arise because markets have *failed* to provide essential services. Example abound."[9] In part, their strategy consists of a *structural adjustment agreement* drafted by the IMF after analyzing each nation's economy. Then the IMF hands each country's finance minister the same four-step program.[10] Step one is privatization, and entails public enterprises being sold off to the private sector. Step two is capital market liberalization, which allows capital to flee, thus allowing for the possibility of a nation's reserves being drained very quickly. Step three is fiscal austerity and market-based pricing, which amounts to raising prices on food, water and other necessities of basic life. Tax collection is increased, while government spending is dramatically reduced.

An example of this is when the IMF eliminated food and fuel subsidies for the poor in Indonesia in 1998, even over the objections of the brutal dictator General Suharto. The result was riots. The same sort of predictable "social unrest" (as the corporate media labeled it) has occurred in Argentina, and, in fact, Stiglitz has termed this "the IMF riot."

Step four in the IMF's program is free trade, which is implemented through arrangements such as NAFTA and the FTAA, the GATT (now the WTO). These restructuring agreements represent an "evolution" in the means of control of "emerging market economies" from the (sometimes messy) coups and imposition of dictatorships via the CIA, detailed by William Blum and others, to the more distant persuasion of economic forces. With Nicaragua, for example, although this took the form of a proxy war, it was followed by an economic blockade and finally the mass infusion of cash to support electoral alternatives (Violetta Chamorro) to the Sandinistas. Economic measures and armaments work hand in hand. At times it has been necessary to resort to outright invasion of countries to turf recalcitrant dictators who will no longer cooperate, such as happened in 1989 with General Manuel Noriega of Panama, but usually the despots have retired quietly and without too much fanfare, as did Suharto in Indonesia. In most cases, it is unnecessary to resort to military action, although Kosovo, Afghanistan and Iraq (again) are recent exceptions. This method has human, social and environmental costs which cannot be calculated, but has its own instrumental 'advantages' such as stimulating the U.S. economy, stabilizing U.S. oil prices and ensuring access to oil, buttressing the Pentagon and munitions manufacturers, diverting the attention of the public away from domestic social and economic matters, and softening finance ministers around the globe to the gentler persuasions of 'restructuring'.

Imperialism and military interventions are certainly not new. Indeed, they date back millennia. But there are several new developments which are noteworthy, such as these restructuring agreements. Another is the WTO which was created in 1995 through the provisions of the Uruguay Round of the General Agreement on Tariffs and Trade (GATT). Prior to this, GATT focused on promoting world trade by pressuring countries to reduce tariffs. As Michael Albert and others explain, the corporate-inspired global agenda was significantly increased by targeting so-called "non-tariff barriers to trade"—essentially any national protective legislation which might be construed as impacting trade.[11] Albert asks,

> [I]nstead of only imposing on Third World countries low wages and high
> pollution due to their weak or bought-off governments, why not weaken
> all governments and agencies that might defend workers, customers, or
> the environment, not only in the Third World, but everywhere?[12]

And indeed, the Canadian government, for example, was pressured by the IMF and others in the 1980s and 1990s when social program spending and deficits were viewed as becoming too high. The real culprit was high interest rates, maintained by the Bank of Canada and serving global capital.[13]

One definitive purpose of globalization is to eliminate the domestic population's 'interference' with the corporate agenda and, on occasion, also non-client governments, whose attempts to take matters into their own hands are typically regarded as a "crisis of democracy," in Noam Chomsky's phrase. Obviously, this is Orwellian Newspeak at its best: the actual exercise of democracy is represented as a crisis demanding intervention. Stiglitz discusses a number of Third World examples, including Indonesia in 1998 under Suharto.

> The IMF is not particularly interested in hearing the thoughts of its 'client countries' on topics such as development strategy or fiscal austerity. All too often, the Fund's approach to developing countries has had the feel of a colonial ruler...[Suharto] was being forced, in effect, to turn over economic sovereignty of his country to the IMF in return for the aid his country needed. In the end, ironically, much of the money went not to help Indonesia but to bail out the 'colonial power's' private sector creditors.[14]

The first thing to note is that the World Bank was delighted with the Suharto government for virtually all of his decades of tenure, up until 1997-98, when even that brutal dictator balked at imposing the stringent economic conditions demanded by the IMF. Suharto was the darling of the U.S. and the West generally, as he killed hundreds of thousands if not millions of people, opened up Indonesia to Western investment, and as *Time Magazine* Asia finally reported after the fact in 1999, he and his family secreted $15 Billion (U.S.) in foreign bank accounts, all on a presidential salary of $1764 (U.S.) monthly.[15] But, ironically, given what happened during APEC 1997, in that year things began to go terribly wrong for Suharto. To begin with, he began to lose control. There were student riots. As Chomsky notes, "If your friendly dictator loses control, he's not much use." But the second thing was that he developed an unexpected "soft spot." Chomsky explains:

> The International Monetary Fund (IMF), meaning the U.S., was imposing quite harsh economic programs which were punishing the general population for the robbery carried out by a tiny Indonesian elite, and Suharto, for whatever reason, maybe fearing internal turmoil, was dragging his feet on implementing these. Then came a series of rather dramatic events... In February 1998, the head of the IMF, Michel Camdessus, flew into Jakarta and effectively ordered

Suharto to sign onto the IMF rules... Shortly after that, in May 1998, Madeleine Albright telephoned Suharto and told him that Washington had decided that the time had come for what she called a "democratic transition," meaning, 'Step down.' Four hours later, he stepped down. This isn't just cause and effect. There are many other factors. It's not just pushing buttons. But it does symbolize the nature of the relationship.[16]

Of course, given the veto the U.S. holds over IMF policies, it's not at all difficult to accept the factual scenario Chomsky describes.

Corporate Hegemony and the Marginalization of Dissent

Little or nothing of the information above may be learned from the mainstream media, working in their vested interests and in their role as agents of public indoctrination and corporate legitimation generally. This is evident from even casual perusal of mainstream media content, but it has also been documented systematically by a range of progressive academics, including Herman and Chomsky, Robert McChesney, Norman Solomon, Robert Jensen, Ben Bagdikian, Russell Mokhiber and Robert Weissman, and economists such as Brian MacLean, William Krehm, and so forth. On a popular level, economic journalist Linda McQuaig has been writing about these developments for more than a decade, most recently in *It's The Crude, Dude: War, Big Oil, and the Fight for the Planet*. Of course, these 'alternative perspectives' on reality are virtually absent from the mainstream.

Two world events in the spring of 2002 demonstrated the apparent futility of either acquiescing to or resisting, the World Bank, WTO and International Monetary Fund (IMF). I refer to the cases of Argentina and Venezuela. Naomi Klein, writing in the *Globe and Mail*, suggested that Argentina was "the IMF's model student throughout the 1990s," and that its "massive privatization" included the selling off of services ranging from phones to trains, such that virtually the only assets yet to be privatized were "the country's ports and customs offices."[17] Jon Hillson, writing in the *New York Transfer*, commented that Argentina,

...like other Latin American debt slaves, has already paid off the principle of its initial loans, but now groans under continental arrears of $750 billion, as interest payments mount. In some national budgets, debt service has reached 40 percent of state expenditures. Buenos Aires has defaulted on, and ceased such payments.[18]

Despite its 'model student' behavior, Argentina wound up wearing a dunce cap and sitting in the corner. It was in economic shambles, while the IMF and neoliberals demanded further "structural readjustments" intended to benefit the interests of corporate capital as opposed to Argentines themselves. The value system underlying such action is remarkably consistent with any number of cases demonstrating the extent to which corporate hegemony endangers fundamental democratic principles and human rights.

In the case of Argentina, a financial reporter for the *National Post* reached out to a spokesperson for the conservative Cato Institute in the U.S., for thoughts on possible remedies. Ian Vasquez told the *Post* that "the Argentine crisis is as much a crisis for the IMF as it is for Argentina. It really has shown the failure of the bailout doctrine." Few would argue with this assessment, but the reasons and rationale offered by the reporter are instructive. For example, consider the following: "The problem with IMF bailouts, its critics suggest, is that instead of providing financial relief while countries sort out their difficulties, they create a 'moral hazard.' The countries know they will be bailed out, so they spend recklessly."[19]

In translation, the term "reckless spending" in this context, refers to money spent on the people, rather than being vacuumed up by international investors. Variations on the theme of 'reckless spending' abound within the boundaries of debate established (and policed) by the corporate media. This in turn impacts both political discourse and spectrums of opinion. Consider a *Reuters* article, carried in the *National Post*, which referred to:

> [The IMF], which since December has refused to throw any more money at Argentina in disgust at its inability to rein in runaway public spending… The IMF has called on Argentina's provinces, widely seen as a morass of corruption and excess, to halt decades of runaway spending. It also wants to see a bank rescue plan in place.[20]

Martin Defends Canadian Interests

Here we see the same alleged litany of corruption and excessive runaway public spending. Another article indicated the Canadian government's position in the crisis. Under the headline "Canada leans on Argentina," the *National Post* article first stated that then-Finance Minister Paul Martin "calls for action," then sets the stage by reporting that "the Argentine government yesterday resisted demands by the IMF for more provincial budget cuts as a condition for a sorely needed aid package, fearful that new austerity measures would lead to another round of deadly rioting." Note the disapproving tone of this description, despite the inherent reasonableness of resisting measures which will lead your people to riot. Also note that "austerity" packages are always presented as a good thing. Eventually, the article turned to the action that Paul Martin prescribed:

> Mr. Martin met Argentina's Minister of Finance and urged him to look into the treatment of Scotiabank and make sure it is dealt with fairly. He told the *Financial Post* he talked with Jorge Remes Lenicov to press his case that the Canadian bank should not be penalized for the country's economic problems. "We made our point very strongly that you cannot discriminate against foreign banks," Mr. Martin said in an interview after meeting Mr. Lenicov during the spring sessions here of the World Bank and International Monetary Fund.[21]

An admittedly "austere" budget from President Eduardo Duhalde in March 2002 which cut spending by about 15 percent was deemed inadequate by the IMF, which indicated that "substantial measures" were still needed.[22] A column in the *National Post*, published approximately a month later, carried a headline and subhead which nicely summed it all up:

> Reform comes first; an IMF bailout won't resuscitate Argentina's economy. Along with cutting government spending, the debt-strapped country needs to severely curtail the influences of provincial governments and unions.[23]

Argentina, by now an old story, has largely dropped from the corporate media agenda, while the story of the people's uprising against the IMF and World Bank goes virtually ignored, except in the alternative media, such as *The Take*, the 2005 documentary film by Naomi Klein and Avi Lewis. Through its policies, the IMF continues to punish the people of Argentina in an attempt to compel them to bend to its will.

Chavez and Venezuela

As for Venezuelans, they had the audacity to elect a "leftist" president in 1998, Hugo Chavez, who soon paid off the country's IMF loans, to fend off economic blackmail. He strengthened the constitution, and used petroleum profits to help the poor and downtrodden who constitute about 90 percent of the country and most if not all of his electors. In the mid-70s, the state-run-oil company kept 20% of its revenue in operating costs and turned 80% over to the state. By 1990 it was 50-50 and in 1998, when Chavez was elected, the company kept 80% and turned over just 20%.[24]

The U.S. government responded, first, by supporting a military and business coup d'etat in 2002, which was reversed when hundreds of thousands of Venezuelans poured into the streets and surrounded the presidential palace, demanding Chavez's return.[25] As this didn't work, they next turned to a purported "national strike," in December, 2002, largely conducted by multinational corporations and wealthy Venezuelans. Workers at a Pepsi-Cola plant in Aragua, Venezuela, took it over against the wishes of management, to prevent joining in the "national" strike. Their slogan was "Fabrica Cerrada—Fabrica Tomada," or "Close the Factories? We'll take them over!" This standoff dragged on for months, but failed to bring the Chavez government to its knees, as planned. Next, they orchestrated a recall referendum held in August, 2004, which failed.

Writing in *Counterpunch*, William Blum summed up the actions of Chavez, which led to the CIA-sponsored coup in April, 2002. Blum writes: "Consider Chavez's crimes":

- Branding the U.S. attacks on Afghanistan as "fighting terrorism," he demanded an end to "the slaughter of innocents," holding up photographs of children killed in the American bombing attacks, he said their deaths had "no justification, just as the attacks on New York did not, either." In response, the Bush administration temporarily withdrew its ambassador;

- Being friendly with Fidel Castro and selling oil to Cuba at discounted rates;

- His defense minister asking the permanent U.S. military mission in Venezuela to vacate its offices in the military headquarters in Caracas, saying its presence was an anachronism from the Cold War;

- Not cooperating to Washington's satisfaction with the U.S. war against the Colombian guerrillas;

- Denying Venezuelan airspace to U.S. counter-drug flights;

- Refusing to provide U.S. intelligence agencies with information on Venezuela's large Arab community;

- Questioning the sanctity of globalization;

- Promoting a regional free-trade bloc and united Latin American petroleum operations as a way to break from U.S. economic dominance;

- Visiting Saddam Hussein in Iraq and Muhammar Ghaddafy in Libya.

Blum concluded, "The United States has endeavored to topple numerous governments for a whole lot less."[26]

Events such as these, involving the IMF and World Bank, are typically (grossly) distorted by the corporate media, in keeping with the neoliberal policies of advanced capitalism which the media represent and promote. As John McMurtry states, the "freedom of international speculators and investors to dictate to governments everywhere how they are to govern" can be seen to be indicative of globalization of the world economy and extends far beyond any one case study.[27] Increasingly, big business dictates government policy and this has given way to harmful consequences, such that there seems to be no limit to examples of the destructive aspects of the myriad policies which can be seen to have evolved from the profit requirements of capitalist production.[28] As Hale points out,

> Most colonized countries have now gained political independence, but this has not brought about effective economic independence. Their economies are still dominated by forces of the world capitalist economic system over which they have little control.[29]

Mechanisms of control which facilitate corporate rule over domestic social and ecological policies "include control over capital, control over patterns of investment, domination of market relations, decisive bargaining power in the labour market, and political clout, including the use of force as a last resort."[30]

The OAS Comes To Windsor

At least since APEC in Vancouver in 1997, the WTO in Seattle in 1999, the IMF and the World Bank protests in Washington, D.C. in April 2000, various organizations, labour groups, and individuals have brought the 'social unrest' of the so-called 'emerging markets' into what we thought were the already-developed market economies of Canada, Italy, the U.S., Switzerland, and so forth. If these are indeed, as Susan George has written, part of an "international citizens' movement which has disturbed the gatherings of the masters of the universe," then it begs the question: how are they reported by the mainstream press?[31]

The 30th General Assembly of the Organization of American States was held in Windsor from June 4-6, 2000. It was the tenth anniversary of former Canadian Prime Minister Brian Mulroney's initiative making Canada a member. It was also the first time the OAS met in Canada, although it met again in Quebec City in 2001, with predictable, similar results. The Windsor convention attracted about 3000 protestors, and about 2200 police, with another 4000 police on the U.S. border side of Detroit. The police arrested 78 people during the OAS Summit, mostly for breach of the peace, though only 15 arrests resulted in charges, and all of these charges were eventually dismissed.

The *Windsor Star* carried a total of about 150 stories and letters about the three-day event. The newspaper's coverage began at the end of May, with accounts of how downtown businesses were preparing for the convention business, while preparing themselves for the expected onslaught of protestors. A study of all the material concerning the OAS in the *Windsor Star* indicated that almost all of the critical, contextual and informative material was contained in the 'letters to the editor' section, restricted to about 100 words or less. News stories, editorials and columns focused almost exclusively on the alleged violence and related topics, with few exceptions.

Topics in the Windsor Star Coverage of the OAS Meeting
- Business preparations, planned closings, boarding of windows
- Neighboring police in nearby Chatham offer backup
- Food preparations for dignitaries, meals to be offered
- Hospitals on alert, 'Code Orange Advisory' at Windsor Regional Hospital
- Emergency plan for city says unruly protestors to be dunked in pools
- One hospital set aside for protestors, another for dignitaries and delegates
- Borders brace for traffic snarl
- Detroit outlaws ammonia, chlorine, slingshots downtown
- Arrested protestors may go to nearby Leamington jail
- CIBC bank boarding up windows
- *Windsor Star* downtown office to close
- Contingency plans for downtown businesses: how to get broken windows fixed

- OAS pavilion showcases children and human rights
- Police undergo teargas training
- Police to use snow plows to remove barricades
- Madeleine Albright to miss Summit, on trip with Bill Clinton
- Barriers to transform Windsor: all protestors fault
- Mayor says barricades necessary for protection
- Number of protestors unknown; estimates range from 3 to 10,000
- Organized labour to bus in people in protest
- Plywood barricades set up downtown
- Shutdown coalition holds teach-in at university
- Several hundred RCMP and OPP officers in student residences
- Mayor urges calm (before storm)
- First protestors arrested in park; tourists ignored
- Radical protestors from Washington plan Detroit protest
- More than 500 police in Windsor and Detroit brace for protests
- Wording on protest signs
- Poverty the enemy, says Canadian Prime Minister Jean Chretien; free trade means prosperity
- Puppeteer protestor arrested
- Film-makers use protest to film backdrop for action scenes
- Bus driver kept delegates on board; feared for safety with protestors
- Warehouse used temporarily for jail
- Business is down, cops all over downtown
- Police say should have required parade permits
- Labour considers formal protest over police use of pepper spray
- OAS brought $10M to city

There were five stories of about 121 in total which mentioned the word 'capitalism'. Four stories mentioned the World Bank, and two mentioned the IMF. Six stories mentioned the WTO. Two stories mentioned 'privatization.' No stories or letters to the editor mentioned the terms: structural adjustment, market liberalization, hot money, money supply, social unrest, prices, fiscal austerity,

MMT, harmonization, 'the race to the bottom', social programs, economic interests, cultural policies, labour laws, giant sea turtles, or hormone-injected beef. Five stories mentioned oil, but two of these were about mineral oil used to treat pepper sprayed protestors, while one story mentioned vegetable oil, one was in reference to 'foil' and the other to 'turmoil.'

The references to 'capitalism' and many of the other key terms were vague, disjointed and de-contextualized. For example, in a report on the diverse objectives of participants at the summit, the *Star* stated that: "First of all, of course, protestors hate even the idea of the OAS meeting unless it is to denounce global capitalism." No further explanation is provided with regard to motivations or what global capitalism actually entails, in this context.[32] The same report contained the following more lengthy explanation and defense of free trade from Richard Bernal, delegate, Ambassador and Permanent Representative for Jamaica to the OAS:

> One of the issues that has come up here and is of concern to us is the operation of the trade unit. The trade unit is very important in terms of doing research for policy and in providing technical assistance to countries in the free trade zone of the Americas. We're very interested in free trade because as a small economy, we're a very open economy. We see the establishment of a hemisphere-wide free-trade area as something we can benefit from.

Another story simply listed some of the wording on protestors' placards as follows: "Hemispheric security? Not with Uncle Death in charge"; "Oppose U.S. militarism of the Americas"; "Human rights now in all the Americas"; "Asylum for workers, no discrimination"; "What world do you protect?"; "Who's streets? Our streets"; "Free trade—free for whom?"; "WTO and OAS—the lies and the mess"; "OAS = terror"; "Funny—I don't recall voting for a one-world government." These cryptic descriptions substituted for serious analysis and background information which may have lent credence to the protestors and would have worked to create an impression of them as something other than radicals and/or threats to public security (and/or the common good).

One of the few attempts to understand the protestors and their causes, published ten days after the summit concluded, contained an interview with a young protestor who said he frequently pulled out his guitar to relax.

It's a good way to take the seriousness out of it all," he says. *"When you're constantly indoctrinating yourself and other people about the dark sides of the world and how everything is just kind of going to hell for everyone who's not a first world consumer, it can get really depressing.* So it's cool just to play music sometimes (emphasis added).[33]

Quotations such as this reinforced the picture of the protestors as radicals, indoctrinated hippies, depressed and, for that matter, depressing.

Another story began, "After a long day of protesting against corporate capitalism, the average protestor isn't likely to shell out for a restaurant meal. That's why Food Not Bombs is on the scene in Windsor."[34] This is open to a multiplicity of available readings, but at the same time, the dominant meaning encoded within the lead implies that the 'average protestor' is impoverished. Concurrently, one could read it as implying that Social Darwinism is very much alive and well in terms of both real-world practice (the agencies of global capitalism and the policies they advance) and the spectrums of thought and opinion advanced by the ideological network (the characterization of these policies, and of the morality/intelligence/social class of those who would dissent). In a non-mainstream interview with one of the protestors who was there on the scene in Windsor, s/he had this to say with respect to the ways in which the slanted discourse above tends to characterize protestors:

I find it incredibly offensive. I've an M.A. in Business Administration, am quite gainfully employed in Toronto, and, for that matter, my yearly salary is in excess of the mean annual income within Canada; whatever that's worth. I went to Windsor because I'm concerned...about economics, debt slavery, pollution, working conditions...women's rights...it's wrong to have such dialogue taking place behind closed doors...I personally try to stay as informed as possible...I've problems with these things and felt like joining in to express my views...this makes me what...*deviant?*...that's generalizing, and stereotyping...it's putting things in the simplest possible terms...

Another *Windsor Star* story illustrates how these 'terms' can be highly critical but de-contextualized. The story quotes one of the protestors as follows:

Our goal was to expose the OAS as part of the jigsaw puzzle of global corporate capitalism and we did that...stop focusing on the minuscule," said Tim Scott, an American union activist arrested Sunday for breaching the peace. "They focus on minuscule acts of property damage. They're not focusing on the lives being destroyed and the tremendous suffering that's happening because of the IMF, WTO, OAS and FTAA.[35]

The terms are not explained—how many newspaper readers would actually know what the acronyms stand for—background details are not provided, and the words of the protestor are simply left hanging there—radical, bald, forsaken, sounding like the slick, pat phrases of the brainwashed. This is especially so when such a quote is combined with photographs and depictions of violent confrontations in which the photo cut-lines indicate that it was "protestors confronting police" and not the other way around. Another problem, of course, is that there are few official spokespersons for the broad anti-corporate globalization movement, so media tend to pick someone out of the crowd, interviewing individual protesters with varying degrees of comprehension and ability to articulate. The media also used the occasion to limit the scope of the movement and to openly question its potential—while purportedly using the protesters' own voices:

> The question on the minds of coalition members is how far their campaign will go. They call it a "global movement" and have convinced some politicians and authors to take notice. Naomi Klein, a Toronto author and columnist, has just published a book about the movement. Worldwide, however, the movement peaks and wanes, with the anti-sweatshop faction being the most influential in initiating policy change.[36]

No quotations are provided here for backup justification(s), to indicate just whose mind the journalist is exploring. Meanings are simply (and flatly) imposed, and successful battles against the MAI are conveniently ignored.

In an article two days after the protests, one reporter described how art was used as a protest medium, "from effigies and wall hangings to street theatre and song." He said that much of the art was crude, "slapdash affairs, literally thrown together with duct tape and wall paint," but that it all had "the same intention: hammer home a message. Rather one-note perhaps, but this week's message was largely along the lines of 'capitalism kills!' " For the journalist, in this case a relatively progressive but exceedingly frustrated former graduate student, this would represent a huge victory: getting these few words of dissent past his editors and into the paper.[37] And he did actually make an attempt to elaborate with an example:

> "The Mexican government formed paramilitary troops to force people off their land after free trade started," says Zapateatro actor Fernando Hernandez, who points out that the uprising in Chiapas started the day after NAFTA began. For indigenous people, there are no other sources of income. They live off the land. Or work in slave labour. The ones who benefit from free trade are the large corporations.[38]

While obviously a very limited picture of what is going on and what the protests are about, this account is nonetheless (obviously) critical, and one that is overwhelmed by the volume of coverage devoted to other events, perspectives and representations: police, violence and pepper spray. The Zapatista uprising also dates back to 1994.

Another exception was a story run on June 2, in the lead up to the convention, as part of the "OAS Countdown" coverage, which was otherwise mostly composed of articles about preparations by police and downtown businesses. The story was about a speech given by CAW president Buzz Hargrove who was quoted about a WTO ruling just the day before which removed preferential tariffs for the Big Three auto manufacturers: the backbone of the Windsor economy. The story was written by the newspaper's labour reporter: a position which has since been eliminated.

> Hargrove said he finds it "frustrating as hell" that governments don't object more to decisions made by "faceless bureaucrats" in organizations like the OAS, WTO, World Bank and International Monetary Fund... For more than a decade, governments have instead been capitulating to a corporate-driven agenda for free trade, lower taxes, deregulation and privatization, Hargrove said. But with incomes of working-class families remaining stagnant or declining at the same time "people are crying out for governments to step in and defend their interests," he said.

Of course, this information is pertinent not just because it is labour's perspective, which is usually ignored, but because the WTO ruling could affect business interests in Windsor.

Any critical references were more than offset by guest columnist material holding these positions and the protesters' views up to ridicule as "collateral noise" and "absurd caricatures," and defending the OAS. "These caricatures are so far off the mark as to be absurd. Worse, they indicate that the persons involved have not asked basic questions about the OAS and have, therefore, forfeited their credibility," wrote John W. Graham, board member of the Ottawa-based Canadian Foundation for the Americas, in a lengthy guest column.

Three more items in the *Windsor Star* should be singled out as exceptions. The first of these was in a column run once every two weeks, by a local, moderately progressive former bookstore owner and former city counselor, Sheila Wisdom. Her column about the OAS ran nine days after the meetings ended. In it, she began by denouncing the radical and violent protesters, and blaming them for creating the violence that obscured the issues. The implication is that if it hadn't been for the (apparent, impending) violence, the media would have been able to focus on the issues, as though it was a choice between the two. "The radical element, by declaring a goal of shutdown," she wrote, "turned the Windsor meeting of the OAS into an issue of power. They aimed to be more powerful than the civil authorities. They aimed to shut down a major world institution." Of course, they were merely aiming to shut down a meeting and not an institution. Thanks to the violent protesters, she continued, "we are still left with questions about what in these relatively obscure international agencies —such as the World Trade Organization, the World Bank and the OAS—inspires such passion in both peaceful protesters and radicals."

Ms. Wisdom quoted the former Premier of Manitoba and former University of Windsor political science professor, Howard Pawley, who "says one reason for the passion is a recent change in mood in some of his students. Where students were apathetic and disinterested only a couple of years ago, he is now seeing a level of political concern that hasn't been seen in decades." We are to take from this decontextualized comment from a thoughtful observer that student activism is the result of a kind of spontaneous combustion on the part of these young people. Pawley then identified alienation and a lack of control on the part of youth, and reintroduced the WTO decision regarding the Auto Pact.

> To Pawley, the underlying anxiety for most groups centres on the growing influence of these organizations. He says that the protesters "don't feel they have a voice." Some international organizations are making rulings that will affect people but there is little or no recourse for those who disagree. An example of this is the recent decision of the World Trade Organization to strike down the remaining elements of the Auto Pact. Three powerful bodies in Canada—govern-

ment, business and labour—had lobbied against this decision, only to lose. This reinforces the idea that power is being shifted from our elected officials to distant bureaucracies. And our old means of democratic influence don't seem to apply.

Here, Pawley identified a major concern: the shift in the locus of power and the ramifications for democracy, although the writer didn't put this in the international context, and only the one example was given. Also, this is but one column in all of the articles provided concerning the OAS, and would not go a long way towards counteracting all of the other misinformation, or overcoming all of the negative portrayals of rage, incomprehensible violence and seeming anarchism.

The second story was carried on the second day of the OAS meetings, and reported on a rally by the Canadian Labour Congress the day before. The story was written by the then-labour reporter, Gary Rennie, and the focus was on how labour denounced the police, and said the only thing missing was the tanks which are present in Colombia, and other Third World confrontations.

The story contained the following brief quotations from labour leaders and the NDP:

"We march for the millions of workers trapped in poverty," —labour leader from Panama

"Let's get the OAS to start standing up for human rights ahead of profit-seeking corporations." —Alexa McDonough, NDP Leader

"What's happening in the Americas is happening to us too," said Darcy. She said the seven deaths from poisoned drinking water in Walkerton resulted from the policies of privatization and cuts to government programs now being urged for adoption in Latin American countries. —Judy Darcy (president of CUPE)

"Francisco Ramirez, a trade union lawyer in Colombia who spoke in Windsor a month ago, is now hiding from death squads in his own country." —Buzz Hargrove.

The last story actually quotes from Noam Chomsky, which, needless to say, is very unusual for the *Windsor Star*. The story quoted some criticisms of the OAS and some praise, concluding that it is "far from perfect," but still "relevent" [sic]. Amid the people quoted we find Chomsky, as follows:

> "The OAS has had a conflicted history…it can't function as a community of equals because the countries are so overwhelmed by the U.S.," says Noam Chomsky, internationally known linguist and philosopher. "Like the UN, it can do only as much as the great powers allow it to do. However, the OAS is an important, if weak barrier against U.S. intervention."

This is the only quotation from Chomsky, characterizing the OAS as "important." It is followed in the story by this protracted opposing view from John Graham, an 'authorized knower' whose lengthy opinion piece was published the same day, along with others.

> The OAS is "far from perfect," agrees John Graham, board member of the Ottawa-based Canadian Foundation for the Americas (FOCAL). But, the Americas would be "much worse off" without it. "The OAS helps iron out the road from dictatorship to democracy and the blessing of the OAS gives legitimacy and credibility to a government when it makes that change," says Graham. Twenty years ago, at least 75 per cent of all Latin American governments were dictatorships or under military rule, he notes. Today, officially, there is only one dictatorship—in Cuba. But the precarious state of many other countries emphasizes the need for a collective watchdog such as the OAS, which helps prevent democracies from backsliding, says Graham… "The OAS is a lifeline for us," says Marcella Diaz, who moved to Windsor from Colombia in 1990. "Without the OAS, there would be no watchdog keeping an eye on what governments are doing and helping them maintain their fragile democracies." Graham, who acknowledged that the OAS needs to be improved, condemned any attempts to shut down the OAS. "The work of the OAS is not made easier by characters running around saying 'shut it down' and accusing it of evil stuff which is not part of its mandate," said Graham. "Many of these people are gulled into thinking it is a nasty association of wicked global imperialists which is nonsense."

Predictably, Chomsky's views as a leading dissident are used in *support* of the OAS and *against* the protesters, as his selected words defend the OAS as "an important, if weak barrier against U.S. intervention," and by implication, criticize those who oppose the OAS. Despite Chomsky's inclusion, the entire article defends the OAS against the "rage" of the protesters, all the while slipping in condemnation of Hugo Chavez and Fidel Castro.

Summing Up the Reportage

Overall, for the *Windsor Star*, organizations such as the OAS are democratic in nature; they represent solutions rather than problems. In its role as a major means of social control, the *Star*, like other corporate media, sees a 'crisis of democracy' in the violent, misguided and indoctrinated embodiment of the protesters, who must be eradicated, so that normalcy: peace, order and 'good government' may return.

The repetitive patterns in these representations, from coverage of labour day, to strikes and the labour movement generally, and for that matter the coverage of the economic picture and class divisions more generally, as well as marginalized groups such as feminists, gays and lesbians, visible minorities, all reflect white corporate, capitalist, patriarchal interests: Michael Moore's *Stupid White Men*.

An intensive analysis of all *Windsor Star* coverage of the OAS meetings demonstrated a lack of important contextual information: for example, about the bodies such as the IMF, World Bank, and OAS, which the protests are all about. In the absence of this information, the protesters appeared to be irrational, and radical, and their causes could be summarily dismissed by reporters, readers, and right-thinking individuals. What coverage existed was predominantly sensationalized, focusing on impending violence, which never occurred. This served to further radicalize the protests, and to justify the neoliberal agenda surrounding free trade agreements and their organizations such as the WTO, *et cetera*. As Ed Herman notes, echoing Joseph Stiglitz,

> There is now an almost religious faith in the market, at least among the elite, so that regardless of evidence, markets are assumed benevolent and non-market mechanisms are suspect...the transnational media corporations have a distinct self-interest in global trade agreements, as they are among their foremost beneficiaries.[39]

The almost exclusive use of right-wing authorized knowers as sources provided the bias of official discourse, and is of course in keeping with the third filter of Herman and Chomsky's Propaganda Model. Where protesters were quoted, it was a means of discrediting them. Finally, even Noam Chomsky himself, a leading dissident, was used as a means of discrediting the protesters and their causes.

The Haïtian Example

One of the countries of the world which has been greatly victimized by "corporate globalization," along with its precursors such as colonialism, and related constructs such as racism, is Haïti. Haïti constantly vies with a couple of other countries, such as Guatemala, for the position of lowest common denominator in the Western Hemisphere, regarding gross domestic product, standard of living, minimum wage, *et cetera*. About 80 percent of the population lives in abject poverty. Up to 70 percent of the population is unemployed or underemployed.

If one relies on the mainstream media to explain this, it is portrayed as an example of a "failed state," indeed, one which remained in 2007 under the supervision and 'protection' of UN Military forces, known by the local acronym of MINUSTA. Despite hundreds of millions of dollars in 'aid money' from Canada, the U.S. and others, despite Canada having supervised elections held in 2006, Haïti is presented as being torn by local strife between opposing factions. Or, more accurately, the problem is depicted as existing on one side alone: the side of the unstable and criminal, deposed president Jean-Bertrand Aristide, and his Famni Lavalas political party. The mainstream view is that gangs of bandits, seemingly created and armed by Aristide, or his party, are engaged in kidnappings, murder and theft. These activities were conducted to keep him in power, and continue now to return him to power, against the wishes of "civil society." Underlying much of this reportage is the unspoken but implied racist perspective that 'these [Black] people are incapable of self-government.' It is somewhat reminiscent of the Afghan insurgents: after all we have done for them, how can they be so ungrateful/incompetent/corrupt?

One would be hard-pressed to find a single mainstream reporter, including those working for public networks such as the CBC and BBC, who do not subscribe to this perspective. A review of mainstream articles in recent years supports this contention. But while this simplistic account has the ring of truth to it, brought about by endless repetition of the alleged facts, in reality nothing could be much further from the truth.

The Historical Context

To understand Haïti, we must go back in history.[40] By the 1697 treaty of Ryswick, the French formally occupied the portion of Hispaniola (Dominican Republic) known as Saint Dominigue (now Haïti), taking it from the Spanish, who had brutally eliminated all of the indigenous population, whom Christopher Columbus had described as "lovable, tractable, peaceable, gentle, decorous."[41] Thousands upon thousands of slaves were brought to do the new colonial master's bidding, and by the 1780s Haïti was the bread basket of France, providing two-thirds of that country's fruit and vegetables, as well as three-quarters of the world's sugar, also leading the world in production of coffee, cotton, indigo, and rum.

The Haïtian slaves rebelled in 1791, ultimately defeating the combined armies of Napoleon's France, Britain and Spain, in a war lasting 13 years. The U.S., which itself was a slave state at the time, lived in fear of a similar uprising, and sent $400,000 to support the war against Haïti. Professor Peter Hallward writes,

> There have been few other events in modern history whose implications were more threatening to the dominant order: the mere existence of an independent Haïti was a reproach to the slave-trading nations of Europe, a dangerous example to the slave-owning U.S., and an inspiration for successive African and Latin American liberation movements.[42]

In 1804, Haïtians celebrated their independence. But France only re-established diplomatic and trade relations when Haïtians agreed, in 1825, to pay their former colonial masters "compensation" of 150 million francs for the loss of its slaves. This was eventually reduced to 90 million francs, but payments consumed 80 percent of the Haïtian national budget, until it was paid off in 1947—to the U.S., which had 'bought out' the debt from France during its occupation which began in 1915.

Haïtians have thus paid their original oppressors three times over, once through the slavery itself, secondly through compensation, or reparations, and thirdly through interest payments.

In 1915 the U.S., under President Woodrow Wilson, invaded and occupied Haïti, and then the Dominican Republic. They abolished the clause in the constitution preventing foreigners from owning property, took over the national bank, ensured more 'reliable' payments of foreign debt, bought out the 'debt' to France, expropriated land to create their own plantations, and created a brutal military to repress the domestic population.[43]

When the U.S. Marines left in 1934, successive military regimes ruled, including the murderous regimes of "Papa Doc" Francois Duvalier (1957-71) and his son "Baby Doc" Jean-Francois, also declared president-for-life in 1971. Jean-Bertrand Aristide was just four years old when Duvalier senior assumed power in 1957. Aristide was a Catholic priest, and follower of liberation theology, who began making popular radio broadcasts in the late 1970s. The conservative and Duvalier-controlled senior clergy sent him abroad for religious re-programming, including studies at the Université de Montréal in Québec. By 1985 he was back preaching in Haïti, and the following year a mass movement chased Duvalier off the island. Duvalier was given shelter in France. Much later, in 2003, the *Montreal Gazette* would admit:

> Human-rights groups say 40,000 to 60,000 political opponents were killed during the 29-year reign of the father and son. Duvalier, along with family and political cronies, also embezzled at least $500 million during his last decade of rule, according to Haïtian government officials and lawyers and American officials. Successive Haïtian governments—there have been nearly a dozen since Duvalier was deposed—retained lawyers in France and the U.S. to help recover the money... As part of an investigation into the looting allegations, authorities raided the villa Duvalier and his wife rented in Mougins shortly after they arrived in France. The authorities say they caught Mrs. Duvalier trying to flush a notebook down the toilet. It logged recent spending—$168,780 for clothes at Givenchy, $270,200 for jewelry at Boucheron, $9,752 for two children's horse saddles at Hermes, $68,500 for a clock, $13,000 for a week in a Paris hotel.[44]

A Reluctant Leader

Aristide resisted entering politics, but eventually, reluctantly, was pressed into service because of his immense popularity with the nation's poor. In open presidential elections in 1990, Aristide became Haïti's first democratically-elected president, winning 67 percent of the vote, to 14 percent for Marc Bazin, a World Bank economist and former Finance Minister under Baby Doc Duvalier, who was the U.S. favorite. Here is Aristide's description of what transpired:

> The emergence of the people as an organised public force was already taking place in Haïti in the 1980s, and by 1986 this force was strong enough to push the Duvalier dictatorship from power. It was a grass-roots movement, not a top-down project driven by a single leader or a single organisation. It wasn't exclusively political, either. It took shape above all through the constitution, all over the country, of many small church communities or *ti legliz*. When I was elected

president it wasn't the election of a politician, or a conventional political party; it was an expression of the mobilisation of the people as
a whole. For the first time, the national palace became a place not
just for professional politicians but for the people. Welcoming people
from the poorest sections of Haïtian society within the centre of traditional power—this was a profoundly transformative gesture.[45]

Aristide instituted education and agrarian reforms, and was clearly on the side
of the poor people instead of the rich. So, in just seven months, a new military
junta with U.S. approval overthrew him, and the brutal General Raoul Cedras,
a former CIA operative, took control. Aristide fled to the U.S., and an estimated
5,000 Aristide (Lavalas Party) supporters were killed in the ensuing reign of
terror, over three years. Economic conditions led to widespread malnutrition.
Waves of desperate emigrants tried to flee to the U.S., which was inundated
with Haïtian boat people. Marc Bazin from the World Bank was appointed
Prime Minister by the Junta, in 1992, in what they termed a "consensus government." Meanwhile, the CIA had launched a smear campaign aimed at
Aristide.[46] Brian Latell, the CIA's chief Latin American analyst, launched an offensive in the U.S. Congress and mainstream media to portray Aristide as
"mentally unstable" and a "murderer and psychopath," while the coup's
leader General Raoul Cedras and his cohorts came from "the most promising
group of Haïtian leaders to emerge since the Duvalier family." Henry Kissinger
went on TV to call Aristide "a psychopath." Right-wing politician Patrick Buchanan called him "a bloodthirsty little socialist."[47] George Bush Sr. had
turned a blind eye to the coup, but by 1994, Bill Clinton was under pressure to
act, in part because the furious Haïtian populace was threatening to overthrow
the military junta, and so Clinton arranged, with a spectacular show of 23,000
troops, and at an estimated cost of $2.3 billion (U.S.), to restore Aristide to
power. Of course, not a shot was fired and it could have all been accomplished
with a phone call. But, Aristide had to agree to a drastic IMF restructuring program. He had to accept amnesty for the coupsters, pardoning those who murdered thousands of his supporters, and poor Haïtians at-large. He agreed to
hold new elections in 1995, after just a year, so his time in exile in the U.S. was
counted as part of his term in office. And, he couldn't run in the next election,
as more than one consecutive term in office is prohibited by the Haïtian Constitution.

The tariff on rice was cut from 50% to 3%, and Haïti was flooded with cheap U.S. rice. Haïti had been self-sufficient in rice, but imports rose from 7000 tons in 1985 to 225,000 tons in 2002. The same thing happened in the poultry sector, costing 10,000 jobs. As part of the IMF's privatization program, in 1997, the state-owned flour mill was sold off to the private sector for $9 million, although its yearly profits were estimated at $25 million. The mill was bought by a group of investors linked to one of Haïti's largest banks. As economist Michel Chossudovsky notes, "this sale will further concentrate wealth-in a country where 1% of the population already holds 45% of the wealth."[48]

Between 1996 and 2000, René Préval, Aristide's former vice president, was elected president, as Haïtians, for the first time, had a smooth transition from one democratically-elected president to another. But Préval's more "moderate" position of greater appeasement of foreign powers alienated some Lavalas supporters.

Aristide, for his part, worked to create schools and improve literacy, but dragged his feet on the IMF's neoliberal reforms. From 1990 to 2002, illiteracy fell from 61% to 48%. Cuba helped to build a new medical school, and the previously soaring HIV infection rate was frozen. Taxes on the rich were increased, and in 2003 the minimum wage was doubled.[49]

THE STORY OF THE CREOLE PIGS

In 1982 international agencies assured Haïti's peasants their pigs were sick and had to be killed (so that the illness would not spread to countries to the North). Promises were made that better pigs would replace the sick pigs. With an efficiency not since seen among development projects, all of the Creole pigs were killed over period of thirteen months.

Two years later the new, better pigs came from Iowa. They were so much better that they required clean drinking water (unavailable to 80% of the Haïtian population), imported feed (costing $90 a year when the per capita income was about $130), and special roofed pigpens. Haïtian peasants quickly dubbed them "prince a quatre pieds," (four-footed princes). Adding insult to injury, the meat did not taste as good. Needless to say, the repopulation program was a complete failure.

One observer of the process estimated that in monetary terms Haïtian peasants lost $600 million dollars.

continued

There was a 30% drop in enrollment in rural schools, there was a dramatic decline in the protein consumption in rural Haïti, a devastating decapitalization of the peasant economy and an incalculable negative impact on Haïti's soil and agricultural productivity. The Haïtian peasantry has not recovered to this day.

Most of rural Haïti is still isolated from global markets, so for many peasants the extermination of the Creole pigs was their first experience of globalization. The experience looms large in the collective memory. Today, when the peasants are told that "economic reform" and privatization will benefit them they are understandably wary. The state-owned enterprises are sick, we are told, and they must be privatized. The peasants shake their heads and remember the Creole pigs. —Aristide[50]

The IMF's Bitter "Economic Medicine"

IMF-sponsored "free market" reforms have been carried out consistently since the Duvalier era. They have been applied in several stages since Aristide's first election in 1990. The 1991 military coup was partly intended to reverse the Aristide government's progressive reforms and reinstate the neoliberal policy agenda of the Duvalier era.[51] The U.S. State Department sought the appointment of Marc Bazin as Prime Minister in 1992, and in 1983 it was the IMF which had recommended Bazin for the position of Finance Minister, because he had a track record of working for the so-called "Washington consensus." This was a term coined in the late 1980s which referred to a reform package for Third World countries, designed by Washington-based organizations such as the IMF and World Bank. It included a neoliberal agenda: tight fiscal policies, tax reform, moderate interest rates, trade liberalization, open foreign investment, privatization of state enterprises, and deregulation. Of course this reads much like the IMF's "structural adjustment" packages, which would be described later by Joseph Stiglitz.

"Free market" reformers were brought into Aristide's Cabinet, and a new wave of deadly macro-economic policies was adopted.[52] Aristide's return was negotiated behind closed doors with Haïti's external creditors. The new government had to clear the country's debt with its external creditors. The new loans provided by the World Bank, the Inter-American Development Bank (IDB), and the IMF were used to meet Haïti's obligations with international creditors. "Fresh money was used to pay back old debt leading to a spiraling external debt."[53] This left no money for social programs, requiring further cuts to programs which were almost non-existent. The civil service was drastically reduced, along with teachers and health workers, leading to further massive unemployment and poverty. By 2001, the unemployment rate reached 70 percent. According to economist Michel Chossudovsky, "The country had been literally pushed to the brink of economic and social disaster."

More than 75 percent of Haïtians are engaged in agriculture, producing food crops for the domestic market as well as cash crops for export. The peasant economy was undermined during the Duvalier era. The IMF-World Bank trade reforms opened local markets to the dumping of U.S. agricultural surpluses such as rice, sugar, and corn, "leading to the destruction of the entire peasant economy." Gonaives, Haïti's rice basket region, with its extensive paddy fields, was forced into bankruptcy. "In matter of a few years, Haïti, a small impoverished country in the Caribbean, had become the world's fourth largest importer of American rice after Japan, Mexico and Canada."[54]

The Second Wave of IMF Reforms

Presidential elections were scheduled for November, 2000. To exert economic and political pressure, the Clinton Administration put an embargo on development aid to Haïti earlier in 2000. Barely two weeks before the elections, the outgoing administration of René Préval signed a Letter of Intent with the IMF, which virtually prevented any departure from the neoliberal agenda. Although Aristide promised electors that he would increase the minimum wage, build new schools and develop new literacy programs, the hands of the new government were tied. "All major decisions regarding the State budget, the management of the public sector, public investment, privatization, trade and monetary policy had already been taken. They were part of the agreement reached with the IMF."[55]

In 2003, the IMF imposed a "flexible price system in fuel," which triggered an inflationary spiral. The Haïtian gourde was devalued. Petroleum prices increased by about 130 percent in January-February 2003, contributing to a 40 percent increase in consumer prices in 2002-2003. Despite this increase in the cost of living the IMF demanded a wage freeze to control inflationary pressures. It pressured the government to lower public sector salaries, including teachers and health workers. The IMF also demanded the phasing out of the statutory minimum wage of approximately 25 cents an hour, in favour of "Labour market flexibility," intended to attract foreign investors. The daily minimum wage was $3.00 in 1994, declining to about $1.50-1.75 (depending on the gourde-dollar exchange rate) in 2004.[56] Haïti's abysmally low wages, part of the IMF-World Bank "cheap labour" policy framework since the 1980s, are viewed as a way to improve the standard of living.

> Sweatshop conditions in the assembly industries (in a totally unregulated labour market) and forced labour conditions in Haïti's agricultural plantations are considered by the IMF as a key to achieving economic prosperity, because they "attract foreign investment."[57]

In 2003, Aristide supported a virtual doubling of the minimum wage from 36 gourdes/day to 70/day—from about $1 to $2 Canadian. According to University of Toronto professor Leslie Jermyn,

> This was a direct threat to the profits of local sub-contractors in the Export Processing Zones (EPZs), people like American citizen Andy Apaid, and their corporate clients, like Gildan of Montreal. On a brighter note, Gildan Activewear will be able to withstand the direct competition of Chinese textiles unleashed when the U.S. dropped its textile quotas in January [2005] because it will be able to take advantage of Haïti's improved minimum wage. Gildan has done very well for itself in our neoliberal world. When it started operations in 1984, 12 t-shirts sold for $28 of which 8% was profit ($2.24), 20 years later, 12 t-shirts sold for $12 of which 30% was profit ($3.60). The price of this profit has been the lives, dignity and freedom of people who are valued only for the cheap labour they can provide during their short lives.[58]

Interest rates skyrocketed. In the northern and eastern parts of Haïti, the hike in fuel prices led to a virtual paralysis of transportation and public services including water and electricity. The collapse of the economy spearheaded by the IMF boosted the popularity of the Democratic Platform, which accused Aristide of "economic mismanagement." The leaders of the Democratic Platform, including Andy Apaid—who actually owns the sweatshops—are the main perpetrators of the low wage economy.[59]

The choices that globalization offers the poor remind me of a story. Anatole, one of the boys who had lived with us at Lafanmi Selavi, was working at the national port. One day a very powerful businessman offered him money to sabotage the main unloading forklift at the port. Anatole said to the man, "Well, then I am already dead." The man, surprised by the response, asked, "Why?" Anatole answered, "because if I sneak in here at night and do what you ask they will shoot me, and if I don't, you will kill me." The dilemma is, I believe, the classic dilemma of the poor; a choice between death and death. Either we enter a global economic system, in which we know we cannot survive, or, we refuse, and face death by slow starvation. With choices like these the urgency of finding a third way is clear. We must find some room to maneuver, some open space simply to survive. We must lift ourselves up off the morgue table and tell the experts we are not yet dead.

—Aristide

The Elections of 2000

In the spring 2000 elections, Aristide's Party, Fanmi Lavalas, won majorities at all levels of government: 89 of 115 mayoral positions; 72 of 83 seats in the chamber of deputies; and 18 of 19 senate seats contested. Aristide himself won the presidential election that fall with 92 percent of the vote. Political opposition to Aristide was confined almost entirely to the elites: the Democratic Convergence, and the Group of 184, with no more than eight percent of the populace. Initially, the Organization of American States (OAS) described the elections as "a great success for the Haïtian population..." but subsequently, the OAS said the elections were flawed because the Haïtian electoral council used only the votes cast for the top four candidates in computing the voting percentages, rather than including all the less popular candidates. This was done in eight senate seat races, in accordance with custom, if not the letter of the law under the constitution. It did not change the results. But under pressure, Aristide asked the offending senators to resign, so new elections could be held. But as the senate seats really were not the "problem," this was not an acceptable solution for the opposition and the American Embassy.

The Clinton administration seized on the belated OAS objection to justify a crippling embargo on foreign aid, involving $500 million (US) from the Inter-American development bank, and others. This, in an economy where the total government budget had fallen to about $300 million annually: $30 each for its eight million citizens, subtracting the annual $60 million payment on the national debt (45% of which was incurred by the Duvalier dictatorships).[60] Imagine if all the Canadian government could afford was $30 for each Canadian? What would happen to our social programs?

Instead of providing the loans and aid money, the U.S. and Canadian governments and others funded opposition parties, and non-governmental organizations which refused to work with the government, for example setting up private schools with the money.[61] Sometimes these NGOs and opposition parties had no supporters, no infrastructure, merely one person as leader, who received the money.[62] Some of them worked actively to undermine the Aristide government, in the interest of "democracy building."

THE ROLE OF THE NATIONAL ENDOWMENT FOR DEMOCRACY (NED)

In Haïti, this "civil society opposition" is bankrolled by the National Endowment for Democracy which works hand in glove with the CIA. The Democratic Platform is supported by the International Republican Institute (IRI) , which is an arm of the National Endowment for Democracy (NED). U.S. Senator John McCain is Chairman of IRI's Board of Directors. G-184 leader Andy Apaid was in liaison with Secretary of State Colin Powell in the days prior to the kidnapping and deportation of President Aristide by U.S. forces on February 29. His umbrella organization of elite business organizations and religious NGOs, which is also supported by the International Republican Institute (IRI), receives sizeable amounts of money from the European Union. It is worth recalling that the NED, (which overseas the IRI) although not formally part of the CIA, performs an important intelligence function within the arena of civilian political parties and NGOs. It was created in 1983, when the CIA was being accused of covertly bribing politicians and setting up phony civil society front organizations. According to Allen Weinstein, who was responsible for setting up the NED during the Reagan Administration: "A lot of what we do today was done covertly 25 years ago by the CIA." The NED channels congressional funds to the four institutes: The International Republican Institute (IRI), the National Democratic Institute for International Affairs (NDI), the Center for International Private Enterprise (CIPE), and the American Center for International Labour Solidarity (ACILS). These organizations are said to be "uniquely qualified to provide technical assistance to aspiring democrats worldwide."

continued

In other words, there is a division of tasks between the CIA and the NED. While the CIA provides covert support to armed paramilitary rebel groups and death squadrons, the NED and its four constituent organizations finance "civilian" political parties and non governmental organizations with a view to instating American "democracy" around the World. The NED constitutes, so to speak, the CIA's "civilian arm." CIA-NED interventions in different parts of the world are characterized by a consistent pattern, which is applied in numerous countries. The NED provided funds to the "civil society" organizations in Venezuela, which initiated an attempted coup against President Hugo Chavez. In Venezuela it was the "Democratic Coordination," which was the recipient of NED support; in Haïti it is the "Democratic Convergence" and G-184.[63]

In a remarkable example of prophecy, leading figures in the opposition, the Democratic Convergence, told the *Washington Post* at the time of Aristide's inauguration in early 2001, that either there should be another U.S. invasion, or: "the CIA should train and equip Haïtian officers exiled in the neighboring Dominican Republic so they could stage a comeback themselves."[64] What was portrayed in the mainstream press as a human rights crisis in Haïti, was in fact "a low-level war between elements of the former armed forces and the elected government that had disbanded them,"[65] with of course, the involvement of the Haïtian elite, and the international community, primarily the U.S.

Canadian Meeting to Decide Haïti's Future

Paul Martin's Canadian government convened a meeting in Meech Lake, in January 2003, of the "Ottawa Initiative on Haïti." It was organized by Denis Paradis, Minister responsible for the Francophonie, and Secretary of State for Latin America. Otto Reich, the U.S. Assistant Secretary of State was there, French Government officials, the president of the OAS, and others, but no Haïtian government officials. In an interview in 2004, Paradis said, "The idea of having this Ottawa meeting was to kind of find ways to help the Haïtian people. So we didn't invite there either the opposition or the ruling party…"[66] After the meetings were held, Paradis confided to *L'Actualite* that the meeting consensus was that "Aristide should go," along with a "Kosovo-model" trusteeship over Haïti, a military occupation and the return of the Haïtian military, "might be necessary." It's quite clear, then, why Aristide's democratically-elected government was not invited to this planning session: they were planning to get rid of him.

With foreign aid and loans to his country cut off, precipitating an economic crisis, by April 2003, the now desperate Aristide called for France to reimburse the 90 million francs paid as compensation for the loss of colonial property in the form of slaves. With interest, he said this now came to $21 billion (U.S.). This request endeared him to neither France nor the U.S.

Mercenaries Put On The Pressure

By late 2003, as predicted—or requested—by the Democratic Convergence in 2001, well-armed 'insurgents' or 'rebels,' really mercenaries, and largely ex-military, were crossing into Haïti and raiding police stations. Their top military leader was Guy Philippe, whose wife, Natale, is a Haïtian-American real estate agent in Wisconsin. He was in the army which was disbanded in the 1990s, and later received training in Ecuador from U.S. Special Forces. He later became the chief of police in the city of Cap-Haïtien. In 2000, he was discovered plotting a coup against Aristide, and fled the country. In December 2001, he led two dozen people in a heavily-armed assault on the presidential palace, killing two policemen.[67] Also leading these thugs was Louis-Jodel Chamblain, a convicted drug dealer, who was convicted of the murder of Guy Mallory, the justice minister in Haïti, and the murder of Haïtian businessman Antoine Izmery, in 1993. Chamblain once led an army death squad, which was accused of massacres. The self-described "political leader" of the rebels was a Haïtian-Canadian named Paul Arcelin, a former professor at the Université de Québec à Montréal (UQÀM). His sister-in-law, Nicole Roy-Arcelin, served in former Prime Minister Brian Mulroney's Conservative government, in the late 80s and early 90s. Philippe and Arcelin call themselves Le Front de Libération du Haïti, and headed a group of perhaps 50 or 60 men.[68] But they didn't act alone. They were supported by the political opposition in Haïti, sweat shop owner Andy Apaid and the Group of 184,[69] the Democratic Convergence, and by the U.S., Canadian and French Governments. As a report by the University of Miami Law School indicated, late in 2004, "Mounting evidence suggests that members of Haïti's elite, including political powerbroker Andy Apaid, pay gangs to kill Lavalas supporters and finance the illegal army."[70]

A long-standing embargo on importing weapons into Haïti, enforced by the U.S., left the Haïtian police poorly equipped to handle attacks by better-equipped soldiers. Recall that the Haïtian military itself was disbanded by the Aristide government when it returned in the mid-90s, so that it could never again overthrow a democratic government. The U.S. Military and Coast Guard transported armaments and other supplies to the "rebels" in the Dominican Republic. Soon, they were crossing over into Haïti, driving SUVs. They began shooting local police, who fled, allowing the rebels to take over some towns. The attacks began late in 2003, and continued into 2004.

THE CIVILIAN "OPPOSITION"

The so-called 'Democratic Convergence' (DC) is a group of some 200 political organizations, led by former Port-au-Prince mayor Evans Paul. The Democratic Convergence together with The Group of 184 Civil Society Organizations (G-184) has formed a so-called Democratic Platform of Civil Society Organizations and Opposition Political Parties. The Group of 184 (G-184), is headed by Andre (Andy) Apaid, a U.S. citizen of Haïtian parents, born in the U.S. Andy Apaid owns Alpha Industries, one of Haïti's largest cheap labour export assembly lines established during the Duvalier era. His sweatshop factories produce textile products and assemble electronic products for a number of U.S. firms including Sperry/Unisys, IBM, Remington and Honeywell. Apaid is the largest industrial employer in Haïti with a workforce of some 4000 workers. Wages paid in Andy Apaid's factories are as low as 68 cents a day. The current minimum wage is of the order of $1.50 a day: *"The U.S.-based National Labour Committee, which first revealed the Kathie Lee Gifford sweat shop scandal, reported several years ago that Apaid's factories in Haïti's free trade zone often pay below the minimum wage and that his employees are forced to work 78-hour weeks."* Apaid was a firm supporter of the 1991 military coup. Both the *Convergence démocratique* and the G-184 have links to the FLRN (former FRAPH death squadrons) headed by Guy Philippe. The FLRN is also known to receive funding from the Haïtian business community. In other words, there is no watertight division between the civilian opposition, which claims to be non-violent and the FLRN paramilitary. The FLRN is collaborating with the so-called "Democratic Platform."[71]

Aristide Appeals to the International Community

By February, 2004, these mercenaries were threatening the capital of Port-Au-Prince. Threatening, but they really didn't stand a chance without more help, despite the arms and supplies, the vehicles and clothing from their military and civilian sponsors. The simple reason for this was Aristide's popularity with the people. Recall that he was elected in 2000 with 92 percent of the vote. But in the end, treachery did him in. As the democratically-elected president, Aristide appealed to the international community and even the United Nations, for support, in putting down this insurrection, this attempted coup d'etat.[72] All that was really necessary was for the U.S. to withdraw its support for the coupsters, and/or for someone to send in a few dozen real soldiers. In other words, a phone call. But the U.S., France, and Canada demurred. They insisted that Aristide must negotiate with the opposition, and make more concessions to them, to find a "power sharing arrangement." In other words, the U.S. really wanted the usual status quo where the wealthy elite run the country. As February wore on, Aristide sat down with international representatives and reached an agreement with them. But, the local elites, smelling blood, wanted Aristide deposed. As this was really what the U.S. and others wanted as well, they threw up their hands. The *Globe and Mail* reported five days before the coup,

> Mr. Aristide agreed to the peace plan on Saturday, but his political opponents have stalled, insisting that only his resignation can guarantee peace. The plan would allow him to remain President with diminished powers, sharing with political rivals a government that would organize elections.[73]

Aristide's personal security was provided by the Steele Foundation of San Francisco, an executive-protection firm which uses former U.S. Special Forces members. Steele's other clients include U.S.-installed Afghani president Hamid Karzai. Following the attempted coup by Guy Philippe and others in December 2001, Aristide increased his security to 60 men, but since then the numbers had dwindled to 19. After all, they were expensive, costing between $6-$9 million (US) annually, and Haïti was in dire economic straits. But now, according to a report in the *Miami Herald*, Aristide called Steele and asked for more men, who were supposed to arrive on February 29th. Reportedly, Aristide made two requests: first for a small group of 25 men to bolster his own security,[74] and secondly for a larger contingent—complete with a $1 million (US) weapons package—to engage the rebels. Unknown to him, the U.S. Embassy in Haïti intervened, contacted Steele and told them to delay their flight to Haïti, which they did, until after the coup d'etat.[75] Aristide is intelligent, but as one would expect from a priest, apparently naïve about security matters. There is a lesson in this: *don't hire your security forces from within the Mafia Don's compound.*

Additionally, Aristide reportedly expected a large arms shipment from South Africa, which was due to arrive on February 29, 2004, and which would help the government to defend itself against the mercenaries.

What They Say Happened

There are at least two versions of what happened next: but only one has any credibility. According to the U.S. Administration, Aristide contacted the U.S. Embassy and asked for assistance in leaving the country. He gave them a letter of resignation, and they drove him to the airport, and gave him a lift to the Central African Republic. This, after they warned him that Guy Philippe's rebels could attack at any time, and they could not guarantee his safety. There are numerous problems with this version of events. For example, first, Aristide repeatedly said that he was democratically elected, and he would finish out his term, so it makes little sense that he would suddenly decide to flee: it flies in the face of all that he stood for. Second, in requesting the additional Steele guards, he does not appear to have been planning to resign. Thirdly, the threat posed by the mercenaries was greatly exaggerated. Aristide had a security force of about 100 officers, plus the 19 remaining Steele guards. He also had the support of the people, numbering in the thousands, who would defend him and their duly elected government to the death against Philippe or anyone else. Fourth, Aristide would not have chosen the Central African Republic, which is closely aligned with France, and where he was initially held as a virtual prisoner, if it was his decision. Fifth, Aristide immediately called his lawyer, and sympathetic politicians and friends from his cell phone on the U.S. aircraft which spirited him away, such as Democratic Congresswoman Maxine Waters. According to these people, Aristide said quite definitively that he was kidnapped or abducted in a coup d'etat. He has been interviewed since, and consistently has told the same story.[76] According to Congresswoman Waters,

> [O]ne thing that was very clear and he said it over and over again, that he was kidnapped, that the coup was completed by the Americans that they forced him out. They had also disabled his American security force that he had around him for months now.[77]

The reaction on the part of the mainstream media is telling: some, not all of them, mentioned Aristide's allegations and then ran the denials by Colin Powell and others in the U.S. Administration. After this, they simply let the whole thing drop. The *Globe and Mail* simply reported,

> Faced with the armed revolt, popular protest and intense pressure from the United States and France, Mr. Aristide signed a letter of resignation early Sunday and was flown to the Central African Republic. His final destination is unknown.[78]

Two weeks later, the *Globe's* Paul Knox was simply referring to the events as "the overthrow" of Aristide, although by this time Knox allowed himself to shed crocodile tears over the Canadian government's lack of support for "a legitimate president under siege by a band of outlaws." Far too little, and far too late. Especially for a reporter who, just ten days before the coup had condemned a "defiant" Aristide, based on a personal interview, and using the usual "denials" of malicious rumour and innuendo. Knox wrote:

> [T]he diminutive former priest is vowing to serve out his remaining two years in office, despite the uprising that threatens to cut off half his country and the clamour of opponents demanding that he step down. Fixing his gaze on a visitor at the National Palace in Port-au-Prince yesterday, Mr. Aristide rejected the idea that the man who helped rescue Haïtians from dictatorship has himself become hooked on power. He denied the accusation, widespread in Haïti, that he funnels weapons to loyalists to allow them to intimidate or even kill dissidents. And he asserted that even his non-violent opponents are trying to engineer a coup d'état against him.[79]

Imagine! "Hooked on power," the paranoid Aristide, a weapons dealer, imagines his opponents are engineering a coup!

Over at the erstwhile progressive *Toronto Star*, Graham Fraser was also bemoaning Canada's "inaction," in what turned out to be a prelude to the Paul Martin government's role in promoting the "Right- to-Protect" policy at the United Nations, which serves to strengthen the ability of the U.S. and others to intervene in sovereign countries, which they deem to be in need of assistance. Fraser wrote,

> Canada hardly contributed to strengthening democracy by choosing, like the United States and France, to stand by while Jean-Bertrand Aristide, the legitimately elected president, was forced out of office by armed thugs. We are now deeply committed, and for a long time.[80]

The *Montreal Gazette* reported that, "Aristide was removed suddenly, and unceremoniously, from the country by U.S. forces, his hated regime in tatters and the country a bankrupt, crumbling mess."[81]

A democratically-elected president was abducted in the middle of the night by the American military and flown off to the Central African Republic, and his protests were greeted with denials, a yawn, and a return to business-as-usual.[82] In Canada, afterwards, the reporting centred on Canada's international peacekeeping role of stabilization, training police and restoring order in Haïti.[83] In the U.S., National Security Adviser Condoleezza Rice told NBC's "Meet the Press," "We believe that President Aristide, in a sense, forfeited his ability to lead his people, because he did not govern democratically." Meanwhile, Jamaican Prime Minister Patterson, chairman of the 15-nation CARICOM, called for an international investigation into the circumstances of Aristide's removal from Haïti. The 53-nation African Union echoed that call.

What Really Happened

Barthélémy Valbrun Jr., director of security services at the National Palace, was a Swede, recommended to Aristide by the Clinton Administration. Later it turned out that he was in the hire of the CIA. In the final days, Valbrun was bought off, as were many of the Haïtian security members who guarded Aristide. When the local people noticed the diminished security, they surrounded Aristide's residence themselves, in the thousands. On February 28, 2004, Valbrun led a number of American soldiers into Aristide's residence. Although there were thousands of Aristide supporters outside, they allowed these men through because they knew Valbrun. Inside, Aristide was in discussions with several foreign diplomats. Once inside, the U.S. military put all of the Haïtians, including Aristide, in handcuffs. They told him there would be much killing, thousands of Haïtians including himself and his family, if he did not resign. He refused. This standoff went on for hours, from the afternoon until midnight. Aristide went on his balcony and urged the people surrounding his home to go to their own homes, that everything was okay, as he was instructed to do. In the early hours of the next morning, February 29th, an American Embassy official, Louis Moreno, assured Aristide that he was being taken to a press conference, and instead he was taken to the airport, where he and his (Haïtian-American) wife Mildred and the Steele Foundation escort were all put on a U.S. plane and at gunpoint, flown out of the country, first to Antigua, and eventually on to the Central African Republic. Aristide had no idea where he was going, until he arrived. Once there, he was kept in comfort but as a virtual prisoner. He obtained a cell phone from someone and began making calls. Later in March he flew to Jamaica, over the protests of the U.S. and French governments, where he stayed briefly before going to South Africa, where he remains. These events have been confirmed by Franz Gabriel, Mr. Aristide's personal body guard and security agent. And this is what Aristide told Congresswoman Maxine Waters, his close friend Randall Robinson, a lawyer and founder of TransAfrica, and others.[84] Canadian troops reportedly secured the airport, while the Americans kidnapped Aristide.

Since that time, Haïti has been an occupied country, a protectorate of the U.S., whose bidding is enforced by the UN Mission for Stabilization in Haïti, known by the acronym of MINUSTA. The day of Aristide's kidnapping, the U.S. named and installed Supreme Court Chief Justice Boniface Alexandre as interim president of Haïti, replacing Jean-Bertrand Aristide in "a transitional government." Vice-President Yvon Neptune has since said that he was not even present when Alexandre was made president. (Normally, as Americans know, the vice-president assumes power in the absence of the president.) Neptune also said Aristide was forced out of office. The U.S. next parachuted in Gérard LaTortue, an expatriate Haïtian and Miami TV talk show host, as the prime minister, and three days later, on March 12, Neptune was tossed out of the government. Within two weeks, Neptune and others were barred from leaving Haïti while corruption charges were investigated. In June, 2004, Neptune was arrested and held without charges. On May 4, 2005, Thierry Fagart, the chief of the human rights division at the UN's Haïti mission, called Neptune's detention illegal. On June 23, 2005, the UN's special envoy to Haïti, Juan Gabriel Valdes, criticized the Haïtian government's handling of Yvon Neptune and called for his release from prison. After spending two years in prison with neither charges nor trial, he was released on July 28, 2006. The allegations against him have not been dropped; he was released on health and humanitarian grounds. Hundreds of other members of the deposed Aristide administration remain in custody without trial.

In the meantime, the Haïtian police and the UN forces, and gangs in the hire of the local business elite have been murdering Lavalas members and supporters and the Haïtian poor generally, with impunity. There has been a concerted campaign to eliminate Lavalas and Aristide supporters, to keep the populace in its place, and prevent the people from attempting to govern themselves. Some of the massacres, captured in photos and on film, have been brutal. Many of them involve teenage youths, but also women, mothers, children and even babies: for example in the Cité Soleil area, in "Operation Iron Fist," on July 6 and 13th, 2005.[85] Some estimate that 11,000 people have been killed since the 2004 coup. The slaughter has been at least comparable, if not greater than that under General Raoul Cedras following the 1991 coup, since described by the mainstream media as having "terrorized the country." This time, the brutal and unforgivable record has been ignored altogether by the mainstream media, or attributed to gang warfare, or Aristide supporters. Even when the UN commander in Haïti, Brazilian officer Lt. Gen. Urano Teixeira da Matta Bacellar, committed suicide rather than continuing to follow orders and supervise the killing in January 2006, the international community looked the other way, treating it as an unrelated, inexplicable event.[86]

The U.S., Canada, the IMF, World Bank and others were so joyous over the restoration of their brand of "democracy" that they reinstituted funding, foreign aid and loans in the hundreds of millions of dollars. In fall, 2004, Paul Martin made the first visit by a Canadian Prime Minister to Haïti, to bestow cash and his blessings on the murderous Latortue regime.

2006 Elections: Defeat in Victory

After five election dates were scheduled for 2005 and 2006, and cancelled, they were finally held on February 7, 2006. Aristide would have won handily, but he was in South Africa. The preferred Fanmi Lavalas candidate, father Gérard Jean-Juste, was in jail on trumped-up charges of murdering journalist Jacques Roche, although he was out of the country at the time. When party members went to register him they were told that he had to register in person, so he could not be a candidate. The entire election was full of such machinations and farce. Lavalas threatened to boycott the election, but in the end many voted for former president René Préval, who ran for the Lespwa party. For the elite, Marc Bazin ran again, as did wealthy industrialist Charles Henry Baker, and Leslie Francois Manigat, another former president. In all, there were 35 candidates, including Guy Philippe.

Although the election was partially funded and supervised by Jean Pierre Kingsley, Canada's chief electoral officer and Elections Canada, it was nothing short of a disaster. Canada and seven other countries established the International Mission for Monitoring Haïtian Elections (IMMHE) in June, 2005. Still, there were numerous serious irregularities, including a refusal by organizers to put any polling booths in the poor district of Cité Soleil, a centre for Lavalas support and home for perhaps 600,000 people. Across the country the number of polling stations was cut drastically, from thousands in the 2000 election to about 800. Coincidentally, the location of polls seriously disadvantaged the poor. But to the chagrin of the powers that be, Lavalas supporters walked for miles and lined up for hours on end, to cast their ballots for Préval.

Early returns saw Préval running away with the election. If he garnered 50 percent plus one vote, this would mean no runoff election between the top two candidates. In desperation, the political masters sent ballot boxes to the dump to be burned, instead of being counted. But they were discovered there and the ruse was up. Now, Préval's lead was said to be just under 50 percent, meaning a runoff election. Negotiations followed, and it was clear that Préval would not be able to win without making concessions to the Americans. Whatever happened behind closed doors, they emerged with a deal: blank ballots would be included in the total calculations, which meant everyone's percentage went up and Préval won with 51.2 percent, Manigat received 12.8 percent, Baker 8.2 percent, and Guy Philippe 1.9 percent. Almost 12 percent of the votes were either blank or invalid. As someone commented, "you don't walk for hours, and line up for hours, only to register a blank vote or make a mistake." Once again, Haïtians had spoken, exercising their democratic right. But as in 2000, the fix was in: Préval had cut a deal.

More than a year later, the deal seems to be that the U.S. Embassy and MINUSTA are running the country. The killings continue. In February 2007, the Canadian government announced a further $10 million in "aid" money going to train Haïtian police.[87] Apparently training them, in part, to kill civilians. Aristide is still in South Africa. Gildan Activewear, of Montreal, announced in March 2007 it was closing its two remaining textile plants in Montreal, plus two plants in Mexico and one in New York, eliminating 1800 jobs. CBC reported, "The Montreal-based company is shifting production to Central America and the Caribbean."[88]

The Haïtian people continue the struggle they thought they had won in 1804.

What Haïtians Really Need

Like Argentina, only more drastically, Haïti is the IMF's model student. Except for its "rebellious" periods, such as its emancipatory war of independence in the 18th Century, and its flirtation with democracy in the elections of 1990, 1996 and 2000, Haïti has been subjected to violent, repressive and murderous rule by foreign and domestic military juntas and dictatorships. It has also been subject to the accompanying economic diktats through the Washington Consensus reforms in the 1980s, and the IMF's market fundamentalism and structural adjustment agreements since the 1990s.

Where militaristic and/or dictatorial regimes have 'failed,' the economic pressures and sanctions have succeeded. Not in improving the Haïtian economy—which has declined dramatically, but in subjugating the Haïtian poor to the local elites, U.S. foreign policy, and global capitalism generally. Haïti's economy, however inconvenient for the local peoples, is perfectly suited to global financial interests. Through the IMF, World Bank and other agencies, they have diagnosed the patient and prescribed free market medicine. The worse things have become, the more of the same they have prescribed. Like the Europeans at the time of Jacques Cartier, they have prescribed bleeding as a cure-all. The sicker the patient gets, the more you bleed him.

This entire story is conveniently omitted from mainstream media accounts. Instead of attributing Haïti's "failed state" to the real cause, which is external intervention in the interests of global capital, all of the blame is focused on the domestic population and its allegedly corrupt leadership, most of whom are desperately trying to pull themselves out of a quagmire created by the IMF and others. Haïti is portrayed as failing to thrive and as in need of even more right-to-protect interference from abroad. Bleed the patient.

What Haïtians actually require is, first of all, to be left alone by the international community, with the sole exception that we must dig deeply into our budgets to pay out *considerable* compensation and untied economic aid to the Haïtian people. All international interests must withdraw, from MINUSTA to the RCMP, the U.S. Embassy, the French Embassy, the Canadian Embassy and all the rest of them, and all of their military forces. And then, we must leave it up to these intelligent, brave, capable people to govern themselves as they are supremely able to do. Should Aristide come back? They will decide. Should Préval continue to the end of his term? They will decide.

One thing abundantly clear is that the international community does not have any right to abduct a democratically-elected president, simply because the wealthy elites in his country, the IMF, and the new Washington Consensus —which includes France, Britain, Canada and others—are not happy with him. And we do not have the right to force structural economic agreements on Haïtians or anyone else, even if it means we have to pay more for our t-shirts.

NOTES

1. A portion of this chapter was previously published in, James Winter and Jeffery Klaehn, "The Propaganda Model Under Protest," in Jeffery Klaehn (Ed) *Filtering The News: Essays on Herman and Chomsky's Propaganda Model*, Black Rose Books, Montreal, 2005.

2. Tony Clarke and Maude Barlow, *MAI: The Multilateral Agreement on Investment and the Threat to Canadian Sovereignty*, Stoddart, Toronto, 1997. P.1.

3. The EPA writes that, "Manganese is a neurotoxin and can cause irreversible neurological disease at high levels of inhalation." Quoted in the article, "Comments on the Gasoline Additive MMT (methylcyclopentadienyl manganese tricarbonyl)" Retrieved from the EPA web site, March 4, 2007. http://www.epa.gov/otaq/regs/fuels/additive/mmt_cmts.htm.

4. For a detailed account of East Timor, see James Winter, "Bitter Paradise," in *MediaThink*, Black Rose Books, Montreal, 2002. See also Sharon Sharfe, *Complicity: Human Rights and Canadian Foreign Policy: The Case of East Timor*, Black Rose Books, Montreal, 1996.

5. For an account of this, see James Winter, "Canadian PM in hot water over APEC 97," *Green Left Weekly*, Australia, November 18, 1998. www.greenleft.org.au.

6. Seth Ackerman, 'Prattle in Seattle: the media and the WTO,' EXTRA! (13:1), Jan/Feb 2000, p. 14.

7. Michael Albert, 'What are we for?', www.zmag.org.

8. Joseph Stiglitz, *Globalization and Its Discontents*, W. W. Norton, N.Y., 2002, pp. 206-7.

9. Stiglitz, *Globalization*, pp. 35, 55.

10. The four step program and the interview with Stiglitz are taken from Gregory Palast, "IMF's four steps to domination," www.zmag.org. See also Gregory Palast, "IMF's four steps to damnation: How crises, failures, and suffering finally drove a Presidential adviser to the wrong side of the barricades," *Observer* and *Independent*, Sunday April 29, 2001. http://observer.guardian.co.uk/business/story/0,6903,480069,00.html See also Joseph Stiglitz, *Globalization and Its Discontents* (Norton: New York, 2002).

11. Michael Albert, "A Q&A on the WTO, IMF, World Bank and Activism" from *Z Magazine's* WTO Primer, www.znet.org. See also Stiglitz, *Globalization*.

12. Ibid., p. 3.

13. Cf. J.J. Moskau, "IMF slams Ottawa's deficit-cutting target as insufficient," *Globe and Mail*, November 29, 1994. The popular economist Linda McQuaig has also addressed these matters in several of her books, such as *The Wealthy Bankers' Wife, Shooting the Hippo, The Cult of Impotence*, and *All You Can Eat: Greed Lust and the New Capitalism*.

14. Stiglitz, *Globalization*, pp. 40-41.

15. Cf. Pramoedya Ananta Toer, "Dictator From Day One: Suharto abused his power from the start, says Indonesia's foremost writer," *Time Asia*, May 24, 1999; John Colmey and David Liebhold, "Suharto Inc. The Family Firm: A TIME investigation into the wealth of Indonesia's Suharto and his children uncovers a $15 billion fortune in cash, property, art, jewelry and jets," *Time Asia*, May 24, 1999.

16. Noam Chomsky, "East Timor on the Brink," Interviewed by David Barsamian, KGNU Radio, Boulder Colorado, September 8, 1999, www.zmag.org.

17. Naomi Klein, "IMF: Go to hell," *Globe and Mail*, March 19, 2002.

18. Jon Hillson, "Reporter's notebook from Argentina," New York Transfer, April 24, 2002. Available online at Argentina Watch (www.zmag.com).

19. Jacqueline Thorpe,"'Financial crisis called a watershed for IMF policy: massive bailouts may end," *Financial Post*, April 29, 2002. The idea of 'moral hazard' is defined as: 'The risk that a party to a transaction has not entered into a contract in good faith, has provided misleading information about its assets, liabilities, or credit capacity, or has an incentive

270 | LIES THE MEDIA TELL US

to take unusual risks in a desperate attempt to earn a profit before the contract settles.' The Risk Institute, http://newrisk.ifci.ch/.

20. Brian Winter, "Argentina mulls re-pegging peso: may risk IMF wrath to stave off banking collapse, more riots," *National Post*, (*Reuters*), April 25, 2002.

21. Peter Morton, "Canada leans on Argentina: Martin calls for action; officials tell Dodge Scotiabank unit could reopen this week," *Financial Post*, April 22, 2002.

22. Gilbert Le Gras, "IMF scrubs quick fix for Argentina: macroeconomic measures still deemed insufficient," *National Post*, (*Reuters*), March 14, 2002.

23. George Bragues, "Reform comes first; an IMF bailout won't resuscitate Argentina's economy. Along with cutting government spending, the debt-strapped country needs to severely curtail the influences of provincial governments and labour unions," *National Post*, April 18, 2002.

24. Justin Podur, "Venezuela's 'National Strike,'" *ZNet*, December 10, 2002. http://www.zmag.org/content/showarticle.cfm?ItemID=2729.

25. This was documented by two Irish film makers who happened to be in Caracas at the time, in Kim Bartley and Donnacha O'Briain, *The Revolution Will Not Be Televised*, Ireland, 2003.

26. William Blum, "The CIA and the Venezuela coup: Hugo Chavez: a servant not knowing his place," *Counterpunch*, Latin America Watch, April 14, 2002.

27. John McMurtry, "A day in the life of the new world order" [letter to the editor] in the *Globe and Mail*, April 1, 1995. Also see any number of books by Noam Chomsky, including *The Noam Chomsky Reader*, New York: Pantheon, 1987; *Language and Politics*, Montreal: Black Rose, 1988; *Necessary Illusions: Thought Control in Democratic Societies*, Toronto, CBC Enterprises; *Deterring Democracy*, New York: Hill and Wang, 1992; *Letters from Lexington: Reflections on Propaganda*, Toronto: Between the Lines, 1993; *The Prosperous Few and the Restless Many*, Berkeley, CA: Odonian, 1993; highly recommended as well is Noam Chomsky and Edward S. Herman, *The Political Economy of Human Rights: Volume One: The Washington Connection and Third World Fascism*, Montreal: Black Rose, 1979.

28. With respect to industrial pollution, Sylvia Hale notes that "In practice, environmental costs, like social welfare costs, are generally left out of business equations. They form hidden diseconomies or real costs that, if actually paid by the companies responsible for the pollution, would greatly reduce their profits, and might well turn these apparent profits into deficits. But such costs are not counted by corporations because normally it is not the corporations that pay them. The people and other creatures whose lives are damaged or destroyed by the pollution pay the price." Sylvia Hale, *Controversies in Sociology*, Second Edition, Copp Clark Limited, Toronto, 1995, pp. 272-273.

29. Ibid, p. 250.

30. Ibid., p. 251.

31. Susan George, "Democracy at the barricades," *Le Monde Diplomatique*, Aug 2001, www.zmag.org. (As translated by Barbara Wilson.)

32. Craig Pearson, "OAS General Assembly: Day 2, participants' summit objectives diverse," *Windsor Star*, June 6, 2001.

33. Quoted in Pearson, Ibid., emphasis added.

34. John Goranson, "OAS General Assembly: Day 2, guerrilla caterers' get food to masses, food was donated," *Windsor Star*, June 6, 2000. That Food Not Bombs was labeled "guerrilla caterers" is also instructive in terms of the predictions of the Propaganda Model.

35. Ibid.

36. Goranson, Ibid.

37. For a description of the role of journalists in the social construction of news, see James Winter, *Democracy's Oxygen: How Corporations Control the News* (Black Rose, Montreal, 1996).

38. Craig Pearson, "OAS perfect medium for artistic ingenuity," *Windsor Star*, June 8, 2000.

39. Edward S. Herman, "The Propaganda Model Revisited," *Monthly Review*, July, 1996.

40. Much of this historical account is adapted from an excellent review article by professor Peter Hallward, written after the 2004 coup. See Peter Hallward, "Option Zero in Haïti," *New Left Review*, #27, May/June 2004, pp. 23-47. See also Hallward's interview with Jean-Bertrand Aristide, "An Interview with Jean-Bertrand Aristide," *London Review of Books*, February 22, 2007. Also, Yves Engler and Anthony Fenton, *Canada in Haïti*, Fernwood Books, Halifax, 2005.

41. Quoted in Noam Chomsky, "The Tragedy of Haïti," in *Year 501: The Conquest Continues*, South End Press, Boston, 1993 pp. 197-219.

42. Hallward, "Option Zero," p. 26.

43. Hallward, "Option Zero," p. 27.

44. Marjorie Valbrun, "Perhaps I was too tolerant," *Montreal Gazette*, April 19, 2003.

45. Quoted in Hallward, "An Interview" p. 2.

46. *Boston Globe*, 21 Sept 1994, cited in Michel Chossudovsky, "The Destabilization of Haïti," *Global Research*, February 29, 2004. http://www.globalresearch.ca/index.php?context=viewArticle&code=CHO20050610&articleId=56.

47. Ben Dupuy, "The Attempted Character Assassination of Aristide," Third World Traveller, From Project Censored, 1999, http://www.thirdworldtraveler.com/Global_Secrets_Lies/Aristide_CharacAssass.html.

48. Chossudovsky, "The Destabilization of Haïti."

49. Hallward, "Option Zero," p. 33.

50. Jean-Bertrand Aristide, *Eyes of the Heart*, Common Courage Press, Boston, 2000. Taken from excerpts on Third World traveller.com http://www.thirdworldtraveler.com/Aristide/Eyes_Heart_Aristide.html.

51. Chossudovsky, "The Destabilization of Haïti."

52. See the IMF press release, "IMF Approves Three-Year ESAF Loan for Haïti," Washington, 1996, http://www.imf.org/external/np/sec/pr/1996/pr9653.htm.

53. Chossudovsky, "The Destabilization of Haïti."

54. Chossudovsky, "The Destabilization of Haïti."

55. Chossudovsky, "The Destabilization of Haïti."

56. Chossudovsky, "The Destabilization of Haïti."

57. Chossudovsky, "The Destabilization of Haïti."

58. Leslie Jermyn, "An Unholy Alliance," a speech delivered to the founding meeting of the Toronto Haïti Action Committee on August 4, 2005. http://www.cpcml.ca/Tmld2005/D35175.htm#5.

59. Ibid.

60. Hallward, "Option Zero," p.39.

61. Yves Engler and Anthony Fenton, *Canada In Haïti*, Fernwood Books, Halifax, 2005. See also, Leslie Jermyn, "An Unholy Alliance," a speech delivered to the founding meeting of the Toronto Haïti Action Committee on August 4, 2005. http://www.cpcml.ca/Tmld2005/D35175.htm#5.

62. From an interview by the author with Jean Candio, a former deputy in the Haïtian parliament, conducted March 9, 2007. Anthony Fenton writes that, "Documents recently obtained from the Canadian International Development Agency (CIDA) show that, with exclusivity, organizations that are ideologically opposed to Aristide and Lavalas are receiving Canadian government funding. The list includes the likes of ENFOFANM, SOFA, Kay Fanm, GARR, CRESFED, PAJ, POHDH/SAKS, and the Haïti branch of the National Coalition for Haïtian Rights (NCHR)." See Anthony Fenton, "Canada's Growing Role In Haïtian Affairs (Part I)," *ZNet*, www.zmag.org, March 21, 2005.

63. Chossudovsky, "The Destabilization of Haïti."

64. Edward Cody, "Haïti Torn by Hope and Hatred As Aristide Returns to Power," *Washington Post*, February 2, 2001; Page A01.

65. Hallward, "Option Zero," p. 42.

66. Anthony Fenton, "Interview With Denis Paradis on Haïti Regime Change," *Dominion*, September 15, 2004. www.dominionpaper.ca.

67. Sue Montgomery, "Mastermind tells how plot evolved: Former Montrealer leads political wing of group that overthrew Haïti's Aristide," *Montreal Gazette*, March 9, 2004.

68. Montgomery, "Mastermind tells…"

69. Apaid, an American, owns Alpha Industries which includes about 15 sweat shop operations, and thousands of employees. He is the sub-contractor for the Montreal-based Gildan Apparel. See, Andrea Schmidt and Anthony Fenton, "Andy Apaid and Us," ZNET, October 19, 2005.

70. Thomas M. Griffin, "Haïti: Human Rights Investigation, November 11-21, 2004,: published by The Center for the Study of Human Rights, University of Miami School of Law, Professor Irwin P. Stotzky, Director.

71. Chossudovsky, "The Destabilization of Haïti."

72. Cf. AP and CP, "Aristide appeals to world for help against rebels," *Globe and Mail*, Feb. 24, 2004.

73. Ibid.

74. Aristide himself said that 25 agents were expected, but that the Steele Foundation told him that the U.S. Embassy blocked them from coming. He also said there were 19 Steele agents with him on the plane to the Central African Republic. This was contained in a broadcast interview with him, conducted by Amy Goodman of *Democracy Now!* March 16, 2004, www.democracynow.org.

75. See Juan Tamayo, "U.S. allegedly blocked extra bodyguards," *Miami Herald*, March 1, 2004.

76. Cf. Amy Goodman, "Aristide and His Bodyguard Describe the U.S. Role In His Ouster," www.democracynow.org, March 16th, 2004.

77. From an interview with Amy Goodman on Democracy Now, March 1, 2004. www.democracynow.org.

78. Paul Knox, "Thousands greet arrival of Haïtian rebels in capital," *Globe and Mail*, March 1, 2004.

79. Paul Knox, "Face-to-face with defiant Aristide," *Globe and Mail*, February 19, 2004.

80. Graham Fraser, "National interest of Canadians tied to failed states like Haïti," *Toronto Star*, March 14, 2004.

81. Sue Montgomery, "Mastermind tells how plot evolved."

82. Cf. Paul Knox, "Aristide flees Haïti," *Globe and Mail*, February 29, 2004.

83. Drew Fagan, "Canada keeps the peace," *Globe and Mail*, March 1, 2004.

84. This account comes from various interviews with Aristide, as well as others he has spoken with, such as Maxine Waters, Randall Robinson, and former Haïtian deputy (MP) Jean Candio.

85. See "Evidence Mounts of a UN Massacre in Haïti," on the Haïti Action Network, http://www.haitiaction.net/News/HIP/7_12_5.html, and "Massacre in the Making," http://www.haitiaction.net/News/KP/8_18_5/8_18_5.html. Also, see the dramatic documentary film produced by Kevin Pina, *Haïti: The Untold Story*, 2005.

86. For an example of progressive reporting on this, see Kevin Pina, "UN commander dead in Haïti amid pressure from elite," by HIP—Haïti Information Project Sunday, Jan 8 2006. http://www.anarkismo.net/newswire.php?story_id=2112.

Also, see www.haitiaction.net, and Kevin Pina, "UN Whitewashes Massacre," The Haïti Information Project and the Haïti Action Network, http://www.haitiaction.net/News/HIP/1_11_6/1_11_6.html.

87. Reed Lindsay, "UN failing to police the police: Peacekeepers: Canadian officers take lead role in frustrating bid to reform Haïtian force," *Toronto Star*, Feb. 5, 2006.

88. "Gildan Activewear closing 5 plants, cutting 1,800 jobs," CBC News, online, March 27, 2007.

Chapter Six

CONCLUSION

USUALLY, BEFORE WE GET TOO many weeks into the Media Literacy course, students will begin to ask, "what can we do about this?" At least, some of them are asking. Some of them are still highly resistant, after all, we are trying to begin to overcome a lifetime of indoctrination in one semester. Trying to get the ball rolling so they can overcome that initial inertia. And some of them have already given up on doing anything, because the problems seem so vast and unassailable.

If students feel helpless, there's good reason for that. As mentioned, the primary lesson they're taught is *conformity*. If they want to do well in school, they must simply learn the material they are going to be tested on. "Arguing takes more energy, doesn't help one's grade, and even violates classroom norms."[1] This is part of our socialization. We are constantly trained in *the art of spectatorship*, and encouraged to practice it. We watch sports, rather than playing them, and we are addicted to watching. We cast a ballot once every four or five years, and then sit back and watch politics happen. Strikers, protesters —people who go out and do something—get a bad rap in the media as "activists" or "militants."

We're *supposed* to feel helpless, so we will know our place and leave the action and the important decision making to the people who know best: the people who really understand complex economics, global geopolitics, treaties, and so forth. This is what Walter Lippmann meant when he wrote in *Public Opinion* in 1920, that the elite class must not rely on force but instead manufacture the consent of the "bewildered herd,"—the people.

Even when you are just 20 years old, it's difficult to overcome a lifetime of training in conformity. So, this is the bigger problem. One of the things I try to do, is to show some examples where individuals and smaller groups and large groups have accomplished great things. Because, the thing to remember is that no matter how great the resources on the other side, no matter what guns and military might they possess, real power is always on the side of the people. That knowledge is what keeps the struggle of the Haïtian people going today, after everything they have been through over the past 300-plus years. So, the people of Haïti are an example, and those of us in our relatively privileged position in Canada and the U.S. should be ashamed if we whine and weep and wring our hands in desperation, knowing what Haïtians have done, and what our governments have done to them, with our acquiescence or manufactured consent. Aristide himself has not been responsible for their gains, as he has described, it has been a popular movement. But he is still a courageous leader and a wonderful example. And there are many others.

I don't like to dwell too much on individuals, because no one really acts alone, and it wouldn't do to engage in what James Loewen terms, "heroification." But when students say, "what can I do? I'm just one person!" I do like to mention some people who have made a difference, not all on their own but they certainly have been a lightening rod for a movement. Here's a short list of names, not meant to be all-inclusive. I don't mind admitting that these are some of my personal heroes.

Rosa Parks	Rachel Carson
Noam Chomsky	Michael Albert
Martin L. King Jr.	Lydia Sargent
Michael Moore	Ed Herman
Linda McQuaig	Mark Achbar
Nelson Mandella	Judy Rebick
Sut Jhally	Michelle Landsberg
Kevin Pina	William Blum
Naomi Klein	Joel Andreas
Mahatma Ghandi	Frank Dorrel
Maude Barlow	Joseph Stiglitz
David Suzuki	

I like to tell the story about the Flint, Michigan boy, Michael Moore, when he was a high school student. He wrote about this in *Stupid White Men*, as I recall. Moore had some serious run-ins with his high school principal, a guy he didn't get along with. So, Moore ran for the school board, got elected, and worked (successfully) to get the principal replaced. Even in high school, Moore didn't accept conformity and spectatorship. Since then, he has gone on to make a wonderful, popular satirical film, *Canadian Bacon*. He's produced a popular television program, the "TV Nation." He's made great documentaries such as *Roger & Me*. He has written the best-selling book of 2002, which spent more than a year on the *New York Times*' bestseller list, *Stupid White Men*. And in the same year, he won an Academy Award for best documentary film, for *Bowling for Columbine*.

Then he went out and produced *Fahrenheit 9/11*, the highest-grossing documentary film of all time, demonstrating, in part, the Bush administration's hypocrisy in dealing with the Saudis and the bin Laden family. Now, you can think what you like about Michael Moore, and you can absorb all of the right-wing flak thrown at him, but he's a genius. And he has had an impact, he has wrought change. Not single-handedly, of course. But he has been a driving force.

Joel Andreas designed, drew and wrote a comic book on the Rockefeller family in the U.S., in 1975, when he was a high school student. Later, he wrote *Addicted to War*, a comic book I use as a university text book, and which has sold more than 300,000 copies. Andreas now is a professor of sociology at Johns Hopkins University.

Frank Dorrell is an anti-war activist from Los Angeles who has produced and distributed *Addicted to War*, along with his own video compilation, *What I've Learned About U.S. Foreign Policy*.

Michael Albert and Lydia Sargent are the founders of *Z Magazine* from Boston, and they operate *Znet*, or zmag.org, which is a wonderful library of alternative perspectives. They archive and email daily articles written by some wonderful progressives and academics, from Noam Chomsky to Howard Zinn. Their monthly magazine was a life-line during the (first) Persian Gulf War, which preceded the worldwide web. Their web site today is a terrific resource.

Naomi Klein wrote *No Logo*, co-produced a great documentary on Argentina called *The Take*, and once gave me a ride in her taxi to a conference in Regina, Sask. (She climbed into the back, giving me her front seat.) Now, she's my hero! Seriously, a great activist.

Obviously, this is just the tip of the iceberg, even on my own brief list, with people like Nelson Mandella, Mahatma Ghandi and Martin Luther King. And then there is Noam Chomsky, who is the first to humbly deny playing any role whatsoever, but he has had a tremendous impact on progressive movements world wide. So, when we shrug our shoulders and deny we can do anything, we're being irresponsible. I look forward to reading in future years about the next Michael Moore, Naomi Klein, or Noam Chomsky, and recognizing their names as former students.

The first step along in this process is breaking our way out of the dogma of conventional wisdom, by asking the tough questions and refusing to continue to conform. This will involve education, and media literacy. Thanks to the internet, the prospect for accomplishing this has improved drastically. But we must be wary of corporate attempts to shut this down, to completely co-opt this new medium as they have all previous ones, including not just newspapers, radio and television, but education, at all levels.[2]

I had an interesting experience in the winter of 2006, when I offered a course on communication and world affairs. It was at the third-year level. Because of current events, I decided to concentrate the course on Haïti, where elections were being held, rather than conducting a broader overview. For the first few weeks, we reviewed the history and context of Haïti. We were fortunate to have Patrick Ellie, former minister of defense in the Aristide government of the mid-1990s, as a guest lecturer in class.

While this was going on, students were to choose topics for a project and seminar presentation. I gave them some examples, and the main requirement was that they choose a project which would have a real effect on the people of Haïti. Of course, to begin with, students simply couldn't come to grips with a real-world assignment such as this. There were about 50 students in the course. Many of them kept coming back to see me, looking for more concrete advice. "What do *you want* us to do," they'd ask. "Whatever *you want*," I'd reply. It was understandably difficult for students to adapt to actually doing something, rather than just studying and talking. In the end, they came up with a very diverse group of projects: from songwriting and performances; to creative art work; video and radio productions; a guerrilla billboard campaign against Gildan Apparel, and an anti-sweatshop petition aimed at the university administration to stop sales on campus. Some students raised funds which they gave to Hearts Together For Haïti, a local Windsor group which helps Haïtians to build schools and other development projects in Haïti. Some students developed a Haïti information campaign and traveled around to local high schools. Others created web sites to inform and/or raise funds. Others raised money with bands or at pub nights. One group worked on draft legislation for Parliament.

Once they got going on their projects, the students seemed delighted with the chance to do constructive work towards social justice. Many told me they appreciated applying some of the things they learned in the classroom, in a good cause.

Reforming The System

Elsewhere, with Maude Barlow, I've discussed a number of remedies for the corporate media system.[3] As was proposed by the 1980 Royal Commission on Newspapers, legislative steps can be taken to limit and reduce concentration of ownership and limit or eliminate cross-ownership of media properties. Other legislative and financial steps can be taken to encourage diverse media ownership. Although limiting the size of corporations flies in the face of the current view that "bigger is better," there are crucial reasons why news media should be treated distinctly from other industries. They produce and disseminate ideas, and diverse views are essential if we are to have a functioning democracy. The way to diverse views is through diverse ownership, which may be encouraged with appropriate subsidies, as we did with the music (Canadian content requirements) and film industries, (Canadian Film Development Corporation) and television programming (Cable TV funding for Canadian programming).

The specific policies will be formulated, further developed and eventually implemented when the public is in a position to insist. We will insist, when we are aware of the problems, and when we have responsible government. What's clear is that these changes are not forthcoming from either the Liberal Party or Conservative Party establishments.

The Family Compact

The first problem we face, as I've briefly discussed, is that we do not have a democratic political system. If we did, we would have elected more than one federal government with a majority of votes (50 percent plus one) since 1960. We must introduce changes to democratize our system, to enact policies which reflect the will of the people, rather than the Family Compact. And there still is a Family Compact. According to *Canadian Business* magazine, in 2006, the number of Canadian billionaires increased to 46, from 40 the year before. The wealthiest families are: the Thomsons ($24 billion), Galen Weston ($7.1 billion), the Irvings ($5.5 billion), Ted Rogers ($4.5 billion), the Desmarais' ($4.4

billion), Jimmy Pattison ($4.3 billion), and Barry Sherman of Apotex ($3.2 billion). Five of these top seven Canadian families are, at least partially, in media holdings.

Implementing policies which reflect the interests of the population at large is called responsible, representative government. I've already discussed Power Corporation's Paul Desmarais and his influence on Canadian prime ministers. This is not a unique example. The man who runs the Thomson family business is John Arnold Tory, as sharp a lawyer and businessman as may be found on Bay Street, and someone the late Ken Thomson didn't merely like, but said he "adored."[4] Tory's father John D. was on the Thomson board with Ken's father Roy. John Arnold's son, John H. Tory, is the leader of the Opposition Conservatives in the Ontario legislature. As U.S. Chief Justice John Jay said, "The people who own the country ought to govern it."

We need trust-busting legislation. We need muckrakers. We need publicly-responsible news media, not profit-oriented, corporate entities. The conflict of interest is far too grave when the information we need to make informed decisions comes to us from the Thomsons, Aspers, Rogers, Desmarais, *et cetera*. Their interests no more coincide with ours than the interests of the people of Haïti coincide with that of sweatshop owner Andy Apaid of Alpha Industries. In Ontario, the Conservative governments of Mike Harris and Ernie Eves froze the minimum wage for ten years, from 1995 to 2005. How does this differ from the stance Andy Apaid took with Jean-Bertrand Aristide? In 2005, the newly-elected Liberal government of Dalton McGinty raised the minimum wage by 4.2 percent. That year, the average CEO's salary in Canada increased by 39 percent.[5]

Proportional Representation

To begin with, we need democracy. But the type of battle we are in for, is apparent from the resistance even to adopting some form of proportional representation (PR), which Belgium has used since 1899. Yes, that's *eighteen ninety-nine*. There are various systems in use around the world, but the idea behind PR is to have the number of seats per party align with the proportion of electoral vote received. This is common sense, and it would avoid ridiculous situations. In the 2004 federal election, the Liberals won 13 out of 14 seats in Saskatchewan, even though they only received 42 percent of the vote there. In the elections in Quebec in 1998, B.C. in 1996, and Saskatchewan in 1986, the party which won a *majority* of seats placed *second* in the electoral vote.

A referendum on proportional representation in B.C. was approved by 57 percent of voters in May, 2005. Although it was passed by a majority, the provincial government wanted it to be approved by a "super majority" of 60 percent, and it fell just shy. So, now they have a system in place which is supported by just 43 percent of voters. Go figure. Another vote failed in Prince Edward Island in November, 2005. The federal New Democrats also failed in a bid to have a national referendum held. The Province of Quebec is also considering PR. In Ontario, a Citizen's Assembly endorsed a mixed member proportional plan in 2007, but the *Toronto Star* termed this "radical," and said, "The system can lead to permanent minority governments and a proliferation of fringe parties."[6] Nonsense. The Liberal government in Ontario said it would put this proposition to a vote during the provincial election in fall, 2007.[7]

In addition to Belgium, some form of PR is used in Australia, Austria, Czech Republic, Denmark, Finland, Germany, Greece, Iceland, Hungary, Ireland, Israel, Italy, Luxembourg, Netherlands, New Zealand, Nicaragua, Norway, Poland, Portugal, Scotland, Spain, Sweden, Switzerland, Venezuela and many other countries.

Countries clinging to the first-past-the-post system include: Canada, the U.S., Great Britain, and India.

Federal and provincial elections using some form of proportional representation would be but a cursory nod in the direction of our electoral ills, but would constitute a first step toward democracy. Another huge impediment, for example, is the amount of power concentrated in the office of the prime minister, through: a veto over party candidates and caucus membership, the ability to parachute candidates into ridings over the objections of riding associations, the sole discretionary appointment of: senators, cabinet ministers, parliamentary secretaries and committee chairs, deputy ministers, supreme court justices, *et cetera*.[8] Even in Britain, where caucus members can at least turf the prime minister, it is a more responsible system. Other baby steps which have been taken in recent years include financial limits on corporate support for candidates, which discourage the blatant purchase of the prime minister's services.

I have dwelt a bit on this electoral reform business for the simple reason that there is precious little chance of enacting meaningful reform elsewhere, until we have some semblance of democracy in place. When we do, we can set about other reforms, to the rules for media and other corporations, trade agreements, foreign policy, the environment, rules for Big Pharma, and so forth. We can begin to address some of the problems highlighted in this book, along with others such as poverty, homelessness, sexism, discrimination, and so forth. By looking at the Cuban and Haitian examples, we can realize that for Canadians, anything is possible, even self-government.

In the meantime, instead of pretending to foment democracy abroad, in Afghanistan and elsewhere, we would do well to tend to the mess we have here at home.

NOTES

1. James Loewen, *Lies My Teacher Told Me*, p. 310.

2. See, for example, James Turk (Ed) *The Corporate Campus: Commercialization and the Dangers to Canada's Colleges and Universities*, Lorimer, Toronto, 2000.

3. Maude Barlow and James Winter, *The Big Black Book: The Essential Views of Conrad and Barbara Amiel Black*, Stoddart, Toronto, 1997.

4. Quoted in, Peter C. Newman, "The Private Life of Canada's Richest Man," *Maclean's*, October 14, 1991, p. 49.

5. Hugh Mackenzie, "Raising the Minimum Wage in Ontario," *Behind The Numbers*, Vol. 7 number 7, January 2007, Canadian Centre for Policy Alternatives, Ottawa.

6. Ian Urquhart, "Radical voting proposal gains steam: Ontario citizens' assembly endorses 'mixed member proportional' plan," *Toronto Star*, February 22, 2007.

7. See Ian Urquhart, "Radical voting proposal."

8. See James Winter, *Democracy's Oxygen*, Black Rose Books, Montreal, 1997; Donald Savoie, *Governing from the Centre: The Concentration of Power in Canadian Politics*, University of Toronto Press, 1999; Jeffrey Simpson, *The Friendly Dictatorship*, McClelland and Stewart, Toronto, 2001.

INDEX

ALSO AVAILABLE from BLACK ROSE BOOKS

POWER OF PERSUASION: The Politics of the New Right in Ontario
Kirsten Kozolanka

The Power of Persuasion looks at how the New Right came to power in Ontario by using lessons learned from its successes in other countries (namely Great Britain, the U.S. and New Zealand), to gain public consent for policies that were economically and socially harmful to a majority of Ontario citizens. Despite widespread protest, which took many forms, the New Right was able to maintain power, and was sustained over the first half of the new government's mandate. Author Kirsten Kozolanka contends that this New Right trajectory is neither haphazard nor narrowly constructed, and that the Conservatives supported their policy platform and legislative agenda with sophisticated communications tools, such as advertising, polling, and marketing, but also by closing down government information channels and legislative processes.

KIRSTEN KOZOLANKA teaches journalism and mass communication at Carleton University in Ottawa, Ontario.

2007: 288 pages, paper 1-55164-288-3 $24.99   ⁂ cloth 1-55164-289-1 $53.99

RADICAL MASS MEDIA CRITICISM: A Cultural Genealogy
David Berry, John Theobald, editors

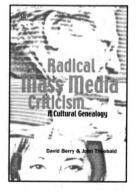

Since the beginning of the media age, there have been thinkers who have reacted against the increasing power of the mass media. This book examines those early mass media critics, and their controversial writings, and links them with their contemporaries to demonstrate the relevance of their legacy for today's debates on media power and media ethics. Included is a look at the work of Karl Kraus, Ferdinand Tönnies, the 'Frankfurt School' (especially Max Horkheimer and Theodor Adorno), the Glasgow Media Group, Marshall McLuhan, Robert McChesney, Noam Chomsky, Edward Herman, Harold Innis, Northrop Frye, David Suzuki, Maude Barlow, and the black American feminist writer, bell hooks. Apart from the editors, contributors include: Slavko Splichal, Hanno Hardt, Joost van Loon, Stuart Allen, Jason Barker, John Eldridge, Robert McChesney, James Winter, Cynthia Carter.

DAVID BERRY is Senior Lecturer in Journalism, Culture and Mass Communications and JOHN THEOBALD is Associate Professor in Modern Languages, both of whom are at the Southampton Institute, UK.

2005: 272 pages, paper 1-55164-246-8 $26.99   ⁂ cloth 1-55164-247-6 $57.99

edited by Jeffery Klaehn

BOUND BY POWER: Intended Consequences

This original work contains exclusive interviews with a range of noted scholars, including Noam Chomsky, Linda McQuaig, John McMurtry, Brian Martin and David Miller, who speak candidly about understanding power, spin and information management, and the costs of dissent. Each of the essays in this collection consider the ways in which power and ideology work within society. They include an examination of patriotic correctness and the repression of dissent in America; U.S. foreign policy toward Cuba; the myth of the neutral professional; academic culture; how dissent is kept to manageable levels in the media; the East Asian Financial Crisis; the near-genocide in East Timor; and the economic, emotional, and familial impacts of workplace injury and the ideology of the Worker's Compensation Board.

Contributors include: Noam Chomsky, David Miller, Linda McQuaig, John McMurtry, David Cromwell, Brian Martin, James Winter, Robert Everton, Jean Chen, Teresa Chen, Valerie Scatamburlo-D'Annibale, Robert Jensen, Peter Eglin, Robert Bertuzzi, and Jeffery Klaehn.

2006: 272 pages, paper 1-55164-282-4 $26.99 ⁂ cloth 1-55164-283-2 $55.99

FILTERING THE NEWS: Essays on Herman and Chomsky's Propaganda Model

Herman and Chomsky's 'propaganda model' argues that there are five classes of 'filters' in society which determine what is news; in other words, what gets printed in newspapers or broadcast by radio and television and whether a news item is going to be used by the media, or not, is going to depend on if it can pass through these filters. *Filtering the News* begins with a critical review, and assessment, of the propaganda model, then applies Herman and Chomsky's model to a range of ongoing news events. In the final chapters, Herman and Chomsky's propaganda model is revisited, and several common criticisms of the model are reflected upon and scrutinized.

By itself, the chapter on the pretentious Dan Rather is worth twice the price of the book. Extremely timely. —Barrie Zwicker, host of *The Great Conspiracy*

Contributors include: Valerie Scatamburlo-D'Annibale, Bob Everton, Peter Eglin, Robert Jensen, Jeffery Klaehn, James Winter, and Robert Babe.

JEFFERY KLAEHN teaches Cultural Studies and Sociology at Wilfrid Laurier University, and is also the editor of *Inside the World of Comic Books* (Black Rose Books).

2005: 248 pages, paper 1-55164-260-3 $24.99 ⁂ cloth 1-55164-261-1 $53.99